the journey of the farmers' rebellion

the journey of the farmers' rebellion

A COMPILATION OF INTERVIEWS ON THE
FARMERS' MOVEMENT IN INDIA, 2020-2021

*Originally Edited, Researched, and Published by
Workers Unity, GroundXero, and Notes on the Academy*

iskra books
olympia | london | dublin

Originally Published by Workers Unity, GroundXero, and Notes on the Academy:
First Edition 2022
Second Edition 2023

This Third Edition published by Iskra Books 2024

Book Retains No Copyright; All Rights Reserved for Book Cover Alone.

10 9 8 7 6 5 4 3 2 1

Iskra Books
www.iskrabooks.org
US | England | Ireland

Iskra Books is an independent scholarly publisher—publishing original works of revolutionary theory, history, education, and art, as well as edited collections, new translations, and critical republications of older works.

ISBN-13: 979-8-3306-9712-0 (*Softcover*)

British Library Cataloguing in Publication Data
A catalogue record for this book is available from the British Library.

Library of Congress Cataloguing-in-Publication Data
A catalog record for this book is available from the Library of Congress

Cover Art, Typesetting, and Design by Ben Stahnke

contents

PUBLISHER'S NOTE / I
A NOTE OF THANKS / VI
ORIGINAL FOREWORD / VII

INTRODUCTION
When the Peasantry Rises / 1
by Ranjana Padhi

The Three Farm Laws and Their Impact on the Peasantry / 19
by Prof. Sukhpal Singh

SECTION I
CONVERSATIONS WITH THE LEADERS OF FARMER UNIONS

Dr. Darshan Pal / 29
Krantikari Kisan Union

Rajinder Singh Deep Singh Wala / 46
Kirti Kisan Union

Harinder Kaur Bindu / 59
Bharatiya Kisan Union (Ekta-Ugrahan)

Surjit Singh Phul / 79
Bharatiya Kisan Union (Krantikari)

Joginder Singh Ugrahan / 94
Bharatiya Kisan Union (Ekta-Ugrahan)

Jasbir Kaur Natt / 111
Punjab Kisan Union

Hannan Mollah / 122
All India Kisan Sabha

Sukhwinder Kaur / 134
Bharatiya Kisan Union (Krantikari)

Manjit Singh Dhaner / 157
Bharatiya Kisan Union (Ekta-Dakaunda)

Kavitha Kuruganti / 170
Alliance for Sustainable and Holistic Agriculture

SECTION II
CONVERSATIONS WITH LEADERS OF AGRICULTURAL AND RURAL WORKER UNIONS

Pargat Singh / 185
Krantikari Pendu Mazdoor Union

Lachhman Sewewala / 195
Punjab Khet Mazdoor Union

Darshan Nahar, Gurnam Singh, and Mahipal / 210
Dehati Mazdoor Sabha

SECTION III
CONVERSATIONS WITH LEADERS OF ZAMEEN PRAPTI SANGHARSH COMMITTEE

Gurmukh Singh / 222

Paramjit Kaur Longowala / 245

SECTION IV
CONVERSATIONS WITH JOURNALISTS, ECONOMISTS, POLITICAL AND CULTURAL ACTIVISTS

Hartosh Singh Bal / 266
Political Editor, THE CARAVAN

Pavel Kussa / 287
Editor, Surkh Leeh

Prof. Sukhpal Singh / 303
Economist, Punjab Agricultural University

Randeep Maddoke / 321
Documentary Filmmaker

Amolak Singh / 328
Cultural Activist

Nodeep Kaur / 335
Labour Activist, Mazdoor Adhikar Sangathan

Prof. Ranjit Singh Ghuman / 355
Economist, Guru Nanak Dev University

380 Days that Shook the Delhi Empire / 373
A Chronology of the Struggle

Glossary / 396

Appendix I / 409
List of Farmer Unions That Led the Movement

The Four Common Demands of the Farmers' Movement

Appendix II / 411
Thirteen-point Charter of Demands of the Left-wing Farmers Unions

Appendix III / 413
List of Rural and Agricultural Worker Unions in the Sanjha Morcha

Eight-point Charter of Demands of the Sanjha Morcha

Salute to all the martyrs of the farmers' rebellion (2020-21).

Publisher's Note
Róisín Dubh, Iskra Books

SEEING MILLIONS OF PEOPLE from the working and peasant classes of India stand up against the fascistic legislation of the Farm Bills was one of the most inspiring events in the years 2020-2021. While the planet was being ravaged by climate change, the George Floyd uprisings, and the COVID-19 pandemic, the farmers of India fought back—and won.

The world witnessed photographs and imagery emerging from the front lines of the protests, revealing the daily lives and day-to-day struggles of the farmers to the rest of the world. Yet despite the proliferation of photographs online, the words of those brave Indian farmers have rarely been read. This brilliant book—*The Journey of the Farmers' Rebellion: A Compilation of Interviews on the Farmers' Movement in India, 2020-2021*, originally published in India in 2022 by our colleagues from Workers' Unity, GroundXero, and Notes on the Academy—uplifts those voices. Whether from farmers, union organizers, activists, the students, teachers, Dalit, women, or elders, they are all here. The diversity of voices in the present volume reflects the fact that the Farmers' Rebellion was, most foundationally, a truly intersectional working class and peasant-led movement.

Those of us who only saw photographs online, in papers, and on social media might wonder what this Rebellion was all about. The Indian government, led by the reactionary Narendra Modi, intended to enforce strict legislation which would negatively impact farmers across the country. Whether they owned the land they tilled or not, the majority of people living and working in the Indian countryside were to be hurt by three distinct 2020 farm act legislations know as the *Farm Bills*. In response to these legislations, a great united front was created, and a yearlong protest erupted.

For over a year, the farmers and their allies occupied highways and border areas, transforming them into sites of resistance and rebellion.

They built makeshift shelters, community kitchens, libraries, and medical stations—creating a remarkable example of bottom-up organization and solidarity. The movement was not just about opposing legislation; it was about asserting the dignity, rights, and survival of millions of farmers who form the backbone of India's food system.

The strength of the movement lay, in fact, in its unity. Farmers from Punjab, Haryana, Uttar Pradesh, and beyond, often divided by caste, religion, and geography, came together to fight for a common cause. Women played a crucial role, not only as participants but also as leaders and organizers, challenging deeply-held patriarchal social norms. Students, activists, labor unions, and international allies lent their voices to the struggle, underscoring the global significance of the farmers' fight against corporate exploitation and state repression.

Despite facing brutal police crackdowns, smear campaigns in state-controlled media, and the cool Delhi winter, the protesters did not waver. Their resilience and determination ultimately forced the government to repeal the Farm Bills in November 2021—a rare and historic victory for people's movements both in India and worldwide. This book, in amplifying the voices of those who fought so bravely, is both a tribute to their struggle and a critical resource for anyone seeking to understand how a diverse, grassroots, bottom-up power can challenge even the most entrenched systems of oppression.

Modi and Singh

The lives of two men are intertwined in the present book. Narendra Modi, head of the current political leadership of India, and Bhagat Singh, the great historical Indian revolutionary.

Singh was born in what is now Pakistan over 100 years ago—yet his words left a lasting impact, inspiring the masses during the farmers protests in 2020. Singh was 16 when he joined the revolutionary movement in 1923. And he was executed eight years later in 1931 by the British government. Camana Lal argued that while Singh was alive, he was as popular as Mahatma Gandhi.[1]

Growing up, Singh was heavily influenced by his uncle, Ajit Singh,

---

1   Camana Lal. *The Bhagat Singh Reader*, p. 15.

particularly his liberatory thought in relation to peasants finding freedom from feudal landlords. Singh then used these ideas as a philosophical base towards which he applied Marx's theory of national liberation.[2] Even at the young age of fifteen, Singh realized that the non-violence of Mahatma Gandhi would not liberate the masses. At sixteen, Singh began to write essays, focusing on the injustices of the caste system, and exploring reasons for which he was an atheist. By 1924, he had risen to the position of General Secretary of the mass organization Naujwan Bharat Sabha.[3]

Singh knew a united front was necessary in order to free the masses from British colonial rule, and, in pursuit of this, he helped to lead the Hindustan Socialist Republican Association (HSRA). Singh became massively popular with the youth—and the British colonial forces took notice. At one point, Josef Stalin wanted Singh to be brought to the Soviet Union, in fear that Singh might be assassinated by reactionaries in India.[4] Singh knew there needed to be both legal and illegal actions in order for real liberation to be achieved, and he also understood that his life would not be a long one. After throwing bombs in the Delhi Central Assembly, Singh was arrested, and the slogans *Inqilab Zindabad* (Long Live Revolution) and *Samrajyavad Ka Nash Ho* (Down with Imperialism) came into being.[5] These very same slogans were chanted during the 2020 Farmers' Rebellion.

During his time, Singh used the British courts as a platform to further the socialist cause and to expose the brutality of British colonialism in India. While in prison, Singh went on hunger strike, boycotting his own trial and winning over the hearts of the Indian public. Singh, along with his other comrades, went to the gallows with heads held high, facing their deaths with dignity.[6] To this day, Singh continues to be revered by Indian and Pakistani peoples alike.

While Singh's actions and words might have inspired farmers in the 2020 Rebellion, the target of protest action was ultimately Narendra

---

2   Ibid., p. 18.
3   Ibid., p. 20.
4   Ibid., p. 23.
5   Ibid., p. 25.
6   Ibid., pp. 35-36.

Modi, a reactionary, conservative Hindu nationalist. When Modi was 8, he joined Rashtriya Swayamsevak Sangh (RSS)—the armed wing of the Hindu nationalist Bharatiya Janata Party (BJP)—later living in its headquarters.[7] Modi rose quickly in the RSS ranks, and eventually joined the BJP in 1987.[8]

Modi became popular among the Indian right-wing when he was Chief Minister of the Indian state of Gujarat from 2001 to 2014. Within the first year of taking office, Modi oversaw the 2002 Muslim pogrom which left almost 2000 dead.[9] While Chief Minister, Modi continued to run on principles of right-wing Hindu nationalist populism, and utilized a US public relations firm to help him manufacture constant contact with Gujarat's population.[10] Modi furthered his program of Hindu nationalism by increasing Muslim discrimination, distancing himself from Muslims, pushing theories that Hindus lived under "1200 years of slavery" in his speeches, and not allowing poor Muslims to access scholarships.[11]

In 2014, with his popularity surging on a wave of Hindu nationalist populism, Modi was elected Prime Minister of India. In his first term, Modi implemented anti-poor policies and discontinued previous pro-poor programs, pushing many back into poverty, including farmers and other rural workers.[12] During his 2019 re-election, Modi became emboldened and made his reactionary tendencies more explicit. His party focused on pushing Islamophobia, labeling it a matter of "national security," while also attacking leftist movements and so-called "illegal" immigration.[13] However, it was during his second term that Modi began to more fully implement his increasingly fascistic policies, such as the Farm Bills, targeting journalists under the guise of "anti-terrorism," and increasing unemployment and poverty rates, while heightening India's

---

7   Jaffrelot Christophe and Cynthia Schoch. *Modi's India Hindu Nationalism and the Rise of Ethnic Democracy*, p. 34.

8   Ibid., p. 36.

9   Ibid., p. 41.

10   Ibid., p. 49.

11   Ibid., p. 52.

12   Ibid., p. 134.

13   Ibid., p. 316.

social and political islamophobia.

Despite the rampancy of Modi's repressive policies, however, the Farmers Rebellion rose victorious. Fighting Modi through the example of Singh, the people created a true united front, composed of a truly intersectional diversity of poor, peasant, and working class peoples.

As you will see in this excellent book, the Farmers' Rebellion was historic *because* it truly reached across caste, gender, age, and class lines. This intersectional movement included women, the youth, the elderly, unions, students, teachers, and individuals from various classes and castes. It empowered so many who had their power taken from them by the Modi government.

Many of the interviews present in this book ask what should happen after such a victory—and the answers are diverse. Some stress the electoral route, while others advocate the continued expansion of the intersectional alliance so that the people might be ready for the next inevitable attack on their rights from the Modi government. One cannot help but to be but inspired while reading this book—and it is hard not to extract important lessons by observing how the people have, either wittingly or otherwise, put Singh's cultural legacy and his revolutionary ideas into practice in the fight against contemporary fascist populism.

A Note of Thanks

OUR FIRST AND FOREMOST thanks to the peasant leaders and activists who took out time from their schedule, interacted with us, gave us the interviews and encouraged us in this endeavor. This book would not have been possible without the voluntary labour and participation of many friends and well-wishers.

We thank Manjit Sharma, Arun Kumar Tripathi, deepani seth, Vikas Thakur, Harshita Bhasin, Sahil Mehra, Manu Akavoor, Simran Narula, Chandrika, Venkat, Gokul, Paroma, Rohan, Adwait, Sarah, Pranjal, Swati Pandey, Nilanjan Dutta, Susmita Sarkar Jhelum, Bama (Bengali feminist magazine), several comrades from Mehnatkash Patrika, Committee for Protection of Democratic Rights (CPDR)-TN and many others for the varied inputs at different stages.

We are grateful to all our friends and comrades who constantly inspired us and gave us hope as we wove the narratives of the farmers' rebellion and victory into the pages of this book.

—*The Editorial Team*

Foreword

Teri chati pe likh inquilab, O Delhi, hum ghar chale!

Lines scribbled on a concrete pillar on the roadside by a triumphant farmer before departing the borders of the national capital on 11 December 2021.

ON 25 MARCH 2020, almost immediately after the national coronavirus-induced lockdown was announced with a four hour notice, we were flooded with visuals. Those visuals were of distressed migrant workers—walking hundreds of miles from their factories and workplaces in cities to their homes in faraway villages. As if these horrors unleashed on them was not enough, they were beaten up by the police, sprayed upon with pesticides, dumped inside makeshift camps and run over by trains while sleeping on the tracks. And those who survived reached their homes only to find prolonged unemployment and starvation.

A few months later, visuals of another journey overtook the national imagination—the farmers travelling through the lengths and breadths of villages across Punjab and Haryana towards Delhi, to encircle the parliament of the country inside the national capital. The trigger was the passing of three farm laws in parliament under pressure from WTO and agro-corporations. Thousands of farmers marching in tractors and trolleys threw away the police barricades, braved the water cannons, crossed wide trenches dug on the highways; they stopped only after reaching the borders leading into Delhi. They set up camps and for the next 380 days and nights they slept in tents and trolleys, cooked in langars and held rallies and demonstrations. Despite state repression, extreme weather conditions and provocations and malicious campaign by the godi-media, they forced the Delhi regime to surrender and repeal the three laws in the same parliament.

If the former impressed upon us the notion that the workers in our contemporary times, fragmented into myriad categories from permanent to temporary, live in conditions of extreme precarity, the latter turned into symbols of courage, resilience, resistance and hope. Consequently, what they demanded from the rest of us was active solidarity.

The Journey of the Farmers' Rebellion is a tribute to the unrelenting struggle of the farmers and their resistance to the pro-corporate agenda of the rulers in Delhi. It is an attempt to bring to the readers a complex yet coherent picture about what this farmers' movement entailed, what it truly accomplished, and what are its possible ramifications for the future of anti-corporate people's movements in our country. And it does so, through the eyes of those who led the movement from the front, and those who stood in solidarity with it.

A movement in which the landed peasantry stood toe to toe against the state and forces of global capital, showed us the ruptures that exist in Indian agrarian society. It exposed the fault lines between the landed farmers leading the movement and the landless peasantry and agricultural labourers. While it absorbed and was moulded by the heavy participation of women farmers, it also amplified their voices, their neglected role as producers and the violence they face. It was a movement that showed us that the road to emancipation and liberation of the toiling masses is long and uphill but one that is filled with optimism and hope thanks to the martyrdom and sacrifices of the farmers who defeated the RSS-BJP regime.

These facets of the movement were often obscured both in the mainstream and the social media representations. Yet another facet which was beyond the horizon of the mainstream media was how the peasant leadership navigated the internal dynamics between various unions, including the coalition Samyukta Kisan Morcha (SKM), BKU (Ekta-Ugrahan) and Kisan Mazdoor Sangharsh Committee (KMSC).

From the very beginning of the farmers' agitation, Workers Unity began conducting a series of in-depth video interviews. An idea arose through discussions among us that these insightful interviews, disjointed as they seem, may provide a coherent perspective on the dynamics of the farmers' movement when woven together. A perspective that comes from those who actively participated in the movement. A consensus was built and a team got formed as the actual work began. We began transcribing the interviews. Some more interviews were conducted to give the portrayal of the movement as unique in its varied dimensions. We have felt throughout that the farmers' movement was not a linear graph before us to be documented but a multi-dimensional protracted struggle in which multiple issues and layers of cooperation and conflicts are intertwined. As collaborative work emerging from the labour of three independent collectives and their comrades, this book tries to outline precisely these unseen dimensions of the movement.

It is not only difficult, but almost impossible to cover every aspect of this movement spread over many states in a single book. For example, the book does not capture views of many of the unions or social forces like *khap* panchayats in Haryana and sugarcane producers' unions in Uttar Pradesh. Their role and participation in this movement needs to be seen and analysed in the context of the distinct nature of the agrarian crisis of these specific geographies, objective social and economic conditions of these places, and in the context of the historical trajectory of their own peasant movements.

History is made by people, and radical transformation of society is achieved through people's struggle; consequently, the focus has remained on the rejection of and rebellion of the farmers against the attempts of the Indian ruling classes to corporatise production, procurement and distribution of agricultural produce in the country. And this could not have been achieved without stressing on the role played by the Left—the political force that led and sustained the farmers' movement.

The spectacularity of the event of the farmers occupying the borders of the national capital was built upon a complicated history of decades of struggle sustained and developed by various Left revolutionary peasants' organisations. We say this, keeping in mind that the Left too is not a homogenous category; it is fragmented, existing in a society dominated by contradictions between the exploited and the ruling class. A keen reader would be able to discern some of these underlying tensions and conflicts that are an inextricable part of the interviews.

While transcribing, translating and editing the interviews, we have taken utmost care to present the views and opinions of the interviewees. The final copies were sent to almost all of them and approved by them before publishing. Most of us are not speakers of Punjabi, the language in which some of the interviewees were most comfortable. Majority of the interviews were conducted in Hindi and were then translated into English. Given the nature of the linguistic diversity and complexities in India, this was, indeed, an extremely difficult task, which raised before us several political questions of a different order. We have tried our best to rise up to them. Yet, in spite of our best efforts, if any discrepancies and errors remain, we are responsible for such.

This project came from a collective political belief. We too retain our faith in the *collective conscience* of the people of this country, even as that collective conscience today stands poisoned through a mix of hatred towards Muslims and other minorities and vulgar-nationalism and has been seemingly programmed towards a willful acceptance of the majoritarian Hindutva rule, backed by a coterie of crony-capitalists.

We believe that this conscience will be reshaped. And it will be reshaped by people's movements like the one, whose footsteps we have tried to document here. We imagine, one day, the two journeys—of the workers and the peasants—will converge and uproot the present repressive structures which enable fascist forces to seize state power.

We hope readers will find this effort to document the triumph of the farmers over the pro-corporate agenda of the fascist rulers useful to engage more in these discussions, current reality and the future before us.

With gratitude and hope,
—*THE EDITORIAL TEAM*

On 26 November, 2020, thousands of farmers marched towards Delhi, facing water cannons and tear gas as the police tried to disperse them at Haryana's Ambala border. The farmers, overcoming police repression and barricades, reached Singhu border. **Photo credit:** Facebook post of unnamed activists.

Tractors and trolleys parked for several kilometers at the Singhu border by the farmers. **Photo Credit:** Workers Unity.

Leaders of farmers' union. **Photo Credit:** Workers Unity.

Farmers preparing food at a langar (community kitchen) set up at protest sites. Photo by Rupinder Singh on *Unsplash*.

INTRODUCTION

When the Peasantry Rises
RANJANA PADHI

> *The moon,*
> *the river,*
> *the flower,*
> *the stars,*
> *the birds.*
> *We can look for them later.*
> *But today,*
> *in this darkness,*
> *The last battle is yet to be fought.*
> *What we need now in our hovel*
> *Is: Fire!*
> —*Murari Mukhopadhyay*

IN THE HISTORY of India's resistance movements, the day 19 November 2021 will be remembered forever. It was on this day that Prime Minister Narendra Modi, the head of the authoritarian regime in Delhi, bowed down before the year-long farmers' movement when he appeared on national media to announce that the union government was taking back the three farm laws that it had brought in. The announcement marked one of the most extraordinary and significant victories of the Indian peasantry in its long and glorious history of struggles.

The unrelenting resistance to the three farm laws, aimed at facilitating the entry of big corporations into the agricultural sector, was manifested in the *Delhi Chalo* march of the peasantry on 26 November and which, when prevented from entering the national capital, led to a three-hundred-eighty days of continuous sit-in on highways bordering New Delhi. Each single day of protest was a demonstration of mounting peasant unity and solidarity around this momentous struggle led by a joint platform of farmer unions, the Samyukta Kisan Morcha (SKM). Those who thought that the days of agrarian revolts in India belonged to the previous century were in for a surprise. After the legendary struggles led by landless peasants of Tebhaga and Telangana, peasant revolts have been sporadic and localised in character even as the agrarian crisis spread, claiming lives of almost four lakh farmers in the last two decades.

The struggle for the repeal of the farm laws culminated in a significant victory and most importantly brought the agrarian issues of rural India onto the national agenda and in national consciousness. The historic movement once again made real the assertion that India lives in its vast rural areas.

Growing Peasant Unrest

The Union government, the ruling BJP party, the capitalist class, the bureaucrats, the pro-liberalisation economists and the lapdog media in unison had touted the three farm laws as a welcome initiation of bold and long-overdue reforms in the agricultural sector that would attract private investment, provide options for farmers to trade their produce outside notified and regulated markets, facilitate them to enter into contracts with private entities prior to production and connect them to big traders and exporters to sell their produce at lucrative prices. They claimed, in a nutshell, that the laws would unshackle the agricultural sector and that linking it to the global market would help unleash its growth potential, bringing in more profits to the distressed farmers.

However, the farmer unions in Punjab saw these laws as a death knell to agriculture and cultivators in Punjab as well as in other states. They viewed the establishment of private markets for trade of agricultural produce as a plan to gradually do away with government regulated agri-markets and eventual dismantle of the Minimum Support Price (MSP) system for food grains, thereby leaving the farmers exposed to the volatility of food grain prices determined by the corporate-controlled the global market forces. They also feared that contract farming would subjugate farmers to a few agro-corporates, and that the combined result of the three farm laws would henceforth not only mean corporate control over agricultural inputs but also mandate corporate control over agricultural outputs. They feared that the laws would accelerate the process of depeasantisation with land owning farmers, particularly the small and middle farmers becoming labourers on their own lands.

The agricultural worker unions in Punjab realised that farming lands going into the hands of the corporates and the dismantling of regulated agri-markets would soon lead to a further shrinkage of the Public Distribution System (PDS) of food grains at subsidised prices. And that even the existing work opportunities in farms, agri-markets and FCI godowns, would disappear overnight leading to yet more unemployment.

The march to Delhi was a culmination of discontent brewing for years in Punjab, irrespective of which political party was in power in the state or at Delhi. Agrarian distress had reached its peak, with rising input costs, low prices of agri-produces and indebtedness caused by loans. Occupying only 1.5 percent of the geographical area of the country, the state used to provide 13 percent of the national food grain output and 40 percent to the central PDS pool. In spite of farmers receiving MSP for both wheat and paddy, the Green Revolution model of capital-intensive agriculture with corporations selling machinery, chemical fertilisers, pesticides and insecticides had resulted in massive indebtedness and suicides due to plummeting profits, stagnant productivity, drastically falling groundwater table and soil degradation. The cost of agricultural inputs outweighed the remuneration of the produce more and more; especially with the government subsidy on agricultural inputs having been slashed as the allocation to agriculture sector in the Union Budget shrunk to 3.84 percent.[1] Added to these woes is the looming threat of the acquisition of agricultural land by corporations in the name of industrialisation and infrastructure development projects. Those who sweated it out in having made Punjab prosperous are left to witness vast tracts of fertile land being given away to corporations like Vedanta or Trident.

The once prosperous land of five rivers continues to be the destination of agro-multinationals for the sale of chemical fertilisers, seeds and pesticides killing the peasants along with the ecosystem. In fact, the daily passenger train from Bhatinda carrying cancer patients to Rajasthan for treatment has earned the epithet of "cancer train." Ironically, the use of chemical pesticides which heralded the arrival of the Green Revolution in Punjab has now become one of the most common causes for disease and also the most common means of committing suicide.

But the blood thirst of global capital knows no limits and it is not merely satisfied with control of agricultural inputs, even the agricultural output—the produce—is being coveted by the corporations. The three laws were pushed through the Indian parliament, disregarding all norms and procedures. But what the corporates and the government did not account for was the resolve, determination and striking power of the peasantry as it laid siege to the national capital for over a year. The threat of corporates taking control of agriculture united all the farmer unions representing the big, middle and small farmers in opposing the laws, and also brought in agricultural worker unions and other sections of society in solidarity. As days passed, the protesting farmers camping at the borders gathered more and more strength subsuming all political and ideological differences and contradictions within the peasantry for a common cause against a common enemy, and built a massive momentum of support and solidarity in favour of their categorical demand for total repeal of the three farm laws and a legally-guaranteed MSP for all crops across the country.

The victory of the farmers is not only over the ruling authoritarian regime at Delhi backed by the fascist RSS and crony-capitalists, but is also a victory over the consistent pressure of international bodies like WTO, IMF, World Bank and World Economic Forum on the Indian government to cut subsidies in agriculture, substantially reduce procurement of food grains for the PDS and open up the sector to global competition by removing all 'free trade distorting' policies. The three farm laws that the farmers' movement forced the central government to repeal were part of this economic agenda of corporate-backed Indian rulers to fulfill the WTO conditions, especially of Agreement on Agriculture (AoA). This deadly attempt to bring all aspects of agriculture under corporate control has been beaten back.

It was the fabled moment of the peasant seizing the reins of the Emperor's marauding horse, by doing which they decisively blocked the pro-corporate fascist agenda of the ruling BJP-RSS combine. Indeed, this victory happened in the aftermath of the repression of the anti CAA-NRC movement, the state-sponsored pogrom of Muslims in East Delhi, the incarceration of Muslim and other student and youth activists in false riot cases. It was a moment of reckoning when Bilkis Dadi of

Shaheen Bagh reached the protest site at Singhu. The farmers' revolt and capitulation of Delhi shattered the media crafted myth of Modi being 'invincible.'

Sustained protests against policies of the neoliberal state seeking reforms in the agricultural sector have taken place earlier. The massive Boat Club Rally of farmers in 1988 led by Mahendra Singh Tikait of BKU had seen lakhs of farmers enter and settle down in the heart of New Delhi for weeks. Their primary demands—loan waivers, higher prices for crops, reduction in power and water tariffs—signalled the early signs of agrarian distress. With their base primarily among largely dominant caste farmers, these movements while demanding remunerative prices for farmers' produce were silent on agricultural wages, indifferent to caste oppression of agricultural workers and opposed to land reform. They were directly antagonistic to the interests of landless agricultural labourers and many were also critical of the government procurement and Minimum Support Price system that today's farmers' protests are battling to defend. There was a sharp political division between the movements over the question of economic liberalisation. While Bharatiya Kisan Union (BKU) opposed economic liberalisation which it saw as a path to corporatise agriculture and ruin India's farmers, the Shetkari Sangathana led by Sharad Joshi in Maharashtra supported the reforms for a liberal and free market for food crops as a way to lessen the grip of the state on procurement and give farmers access to international markets. In South India, the Karnataka Rajya Raitha Sangha (KRRS) led by M. D. Nanjundaswamy opposed the entry of multinational seed and processed food companies into Indian markets. It organised and led huge protests against the multinational seed company Monsanto. It also questioned the prevalent agrarian model and its fallouts.

In Punjab, the present farmers' movement can be seen in the context of both the historical militant peasants' struggle from the pre-independence days, starting from the Pagdi Sambhal Jatta movement in 1907, the Pepsu Muzara movement in late forties to early fifties, and the farmers' agitations post liberalisation in the mid-nineties until now demanding loan waivers, free electricity, compensation to families of farmers who committed suicide, increase in MSP, the struggle of landless Dalit farmers for panchayati common lands, the struggle of agricultural workers for social security, the hike in farm wage, and so on.

The massive nationwide support to the farmers' movement also happened in the wake of the recent mass protests by farmers in the states of Maharashtra, Rajasthan, Madhya Pradesh, Tamil Nadu and Karnataka. The formation of the All India Kisan Sangharsh Coordination Committee (AIKSCC), which was triggered by the death of six farmers in a police firing on 6 June 2017 in Mandsaur district, Madhya Pradesh, is significant in this context. AIKSCC rapidly covered ground in large parts of the country highlighting the widespread agrarian distress with two central demands: MSP legislation and complete relief from indebtedness. In 2018, over sixty thousand farmers, including agricultural labourers and indigenous (Adivasi) cultivators under the leadership of Left-affiliated farmer unions under AIKSCC marched to Mumbai, India's financial capital. Even in states like Madhya Pradesh, Odisha and Chhattisgarh, the systemic violence is borne by marginal farmers and sharecroppers whose suicides are less reported to the world outside.

The Long March

As soon as the three ordinances were promulgated on 5 June 2020, various farmer unions in Punjab, constituents of AIKSSC, initiated the protests by launching campaigns against the ordinances. In the face of pandemic restrictions, peasant communities took to the rooftops for a one-hour protest daily for two entire weeks. Later, rallies and demonstrations were held almost every day. Memoranda were submitted to BJP leaders and union ministers from Punjab, their houses were gheraoed, effigies of the NDA politicians were burnt on the streets, and a statewide *rail roko* (rail blockade) campaign took place for weeks. A successful bandh on 25 September, 2020, reflected the massive support of the people of all sections including students, youth, traders and shop owners towards the farmer unions. Every farmer union in Punjab came out to oppose the ordinances.

But after the ordinances were brought in the form of Bills in the parliament, hurriedly passed in both houses without any discussion through voice vote, the call for a long march to reach Delhi on 26-27 November 2020 was announced by SKM. The passing of the Bills acted as a catalyst that triggered the do-or-die battle to get the laws repealed. This battle crystallised in thousands of farmer unions and supporters marching in tractors and trolleys away from their homes and hearths for an indefinite period of time. As they marched towards the nation's capital, they were joined by farmers from Haryana, UP and Rajasthan.

The rulers in Delhi tried to stop the farmers through their state government in Haryana. The digging of trenches on highways to block the entry of farmers' tractors and trolleys from marching to Delhi was reminiscent of mediaeval wars when kings fortified the kingdom from an advancing enemy. Only this time it was a case of a state fortifying itself from its own citizens—the *annadatas*. Farmers crossed all hurdles set up by the Haryana Police, including a seven-foot-tall barricade at the Rohtak toll plaza, large boulders, huge metal containers and sand-laden trucks across the highways leading to Delhi. They braved the water cannons and tear gas shells. The Delhi Police put up multiple layers of barbed wire and steel barricades at Haryana-Delhi border points. The farmers set up camps on the Singhu and Tikri borders.

The farmers outwitted every malicious move of the state like disrupting water supply and electricity and jamming of Internet connectivity at the protest camps. They simply dug borewells for water, brought in generators for electricity and set up their own routers for Internet connectivity. Many even grew vegetables on the sidewalks. News and images of *annadatas* unyielding to give in an inch till the farm laws are revoked ignited hope and inspiration. The spectacles of brutal police violence on farmers galvanised support and solidarity from remote villages in India to cities abroad.

The year-long protests were a demonstration to the entire world of the peasant community's unity, tenacity and creativity in its battle with a ruthless authoritarian state. The farmers' struggle evolved with ingenious strategies like the boycott of corporate products and dharnas at petrol pumps and malls owned by big corporates like Adanis and Ambanis, and keeping the toll plazas free in Punjab and Haryana. Such protests targeting corporate houses backing the authoritarian Delhi regime made more and more people and the youth enraged at corporates that supported laws aimed at dispossessing the peasantry.

The kisan protest stages at the different border sites—Tikri, Singhu, Ghazipur, Shahjahanpur and Palwal—prudently prevented any vote-seeking politician from making use of the protest for their own propaganda. The strength of the SKM lay in its alliance building efforts and democratic functioning. The collective leadership that emerged made strategic moves, boosted mobilisation capacities and exercised caution and restraint in the face of a ruthless state apparatus.

SKM also kept the mainstream corporate media at bay, which had begun projecting farmers as Khalistanis, Maoists or only as rich farmers, in total sync with the hysteria whipped up by the BJP-led government. There emerged creative ways of communicating with people from within the protest. Newsletters like *Trolley Times* and *Karti Dharti* sprang up. The dissemination of news about the movement through social media by a dedicated team of volunteers engendered support and solidarity; SKM daily updates reached a wide audience across the country and abroad. In this way, the movement successfully challenged the narratives spun by mainstream media in its attempts to spread lies and vilify the protests.

Democratic and left forces within the SKM used the protest stages to highlight other pressing issues facing the people of this country. In less than a month of being in Tikri, BKU (Ekta-Ugrahan) expressed solidarity to political prisoners and demanded the scrapping of UAPA. When labour activists Nodeep Kaur and Shiv Kumar were arrested and tortured in prison, BKU (Krantikari) protested against their arrests and campaigned for their release.

The farmers' movement also challenged the divisive religious ideology of the BJP-RSS. The Kisan Mahapanchayat in Muzaffarnagar resonated with slogans of three different faiths: *"Allahu Akbar,"* *"Har Har Mahadev"* and *"Jo Bole So Nihal."* Ambedkar Jayanti was celebrated at the protest sites. The majority of people locked up in the confines of the four walls by pandemic restrictions witnessed on TV and mobile screens a rebellion that was indeed a festival of the masses. The peasant community danced and sang, nurtured and cared for the sick and ailing. While in protest, they cooked in the langars to feed the mass gatherings, passers-by and the police personnel too. Migrant workers walking back home during the lockdowns sought refuge at the protest sites.

Each single day became a test of the movement's tenacity and tactics. The movement faced its severest challenge when the planning of the 26 January event of marching into the capital went awry. A section of the protestors entered Delhi city, reached the Red Fort and hoisted the *Nishan Sahib* flag. The state and the media were successful in orchestrating a vicious campaign denouncing this incident as handiwork of "anti-national elements, who had taken over the farmers' movement." Our collective breath remained suspended for more than 24 hours of what would follow. The delegitimisation of the people's movement by first declaring it either Khalistani, Maoist, terrorist or worse by craftily engineering a disturbance from within the protests is a time-tested tactic of the Indian state and its allies. The brutal repression and arrests carried out on the Muslim community in northwest Delhi a year before and the forceful disbanding of the protest site at Shaheen Bagh was fresh in our minds. However, the 26 January fiasco did not prove to be as detrimental as BJP-RSS and the corporates had intended. In fact, unity flourished at precisely this moment of crisis. There was cheer and jubilation as thousands of sugarcane producers marched from UP in solidarity with the farmers' protests. Farmers from Haryana joined the protest sites in even greater numbers. The most amazing support came from agricultural workers unions and landless farmers organisations from Punjab.

The SKM leadership, in turn, became more alert to provocations set up by anti-farmer elements. It swiftly dealt with any incident that could give the powers that be a ruse to denigrate the movement. When a young woman who had travelled from West Bengal was sexually assaulted by members of the Kisan Social Army, the SKM helped the father file an FIR against the accused. On 26 June, while observing Emergency Day, protesters marching to the Raj Bhavan in Chandigarh broke barricades and faced both lathi charge and water cannons. But they held back from any more confrontation. There was yet another brutal lathi charge by the Haryana Police on farmers protesting against a BJP meeting attended by the Haryana CM. But the farmers staunchly and peacefully carried on a protest until action was taken against the SP who had ordered the lathi charge.

When some farmers were run over by a speeding vehicle belonging to the son of the Union Minister of State for Home Affairs, Ajay Mishra Teni in Lakhimpur Kheri in UP, SKM demanded an immediate inquiry and resignation of Ajay Mishra. The pressure on BJP was tremendous and justice for martyred farmers of Lakhimpur remains an unfinished chapter of this movement. Again, when Lakhbir Singh, a Dalit, was lynched to death by the Nihang Sikhs for allegedly desecrating the Granth Sahib, SKM opposed the killing and demanded an enquiry. The modus operandi of BJP and its allies in manufacturing such incidents got exposed time and again to the entire world.

When the state did everything to agitate, insult and divide the farmers, SKM was remarkable in demonstrating restraint and discipline in mass actions. There is no doubt that this discipline is ingrained in the ethos and culture of Punjab when they are up against an enemy. A total of 733 peasants died in the protests; an average of two deaths per day.[2] Most of them happen to be landless or small peasants.

Sikhism has fought so many wars to establish itself as a religion that the deeply embedded ethos of *sewa* (service), sacrifice and endurance became the mainstay of the protest sites. The unique amalgamation of farmer unions with thousands of volunteers of the Sikh faith helped the farmers brave the chilly nights, the scorching heat in summer and the torrential monsoon rains flooding the makeshift tents. The movement also aroused all-encompassing support from its wide flung diaspora. Resources to sustain the protests poured in, protests took place outside Indian embassies, families back home were urged to continue the sit-in at the borders till demands were met. In short, the solidarity to the struggle of the farmers against the government went global.

It was an exemplary exposition of an extra-parliamentary, peaceful but militant mass movement. Its militancy was based on people's massive mobilisation and participation. So strong was the determination of peasants that forces within SKM who favoured compromise and to settle short of repeal of the three farm laws were silenced and dared not express their views before the peasants for the fear of getting isolated as traitors.

Most incredible was the way in which the movement triggered hopes and pertinent queries among the left and democratic forces like nothing else in recent years. Dreams of a future egalitarian society are inextricably tied up to one's location in the social structure and in the political economy. The stakes in agrarian struggles are determined by graded inequalities within the peasantry. Be it about women's participation being a step closer to emancipation or not, the re-emerging demands of land to the landless farmers, the rights of agricultural labourers, the sustainability of the prevailing agrarian model or the alliances with other struggling sections, open discussions took place, expressing hope and optimism.

The Churning Within

While the farmers' demand for a legally guaranteed MSP for all crops strikes at the heart of the imperialist agenda to allow global capital a free run in Indian agriculture, the emerging demand and struggle for redistribution of land by agricultural labourers and small peasants has sharpened the conflict between feudal forces represented by land-owning big farmers and the landless peasantry in villages across Punjab. The slogan of the 1930s—*Land to the Tillers*—is yet to be realised by large sections of women and men within the struggling peasantry. Until today, upper and middle caste farmers continue to usurp government land allocated to Dalits. These agricultural labourers, who have been historically denied access to land, are today forming collectives and are challenging the power dynamics by bidding for village common lands under the leadership of Zameen Prapti Sangharsh Committee (ZPSC) and Krantikari Pendu Mazdoor Union (KPMU). They along with various left and revolutionary farmer unions are raising the demand to implement the Land Ceiling Act to redistribute excess land among the landless and small peasantry.

While a significant section of landless peasantry was forcefully transformed into agricultural labourers during the Green Revolution, the long-term impact continues in the ongoing exodus of thousands of Jat Sikhs also—small and marginal farmers—from agriculture. Since 1991, about 53 percent of marginal farmers, 18 percent of small farmers, and 11 percent of other farmers had left farming as it was non-remunerative.[3] A sizable percentage swell the ranks of the agricultural labourers while others migrate to cities in search of work. This process of depeasantisation further blurs the distinction between agricultural workers and landless peasantry. As Balagopal had said in the context of undivided Andhra Pradesh: Just as it is impossible to differentiate the rural rich into feudal and capitalist landlords, it is equally impossible to differentiate the rural poor into the capitalistically exploited agricultural proletariat and the feudally exploited landless peasantry.[4]

Unsurprisingly, the participation of landless farmers and agricultural workers, in most cases Dalits, in the protests was erratic because of fissures between landed peasantry and agricultural labourers in June 2020. Participation was tough also due to the exigencies of life; how many days of wages could agricultural labourers forgo to take part in the protests? Both landless peasants and agricultural workers face daunting challenges. The antagonism reached the peak, just months before protests broke out against the three laws, when farmers facing a shortage of migrant labourers due to the lockdown refused to pay local labourers higher wages. In such a situation, upper caste farmers invariably announce a social boycott of labourers who then cannot enter the fields for their work and livelihood.

Bargaining wage rates with local authorities is an uphill battle mainly because big farmers prefer to hire labour from other states, especially Bihar and UP. The pandemic lockdowns severely affected the income of agricultural workers. Yet, when the lockdown was lifted the big farmers invested in bringing back workers from Bihar instead of hiring local labour.

Therefore, even as farmer leaders called attention to the impact of the three farm laws on the landless peasants, agricultural worker unions could not relate entirely to the call. True, the dismantling of the *mandis* (agricultural produce markets) and the near imminent collapse of the PDS would push the working poor to starvation. But it is not as if anybody lives on food alone; the struggle of all oppressed sections is for dignity as well.

The recognition of labour through fair wages and guaranteed employment is uppermost on the agenda of the agricultural worker unions. The farmers' movement provided the impetus for seven agricultural worker unions to come together in August 2021 on a common platform called the Sanjha Mazdoor Morcha. The most pressing demand is that of Rs 700 as daily wage; guarantee of at least 200 working days of work under MGNREGA and stemming the corruption within MGNREGA; access to loans from cooperatives; and 300 yard plots for landless labourers.

The long-term impact of capital-intensive agriculture has been borne by the landless, as is also evident in suicide rates. Of the 16,000 agriculture-linked suicides in Punjab between 2000-2018, 9,000 are farmers while 7,000 are agricultural labourers. Almost 79 percent of suicides among labourers is attributed to the burden of indebtedness.[5] Peasant suicide is the starkest pointer of the agrarian crisis; besides this, hundreds of thousands more are struggling for sheer survival amidst misery, hardship and uncertainties.

The percentage of suicide of women among agricultural labour is at 12.43 percent while it is 8.2 percent among farmers.[6] The reasons are significant: the proliferation of the microfinance sector in Punjab in the last ten years has led to increasing indebtedness among landless women of whom almost 90 percent are Dalit women.

The grim reality is, there are almost 12.88 lakh women borrowers today.[7] Loans that are availed for whatever official reason on paper are mostly spent on running the household, in medical emergencies, arranging dowry for marriages and so on. Women fall prey to the exploitative rate interests of microfinance companies who offer fresh loans all the time. It's a shame the way in which banks, finance companies and corporations are living off the poor, and the poorest of poor women. And that in government and in NGO lexicon, it is called women's empowerment. The state-capital nexus can be fathomed in its entirety from the vantage point of labouring women.

On the other hand, this precariousness of life that women endure gives them the tenacity to scoff at the Supreme Court's patriarchal questioning on 11 January 2021 as to why women are "kept" in these protests and that they should be "persuaded" to return. The truth of course is that women joined these protests spontaneously. On 16 December, 2020, hundreds of women held up photos of male kin who had committed suicide. Even if peasant unions project them as "widows" or as "victims," the truth is still starker. They bear the scars of surviving the Green Revolution whose social and cultural impact was as devastating as its destruction of the agrarian political economy and ecology. These women are political prisoners of a patriarchal system where the semblance of protection purportedly given by the institution of marriage is undermined by the agrarian crisis that drives farmers and agricultural labourers to suicide. Who stops to think that the burden of patriarchy is heavy on the male peasantry and working class as they sweat it out to also fulfil dowry and wedding expenses?

It is evident that issues around women's reproductive roles, son preference, domestic violence, sexual division of labour and dowry are yet to become rallying points in agrarian struggles, indeed they are not likely to be viewed as pertinent. Lived experiences have always shown how patriarchal structures become more rigid in times of economic crises, especially in the agrarian crisis in the Indian context.

Be that as it may, during the protests, women were present as a powerful force and lent vibrancy and colour to the stage meetings held every day. Their statements and assertions on stage, in hundreds of interviews, behind cameras and the media, nationally and internationally, resonated with the women of Shaheen Bagh calling out the CAA. The Prime Minister's *Beti Padhao, Beti Bachao yojana* rings hollow at such moments. On 18 January 2021, when women from Haryana and Punjab drove tractors into the national capital, they made history that should be taken note of by all anti-patriarchal struggles. A long and tedious debate among peasant organisations and earnest academics was given a joyous burial: whether women are seen as farmers or farmers' wives. At last, the verdict lay in the claim of an identity, long overdue, of *"mahila* kisan.*"*

Whether it is Bodhgaya in Bihar, Nandigram and Singur in West Bengal, or Gandhamardan and Baliapal in Odisha, women have always joined *en masse* when land, natural resources or productive assets are at stake. Agrarian conflict in particular has its own history. Women have always participated in such mass movements whether it is for the share of the harvest as sharecroppers as in the 1946-1947 Tebhaga movement in Bengal, or in the armed uprising of the people of Telangana from 1946 to 1951 as they rebelled against the exploitation and oppression of the policies of the Nizam of Hyderabad and demanded the abolition of intermediaries, regulation of tenancy, and land ceilings. As landless peasants and sharecroppers, women are part of a history in which they have made enormous sacrifices. The farmers' protests would have been impossible without the involvement of all sections of the peasantry, especially women. And rightly so, as they also have a claim in shaping an egalitarian future today.

International Women's Day on the National Highway at the Tikri and Singhu borders saw thousands of women demanding the repeal of the farm laws and shaming the Prime Minister.

In effect, women were questioning the dominant agrarian political economy. The rich legacy of March 8 broke new ground as it was vindicated with voices of peasant women. Women from Punjab, Haryana and UP danced on the roads exuding energy and exuberance. Indeed, a revolution without dancing is not a revolution. The abundance of joy brought by women's presence to the doorsteps of the national capital is inseparable from the consciousness of the lived reality of working class and peasant women. For women want both the bread and the roses. In the year-long sit-ins at Tikri and Singhu, at the barricades in Dhinkia, in jal satyagrahas in Maheshwar Dam, on the sands of Kudankulam and so on, these are labouring bodies never ever free from the tyranny of household labour and the diktats of caste and patriarchy.

Yet, the most bitter truth of our times is that the recognition of the labour of the majority remains stubbornly elusive. A landless farmer who tills the land of others is never free from facing discrimination from the landed peasantry, similar to the way women feed and nurture families even as they remain vulnerable to domestic violence and abuse. Landless Dalits question why the SKM should be fine with concessions in wheat and dal or subsidised electricity only for them and not set higher demands.

Indeed, it is misleading to emphasise that the Essential Commodities Act amendment would affect women or workers the most. Price rise in commodities affects all across the spectrum. Food is cultivated, processed, stored, rationed and also cooked. By reducing the woman's role to a cook or the landless labourer to a mere consumer, such analyses obscure the role of the landless and women in agrarian conflicts, and their claim to history, on whose backs the most historical struggles have been fought against the zamindari system. Even until today, their access to land continues to be suppressed under larger narratives of resistance.

Challenges Ahead

True, the peasantry has fought back to protect land, labour and the produce from the stranglehold of the ruling class. But that umbilical cord which connects a peasant to land through their labour has been severed in states like Bihar due to years of devastating policies of the state as well as central government. Due to ever increasing fragmentation of land, uncertain productivity and a complete absence of MSP, a small and marginal farmer in Bihar and Jharkhand has to mutate one's identity for part of the year as an informal labourer. The psychological toll of such a schizophrenic existence deepens the sense of alienation from land and from dignity.

The entire agrarian political economy is undergoing deep turmoil. The future of this movement will depend on how the contradictions between landed and landless farmers are resolved on the ground. Far from overlooking or diluting the interests of the landless, we need to strengthen their position and class unity to such an extent that the middle and rich peasantry see no future for themselves without an alliance with them.[8] The struggles of farmers can be fully realised by forging decisive and enduring alliances with all sections of the peasantry.

While the alienation of farmers is deepening, the state-industrial-military complex is usurping fertile agricultural land and natural resources dispossessing entire habitats. In states across the country, subsistence producers, fisherfolk, forest dwellers, the Adivasi and Dalit peasantry are resisting the territorial advancement of the neoliberal regime. The fight for *Jal, Jangal, Zameen* rages across the forests and mountains of Chhattisgarh, Jharkhand, Odisha and Telangana. Working class communities in the metros as well as in other cities and towns are fighting forced evictions every day.

The anti-corporate struggle led by the peasantry has to unify with the working class movement. The systemic assault on labour laws, which has paved the way for unhindered capital accumulation, has undermined the hard won battles of the working class, some of which had been waged even before Independence. When industrial workers who produce the most cherished products of the neoliberal regime—cars, air conditioners and motorbikes—undergo years of incarceration for asserting labour rights, it is not difficult to imagine the plight of workers in the vast unorganised sector who have in the first place been bereft of any protective legislation. Therefore, when the *Mazdoor Kisan Ekta*

Zindabad slogan resonated in the farmers movement, it was yet another historical moment.

By bringing the agrarian crisis onto the national agenda, the farmers' movement has rekindled these issues in people's consciousness. Now the ground has been created for peasant resistance to take a further stride in addressing the agrarian crisis as being inextricably linked to the political, social and economic structures of Indian society.

When seen in its totality, the movement has broadened the canvas and horizon of issues beyond the three laws that it set out to oppose. Its most significant contribution is in giving hope for a broad democratic movement in this country. And therein lies the victory of the Indian peasantry.

To conclude, let us reiterate the common refrain of women in these protests: "Future generations will not forgive us if we do not resist today."

> *Utthega an-al-haq ka nara*
> *Jo main bhi hoon, aur tum bhi ho*
> *Aur raaj karegi khalq-e-khuda*
> *Jo main bhi hoon aur tum bhi ho*
> *Hum dekhenge*
> *Lazim hai ki hum bhi dekhenge*
> *– Faiz Ahmad Faiz*

About the Author

Ranjana Padhi is a political activist and author currently based in Bhubaneswar. She has authored Those Who Did Not Die: The Impact of the Agrarian Crisis on Women in Punjab *(Sage Publications: 2012) and co-authored* Resisting Dispossession: The Odisha Story *(Palgrave Macmillan and Aakar Books: 2020).*

Endnotes

1. The percentage of the budget spent on agriculture was 14.9 percent during the First Five-Year Plan (1951-56). It declined to 12.3 percent during the Fifth Plan (1974-79), and further to 3.7 percent during the Eleventh Plan (2007-12).
2. See List of Deaths in Farmers' Protest at Delhi Border since 24 November 2020 (hu-

mancostoffarmersprotest.blogspot.com).

3. Sukhpal Singh and Shruti Bhogal: Punjab's Small Peasantry: Thriving or Deteriorating? Economic & Political Weekly Supplement, June 28, 2014, Vol XLIX, Nos 26 & 27.

4. K. Balagopal: Probings in The Political Economy Of Agrarian Classes and Conflicts, 2021, Perspectives, Hyderabad.

5. Sukhpal Singh, Manjeet Kaur, H S Kingra: Agrarian Crisis and Agricultural Labourer Suicides in Punjab, Economic & Political Weekly, March 27, 2021, Vol LVI, No 13.

6. Ibid.

7. Vivek Gupta: How Punjab's Rural Women, Neck-Deep in Debt, Are Trapped in Microloan Cycles, The Wire, February 18, 2021.

8. K. Balagopal: Probings in The Political Economy Of Agrarian Classes and Conflicts, 2021, Perspectives, Hyderabad.

The Three Farm Laws and Their Impact on the Peasantry

Prof. Sukhpal Singh

> What were the three farm laws and why were they resisted with such fervour and determination by the farmers? For readers, who are not familiar with the content of the three farm laws, we start this volume with a brief introduction to those laws and their likely impact on different sections of the peasantry by Prof. Sukhpal Singh. We think this will help us comprehend the anxiety and rage that triggered the unprecedented farmers' rebellion.
>
> – *The Editorial Team*

THREE ORDINANCES were passed by the Narendra Modi-led central government in June 2020, which would have a huge impact on agriculture in India. In September they became the three 'farm laws'— the Farmers Produce Trade and Commerce (Promotion and Facilitation) Act, the Farmers (Empowerment and Protection) Agreement on Price Assurance and Farm Services Act and the Essential Commodities (Amendment) Act (ECA), which amends the Essential Commodities Act, 1955.

I. The Farmers Produce Trade and Commerce (Promotion and Facilitation) Act

According to the Indian Constitution, the central government cannot enact laws related to agriculture. It is mentioned in Article 14, 26 and 28, and in the Seventh Schedule of the Constitution that only the state government can enact laws related to agriculture. There are three lists— State List, Union List and Concurrent List. Agriculture falls under the State List. It is stated that the central government may provide a model based on which states can form their own laws. However, in this particular case, the central government did not provide any model; it directly passed the laws. This new Act basically bypasses the Agricultural

Produce & Livestock Market Committee (APMC) Act, and in order to make a law, the central government has intentionally added trade and commerce to it. However, the farmers do not directly engage in trade and commerce and they produce natural grain and not food-stuff. In this regard, this law is both unconstitutional and anti-federal.

The law aims at providing freedom of choice to the farmer and the trader. This means that the farmer can go anywhere to sell their produce to anyone. However, even before these laws, the farmers had the choice of selling their produce to anyone and anywhere. With this law the ambit of freedom to sell extended to include private players also. On the one hand, the central government says that it aims to create one nation, one market, one religion, one vote. On the other hand, this law creates two markets in agriculture—a private market and a government market. The government says that both will function simultaneously. However, there is an important difference that the private markets will not levy any tax, whereas the government markets levy a tax, which will ultimately lead to an end of the government market. For example, in Punjab, the state government charges 8.5 percent tax, of which 3 percent is for rural development funds, 3 percent is market fees and 2.5 percent is commission of agents. This tax is levied by all the states. The burden of paying these taxes lies with the purchaser of the agricultural produce and not with the farmers. So, given this fundamental difference that there is no tax on buyers in the private market, they will be able to offer lucrative prices to the farmers, who will then sell their produce in the private market. For example, there is an approximate tax of Rs 150-175 on one quintal of wheat or paddy. As long as the buyers are able to offer a price greater than that offered by the government *mandi* (agricultural produce market) by less than the tax amount, it will be beneficial for both farmers and the buyers. Slowly, the government will introduce targeted procurement, limiting the amount of produce procured by the government, and then this will put an end to the regulated markets and public procurement at Minimum Support Price (MSP).

Another important aspect related to this Act is that it gives farmers the freedom to sell anywhere. However, our data tells us that agricultural markets are already integrated and interlinked, and small traders have played an important role in achieving this integration.

With these laws, the small traders will be *replaced* by companies. This is the only difference that these laws will be able to achieve. It will not have any beneficial impact on farmers as 86 percent of Indian farmers are small and marginal, who do not have the means to arrange to sell in any desired market. Currently, this is being done by small traders; after these laws, this will be done by the companies. In all, this will put an end to the regulated market system, MSP and state procurement, and only a handful of private companies will remain in the market as the main buyers of agricultural produce.

2. The Farmers (Empowerment and Protection) Agreement on Price Assurance and Farm Services Act

In short, this is called the Contract Farming Act. According to the law, there can be two forms of contract farming that can be implemented in practice. In total there are five different kinds of contract farming systems. However, in most countries the following two are followed: first, when there can be a contract on the basis of the farm produce and second, when the company leases the land from the farmer.

Within the first form, the farmer will be provided with a package of inputs like seeds, fertilisers, technological inputs and directions on what to produce and how to produce. The price of the final produce will also be fixed within this contract. One issue with this is that the kind of crop to be grown will not be decided by the requirements of the people but that of the company. Another issue is that the company also fixes the price based on certain parameters like size, quality, grading, etc. The company in contract with the farmers will make specific demands to the farmers with regard to the produce. For example, they may want a specific size and colour of tomato, potato or chilly. However, agricultural commodities are produced naturally and fixing such parameters leads to various problems, the biggest being wastage of the produce. Across most developed economies, the agricultural sector is not able to meet these parameters as its product is not an industrial product, rather a natural product that renders each single commodity different from the other. So, the company only procures the products from the farmers that meet these strict quality parameters, and does not purchase the rest. One may argue that the farmer then can sell the remaining produce in the market.

But that too is not possible since the contract does not allow farmers to sell their products in the market. A large proportion of the produce that the company does not purchase and that the farmers cannot sell in the market gets wasted. On the one hand, a shortage in supply leads to price rise, and on the other, it leads to wastage of food while there is a huge population facing starvation. Even if there is demand for food, the contract restricts the farmer from selling in the market.

The second form of contract farming is when the company leases the land from the farmer. Initially companies lure farmers by giving long-period contracts (like five years) and paying higher rents. Since the first law tries to bypass the APMC Act and farmers are not able to avail the MSP, they are induced to engage in contract farming to get higher rents as compared to the income from cultivation. However, whatever is the rental value of the land according to the contract, there is also 18 percent GST (Goods and Services Tax), an indirect tax levied by the Indian government. This is deducted from the rental amount paid to the farmers. For example, if the rent for one acre of land is Rs 50,000, the farmer will receive only Rs 41,000 as rental amount after deducting 18 percent GST (Rs 9,000). It is possible that the company will reduce the rent that it pays on the land simply by taking advantage of the fact that the farmer will find it extremely difficult to start cultivation after a gap of five years. Moreover, there might even be new technological advancements that have come in the interim. For example, before the Green Revolution, bullock carts that were majorly used in the cultivation process got replaced by tractors. With the enactment of the three farm laws, the use of tractors may become less important due to the advancement in artificial intelligence, which is likely to introduce a high-tech mechanised system in highly fertile areas of Punjab, Haryana, Western UP and the entire Indo-Gangetic plains, which are the areas that benefited from the Green Revolution. No farmer will dare use tractors. Today we cannot imagine a farmer using bullock carts since it is more expensive to use outdated technologies due to high unit cost. Due to these factors, the farmer will be driven out of agriculture and will be forced to sell the land and join the ranks of labour.

Another important claim being made by the central government is that these laws aim to remove the middleman. In effect, a new kind of middleman will replace the old ones. The new middleman will belong to the companies, for example, there will be suppliers, processors, agents, franchisees, even Farmer Producer Organisations (FPOs). Across Europe and America, it is largely accepted that suppliers are the main exploiters as they are the ones who monitor and enforce quality parameters. Wherever this has happened, such problems have surfaced.

It is argued that if contract farming can work for perishable commodities like milk, why can't it work for other food items like grains, fruits and vegetables? However, the milk sector in major milk producing states like Punjab, Gujarat, etc., is largely dominated by cooperatives like Verka and Amul which are the price leaders in the market. Until and unless the government intervenes in leading price discovery of agricultural commodities and provides competition in the market, contract farming may not really work for these agricultural commodities. In fact, documented examples and technical papers testify how farmers who engage in contract farming earn less than the farmers who do not enter into contracts. Contract farming basically serves the interests of the companies. Punjab and other states that fall predominantly under agrarian economies should promote a cultivation model that would also generate employment. Compared to other sectors, only the agricultural sector has the capacity to provide employment.

3. The Essential Commodities (Amendment) Act (ECA)

The Essential Commodities Act (ECA) was enacted in 1955 to provide food at affordable prices to the people. There are several items like drugs, chemicals, fertilisers, seeds, fodder, vegetables and fruits, petroleum, etc., mentioned in this Act. Within this Act, it is prohibited to store these essential commodities. With the 2020 amendment in ECA, agricultural commodities have been removed from the essential commodities category, which will now allow the storage of these commodities. There are certain emergency situations under which storage is not allowed, for example, if the price of highly perishable commodities increases by 100 percent or the price of grains by 50 percent. However, even under these circumstances, there are certain areas where storage is allowed. If you are a processor, exporter or a supply chain agent (distributor, providing storage, transporter or any other part of this chain), the storage of agricultural commodities is not prohibited. If the prices rise beyond 50 percent or 100 percent, even then storage is allowed, depending upon the export capacity, processing capacity, etc. It is not mentioned clearly whether this capacity is measured monthly or yearly. In agriculture, prices increase in the month before harvesting. Since there is no prohibition on storage, they will store the commodities and put upward pressure on the prices. This will majorly impact the working class because if the price of food commodities increases by 50 percent or 100 percent, then a major proportion of their income will be spent on food. It has been estimated that as a result of the price rise, for 90 percent of the people in India, total annual expenditure on food out of their yearly income (for the entire family) will increase by Rs 31,000. While this happens, their incomes are not going to rise. Rather their incomes will decrease as unemployment will rise because of these laws. Thus, a rise in price will lead to a fall in their real incomes and these people may fall below the poverty line. Whenever there is a small increase in the prices of agricultural commodities, there is always a corresponding increase in the population living below the poverty line.

A significant proportion of the income of the labour class both in urban and rural areas is spent on purchasing food. In the market there are two situations that are bad—monopsony and monopoly. When there are only one or two buyers in the market (monopsony), they will be able to purchase at a low price from the farmers because there are a few buyers to whom a large number of farmers are willing to sell their produce. Also, there will be a handful of companies selling agricultural commodities in the market. The laws will create these worst situations in the market where there are only a few buyers of agricultural produce (from farmers) and only a few sellers (to consumers) of these commodities; in short, the companies will exploit both consumers and farmers. The government has extended the logic that the Public Distribution System (PDS) will continue and they will keep on purchasing under this system in order, to maintain buffer stock as well to provide food under the Food Security Act. However, the government may start purchasing the required quantity from the private market. The farmers will sell their produce to private markets and the government will then purchase the commodities from the private market. There will be no hue and cry about this. The MSP for wheat is Rs 1,925 per quintal, but the economic cost (which includes what the farmer gets, the procurement cost and distribution cost) is Rs 3,000 per quintal. So, the government will purchase from Adani and Ambani (and may even distribute through PDS) and no one will object to this arrangement. Earlier there was universal PDS, later it was converted to a targeted PDS system, under which only 67 percent of the population is eligible to receive food.

There are four major agri-business companies called A,B,C and D (ADM, Bunge, Cargill, Dreyfus) that control the world agri-business market. We know that the world's most profitable business is the pharmaceutical industry followed by agri-business. These companies want to enter India and tap this large market. Similarly, domestic companies like Ambani and Adani want to enter the agri-business market. However, since they don't have the technical knowledge, they want these major global agri-business companies to enter India in order to collaborate with them. In this way, the domestic companies can control both the input and output market in the farm sector.

About the Author

Professor Sukhpal Singh is Principal Economist in Punjab Agricultural University, Ludhiana. The content of this article has been taken from his interview conducted by Workers Unity on 30 March 2021 at Ludhiana.

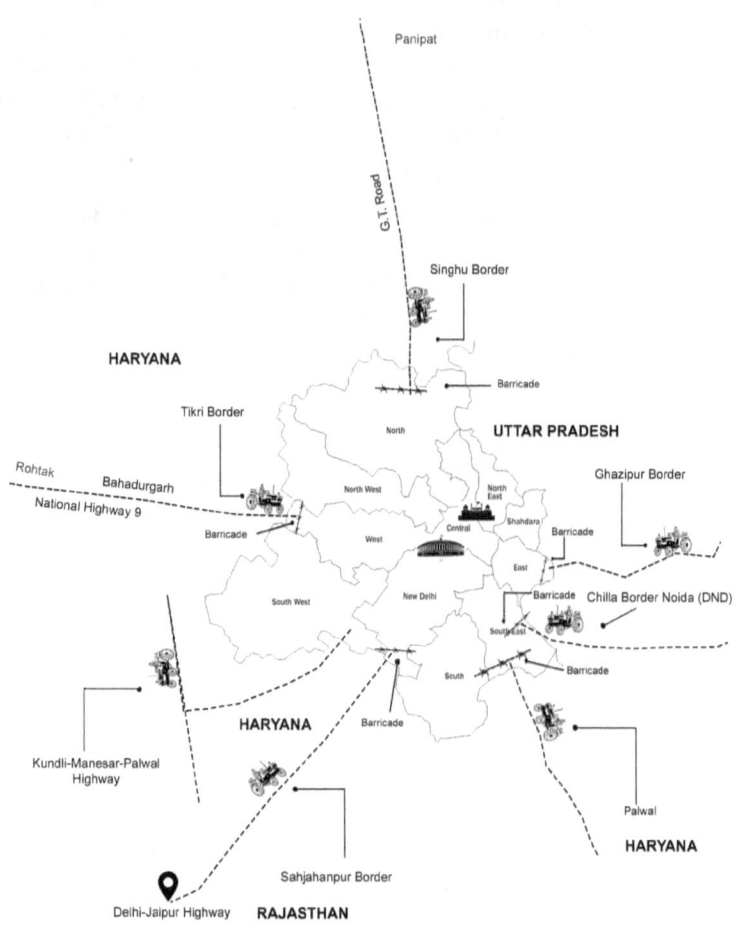

Map showing protest sites of farmers at the borders of Delhi. **Map design:** Vikas Thakur.

SECTION I

CONVERSATIONS WITH LEADERS OF FARMERS' UNIONS

On January 26, 2021, lakhs of farmers marched on tractors decorated with the national flag and the flags of the kisan unions on the outskirts of Delhi. The Kisan Tractor Parade was organised in all the states. **Photo credit**: Workers Unity.

This Struggle has Established that the Farming Community Can Play a Central and Leading Role for a Democratic Change of Indian Society

DR. DARSHAN PAL, KRANTIKARI KISAN UNION

> DR. DARSHAN PAL is the President of the Krantikari Kisan Union (KKU), Punjab, a leader of the Samyukta Kisan Morcha (SKM) and a leading member of the All India Kisan Sangharsh Coordination Committee (AIKSCC). He is a people's doctor and an organiser of the peasantry in Punjab. Darshan Pal's major role in keeping the farmers' movement united, strong and active was the manifestation of his long years of experience in building alliances and joint coalitions with the vision of a broad democratic movement in the country. The unity of the peasant unions in Punjab for the repeal of the three farm laws paved the way for a broader unity among peasants and diverse struggling sections in India.
>
> This interview is a consolidated outcome of several interactions with Darshan Pal by WORKERS UNITY, ARUN KUMAR TRIPATHI, and GROUNDXERO.

QUESTION: *Darshanji, in recent times, there have been very few people's movements that have lasted for such a long duration with such intensity. The capital city of the country has been surrounded by protesting farmers for nearly a year. So many farmer organisations have come together under the umbrella of Samyukta Kisan Morcha (SKM). Can you tell us briefly about the agrarian crisis that precipitated this struggle?*

DARSHAN PAL: First, I would like to thank you on behalf of our Krantikari Kisan Union (KKU). Let us go through the issues one by one.

If you consider the current situation of agriculture in India and even the rest of the world, you will notice that the agrarian sector is in a state of crisis everywhere. The sector is profoundly sick. And its condition has become so serious that now it is like a serious patient who needs to be admitted to the ICU (intensive care unit) immediately. All those associated with agriculture—the farmers and the agricultural workers too—are in urgent need of receiving radical treatment. They need oxygen, they need life-support systems—just to survive.

So, the farmer organisations in various parts of the country were already engaged in various struggles, raising issues and demands concerning the farmers and agricultural workers, even prior to this movement. I am from Punjab, where during the period of globalisation in the '90s and even earlier from the time of the Green Revolution, our ruling classes in their own interests, in the name of development and reform, introduced certain policies and changes in the sector. We had a problem of scarcity of food grains in the country that led to frequent famines, malnutrition and even death due to hunger. To overcome these problems, they implemented a model of agriculture, directly copied from the western countries. In Punjab and Haryana, *mandis* (agricultural produce markets) were built, HYV (High Yielding Variety) seeds were introduced, so were inputs like fertilisers, pesticides, insecticides, etc. I have seen with my own eyes how bulls were replaced by small machines; double furrow ploughs which followed the single furrow ploughs were in turn replaced by tractors. All these changes necessitated investment of capital into farming to access the new technology and inputs, and the farmers became dependent on the moneylenders and banks or finance companies for securing capital for investment in order to produce crops. The farmers soon became dependent on agencies outside of agriculture.

As this system progressed, the major change was that the 'terms of trade' turned against the farming community. The apparent benefits that the farmers were getting from increase in yield and conversion of barren land into fertile land were accompanied by increasing 'input cost.' The farmers were indeed making profits and earning more in comparison to the earlier model of traditional farming. But after a point, profits stagnated—reached a plateau—and then started dipping. Eventually, the rate of increase of profit became negative and farming became what we now call *ghaate ka dhanda* (loss making profession).

So, the first symptom of the agrarian crisis, or this sick model of farming, was that growth of profit became negative and farming turned unprofitable. Now this model required huge capital investment by the farmers to reap its benefits. The farmer had to take loans. He needed to mandatorily pay back the loans with interest. But, with rising input costs, stagnating yield and falling rate of profit, his outstanding loans started rising. Gradually, he fell into a debt trap. Indebtedness of the farmers is the second symptom of the agrarian crisis created by this sick model. More than two lakh farmers of Punjab sold out their land and turned landless labourers, which is the third symptom of the crisis known as depeasantisation.

QUESTION: *When did this agrarian crisis become the most severe? Was it in 1991, when liberalisation of the Indian economy started? Was the crisis present even before the Green Revolution? Had it intensified during the '90s or now when the three farm laws were passed by the Narendra Modi government? In short, tell us whether you organised this movement because there is a crisis right now.*

DARSHAN PAL: You see, the crisis did not happen because of the three farm laws. The crisis began in the late '70s and '80s, when the cost of production started to increase. By the '80s, we used to say that the 'Green' of the Revolution had started turning 'pallor'! Economic reforms in the '90s accelerated, deepened and widened this crisis further. Subsidies on fertilisers and other inputs were slashed. Import of good grains was allowed. Health, education and other public services were privatised. Farmers were committing suicide. There was massive indebtedness. Farmer organisations were only fighting against these symptoms. Some were fighting for compensation to the families of the suicide victims, some on taking measures for stopping of suicides. Many organisations were agitating to reduce the cost of production by subsidising inputs, while others were demanding an increase in the support price of the produce and some were raising the issue of freedom from indebtedness.

QUESTION: *You mean, the struggles were fragmented...*

DARSHAN PAL: People do understand the comprehensive nature of the crisis, how the various symptoms were connected to the Green Revolution, but it is difficult for a single organisation working in a particular region to challenge the entire agrarian model on its own. The organisations are small, their vision is narrow and also they have limited capacities and resources.

Farmer organisations, say for example, those belonging to the Left, were for years discussing and debating contradictions between big farmers, middle farmers and small farmers, the antagonistic relationship between landless agricultural workers and the landed peasantry. Some organisations refused to include MSP (Minimum Support Price) in their agenda, saying that MSP ensures profits mainly to the big land-owning farmers. They felt that instead, they should concentrate on the struggle to reduce the cost of inputs. Thus, the Left organisations were divided into various camps based on their ideology, their political outlook and their way of functioning.

But farmer organisations were active at various places. You see, wherever a farmer organisation was formed, be it by Mahendra Singh Tikait in UP, or Joshiji in Maharashtra, Ghasi Ram in Haryana or Rajewal and Bhupindar Mann in Punjab and Prof. M. D. Nanjundaswamy in Karnataka, you will see that there is a common thing—all these unions came to the forefront at a time when after capital's intervention into the agrarian sector had led to the cost of production rising, profits falling and crops being left unsold in the *mandis*. The same is also true for Tamil Nadu and other states. So these farmer organisations and kisan leaders emerged as the agrarian crisis started unfolding in regions where this new model of agriculture was put into practice.

These leaders launched many struggles and tried to coordinate amongst themselves, but due to their individualism and personality cult, even when they came together, it always resulted in internal conflicts and eventually they would split and the struggles would disintegrate.

The percentage of Indians dependent on agriculture is quite high, both in developed and underdeveloped regions. More than 58 percent of India's population, in some way or the other, is dependent on agriculture. Apart from economic exploitation there exists non-economic coercion. Exploitation based on caste and gender is a fact in rural areas. It exists in urban areas too, but there it is relatively less.

But, in spite of uneven development across regions in India, the people involved in agriculture—peasants or farmers, landed or landless—developed an identity that they belong to the same community, the same class. We identified this common sense of identity and community feeling, and stressed on getting all the sections of the agrarian society involved in support of the movement.

QUESTION: *Do you see any major difference between the United Progressive Alliance (UPA) government under Manmohan Singh and the current National Democratic Alliance (NDA) regime being led by Narendra Modi? Have corporations become more influential now?*

DARSHAN PAL: The process of restructuring the Indian economy in the name of globalisation, liberalisation and privatisation, and especially fitting the agrarian economy inside that restructured economic model, began from Manmohan Singh's time. I still remember the struggles by farmer organisations against the Dunkel Draft[1], the WTO (World Trade Organisation) and specifically against the Agreement on Agriculture (AoA)[2] and the demand to keep Indian agriculture out of the WTO. At that time there was a split in farmer organisations depending upon the stand taken by its leadership in support of or against the WTO. The laws that were passed in parliament at that time were for the benefit of the multinational corporations, be it about pesticides or high-yielding seeds. The privatisation and disinvestment of PSUs (Public Sector Units) was started. But the process was moving slowly. The pro-corporate reforms were started by the Congress government, were taken forward by all the subsequent governments, and now they have been exponentially accelerated by the Modi-led BJP government. The all-out privatisation of PSUs happening now would have been difficult to pull off in those days. Selling the railways would have been unthinkable at that time.

QUESTION: *You mean both Congress and BJP have had the same policy direction, the difference is in the speed of their implementation.*

DARSHAN PAL: Absolutely. Globally, these trends can be stopped only by people's movements, be it in a small country or a large one. Whether to work under the dictates of the WTO and allow the corporates to take all natural resources and public wealth—these decisions have led to changes in policies and laws. We were all trying to fight against some policy implementation here, some corporate penetration there, and so on. What I want to say is that the farmer unions that came out of the struggles in the '80s could neither unite nor coordinate nor advance these struggles. These farmer leaders lacked the vision that could look through the global phenomenon of corporatisation and prepare the people against it. During the first phase of globalisation, there were massive movements like against the Iraq war, WTO, etc., all over the world. The Iraq war was opposed by perhaps one and a half million people in France alone. It became a global protest. Then there were all those struggles in Tunisia, Egypt, Syria—the Arab Spring. Even these movements did not have much of a clear-cut orientation about the future.

Similarly, the farmers' movements in India back then lacked orientation. So, the movements eventually faded out. The BKU (Bharatiya Kisan Union)[3] split into numerous factions. Also, after a point, the old way of organising struggles needed to be changed. The new model of development had to be understood well.

The turning point was the incident on June 6, 2017 in Mandsaur district of Madhya Pradesh, where six farmers became martyrs. These six were not part of any farmer organisation. There was a protest against farmers not getting remunerative prices for wheat and waiver of their loans. And, the agitating farmers in Pipliya Mandi, in Mandsaur were lathi-charged and fired upon. This incident unified several farmer leaders and organisations. It was then that the farmer organisations with different ideological outlooks came together—from radical Left to far Right. A big meeting was held on 16 June 2017 at the Gandhi Peace Foundation in Delhi, and for the first time, I saw kisan *sangathans* (farmer organisations) of different ideologies, political orientations and beliefs had come together on a single platform. There was discussion on a lot of issues in that meeting and an agreement was reached on two issues—indebtedness of farmers and guaranteed procurement of crops at MSP. A possibility of forming a united *morcha* (front) of farmer organisations appeared for the first time, based on these two issues. This was the *morcha* that later came to be known as the All India Kisan Sangharsh Samanvay Samiti or All India Kisan Sangharsh Coordination Committee—AIKSCC. AIKSCC was constituted in this meeting. Following this, protest marches started on 6 July from Mandsaur, and rallies were held all over India under the banner of AIKSCC. Two kisan *sansads* ('farmers' parliament' sessions)—the first on 18 July and the second on 20 and 21 November 2017, took place in Delhi. When the three farm laws came in June 2020, it was this Kisan Sangharsh Samiti or AIKSCC that protested widely, and a decision was taken that a nation-wide movement should be organised against the laws.

Question: *Modi's rule is based on Hindutva majoritarianism and corporatisation. A combination of these two are deciding the policies these days. The rulers are confident that the policies that they make will not be opposed by the people. But it is turning out to be counter-productive. People felt that rule based on majoritarianism signalled the end of democracy. Perhaps that is one reason why the farmers' movement could come this far. So on the one hand the matter is about the economy and on the other about democracy. You have spoken about the economic side. But this movement has also raised the subject of democracy, fundamental rights of the citizens to protest, etc. How do you see the farmers' movement in these terms?*

Darshan Pal: There are several factors which I would like to mention here. When we thought of starting the struggle against the three farm laws, we were not very optimistic. *Mandis*, MSP and debt are definitely agrarian issues. But these mainly impacted farmers in Punjab.

If it was not for the AIKSCC which initiated the process of organising protests against the three farm ordinances during the Covid-period, perhaps we would not have been where we are now. In fact, it is the AIKSCC which invited all other farmer unions and organisations to be part of a joint front to oppose the ordinances. This was a decisive first step which gave birth to this struggle. When we started this struggle, we absolutely had no inkling or agenda that this was a struggle to save democracy, or a struggle against religious majoritarianism, or that we were launching an anti-fascist struggle.

Our entire objective was to resist the three farm laws. In fact, I now think that in addition to opposing the three laws and demands for an guaranteed MSP, we should have also added a demand for erasing debts of all farmers. This was an error on our part, in my opinion.

I should finally add that the specificity of Punjab has played an important role here and it is hard to envisage how this struggle would have developed, had it not been launched by the farmers of Punjab. Punjab is a border state, its contribution to the agrarian GDP is one of the highest in the country, and as we know it was one of the main laboratories for the Green Revolution. Then there is the specificity of Sikhism in which fighting against any socio-political injustice is very much part of its ethos and we have seen a history of sacrifices and martyrdom from people of Punjab at various stages of history.

In my opinion, and this is something I have experienced over the last decade, and especially in the last year, the Indian peasantry in many ways is a single such group which has a scope of unifying, possessing a strong striking power and some common objectives. There is so much unevenness in the agriculture sector—so many sections between farmers on the basis of land, caste, culture and language. But I still feel that there is a lot more that unites farmers in Tamil Nadu and Punjab than what divides them. That is, there is a real scope (and we now have had some solid evidence over the past year) that this possibility will materialise. Farmers all over the world are going through a crisis in this so-called era of neoliberalisation. In India, farmers in Punjab and in Tamil Nadu and in other places are committing suicide. And the enemy is a common one. I strongly believe that these factors will ensure that the farmers' struggle will play a vital and a central role in a larger people's movement and in reshaping the society. In fact, the way this movement got support from many sections of the society, not only from the working class but also the intellectuals, youth and students for example, is enough evidence to show that people can unify around the pillar of the peasant movement.

QUESTION: *How were the protests in Punjab organised? Were they spontaneous? Tell us about the process of formation of SKM and the march to Delhi by the farmers.*

DARSHAN PAL: The three ordinances were brought on 5 June 2020. To be frank, the kisan organisations in Punjab did not take up the issue of these ordinances seriously. I remember that I had sent the text of these ordinances to a working committee member of AIKSCC in Bangalore. We immediately discussed it among ourselves and gave a call for two or three types of actions. Firstly, to write letters to the PM opposing the ordinances. Secondly, to hold protests in front of the offices of the parties in the NDA in Punjab and throughout the country.

However, maximum mobilisation was taking place in Punjab, while in other states due to lockdown restrictions, mobilisation was at a much lower level. There was only token participation. In Punjab the mobilisation was at a large scale. The ten constituents of the Punjab chapter of AIKSCC gave a call that kisan *sangathans* (organisations) in Punjab will hold demonstrations in front of the offices of the NDA partners with a demand charter drafted by us based on guidelines from the AIKSCC.

The Punjab Tractor March was organised perhaps in the last week of July, on the 27th. And for the first time we felt that a lot of youth were coming forward, while in the earlier times, older people mainly participated in farmers' protests. Thousands of youth playing loud music drove tractors at a fast speed towards the houses of BJP and Akali Dal leaders. Such programmes were repeated and once again the youth came forward in large numbers. The pressure built up by the farmers and youth in Punjab was so intense that Akali Dal was compelled to break its alliance with BJP. Harsimrat Kaur, the lone minister in the Union Cabinet from Akali Dal, had to submit her resignation. The society as a whole in Punjab, including youths, religious organisations and political parties, was joining the protests opposing the three ordinances.

Besides the ten kisan organisations (the members of AIKSCC) in Punjab, several other farmer organisations held meetings and decided to work together. This led to the formation of the *morcha* of 28 Punjab-based organisations. This *morcha* gave a call for a Punjab Bandh on 25 September 2020. The bandh was very successful and it was also a turning point.

From the people's response to the tractor march and Punjab Bandh, it appeared that Punjab was ready for a big battle with Delhi. In this situation other organisations in Punjab joined the movement. BKU (Ekta-Ugrahan) and Kisan Mazdoor Sangharsh Samiti also announced that they were with the *morcha*. Many smaller organisations also joined. This was the beginning of the direct battle with Delhi.

The protests intensified and became more widespread in Punjab when from 1 October an indefinite call was given and all the railway tracks in Punjab were blocked. All toll plazas in Punjab were occupied. It was decided to boycott all products and services of Adani and Ambani—seize all petrol pumps run by them and sit on dharnas (sit-ins) outside their malls. We had already declared that if anybody from BJP and Akali Dal tried to come, we would prevent them from entering the villages. It was this fear which had forced the Akali Dal to exit from the NDA. The BJP elected representatives and their leaders were being gheraoed and indefinite dharnas started in front of their houses and offices.

Both the central and the state government were shaken. The Punjab government called a special session of the Assembly [on 19 October 2020]. Barring two BJP MLAs, the MLAs of all the political parties in Punjab joined a procession to submit a resolution opposing the laws to the Governor. This meant that all the political parties except the BJP were forced to take a stand in favour of the kisans; this included the Punjab government also.

Feeling the heat, the central government invited us for a meeting with the Union agriculture secretary, who will explain to us the benefits of the Acts. We decided not to take part in this meeting and boycotted it. The struggle was in full swing in Punjab. Railway tracks were kept blocked. BJP members were not allowed to move around freely. Then we got another invitation from the central government promising that we would also be given time with the Agriculture Minister in Delhi. We went from Punjab for the meeting. But the minister was not present, so we boycotted the meeting, burned copies of the laws in front of Krishi Bhawan and returned back.

AIKSCC gave a *Dilli Chalo* call on 26-27 November 2020. We decided that the *Dilli Chalo* programme would not be limited to only the constituents of AIKSCC but let all the kisan organisations come together in the struggle.

On 7 November, a meeting of the big kisan organisations was held in Gurudwara Rakab Ganj. An umbrella body named Samyukta Kisan Morcha (SKM) of different farmer organisations from across the country was constituted. Rakesh Tikait remained outside the SKM. Some kisan organisations from UP had also not joined. Two of the Punjab organisations, BKU (Ekta-Ugrahan) and Kisan Mazdoor Sangharsh Committee also remained outside SKM.

On 14 November, a meeting with the Agriculture Minister and the Railway Minister also failed. Our agitation in Punjab had stopped all goods as well as passenger trains. It was sowing time for wheat and fertilisers were urgently needed. Coal was necessary to run power plants. Diesel was also needed. The Union government was screaming that military supplies were not reaching Kashmir. We were willing to lift the blockade on goods trains. But we remained resolute on the *rail roko* (rail blockade) for passenger trains. The Minister of Railways was obstinate. He threatened to stop all supplies from and to Punjab. The talks broke down.

The preparations for the Delhi March began in full swing. The farmers had already started to decorate their tractors; they had equipped their trolleys with all necessities and converted them into mobile-homes. The great unity of the people of Punjab was achieved. In the past also, the Sikhs had a long history of sacrifices. They had rebelled against the Mughal and British rulers in Delhi. The fight of Punjab again was with Delhi. They felt politically and spiritually energised.

We knew that we would not be allowed to enter Delhi. We had decided we would camp wherever they stopped us outside Delhi and hold our dharna. After two-three days of dharna, a committee of seven persons will consult with all organisations and decide what had to be done after that. But fate had something else in store for us.

In four or five places at the Punjab-Haryana border barricades were put up by the administration. It was our plan that we would stop there and camp there, hold rallies and block the highways. But on 26 November, especially the way the youth participants were energised, they wanted to reach Delhi at any cost. My personal feeling is that the mood was such that if at that time any of the kisan leaders had opposed the youth even a little bit, then surely the youth would have rebelled against the leaders also. Kisan leaders understood the sentiment and showed their farsightedness. The Haryana and Delhi police tried their best to stop us. They used tear gas. They used water cannons. They dug huge 15-25 feet deep trenches on the highway. They laid huge boulders on the roads, placed large containers to block the marching tractors and trolleys. The marching farmers and youth overcame all obstacles. After two nights and one day, the kisans and the people of Punjab reached the Singhu and

Tikri borders, just outside Delhi. Thousands of those who were supporting us with water and food, those who ran the langars, and those who were providing us medicines and other support also reached there. It felt that it was not only the kisans but the whole of Punjabi society which had converged there.

Even when the marchers camped outside Delhi, there were a lot of conspiracies hatched against them by the government in Delhi. The leaders were called Khalistanis, separatist, Maoists, and so on. They suggested that roads be opened for the protesters to drive to an open ground in Burari in an obscure corner outside the city. But most of the kisan organisations rejected such proposals and decided to camp at the borders. The two big dharna sites of kisans were established at Singhu and Tikri borders where the majority of people were from Punjab. At the Ghazipur, Shahjahanpur and Palwal borders, the participants were mainly Punjabis to start with. At the Ghazipur border, where Tikait had come with some 100 to 150 supporters, the highway to Delhi was initially blocked mainly by Punjabi migrants who had come from the Terai region of UP and Uttarakhand. Even at the Shahjahanpur border, people who had gathered there at the start were mostly Punjabi migrants from Hanumangarh and Ganganagar districts of Rajasthan. The contribution of the Sikh community in shaping this struggle is immense.

QUESTION: *Thanks for explaining how this historic movement started. As you pointed out from day one the Indian state has tried to build a narrative that Khalistani elements and outside forces were leading and planning these protests. We also saw how the entire narrative was built around the events on 26 January. It was also said that radical Left groups had hijacked the struggle. There was also this episode with the Nihang Sikhs, who killed a person at the Singhu border. Will you comment on this?*

DARSHAN PAL: As I said earlier, when the protest began, the entire agenda was about repealing the farm laws and getting a legal guarantee for MSP. Now as the farmers and people of Punjab and their various organisations got involved, be it religious organisations or communists, they had an aspiration that the movement should take shape as per their ideologies and dreams. As Sikhs are the largest population in Punjab, I have no hesitation in saying that Sikh religious organisations and even certain fundamentalist groups, whom you may call Khalistanis, were present simply as, a large section of Punjab's population was involved in this struggle. The same with the communists. Punjab has a history of communist movement and as it is, the Left leaning farmer unions were already involved in AIKSCC. They continue to play a vital role in this struggle. In fact, I would like to criticise the communists in the context of the situation that we are witnessing in the country today. In my opinion, they should have put all their physical and ideological energies into the movement, which they have not done. So I have an opposite view about the involvement of communists from what the state has, in the sense that I think they are less involved than they should have been.

About 26 January incidents, I just want to say that it was not a question of some conspiracy. All religious places, be it temples, mosques or gurudwaras, have a deep relationship with the farming community, since after all farmers are the ones who provide food supplies to them for the devotees. So the fact that various Sikh religious groups got involved on 26 January has nothing surprising in it.

Now coming to the issue of killing by Nihangs (a Sikh religious order), we certainly believe that this should not have happened. What happened to the person who was brutally killed by the Nihangs is certainly unacceptable and even if he did something wrong, they should have handed him to relevant authorities.

QUESTION: *We would now want to ask you about the relationship of political parties with this movement. The movement has kept all political parties and leaders away from the protest platforms. But how long can a movement sustain itself without challenging the political class and system which makes such anti-farmer policies?*

DARSHAN PAL: First of all, it is incorrect to say that this movement is apolitical. And this is true for all such large-scale mass movements which have taken on imperialists and big corporations. It is true that our movement has nothing to do with electoral politics. But even here, I would mention that each organisation has a concrete political stand of its own. For example, BKU (Ekta-Ugrahan) may have a position that all politicians are thieves, and so they may tell their members not to vote for any party. BKU (Krantikari) may tell their members to boycott elections as per their politics. So in whichever way you look at it, I think, to say that the movement has stayed away from politics is incorrect.

QUESTION: *Can you comment on the sudden withdrawal of the three laws? What do you think were the reasons for the government to take this step? Do you support the decision of SKM to suspend the movement without getting a legal guarantee for MSP?*

DARSHAN PAL: I think the sudden withdrawal of the laws on 19 November by the Prime Minister was mainly due to the fact that the people who were sitting on the borders were from a state which has its borders with Pakistan and Jammu and Kashmir. Also the majority of people from that particular state belong to the Sikh community which is a minority community in India as a whole. Secondly there were elections going to be held in five states and for the BJP government in the centre, Uttar Pradesh (UP) was and is a politically strategic state. They thought that if the movement of the farmers in the form of camping at the Delhi borders continued, it would affect the minds of the people in the neighbouring states and the people of UP would become hostile to the BJP. They were aware that if they tried to repress it, that would negatively affect them and there would be resentment not only in India but across the world.

There was actually a lot of discussion among the various organisations amongst the constituents of the SKM on whether we should suspend the *morcha* immediately after 19 November or we should take a commitment from the central government regarding continuation of MSP and about the withdrawal of cases framed against the farmers of different states all over India. Lots of discussions took place and it was decided that only when the Government of India will send a formal letter to SKM mentioning in writing its commitment to form a committee for MSP guarantee and agreeing to withdraw the cases framed against the farmers, should we suspend the agitation. I was against withdrawing the movement immediately after the announcement by the Prime Minister which some of the Punjab organisations were asking for.

Question: *What do you think the movement achieved aside from repeal of the laws? Punjab is back to where it was—suffering from indebtedness, suicide and unemployment.*

Darshan Pal: The repeal of the three laws is undoubtedly a great achievement of the farmers of India, particularly the farmers of Punjab and their organisations. You are right. For the farmers of Punjab indebtedness, suicides, unemployment remain as before but the farmers of Punjab while participating in and leading a long struggle have contributed to so many achievements of the movement. For example, this movement has for the first time united the farmers of India with different ideologies, programmes, beliefs and organisational structures. It is for the first time that a movement has brought to the focus the corporates like Ambani and Adani as the enemies of the Indian people. It is for the first time that people have boycotted their products and services in this part of India. It is the movement which has brought the Muslims and Jats of Western UP together against the BJP and brought the Gujjar and Minas of Rajasthan together as farmers. This *andolan* for the first time focused on the issue of MSP as the main issue of the farmers of India. It has brought all the farmer organisations of India together. It has for the first time challenged the fascist and autocratic regime of Modi and Amit Shah. It has built the confidence and self-confidence in the minds of the people at large that they can fight, they can struggle against this regime. This struggle has established that the farming community of India can play a central and leading role along with other toiling masses such as workers for a democratic change of the Indian society.

The leading role of Punjabi farmers and particularly of Sikh masses indicate that Punjab will play an important role in the struggle for protecting and developing the federal values and democratic institutions and values of Indian society along with the Indian masses.

About the Interviewer

Arun Kumar Tripathi is a senior journalist and writer. His interview of Dr Darshan Pal in Hindi has been published in the book *Sankat Mein Kheti: Andolan Par Kisan* by Vani Prakashan, New Delhi.

Endnotes

1. Dunkel Draft refers to the draft proposals of Arthur Dunkel, director-general of GATT, at the Uruguay round negotiations of GATT in December 1991. The draft put together the results of negotiations and provided a solution to issues on which negotiators failed to agree. The Dunkel Draft was accepted and became the foundation of World Trade Organisation (WTO).

2. Agreement on Agriculture (AoA) was signed as part of the WTO deals giving market access, reducing export and government subsidies on agricultural products. High subsidies are seen to be distorting global trade.

3. Formed in 1978, by Chaudhary Charan Singh, the Bharatiya Kisan Union (Indian Farmers' Union), abreviated as BKU, provided a platform to big and middle farmers across different castes and religions in North India.

Farmers holding a placard opposing the three farm laws. **Photo:** Workers Unity.

Ghazipur border, 27 January 2021: BKU leader Rakesh Tikait's emotional appeal resulted in thousands of sugarcane farmers from western UP marching to Ghazipur border to join the protest. **Photo:** Workers Unity.

The Movement has Helped the Farmers Understand the Value of United Struggle

RAJINDER SINGH, KIRTI KISAN UNION

> RAJINDER SINGH DEEP SINGH WALA is the Vice-President of Kirti Kisan Union (KKU), which is active in about 15 districts of Punjab, and has built up its organisation primarily amongst small and marginal farmers. KKU also fights and campaigns against all kinds of communal forces, be it the Sikh ultra-nationalists demanding Khalistan, or the RSS-BJP attempting to convert India into a Hindu state. At 38, he was the youngest member of the panel of leaders who attended several rounds of talks with the Union government regarding repeal of the three farm laws.
>
> WORKERS UNITY and GROUNDXERO had several discussions with Rajinder Singh during different phases of the movement. This interview is based on those conversations.

WORKERS UNITY: *Rajinderji, could you please share with us a brief history of the current farmers' movement? Can you tell us how it started and how the farmer unions came together?*

RAJINDER SINGH: The struggle started with the Modi government issuing three separate ordinances on 5 June 2020. In May, as soon as the discussions began around those ordinances, we opposed them and started planning on how to mobilise the farmers and the modes of fighting back. The struggle, in many ways, began from the grassroots. First, district level protests against the ordinances were held by individual organisations. Pamphlets were distributed. We arranged street meetings in the villages. Then, the constituents of AIKSCC in Punjab held five big rallies at Moga, Barnala, Patiala, Phagwara and Amritsar. We also organised several rallies, including torch rallies and *dhol* (drum) marches. On 27 July 2020, we organised a big tractor march, driving towards the residences of Akali Dal and BJP leaders. Henceforth, we started to gherao the BJP leaders' homes regularly. These parties were in power at Delhi, and they were the ones who were responsible for bringing in these laws.

After the hugely successful Punjab Bandh on 25 September 2020, the protests became even more widespread. All sections of the population not only supported but actively participated in the bandh. This gave a big boost to the struggle. After this, the joint platform SKM decided to block rail traffic in Punjab indefinitely, the roads to BJP offices and the houses of its leaders. Dharnas were held at nearly 150 places in Punjab, outside the businesses of Ambani and Adani and toll plazas. The struggle was directed against the BJP government, BJP party and the corporates, particularly Ambani and Adani—the pet cronies of Modi.

Once the ordinances were passed in the monsoon session of parliament in September, SKM issued the *Dilli Chalo* (march to Delhi) call on 26 November 2020. And since we reached Delhi and camped on highways at its borders, the influence of our movement grew countrywide, bringing in protesters from Haryana, Rajasthan and UP, as well as from other states.

But before we began the fight against the farm laws, we had to win another battle—against the fear of the coronavirus. The central and the state government were both implementing various anti-people policies, and the people impacted by them were being forced to stay inside homes. This was done by imposing lockdowns, corona-curfews and various restrictions on the movement of ordinary people. During the second lockdown, we gave a call to hold protests in the villages, in the streets, in front of houses. We did mass mobilisation in rural areas on May Day. We decided to break lockdown restrictions and violate the corona-curfew. We took out rallies and held protest gatherings. Thousands of cases were lodged against us, our comrades were even jailed. Other parties and organisations also started mass mobilisation and the government had to reconcile with this trend. Slowly, the fear about the virus was gone. So, in June, when the ordinances came, we said these laws are more dangerous than the virus, people believed us and they joined the protests.

In Punjab, the movement, however, developed gradually and in phases. In fact, this kisan *andolan* (movement) was a continuation of our decades of past struggles against the New Economic Policies introduced by Manmohan Singh, since the early nineties. We had opposed the Congress government's policy of privatisation of public health and education. We had campaigned among the masses that these policies would, in future, mean that they would not be able to access hospitals and send their children to schools. The corporates would take them over. People saw that happen. We told them there would be no government jobs in future. People saw how acute the problem of unemployment is in Punjab. So, when we said that these farm laws imposed on us by Delhi would now take away our land and roti, people trusted us. Also, historically, Punjabis don't trust the Delhi *hukumat* (regime). To us, more than Pakistan, Delhi is our enemy.

WU: *More than 30 farmer unions from Punjab came together to oppose the farm laws. What was the process that united them?*

RAJINDER SINGH: The process started in 2017, after the incident in Mandsaur[1], in which six protesting farmers were killed in police firing. The All India Kisan Sangharsh Coordination Committee (AIKSCC) was formed in the aftermath of this incident to protest against those killings and organise countrywide agitations based on common demands of the farmers. There are 10 farmer unions from Punjab in AIKSCC. We call them *Punjab Chakra* (Punjab Circle). On behalf of those ten, we had announced the Punjab Bandh on 25 September 2020, demanding scrapping of the farm ordinances. As protests gathered momentum, other organisations too became keen to join the struggle. We also approached them and asked them to start an united struggle. The bandh on 25 September was supported by all the farmer unions across Punjab. For the first time in the history of Punjab, nearly all the farmer unions had come together on one single issue. In a meeting at Moga, 30 farmer organisations in Punjab decided to form a joint platform to lead the struggle. The joint platform was finalised at a meeting in Delhi. The Ugrahan group stated that they would go for only coordinated action, but not be a part of this united platform. And since then, we have been working together under a united platform named Samyukta Kisan Morcha (SKM) which led this historic kisan *andolan*.

WU: *Within the SKM there were forces representing the rich farmers. In fact, they were in the majority. Also due to their class character they are prone to make compromises with the government. How did forces like*

KKU ensure both the unity of the SKM and the non-compromising nature of the struggle for such a long period?

RAJINDER SINGH: This struggle had multiple class leadership. SKM had representatives of small peasants, middle peasants, rich farmers and even landlords. There were sections and leaders within the SKM who were ready to compromise, accept the amendments to the laws suggested by the government and withdraw the movement. But in this movement, the participation of marginal and small farmers and their unions was also very significant. They were also in leadership. For example, our organisation was one such. The Left revolutionary forces like us stood firm in our resolve to accept nothing short of a total repeal of the three laws. But we were also determined to preserve the unity of the SKM. To us, apart from the issue of total repeal of the laws, every other tactic to be used during the movement was flexible and negotiable. Also, there was tremendous pressure from the farmers and people that prevented any leader from clandestinely striking any deal with the government. And it was because of the mobilisation of thousands of farmers by the Left forces including us, and the relentless fight inside the SKM against the pro-compromise forces, the struggle continued and stayed united for over a year till the laws were repealed. The government tried several tricks to break our unity, but it failed. Of course, the tenacity and determination of the farmers was the primary factor.

The national media projected certain faces as leaders of the movement. There were some leaders who had nothing to do with peasants or farmers, their main concern was to highlight that they were in command. They live around Delhi, have friends in the media and are seen more in TV studios than among the struggling masses. But it didn't matter to us. For us, the deciding force of this movement were the farmers sitting for days and months at the borders—Singhu, Tikri and others. Over 650 persons from Punjab alone were martyred during this movement. A study[2] has revealed that 95 percent of the martyred farmers owned less than three acres of land. This also exposed one of the many lies spread by Modi and the media that only rich land-owning kisans are opposing the laws.

WU: *The three laws have been repealed. But the condition of the marginal* *and small farmers, the structural factors causing the agrarian distress in Punjab have remained unaddressed. Are there any specific thoughts about a long-term movement to address the root causes?*

RAJINDER SINGH: The fact that the three laws have been repealed, obviously does not signify the end of all the problems faced by the peasantry in Punjab. Their situation will not change much. But the movement has helped the farmers understand the value of united struggle. We will continue to work on building a nation-wide movement based on the demand of MSP (Minimum Support Price) for all crops. Also, the farmers in Punjab are facing a total debt of about one lakh crore rupees. This means the average debt on a farmer is about ten lakh rupees. A few years ago, the various *jathebandis* (unions) in Punjab had organised a struggle demanding a waiver of this debt, and it was because of that struggle, the Punjab government had promised to waive it. But, the debt still exists to this day. Now, after the victory over Modi, there is a strong basis for continuing with that struggle with more intensity in Punjab.

We have some demands for the marginal and small farmers too, such as giving them land, providing them farming equipment for free, zero-interest loans etc.

There is another important issue which exists in the entire belt, where the Green Revolution model of agriculture is being practised. One must understand that the Green Revolution model is not only pro-corporate and anti-farmer, it is also anti-environment. We call it 'Green Massacre' which has destroyed both farming and the farmer community. We are discussing how to implement an agrarian model that would satisfy the interests of the farmers and would also be at the same time environment-friendly. The future peasant movement will have to address this crucial question.

In future you will see a large-scale united movement by farmers—in particular based on the demand for MSP for all crops and debt waiver.

WU: *Farmer organisations had protested not only on the issues that directly affected the farmers, but other issues like violation of human rights, anti-working class labour codes, etc., were also taken up during the movement. For example, at the Tikri border, the farmers protested the incarcer-*

ation of human rights activists and intellectuals in the Bhima Koregaon case. After this the government tried to label the protesters as Naxalites and Maoists. What is the Kirti Kisan Union's opinion on this?

RAJINDER SINGH: They called us Khalistanis and Maoists. But flags of all colours—yellow, red and green—furled side by side during the movement. So, their IT cell and *godi*-media (lapdog media) propaganda did not quite work out in the way they had hoped it would.

We agree that the issue of human rights is very important and crucial. The farmers' struggle grew beyond the three farm laws. It developed into a movement to halt the fascist drive of the Modi government. But we were of the opinion that the farmers' movement alone couldn't lead and achieve that goal. It would be an act of imposing our own aspirations on the movement. At that time, we also didn't want our focus to shift anywhere other than those four primary demands[3]. We were of the view that the success of this struggle would help reclaim the democratic space that had been snatched away from the people of this country by this regime. Our success will be valuable to all those fighting against human rights violations as well. Our success will go in favour of all those who are being targeted and oppressed by the RSS-BJP.

WU: *Agricultural workers comprise an important part of the peasantry in Punjab, as well as in the rest of the country. Do you think that the issues of agricultural workers should have been raised by the farmer's movement?*

RAJINDER SINGH: We consider the three farm laws as a package, a weapon to kill the farmers, agricultural workers and consumers. There are people who think that these laws are only against the land-owning farmers. But this is not so. We have published many articles, distributed pamphlets and held meetings in villages explaining to people how these laws would impact the agricultural workers, non-farm rural workers and even small shopkeepers; what impact it would have on loss of employment. Even urban workers in the unorganised sector will suffer.

Let me share some information. The Economic Survey of Punjab (2019-20) says that 1,39,95,000 people from 36,50,000 families in the state are dependent on the PDS (Public Distribution System) for getting subsidised food grains. This number makes up nearly half of Punjab's total population. These people solely depend on the government ration shops for cheap food grains. Now, if the government does not buy food grains from farmers in *mandis* (agricultural produce markets) at MSP, then consequently, it will not be able to provide subsidised ration to the poor. So bypassing notified *mandis* means not only will farmers not get MSP for wheat and paddy, it also implies the government will not procure food grains for public distribution.

The FCI (Food Corporation of India) was created with three main purposes. First, they will buy food grains from the farmers at MSP. Second, they will supply food grains for the PDS to states for supply through ration shops. Third, the government would store enough food grain with the FCI to use it as a buffer stock for emergencies, to control market prices of food grains and prevent hoarding by traders. Now, let's see what a commission[4] under BJP leader Shanta Kumar, who served as BJP's Chief Minister of Himachal Pradesh, has to say about the FCI. He simply recommended the FCI to be replaced by private companies. So, eventually, the whole process of procurement and distribution of food grains through FCI is going to be stopped. Currently, there are about 11 schemes to provide food grains to poor people at a cheap price. What will happen to millions who survive on these schemes? If PDS is ultimately abolished, the agricultural workers will suffer the most.

Secondly, in Punjab, there are 4,016 *mandis*, in which paddy and wheat are bought and sold. About 4,50,000 labourers work in those *mandis* during the sowing and harvesting seasons of both rice and wheat. If trade in food grains gradually shifts to private *mandis*, most of those 4,50,000 labourers will lose their jobs. Similarly, in Punjab, thousands of employees work in the *mandi* committees, they will also lose their jobs along with the commission agents. There are 43,000 commission agents in Punjab alone. Each of them has clerks, *munims* (accountants), peons and other staff. Most of them will become unemployed. Already, in rural areas of Punjab, unemployment has gone up so high that the people get work through MGNREGA only for 25 to 27 days in a year on an average—nowhere close to the 100 days promised in the scheme. The labourers get work in the farms at best for two months—during the rice sowing and wheat harvesting seasons. Now if the government *mandis* are bypassed, FCI is dismantled and the PDS gradually abolished, then starvation will become unavoidable in villages.

Thirdly, there is the issue of contract farming. This will lead to formation of very large sized farms, which will further reduce the number of available jobs in farming. More farmers will lose land and become labourers. Where will they find jobs outside agriculture? Neither labourers nor farmers will find work. With an excess supply of labourers and less demand, agricultural wages will also fall.

Wherever in the world the corporate farming model has been implemented, entire regions have been turned into slums. In America, there are only a handful of peasants. There are more prisoners than peasants in that country. Now, suppose we implement such a system here. According to the 2019 Land Revenue Statistics, there are some 10 lakh land-holding families in Punjab, whereas there are 24,000 prisoners. If we try to be like America, the figures might get reversed here too!

Another important issue is that only 3.5 percent of the land in Punjab is owned by the Dalits. Most of them are landless agricultural workers or non-agricultural workers. There is 165,000 acre panchayati land, which the activists of the Zameen Prapti Sangharsh Committee have been struggling to claim. One-third of that land, i.e., about 55,000 acres, should legally go to the Dalits. But with corporates eyeing agricultural land, panchayati land will also go into their hands.

Also, take the case of amendments in the Essential Commodities Act. This law said that the government would control hoarding only if there was a situation like war, drought or famine, or when there is an 'extraordinary' price hike. Now, what is that extraordinary price hike? The new law said, if the price rise was 100 percent for perishable products and 50 percent for non-perishable products, then it would be considered as an extraordinary price rise. That is, if today the price of onion is Rs 80 per kg and if the price becomes Rs 160 per kg, only then it will be considered an extraordinary price rise.

Now tell me, who is going to get affected by all this? So these set of laws are not only anti-farmer, they are equally anti-worker. They will kill farmers by doing away with MSP and starve workers by abolishing PDS. These laws are against anyone who eats roti. And we all eat roti. We had discussed these issues with the agricultural worker unions. We think we should fight together; we should bring the issues of agricultural workers in the movement.

Let us try to understand the politics behind these laws. Big corporations are keen on getting control of the entire food business, from farm to consumer. And the government wants to hand this over to them! Now, if I want a new car, but I don't have enough money to buy one, then I will travel by public transport—a bus or a train. Or I will travel by my old car. If I want a new house and I don't have money, I will stay in my old house. But, one can't do without food, without their roti. And if this entire roti business gets owned and controlled by the corporate, no doubt they will earn huge profit. But it can be said without any doubt that the situation will be adverse for everyone else. Prices of all food commodities will rise.

So, it can be said that we, the farmer unions, were actually fighting everyone's fight. They tried to divide our movement, but the farmers, the workers and even the small shopkeepers in Punjab understood that these laws would not spare anyone.

WU: *Meanwhile, along with the farm laws the Modi government has also enacted four labour codes. These codes are equally oppressive and meant to snatch away the rights of the working class. But a strong workers' movement by the trade unions is not taking off. Do you feel that the farmers' movement should have also addressed the issue of the labour codes?*

RAJINDER SINGH: The movement by the farmers has proved that everything is possible. They [the BJP] used to say: "*Modi hai to mumkin hain!*" (Modi makes everything possible). We said: "*Unity hai to mumkin hain!*" (Unity makes everything possible!) Also, it is now clear that Modi can be compelled to take back anti-people laws. But the trade unions must work for that. So far, they haven't been able to do anything about the Labour Codes. The largest section of the workers belong to the unorganised sector. The worker unions haven't been able to mobilise them against the labour codes.

Another reason behind the failure is that the trade unions, even if they belonged to the Left groups, didn't organise any significant struggle in the last few years. Once it was proposed during the movement that the trade unions and the farmer organisations should work together, and the abolition of the Labour Codes demand should be added to the demands of the farmers' movement. But at that point, everybody decided that this was a movement that had been built by the farmers on their issues. Only if the trade unions build a workers' struggle, can these two forces come together. Demands can easily be added, but there must be a struggle on the ground behind the demands. The farmer unions can't build and lead workers' struggles, even though we are opposed to the Labour Codes.

WU: *A few corporate houses were directly targeted in this movement. For the first time, we saw people talking critically about corporate control on government policies. People even raised questions regarding the neoliberal development paradigm. In terms of the farmers clearly taking on the corporates, do you see any clear difference between this movement and the earlier peasant struggles in Punjab? How significant is this development?*

RAJINDER SINGH: Yes, this is a very important issue that you have brought up. In this whole movement, two very important things took place. First of all, the BJP stands upon two pillars—the corporates and the RSS. The politics of RSS is about dividing people—Punjab vs. Haryana, Hindu vs. Muslim vs. Sikh—that's all their agenda is about. This RSS politics of creating communal divide and hatred was defeated, as all kinds of people—Hindu, Muslim, Sikh—from Punjab, Haryana, Uttar Pradesh, Rajasthan, Himachal Pradesh, etc., united to fight against the three laws. This united mass struggle has perhaps even surpassed the inter-community brotherhood that rose in response to the 'divide and rule' policy of the British rulers. This movement has pushed its way above all possible communal and divisive politics. When people from Punjab came to Delhi and received the hospitality provided by the people in Delhi and Haryana, the bonds they shared became stronger. RSS-BJP kept instigating the Punjab vs. Haryana conflict, but soon lost their plot. These laws were bound to be repealed. But the way this movement handled communal hatred is of greater political significance.

Secondly, we told people, Modi is in a hurry. There is pressure on him to pass these laws by the WTO (World Trade Organisation). It had given India five years to abolish government purchase of food grains and reduce all subsidies related to agriculture by December 2018. People understood the real forces behind those laws were the corporates and they directly targeted their business interests in Punjab. For example, thousands in Punjab gave up Reliance Jio SIM cards in response to boycott calls of its products. Reliance Jio even tried to derail this popular boycott, by claiming that this campaign was being run by their business rivals and they were the ones who were enticing Jio customers to switch. Silos of Adani group were gheroed. Toll plazas were prevented from collecting taxes. Retail chain stores of Reliance were shut down, their petrol pumps closed. Slowly, the boycott call spread from Punjab to Haryana and parts of Uttar Pradesh. The corporates were alarmed. For the first time, they felt the heat of people's anger.

In both respect, keeping itself above caste-religion-region divide and directly targeting the corporate business interests, this movement was markedly different and potentially more significant than the earlier peasant struggles, which targeted the ruling political parties only.

WU: *The farmers all across the country have shown their support to this movement. Haryana and UP were in the front row in their support; there also was big support in Maharashtra and Rajasthan. But in the states in the East and South of India, the support was more of a passive nature. You must be aware that the Bengal peasants have a glorious history of past struggles. Why was it so?*

RAJINDER SINGH: The farmers' participation and solidarity actions was determined by the organisational strength of the farmer unions in those states right from the very beginning. In Punjab, there was a sense of continuity, because for a long period of time, various struggles were being organised there by the farmer unions on many issues. In West Bengal, for example, the condition of the Left has worsened, particularly, after the Singur and Nandigram movements. The peasants began to see the Left, I mean, the CPI(M), as land-grabbers. Even today, they are in no position to organise the farmers. The non-parliamentary Left is also very weak in Bengal.

Apart from the organisational strength, there is also another important reason. The demand for MSP and *mandis* is the concern of the farmers in the Green Revolution belt. Many have claimed that these demands are relevant for the farmers of the entire country. But that's not exactly the case. These demands came from the areas with farmers having at least some amount of surplus production. Even now, a large section of the farmers in the country produce crops for their own consumption—sometimes not even enough for that. The demand for MSP does not concern them. MSP is a demand of the farmers who are directly connected to the *mandis*. In other places, land reforms, government investment in developing infrastructure for the farmers, etc., are the important issues. It was not possible to come up with a single issue that would be relevant for all the farmers in this vast and diverse country.

Perhaps contract farming could be one issue that would have made everyone come together. But, MSP remained the prime focus of the movement and contract farming was not really discussed much. The issue did not become prominent. Even the issue of PDS in relation to the Essential Commodities Act did not come to the forefront. We also did not see enthusiastic reaction from the farmer unions of South India. For example, we heard reactions like, "Contract farming is voluntary. So why is it such a problem?" The farmers in Punjab were quite vocal against it—"No! Contract farming would imply loss of our land." Same reaction came from the farmers in Haryana. But in other states, the unions did not take it so seriously. This was clearly due to a lack of organised work by them in those states.

However, even without a pan-national issue, the victory of the movement has generated a hope that the 'Modi era' could come to an end. In the past seven years, the Modi government never admitted its mistakes and accepted defeat. This is the first time they were forced to listen, step back and at last withdraw the laws that they had enacted. The farmers' victory has shattered the myth of the invincibility of Narendra Modi's aura.

Endnotes

1. On June 6, 2017, six farmers fell prey to police bullets in Mandsaur in Madhya Pradesh, while they were protesting against the then BJP government, led by Shivraj Singh Chouhan. The farmers were demanding better prices for their crops and a loan waiver. Subsequently, the farmers' agitation gripped the entire state, as protests broke out, and the issue

grabbed the national headlines. AIKSCC was formed in the aftermath of this incident.

2. A report on a study by economists Lakhwinder Singh and Baldev Singh Shergill, associated with Punjabi University, revealed that 80 percent of those who died due to various reasons like suicide, accidents and extreme weather while participating in the protests were marginal farmers. The remaining 20 percent were small farmers and landless cultivators. The study tracked 460 deaths between December 2020 and August 2021 and its conclusion challenges the claims of the Modi government, the media and some experts that the farmers' movement was primarily driven by rich land-owning farmers.

3. The four primary demands of the farmers' movement were:

i) Repeal of three agricultural laws passed by the Union government. The three agricultural laws include the Farmers Produce Trade and Commerce (Promotion and Simplification) Act 2020, the Farmers (Empowerment and Protection) Price Assurance and Agreement on Agricultural Services Act 2020, and the Essential Commodities (Amendment) Act 2020.

ii) Legal guarantee of Minimum Support Price (MSP) to ensure procurement of crops from farmers at fair price.

iii) Withdrawal of the Electricity (Amendment) Bill 2020, as farmers feel that they won't get free electricity due to the amendment.

iv) End the monetary fine and jail sentence for stubble burning.

4. In August, 2014, the Government of India (GoI) set up a high-level committee, with Shanta Kumar as the Chairman, to suggest a restructuring or unbundling of FCI. The committee proposed a drastic reduction in state support for both food grain procurement and the public distribution system that provides subsidised food grain to the poor. It is against this background that the farmers in Punjab and Haryana, who depend on MSP procurement, perceived the move to allow private *mandis* as a plan to gradually abolish the MSP system and government support from agriculture.

If We Fight Along with Our Men and Protect Our Land, then Our Equal Claim and Rights Over Land May Happen in the Future...

HARINDER KAUR BINDU, BHARATIYA KISAN UNION (EKTA-UGRAHAN)

> HARINDER KAUR BINDU is a state committee member of BKU (Ekta-Ugrahan). She mobilised thousands of women at the Tikri border protest site in a sustained manner and has emerged as one of the most prominent women leaders of the farmers' movement at Delhi borders. She spent many years in the Pendu Khet Mazdoor Union, which is an agricultural worker union. She had been drawn to politics at an early age, especially after the brutal murder of her father by Khalistani militants in 1991.
>
> GROUNDXERO interviewed her on 31 January 2022.

GROUNDXERO: *First of all, I, on behalf of GroundXero, would like to congratulate you on the victory of the farmers. You played an important role in this historic movement. Can you tell us a little bit about yourself, and how you became involved in activism?*

HARINDER BINDU: I am only a soldier of this movement. The credit for the victory of this movement should go to all the farmer organisations who fought together for over one and a half years, to the thousands of farmers, agricultural workers, youth and students, to all those who stood by the farmers throughout this struggle. The credit should go to the persons who were martyred during the course of the struggle—more than 700 in number.

As for me, I hail from Ramgarh Bhagtuana village in Faridkot district of Punjab. We were five siblings—one brother and four sisters. My older sister died at an early age, I am the second child; I have three younger siblings—two sisters and a brother. My father, Megh Raj Bhagtuana, was a local leader of an organisation called Naujawan Bharat Sabha. It was founded by revolutionary freedom fighter Bhagat Singh to mobilise workers and peasants against the British Raj.

My father, along with the young people of the village, used to work on many social issues, mobilising people to fight for their rights and solving their problems. He believed in communist ideology. So, in our family there were always discussions on Bhagat Singh, Mao and Lenin and on revolutionary ideas like Marxism. I used to listen to all of these discussions even when I was still a kid. They used to hold street plays, protests and rallies in our village. I remember one such rally—a woman who was working in the village school as a maid was raped. My father mobilised the villagers, took out rallies demanding justice for that woman. I was always interested in attending such programmes.

GX: *Those were the days of the Khalistani movement in Punjab. Do you remember those days?*

HARINDER BINDU: How can I forget those days! My father became a *shaheed* (martyr) fighting the Khalistanis. And see, today, Modi and his *godi*-media (lapdog media) are labelling us as Khalistanis!

GX: *Sorry, I had no idea...*

HARINDER BINDU: It's okay. I was born in 1976. So I was very young then. In 1984 anti-Sikh riots happened. We used to hear that in Delhi, Sikhs were set ablaze on roads with rubber-tyres tied to their necks. You can imagine the atmosphere in Punjab. It was a time when we heard a lot about terrorists. My father was opposed to the Khalistani demand and the violent methods adopted by them. He used to say it is one's right to place demands before the government, but there is no need to attack and kill Hindus. He opposed the Khalistanis when they tried to impose rules regarding one's dress, hair, smoking and eating habits. He said that this was not the right way to achieve anything. Meanwhile, the police were doing fake encounters, filing spurious cases and torturing youth in custody. He opposed both the religious killings and the police encounters.

My father and his comrades formed the Jabar Te Firqaparasti Virodhi front (Front against Communalism and State Repression). Some of the leading activists of Punjab joined the front. The organisation used to hold long peace and anti-communal marches and I used to join them even as a kid. They staged plays of Gursharan Singh in villages to promote unity and harmony between communities. I loved the slogans they raised—*Hindu Sikh ladan ni dena, mud santali banan ni dena* (Won't let Hindus and Sikhs fight, Won't let 1947—the Partition—happen again), *Na Hindu Raj Na Khalistan, Raj Kare Mazdoor-Kisan* (Neither Hindu rule nor Khalistan, we want rule of workers and peasants). From that young age, I became passionate about people's issues and felt a connection with them. It was all going fine.

Then, on 9 April 1991, a rally was organised by the Front in Sewewala village of Faridkot district. A group of young people were staging a play and singing revolutionary songs. All of a sudden, a Khalistani armed group arrived and opened fire. While 22 persons were wounded, they killed 18 people. My father was amongst those who were killed.

When I saw my father's bullet-ridden dead body, I promised to myself that I would fulfil his unfinished dreams. I wanted to avenge his death by making the movement stronger and taking his message of unity amongst even more people.

GX: *But you were too young! Just a school-going kid...*

HARINDER BINDU: I was then 14, and in Class IX. I joined the Front and started to visit villages. I began addressing social issues and fighting for small demands. I was successful in shutting down a liquor shop in a village.

For three to four years, this movement against Khalistan went on. Whenever there was any meeting or program, I used to go and work as a security guard. I had learnt to fire a 12 bore rifle. I also worked as a security guard during a big program that was organised in memory of the revolutionary poet Pash who was also killed by the Khalistanis.

I somehow managed to pass the matriculation exam. I had to share the responsibilities to run the house because our condition became quite tough after my father's death. My family was amongst the many who had received some land in the 1950s during the Pepsu-Muzara movement. Today, the corporates eagerly await the opportunity to occupy such lands. The kisan *andolan* (movement) is determined to defeat their attempt at this reversal of history.

GX: *When did you start working for BKU (Ekta-Ugrahan)?*

HARINDER BINDU: That happened many years later, around 2006. Before that, in 1993, a labour organisation—Punjab Khet Mazdoor Jathebandi was formed. I joined that *jathebandi* (union) and used to work with agricultural workers, mostly Dalits, who worked as daily wage labourers in the farms. We also fought for affordable bus fare, education of girls and other issues facing Dalits and labourers. I used to stay in the houses of the labourers with other comrades and explained to them the causes of their exploitation and their rights.

I had to hear taunts about the ridiculousness of a girl from a Hindu family working with Dalit agricultural workers. I didn't care. I worked there till 2006, then joined Ugrahan *jathebandi* and started attending their meetings and programs.

Then I got married. At that time, in Punjab, a movement was going on against the privatisation of electricity services. I became a part of that movement. We raised awareness in the villages about what privatisation means. We explained to people that if private companies take over electricity distribution, electric bills will increase and poor households would be unable to afford electricity. We organised a big mobilisation in Chandigarh where 25,000 to 30,000 people gathered in protest against the privatisation of the electricity board. I arranged buses to take people from Gurdaspur to Chandigarh; a large number of women also participated in that protest. It was a big protest. There was a lathi-charge; some farmers even died.

My marriage didn't last long, I was divorced. In 2010, I came back to my own district, Bathinda and started to work there. After divorce, I dedicated myself to working full time for BKU (Ekta-Ugrahan) under Jhanda Singhji's guidance. I knew him, as he used to work with my father in Naujawan Bharat Sabha.

I have a 14-year-old son who stays with my brother in Punjab. He once came to the Tikri border.

GX: *You are the chief of the women's wing in BKU (Ekta-Ugrahan). How did you start organising women in the villages? Tell us about the issues you raised and some of the important women's struggles organised by BKU*

(Ekta-Ugrahan).

HARINDER BINDU: Our union has been organising women since 2012. In 2012, we formed a women's *jathebandi* in Bathinda. We formed a village committee, a block committee and then a district committee, all comprising of women. Since then, I've been working continuously to increase women's participation in the organisation and the movement. When I started working, a *suba* (state) leader bought me a car. A loudspeaker was fixed to it and I started visiting village after village, addressing people, meeting women and organising them in our union. We staged street-plays during the day and held torch rallies at night. We addressed issues related to women like loans, suicide, torture at home, alcoholism, etc. We held a huge '*Rang De Basanti*' conference to infuse the thinking of Bhagat Singh among youth and women. Women came in yellow *dupattas* (scarves) while men wore yellow turbans. Yellow was the favourite colour of Bhagat Singh.

Our women's committees fought against the microfinance company agents who used to come to villages to provide loans. We organised women against attempts to disconnect electricity lines to houses whose bills were pending. We would never let any of the farmers in our *jathebandi* have their land seized due to *karza* (debt). At the end of the day, the land belongs to the farmer who works on it.

In 2012, we gathered farm widows in Bathinda's Haji Rattan Gurudwara—3,000 widows from farmer families showed up. By then, thousands of farmers and agricultural workers had committed suicide. Each woman carried photographs of her loved ones—her son, her husband, her father-in-law—all who had committed suicide due to debt. We demanded that the government pay Rs 5 lakh as compensation, provide a job and waive debts of such families. Finally, in 2014, the Punjab government sanctioned money, so that every such family would get a compensation of Rs 2 lakh. Now, the compensation is Rs 3 lakh.

I'll tell you about another incident. In 2014 a girl from a *mazdoor* (worker) family in Gandhar village of Muktsar Sahib district was raped by a dominant caste landlord. We took about 4,500 women on a protest march to Faridkot demanding arrest of the accused. All women members of BKU including those from dominant caste background marched together, rising above the usual caste solidarities that mark such cases.

During this protest many women were arrested but they relented only after the accused was arrested by the police.

We worked at the grass-root level to raise consciousness in women. We went to villages, to *mandis* (agricultural produce markets), to gurudwaras—all with the aim of raising consciousness that we women have to form our own *jathebandi* on the basis of our shared solidarity. When women started joining in the protests, various political parties and village *pradhans* (chiefs) objected. But we ignored them and kept organising the women and that is how we reached a point where women played a significant role in the success of the farmers' movement.

GX: *Why did you think that there should be a separate wing for women in a farmer union like how it is now in BKU (Ekta-Ugrahan)?*

HARINDER BINDU: The farmers' fight is against feudalism, capitalism and imperialism. We believe that the male farmers cannot fight this battle all by themselves. Women, who form a major part of our society, must join the struggle. If women had not participated, it would not have been possible to win the present struggle. Being the most marginalised in village society, women face all kinds of oppression—social, political and economic. So, to make women free and independent, it is important to organise them and build their own wing within a farmer organisation. They face discrimination at every step. Even in their own households, their opinions are not counted and their views are not considered. To win struggles, we need to unite and organise women just like the male farmers. In this respect, BKU (Ekta-Ugrahan)'s thinking is different from other unions.

GX: *Women constitute a major part of agricultural workers. Even in land-owning families women put in a lot of hard work in farming and other farming-related activities. Yet farming is widely seen as a man's occupation and just 13 percent women own any agricultural land. Women have no rights even over the land they own. So why did women think it is necessary to be a part of the farmers' movement which is predominantly a male bastion?*

HARINDER BINDU: I know that property rights regarding agricultural land for women are complicated. As far as land ownership is concerned, even the majority of men in the villages don't own any land, or at most have four or five acres. It is the *jagirdars* (landlords), the big politicians like Badals and Amarinder Singhs, the MLAs and ministers, who actually own all the big farms and fields. Ordinary farmers don't own much land[1]. And women don't own land at all. We women might legally have land in our name on paper, but we don't have the rights to decide about what portion to contract out or to sell, we independently can't take loans on its basis, we can't do anything according to our own will. When a woman claims her share of agricultural land from her family, in most cases, she is cut off from the family and is considered to be a bad woman. Property rights exist on paper, but not in reality.

Even then, we women realised that it is our duty to protect the lands of our family, of our fathers, husbands and brothers from going into the hands of the corporates. If we fight along with our men and protect our land, then our equal claim and rights over land may happen in future just like it happened in China after the revolution. That kind of struggle we have to build up and carry forward. We may not have land rights and women's labour may not be visible still, but we're visible in the protests, and we are sure that in future we will win our rights as independent farmers by being part of the overall struggle. The direction of our movement is also towards that end.

GX: *What steps do you take to ensure that women feel comfortable in joining your* jathebandi? *What role do the male union members play in this regard?*

HARINDER BINDU: In my 30 years of experience, I've seen that women were made part of every peasant movement and not merely to add to the numbers. Our male companions in the movements went to villages, made the women aware of the issues, explained to them how the issues affected them equally, and sometimes more than the men, they encouraged the women to join the protest meetings and rallies. Men also took the initiative to change the atmosphere within the *jathebandi*. One of our leaders used to drink alcohol and used foul language during fights and arguments. But it came to an end when he understood that if we want to take women along with us in the movement, we would have to stop consuming alcohol and stop abusing them at home. When wives of our leaders realised that their husbands would be sober at home, not consume alcohol, not create a scene and not torture or abuse them at home, they reached out to more women in the village and encouraged them to join the *jathebandi*. They told other women that if their husbands could leave alcohol, then others' could too. In this way, women's participation in our *jathebandi* grew in numbers. It's true that it took a long time to change the overall atmosphere. It was not easy.

Secondly, for example, we always organise a separate bus when we take women to a rally, because they gain confidence when they travel and participate on their own. Also, men are still not sensitive or responsible in their behaviour towards women. Since we are concerned about the honour, respect and comfort of women, we have to be strict and mindful about our male comrades' conduct within the union.

GX: *Since women's participation is increasing in the movement, do you think there should be separate independent unions for them, or is just having a women's wing within the farmers'* jathebandi *enough?*

HARINDER BINDU: We believe that if we want to make women's participation in the movement stronger, we have to do that by staying within the same *jathebandi*. If we talk about Punjab, a member from every household has participated in the farmers' movement. Since we already work with the farmers, it was possible for their daughters, wives and mothers to join us at Delhi borders. They have faith and trust in us because they know and believe that in our *jathebandi* the atmosphere is safe and good and there won't be any misbehaviour with women.

Earlier it was common that men couldn't meet women easily or women couldn't call any man to their houses. Such attitudes have started to change. Women now go to the villages, organise meetings with other men, arrange rallies, give speeches, go to jail. These are noteworthy changes. They are now an important part of the *jathebandi* and the struggles.

GX: *You are a woman leader in a male-dominated farmer union. In your union, have you ever faced any problem or barrier from the male members* *and leaders? How do they take you as a leader or rather a woman leader?*

HARINDER BINDU: In our *jathebandi*, we first had to struggle to change the male members' thought process, their outlook towards women and their patriarchal mindset. Our *jathebandi* had decided that it would take women along and make leaders out of them. So I didn't face any problem. Yes, initially I faced some problems from my family, like any woman does when she decides to come out of the house and work independently. Now it has been 30 years since I started working. I stay at my home and village only for short spans. I started by working with the labourers and Dalits—they all treated me like their daughter and sister...

GX: *In a feudal and patriarchal society, receiving love and respect like a daughter or sister from men is not uncommon. How do those men respond when Bindu as a leader, a woman leader, is asking them to listen to her, carry out her instructions and work under her leadership—does that create any problem?*

HARINDER BINDU: You see, it is true that I'm a woman leader. When I sit in protest demonstrations or arrange programs, the police often arrest me. When I'm put in a jail with my other male comrades—society considers that as a bad thing for a woman. In the beginning, I also used to feel bad about that. Later on, after my release, the same villagers—both men and women—gathered and welcomed me with garlands and shouted slogans in my support. Even now, when I organise and lead any big protest, the police come to my place. So, I leave home at night and take shelter in others' houses, sometimes I even have to disguise myself to avoid arrest. This is part of my life as I've chosen this path. People provide me with shelter when the police come looking for me. They do not ask me to leave out of fear of the police. They open their doors to offer all help. I have never felt being a woman has been any handicap for me, both in the villages and inside the *jathebandi*.

GX: *Coming back to the farmers' movement, while the participation of women was markedly visible, they were projected mostly as farmers' wives, mothers and daughters. There was very little focus, both by the media and* *also the movement itself, to acknowledge their presence in the protests as equal stakeholders fighting against the three farm laws. What do you have to say about this?*

HARINDER BINDU: This is absolutely right. There were a huge number of women visibly present at the protest sites. They came from across all villages in Punjab. They stayed back at the camps, facing all odds. Yes, they were mothers, wives, daughters and sisters of male farmers, but they were also fighting against the farm laws. It was their issue too, but their presence as equal stakeholders in the movement did not come to the forefront.

The world took notice of the women farmers and agricultural workers when on 8 March 2021, International Working Women's Day, almost 80,000 women gathered at Tikri border, donning bright yellow *chunris* (scarves) and spoke about their issues. The women organised the event, hosted the programme and delivered speeches. That was the day everybody came to know not only about their huge presence, but also that they too were fighting for farmers' rights.

GX: *Also thousands of women participated in the Mahila Kisan Divas...*

HARINDER BINDU: In these one and a half years of the movement, almost the whole of Punjab has participated, as have a large number of women. We celebrated Mahila Kisan Divas (Women Farmers' Day) on 18 January [2021] when women's mass participation became markedly visible for the first time. It was observed at Singhu and all other borders. This was the first time that hundreds of women travelled far from their homes to live for weeks at the protest sites. Women spoke on the stage on that day. At Tikri, men were doing what is seen as women's work—cooking, cleaning and washing—while women were delivering rousing speeches on why the three black laws must be repealed.

In Punjab, we observed Mahila Kisan Divas in the grain markets of Bathinda, Barnala, Sangrur and Moga. Two very large gatherings of women, in thousands, took place on that day—one was in Barnala in the village of BJP leader Harjit Grewal who talked a lot against the farmers, and another in a village in Sangrur. On that day thousands of women came out from their houses, boarded the buses on their own and reached these two villages. There was a gathering of 20,000 to 25,000 women in Barnala and 10,000 to 15,000 women in Sangrur. Everything was arranged and run by women, only one or two speakers were men. Even at the Tikri border, the women had organised everything for the event and managed the stage.

GX: *Was women's participation in such huge numbers spontaneous? Or were they brought in by their male family members? Or was it the ground-level organising work done by activists like you that led to the mobilisation of women at the borders?*

HARINDER BINDU: This is a very good question. On seeing women's participation in the farmers' movement, many people were surprised. They wondered how such a huge number of women turned up. Did they come all by themselves, spontaneously?

Before this movement, we had fought on many social issues, like farmers' suicide, loan waivers etc. And women had participated in those struggles. After the ordinances were brought, we had arranged meetings, rallies, street plays in villages, where we have our organisation, to make people, including women, aware of the three farm laws passed by the Modi government. We went to the villages, played *dhol* (drum) to gather people, shouted slogans and then when people joined, we talked about the laws and their harmful impact.

We visited every household in the villages and told the women that we are organising meetings, and asked them to join us. This time, we went some extra miles to make the campaign more intense. We didn't leave the campaign even during the Covid period, when the epidemic was at its peak, and everybody was shut inside their homes. I personally went to their homes and explained to the women that we may not go to the main road or the cities, but we can at least go to our own roofs, maintain distance and stand there and protest. When Modi asked us to bang utensils, light candles and torches during the lockdown, we went to the roof, banged vessels, utensils and shouted that these are empty, we didn't have anything to eat, we needed food. In about 600-700 villages, all the family members, irrespective of age and gender, went to the roof and banged utensils and shouted slogans against the Modi government.

We didn't waste a day in making people aware of the anti-farmer laws. Before coming to the dharna in Delhi, we held protest marches in almost 1,500 villages—women's marches, torch marches at night, where 500, 700, 1,000 women joined. A team of 10 to 15 women would visit the homes in a village and tell them we are going to Delhi and will return only after making Modi take back the laws. We would also tell them it will be a long battle, so we need rations. From every village, every household, we gathered rations—food items, vegetables, spices, whatever was needed. We repeated the same words—*26 November Dilli Chalo* (march to Delhi on 26 November). Women from nearly every family joined us.

When we organised a press conference in Chandigarh, we had told the press that our organisation would mobilise nearly two lakh farmers and there would be 30,000 to 40,000 women joining us. It actually happened and then it became news that a huge number of women are also present in the farmers' protest sites on the Delhi borders. It took a lot of effort, a lot of hard work to get to this point. When we did the *rail roko* (rail blockade) in September 2020 for over 70 hours—at that time not too many women were part of the protests. Maybe 100-200 women had joined us at that point. But their participation increased as the movement went on.

GX: *The camps on the highways at the borders were like mini-towns and villages. Apart from doing household work like cooking, cleaning, washing, etc. what other tasks were women performing? Did women participate in the decision-making process?*

HARINDER BINDU: At Singhu border huge langars were set up. At Tikri border, a long stretch of 19 to 20 kilometres was covered by the protesters and the farmers ran their own langars. The men did all the work that a langar needs, like cooking, making rotis and washing utensils. We had also made it clear that women were not at the protest sites to do household chores. Young men, who didn't even pour a glass of water to drink at home, when they participated in the protest, they asked the women not to do such work.

Later, when the movement became protracted, and the camps became our temporary homes, the women told the men that they would help them now. The difference was that men and women worked together—cooked together, washed clothes together, served food together, and went to the dharna stage together. Women conducted discussions amongst themselves and spoke on the stage.

Our routine was something like this—waking up in the morning, preparing tea, making food, washing clothes (men and women did these together) and then at 10 am we used to go to the main dharna stage. Till 3 to 3.30 pm we were at the stage, listening to the speakers, presenting our own speeches etc. One thing must be mentioned, the women who were never allowed to speak, they spoke, sang songs and played music, many even started writing. There were many women who were illiterate, but they spoke fearlessly on the stage, placed their demands and criticised the government.

In our *jathebandi*, every day there used to be a state-level meeting where men and women participated equally. Women like me who are in the leadership participated fully. It used to be at 9 am in the winter and at 8 am during summer every morning. We discussed the daily situation. Women's participation and their opinions were considered with due importance.

Women leaders will emerge only when we bring in more women to the protests and into the union. The farmers' movement has shown this. After the victory of the movement, our organisation has gained much recognition. From 600 villages, we now have committees in 2,000 villages. We can easily mobilise 70,000 to 80,000 women now. Earlier there were only five or six women who would come forward and take part in leadership. Now there are hundreds of women organising and speaking at rallies and meetings in the villages. The number of women has also increased in our block and district committees.

GX: *In between came the Supreme Court of India's direction that the elderly and the women must be sent back to their homes from the Delhi borders, keeping in mind their safety and health condition. The remarks created a huge controversy and protests. Tell us how the women at the protest sites responded to these remarks from the Supreme Court?*

HARINDER BINDU: The BJP government was not able to remove us from the protest sites. Thousands of farmers, their entire families were camping on the highways, saying they would leave only after the three laws were taken back by the Modi government. So, the government tried to use the Supreme Court to evict us like they had done in the case of protest at the Shaheen Bagh[2]. It made the Supreme Court say that the women, the elderly and the children should be sent back to their homes. This boomeranged. Women demanded that the judge who passed this verdict should visit them at the borders. They said, "The judge must understand that we haven't come just like that... nobody forcefully brought us here with them. The judges must come and talk to us, ask us why we are here. We are women of the *jathebandi*. We have our organisations. Who is the Supreme Court to send us back home? What does it think of women?" Thus, we, the women, answered back from the movement spots to the Supreme Court. We announced to the press and on social media that this is also our movement and we know how to fight it. We are from the *jathebandi*, we have joined the protests on our free will, knowing everything—we know how to fight against the cold, fight against the BJP and also how to fight against the patriarchal verdict from the Supreme Court.

GX: *After coming back from the movement, are the women claiming their space, their rights within the household? Is there some change in the attitude of men towards women?*

HARINDER BINDU: Yes, yes definitely. Women who joined the movement, saw it from close quarters and listened to various speakers, soon became aware of their rights and learnt how to assert and claim those rights. Let me give you a small example. The Punjab government has introduced a scheme where women can travel free on buses by showing their Aadhar [identity] card, but often the male conductors and drivers heckle them on this issue. After returning from the protest, the women are asserting that this is their right and if the conductors and drivers harass them, they will unite and stop the bus service. When political party leaders visit their villages seeking votes, women tell them, "We don't want a free bus ride or your 1,000 rupees dole. We want our rights on land. We want loans, we want jobs."

GX: *But are the women standing up against domestic violence and discrimination within their own families?*

HARINDER BINDU: It won't change so easily. Farmers' families go through a lot. There are issues of unpaid debt, lack of income, no rations at times, children's school fees can't be paid, treatment of sick family members become impossible—all these tensions flare up within the four walls of the home and fights do take place between the husband and wife. Women have to deal with alcoholic husbands, sons who have become drug addicts, and nasty fights do take place. But I've seen personally that in families which participated in the farmers' movement and stayed at the borders, the atmosphere inside their homes is changing. Earlier, even if the woman was sick or had given birth, she would have to do all the household work. But, now the men are helping them, they are participating in household work. They are trying to help women in little ways like chopping vegetables, cleaning, etc. The efforts may be still small, but the attitude has started to change. Earlier, women had to take permission from the male family members before they went anywhere. They still have to ask, but there is a difference. They only let the family know about their plans and go out with their friends, maybe to cinema halls or to rallies and demonstrations.

GX: *Another highly marginalised section are the Dalits, particularly Dalit women. Our patriarchal and casteist society treats them in the most cruel manner. How do your organisation and the women's wing fight for them?*

HARINDER BINDU: Dalit labourers have formed a united *morcha* (front) of their own in Punjab, just like the farmers formed the Samyukta Kisan Morcha (SKM). For the first time in Punjab, seven rural and agricultural worker unions have joined hands to stage protests and raise their demands. In our state committee meeting, we decided that we would extend our full solidarity to their movement. In Patiala [August 2021], almost 10,000 labourers, including many Dalit women, had held a three-day protest programme. We felt that they were fighting their own struggle and we had to make our solidarity relations with them stronger. So, BKU (Ekta-Ugrahan) had arranged a langar for them. The Jat women cooked food in the langar, while our male Jat farmers and farmer leaders served them [the Dalit labourers] food and washed their utensils. The important thing was that the agricultural workers had also united and raised their demands.

In a particular area in Punjab, the land-owners behaved in the most cruel manner with the labourers, especially with women labourers. They sexually tortured the women labourers, injured their private parts and some women had injuries in the uterus. They were oppressed in the name of caste. Then, our *jathebandi* stood by them when they protested. We supported them financially and socially.

I mentioned the incident in Muktsar earlier. A Dalit labourer whose daughter was studying in class IX was raped by a politically influential landlord. He was not arrested. To give justice to this girl, we, along with Punjab Khet Mazdoor Jathebandi, staged protests. The dominant caste women, farmer leaders, and male farmers—all joined that protest. The protests went on for quite a few days. The Punjab Police would come and arrest the women from the protest and take them to the police station. Our leaders were arrested and were kept in custody for four months. They would keep on charging us with fake cases one after another. But the protests continued till that Jat landlord was arrested. So, it is not something new for us to fight and support Dalit labourers, both women and men, on economic and social issues.

During the farmers movement, on 21 February 2021, we organised a joint *maha* (mega) rally of farmers and labourers in Barnala grain market. There were almost 2.5 lakh people who joined us, amongst which almost 80,000 were women. The women were mostly Dalit labourers and from farmer families. We have decided that whatever funds our organisation will have, we would donate a portion of that to the Dalit labourers' movement to make their struggle stronger.

There were cases where Dalits were being harassed, even lynched, in the name of protecting cows, especially in Uttar Pradesh. A committee in Punjab was formed, we joined that committee and participated in a rally demanding—"Give us land and we will stop skinning cows." We also joined their protest against the attempt by the Modi government to dilute the provisions of the Scheduled Castes and the Scheduled Tribes (Prevention of Atrocities) Act.

Not only Dalits, we also extended solidarity to the struggle of the Muslim community. We held massive demonstrations against the CAA (Citizenship Amendment Act) in Punjab. Protest at Shaheen Bagh brought Muslim women out on the streets against the CAA and their struggle inspired us. We went and stayed at Shaheen Bagh for a few days. Unnerved by the farmers' support to the anti-CAA movement, the BJP leaders and *godi*-media had said that the protesters at Shaheen Bagh were part of the '*tukde-tukde gang*.'[3]

We consistently take stand against all atrocities. Our relations with Dalits have now improved. A mutual trust is being built.

GX: *The movement compelled the government to withdraw the three laws. The government also said that it would constitute a committee to look into the issue of guaranteed MSP (Minimum Support Price) for all crops. Are you satisfied?*

HARINDER BINDU: In his characteristic arrogant style, PM Narendra Modi announced that those three laws had been withdrawn. He never met the farmers or held any discussion with them. We welcomed the announcement, but said that the laws should be withdrawn in parliament because we do not trust him. After the government gave in writing that all the remaining demands would be addressed within 15 January 2022, SKM decided to vacate the borders [11 December, 2021]. The farmers went back to their homes. SKM stated clearly that the movement had only been temporarily withdrawn and the struggle for MSP would continue.

But the government did not keep its promises. In the Lakhimpur Kheri case, instead of punishing the perpetrators, the police and BJP leaders were tormenting and harassing the farmers. In a review meeting [15 January], SKM had decided to observe a 'Day of Betrayal' on 31 January all across the country. Today, we observed that day. Men, women and young people gathered in front of the district headquarters in Punjab and other states, protested and burnt effigy of the Modi government.

This movement won't stop with only the three laws being withdrawn. The major demands of implementing MSP on all the crops will have to be met. SKM will decide on the future course of the movement after discussions with the farmer unions. Even though we won a significant victory, there is no question of being satisfied. The struggle will continue.

GX: *But the SKM split vertically on the question of participating in the elections in Punjab...*

HARINDER BINDU: Yes. It became confusing when many *jathebandis* that were part of the SKM, decided to form a political party and contest the elections. This decision was against the declared position of the SKM. Our stand regarding participation in the elections remains the same. We don't support any political party nor do we participate in elections. Our members can exercise their right to vote individually, but they cannot influence others into voting for any one particular party or candidate. If any member does this, we suspend their membership. We continue with our agendas to intensify the mass struggle for people's rights, for farmers' rights.

GX: *What was it like on returning back to Punjab? What is keeping you busy these days?*

HARINDER BINDU: We celebrated because we have won, we have defeated Modi. We sang, danced, and did *bhangra* (Punjabi folk dance).

Every day we organise meetings either at block level or district levels, and hold sit-in protests on various farmer issues. I went to the toll plaza where thousands of farmers were protesting. Our movement against the Punjab government to implement their promises to fulfil our demands and to claim compensation for the farmers for the loss of cotton crop was on even before we left for Delhi. We resumed the protests after returning to Punjab. For five days, starting from 20 December, we completely blocked the secretariat in Bathinda, we didn't allow any officials to enter the building for those five days.

Then on 5 January 2022, when PM Modi visited Punjab, we held protests against his visit. As per SKM's decision, protest marches were organised in every district headquarters in Punjab, and Modi's effigies were burnt. On every road he was supposed to travel, people gathered and shouted "Go back Modi." Modi literally fled from Punjab, realising the people's mood.

We have won Rs 5 lakh compensation for each family whose member was martyred during the farmers' movement at Delhi, and a job for one of the family members.

I am out on the road every day doing organisational work. I don't really have time to stay at home. My home is on the road, within the struggle.

Endnotes

1. As per the last Agriculture Census (2015-16) report, there are 10 lakh operational land holdings in Punjab. One-third of the farmers in the state have land holdings between 1 to 2 hectares, another 33.67 percent of the farmers have holdings between 2 to 4 hectares, 27.92 percent have holdings between 4 to 10 hectares and 5.28 percent have large holdings of above 10 hectares. One hectare of land is equal to 2.47 acres. Two-third of the farmers don't own much land and fall in small or marginal or semi-medium category.

2. The Shaheen Bagh protest was a peaceful sit-in by Muslim women at Delhi, that began on 15 December 2019 and lasted until 24 March 2020. The protest began in response to the passing of the Citizenship (Amendment) Act on 11 December 2019 in parliament and a brutal crackdown by Delhi police on the students protesting against the Act at Jamia Millia Islamia University.

3. '*Tukde-Tukde* gang' is a pejorative catchphrase used in India by the ruling Bharatiya Janata Party (BJP) leaders and its cadres accusing their critics for supporting sedition and secessionism. The term is generally used to refer to the radical Left and Muslim activists, who oppose the communally divisive and ultra-nationalist politics of the Narendra Modi government.

Graphitti at Singhu border. **Photo:** Workers Unity.

Woman farmers gathers in large number at Singhu border. **Photo:** Workers Unity.

Redistribution of Surplus Land is an Absolute Necessity to Save Punjab's Landless Farmers

SURJIT SINGH PHUL, BHARATIYA KISAN UNION (KRANTIKARI)

> SURJIT SINGH PHUL is the state President of Bharatiya Kisan Union (Krantikari), which was formed in 2004. It has been working among marginal, small and landless peasants in and around ten districts, mainly in the Malwa region. Phul was booked under UAPA by the Punjab government in 2009 when he was accused of being linked to Maoists and placed under "intensive interrogation" in the Amritsar jail. He was brutally tortured and suffered grave injuries. There was a concerted campaign by farmer organisations across Punjab demanding his release.
>
> On 9 and 14 December 2021, Surjit Singh Phul was interviewed by WORKERS UNITY.

WORKERS UNITY: *Tell us about your organisation, BKU (Krantikari), about its history and the kind of work it does.*

SURJIT SINGH: I have been actively working in the peasant movement since 1984, under various leaderships and farmer organisations. In 2004, some of us decided to form a new union, BKU (Krantikari). Our idea of forming a separate union was based on the fact that we wanted our work to be grounded on what one could call revolutionary principles and politics. Our main idea was that most farmer unions (including the Left ones) are often infected with economism and get mired in reformist practices and we wanted to avoid this. In a nutshell, our policies and practices are based on ideas of direct struggle for gaining farmers' rights. And it is something we have tried to never compromise.

Our orientation is such that mostly small and middle farmers join us. Big farmers do not join us due to our class orientation. We take up issues of all farmers, for example one of the issues we have been fighting for is the implementation of Swaminathan Commission's[1] recommendations including the correct calculation of MSP (Minimum Support Price). This will obviously benefit all classes of farmers but big farmers usually do not join or work with us.

We work in ten districts of Punjab, eight districts in the Malwa region and two districts in Amritsar. There are some other districts where we have just started our work but we still do not have a full-fledged organisational structure in these areas.

WU: *Let us now start with the farmers' movement and the repeal of the three laws. How do you view this sudden decision of the Prime Minister to repeal the laws and how do you see the movement shaping up from here on?*

Surjit Singh: Let us first emphasise that this repeal of the three laws is a clear victory of the movement. This victory is in our bag and the laws are now a thing of the past. So we have a clear marker that this phase of the struggle is over and it has ended with victory for India's farmers. It is certainly a partial victory but a clear one.

We should also remember that we have lost more than 700 people and the amount of money spent in this movement will go into tens of crores. So when media people ask us if we should now thank the Prime Minister, I would like to remind them of what we have lost collectively. Had he repealed these laws on the 26 November 2020, when it was absolutely clear that farmers were against it, we would have thanked him. The decision to withdraw the laws is good but it has come too late.

Some other demands, the most important being the demand for legal guarantee of MSP, are still pending. They have assured that they will discuss the issue of legal guarantee of MSP but there is no clarity on the issue. So far all we know is that a committee composed of representatives from the Samyukta Kisan Morcha (SKM), the government and other experts will be formed soon to start discussion on the MSP issue. But what we call 'terms of reference' of such a committee are not clear at present.

WU: *What is the situation with the Electricity Amendment Bill and the stubble burning fine which the Centre had agreed to withdraw as early as December 2020?*

Surjit Singh: In our third or fourth meeting with the Indian government, these two demands [to withdraw two of the three laws regarding the Electricity Amendment Bill and stubble burning fine for farmers] were accepted. However, these were ordinances which were not yet tabled in parliament. The agreement is that the government will discuss those Bills with SKM before tabling them in parliament. So this fight is not really over yet. But I want to add that as far as the three laws were concerned, a lot was dependent on these laws for big capitalists in India and for multinational corporations abroad. So, this repeal is a big step and other pending issues regarding these ordinances are relatively smaller issues.

WU: *On the decision to end the protest, we heard from several sources that after the announcement of the repeal of the laws, there was a lot of discussion among SKM members, and on the decision to continue the protest or end it there was initially no consensus. We also heard about a possibility of a split among SKM members after this decision was reached to end the protest even though MSP guarantee was not given. Can you give us your views on this?*

Surjit Singh: All the decisions within SKM are democratic and are taken after discussions with all its constituent member organisations. I think it is important to understand that the protests are not over but have been suspended for the time being. As you know, we (all the constituent organisations of SKM) will meet again on 15 January [2022] in Delhi[2] and assess to what extent this government is adhering to its signed commitments. They have agreed to six of our demands including constituting a committee to decide on MSP, withdrawing all police cases and providing compensation for the families of martyred farmers. By 15 January next year, we will see if the government is acting on its promises or is cheating the farmers again. Depending on how they act on the six agreed demands, we will decide on the next course of action in our meeting.

WU: *Is it not true that some of the unions did feel that after such a morale boosting victory, the struggle for MSP should have progressed a bit more* *and the protests at borders should have continued for a few more months?*

SURJIT SINGH: In fact, we felt the same way. But it should also be clear to us that this government is not going to agree to the demand of giving legal guarantee of MSP so easily. However, we could have continued the movement for a couple of months more and tried to put pressure on the government to at least start the process of discussion on the MSP demand.

WU: *Can you elaborate on this? What according to you could have been the next immediate goal of these protests, had they continued? I mean regarding implementation of MSP guarantee demand.*

SURJIT SINGH: We felt that terms and conditions under which the MSP committee would be formed and mandate given to it needed to be decided and made public. The minimum mandate this committee must have is to declare an MSP for as wide a section of the agrarian population as possible. At present only a small percentage of farmers in the country get MSP for their crops. We also felt that had the protest continued, SKM could have had a direct say in the formation of the committee. This would have marked the beginning of what will surely be a very long process and struggle for our demand of nationwide MSP for as large an agrarian population as possible.

WU: *Many communist organisations in Punjab have been working among the landless farmers. Organisations like Zameen Prapti Sangharsh Committee (ZPSC) and Krantikari Pendu Mazdoor Union (KPMU) have been at the forefront of many struggles. Due to the work of the communists, a sizable section of landless farmers also participated in farmers' protests. They have their own demands such as ownership of panchayati common land, implementation of Land Ceiling Act and demand for a living wage, etc. What are your views on this? And how do you think SKM can join forces with the platform of the seven agricultural worker unions to take this struggle into its next phase where demands of all strata of the peasantry are unitedly raised?*

SURJIT SINGH: We have tried to increase the participation of landless farmers and agricultural workers in this movement. There is a simple reason for this. The Essential Commodities Act would have had a devastating impact on agricultural workers. Had the APMC (Agricultural Produce & Livestock Market Committee) markets been dismantled, the various grain distribution schemes like cheap ration, which directly depends on the existence of these *mandis* (agricultural produce markets), would also have disappeared. This would have placed the lives of the poorest farmers and agricultural workers in an even more precarious condition. And so our efforts and emphasis from day one was to increase the participation of the marginal and landless farmers in this movement and place their demands on an equal footing with the demands of the landed farmers. However, in spite of our efforts their participation was less than what it should have been. One of the primary reasons for this is that many of the unions in SKM, especially from Haryana and UP, have a very confused understanding of the rights of landless farmers or agricultural workers. It is indeed true that all the farmers, from landless to big farmers, whom you may as well refer to as landlords, are facing severe problems today. However, the agrarian crisis most acutely hits marginal and small farmers as well as agricultural workers. So we believe that farmers cannot be liberated unless there is unity between various classes of the peasantry.

WU: *Can you tell us about your relationship with unions of agricultural workers who are called landless farmers as well?*

SURJIT SINGH: Our coordination with KPMU, which has been working among landless farmers since 1998, is very close. Even in a recent three-day programme of various agricultural worker unions in Patiala, BKU (Krantikari) participated. We set up a langar and made it compulsory that all our units send some representatives to attend that programme. This was to show solidarity to the struggle of agricultural workers, but even otherwise, we have a close coordination with KPMU, and we agree with all their demands.

WU: *How important is the question of land redistribution among the landless farmers according to you?*

SURJIT SINGH: It is of utmost importance. We clearly believe that land redistribution is one of the prime issues.

WU: *I would like to again draw your attention to what Pargat Singh of KPMU said once. He said that the principal contradiction in Punjab is between landless and big farmers. He was talking in the context of the panchayati land in the village. This common land is leased annually, 33 percent of which is reserved for Dalits. As we know, although on paper, this right has been given to Dalit farmers of Punjab, in practice, this land goes to big farmers who simply put dummy Dalit candidates during auction. Do you agree with his assessment?*

SURJIT SINGH: Absolutely. But I would also like to add something to this. As you said, 33 percent of the panchayati land (land belonging to village council) which is up for lease every year is reserved for Dalits. However, what landlords, big farmers and even people with political powers, say sarpanch, do is to put dummy Dalit candidates during the auction. These are basically Dalit farmers who are working as agricultural labourers on these landlords' farms. Organisations like KPMU and ZPSC have been fighting precisely against these fraudulent caste-based exploitative and discriminatory practices in many villages. In a village in Sangrur district, a Dalit even died in the violence perpetrated by big farmers.

However, my point is that land redistribution and not simply leasing of panchayat land on rent is an absolute necessity. If we look at violations of the Land Ceiling Act in Punjab, there is a massive amount of surplus land. This needs to be redistributed among the marginal and landless farmers.

WU: *There is a question often raised by those who think that land redistribution is not an answer to the agrarian crisis. Their argument is that even landed farmers are in debt and an increase in the land holding of a marginal or small farmer will not solve his or her problems and may even increase indebtedness. Do you agree?*

SURJIT SINGH: I do not agree. Indebtedness exists mostly among small and marginal farmers. If we look at the number of farmers' suicide in Punjab over the last several decades it is mostly among these farmers. It is true that big farmers are also in debt, but because they have land, they have the basic means to negotiate such a debt, which small and marginal farmers do not. By doing a redistribution of all surplus land, not only will the asset of small farmers increase which will give them some protection and will certainly reduce the number of suicides but it will also increase employment opportunities for agricultural workers and their bargaining powers, as land will not be concentrated in the hands of a few.

So to repeat our organisation's views, redistribution of surplus land along with implementation of 33 percent reservation of Dalits for panchayati land is an absolutely primary demand that the Punjab peasantry should raise.

WU: *Let me now slightly change the topic and take you back to the events of January 26, the protesters marching into the Red Fort and the supposed presence of 'religious extremists' and Khalistani groups on that day. We saw how people like Lakha Siddhana and Deep Sidhu provoked farmers to march towards the Red Fort. You and BKU Krantikari were also accused of violating SKM's decision regarding the route of the tractor rally and as a result you were even suspended for a month from the SKM. How do you analyse the events on that day and what were primarily your disagreements with other SKM leaders?*

SURJIT SINGH: It was SKM's decision to do a tractor march on the Ring Road on 26 January. We were not going to enter the Red Fort or interfere with the official Republic Day parade. Lakhs of people from various villages of Punjab came in tractors to participate in that rally. They did not come as Khalistanis but as ordinary farmers responding to the SKM's call. But on 25 January, SKM changed the decision and announced that instead of Ring Road, we would take an alternative route completely outside Delhi.

People had spent approximately Rs 10,000 on diesel to travel from various parts of Punjab to Delhi in order to participate in the rally whose route had been announced. Many of them refused to obey SKM's last-minute change of decision. This was what we had communicated to the SKM leadership. The fact that farmers came with a resolve that a big gathering and tractor rally inside Delhi would result in putting pressure on the government to repeal the farm laws was important. But SKM's decision was final and the route had been changed. Even on the decided route, police had put up barricades which farmers broke and in anger many of them drove towards the Red Fort. I would like to remind everyone that it is not only Sikh farmers but also UP farmers, who started from Ghazipur border, went to the Red Fort, and in fact many of them reached there even before the farmers from Singhu border. So this was not some Khalistani conspiracy as the government had claimed.

Now coming to the question of our coordination with Khalistani elements, we were and are with the farmers. Most of the protesters who went to the Red Fort were farmers. They were not from outside farming communities. They were not Pakistanis or anything like that. They all participated in the rally with the common goal of repealing the farm laws and we—BKU (Krantikari)—supported them even on that day.

WU: *But this brings us to the question which has emerged during this movement once again. That is the nationality question for Punjab and the related issue of demand for a Khalistan state. What do you think about this?*

SURJIT SINGH: India is home to many nationalities and religions. And the way the state treats religious minorities, be it Sikh or Muslim, there is a deep sense of injustice and anger in these communities towards the Indian state. And I would say that this anger was channelised in the right way during the farmers' movement. For people of Punjab—let us not only look at Sikhs but people of Punjab as a whole—their relationship with New Delhi has always been tense. Going way back into history, our ninth Guru Tegh Bahadur was arrested on his way to Delhi and taken to Delhi along this very route and was beheaded there. His body was brought back by his followers to Punjab along this very same route. There are many other historical events which have caused a deep-seated anger in the people of Punjab towards Delhi which to them represents the power centre of the Indian state.

Now, it is true that SKM mobilised farmers with a *Dilli Chalo* campaign with a concrete objective of repealing the farm laws. But the fact that "We have to fight with Dilli to win our freedom" is an emotion which is always present in Punjabi society.

WU: *But what about the violence on 26 January and the accusation that it was a result of Khalistani elements and a BJP conspiracy? It was even claimed by SKM that celebrities like Lakha Siddhana and Deep Sidhu were in fact BJP stooges.*

SURJIT SINGH: In a democratic protest, like the one we have seen over the last year, the protest takes many forms. However, one thing we need to remember is that there was no violence by farmers on anyone on that day. Let me explain this a bit more. No farmers snatched guns from policemen present there and shot at them. Farmers with their tractors dismantled the barricades for sure. But even where police were outnumbered, farmers did not attack them. Inside the Red Fort, the number of farmers was many times more than the police force present there and in spite of all the provocations, farmers did not indulge in any violence.

About people like Lakha Siddhana[2] and Deep Sidhu[3], there is no evidence that Lakha Siddhana even went to Red Fort. There was certainly a possibility that Deep Sidhu was a BJP stooge but if we look at his bail order, it basically says that there was no link of Sidhu with those who were seen agitating the farmers to move towards the Red Fort. So we cannot say with certainty that they were really working for the BJP.

I should also add that after 26 January, it was claimed by some SKM leaders that all the students, youth and farmers who went to Red Fort were traitors and were harming the movement. This was completely wrong.

WU: *So you disagreed with SKM's public response to the events of 26 January?*

SURJIT SINGH: Totally. On the very next day, from the Singhu stage it was said by some farmer leaders that certain student groups and farmers groups were traitors. This was absolutely wrong. Let us forget celebrities like Siddhana and Sidhu. In fact on 28 January when BJP sent their goons to attack one of the stages at Singhu border and even fire-bombs were thrown on farmers, several leaders said, "Let it happen. These groups deserve it." But the overwhelming emotion among farmers was rather opposite, that we cannot tolerate this attack on fellow farmers. We must stop it.

So some of these initial responses that came from some of the leaders of SKM, I totally disagree with.

WU: *And why were you specifically suspended?*

SURJIT SINGH: It was basically about the first impression of our role in the events of 26 January. An inquiry was constituted by SKM in which I gave my statement that I had not gone to Red Fort and had in fact returned from a specific point much before the Red Fort along with a few other leaders. The committee did not find any evidence that I had been to Red Fort, let alone instigated the farmers. But thanks to the first impression and our insistence of going along the designed route, I was suspended.

WU: *The stated programme of SKM was to do a tractor rally on 26 January and a parliament march on 1 February. The march did not happen. Your organisation put a lot of pressure on SKM to do the parliament march. Why did you insist on it?*

SURJIT SINGH: Such a protracted movement requires concrete intermediate goals otherwise the protests can stagnate and the morale of protesters can go down as time goes on and the situation does not change. Our idea was to maintain the pressure on the central government which had by and large started ignoring our presence on the borders. This is why we insisted on holding the parliament march, as was collectively decided.

WU: *During this movement, the issue of Sikhism's relevance in the farmers' movement and even the demand for Khalistan by certain religious extremists came to the forefront over and over again. What are your views on this?*

SURJIT SINGH: Let us first understand this in the context of state propaganda. The modus operandi of the Indian government has been to malign this movement. Sometimes they say it is led by Khalistanis, sometimes by Maoists and so on and so forth. There is no truth to this, and it is all baseless propaganda.

Let me also emphasise that no organisation in SKM ever claimed that we should be given the leadership of SKM. There are many leftist organisations in SKM and none of them ever demanded that we should have the main say in decision making of SKM. Sikh organisations have given support to this movement. They have conducted langar and given other material support but never said that they should be given the decision-making rights in the movement.

WU: *But we cannot ignore the presence of Khalistani elements on the protest sites of Singhu. We also saw pictures of Bhindrawale on tractors and tents. Now we all remember that Khalistanis considered Punjabi communists to be their direct enemies in the 1980s and in fact many communists were murdered by Khalistanis. So how do you view this entire development?*

Surjit Singh: I agree with everything you said. Khalistani and religious extremists did have a direct antagonism with the communist movement in the past. I of course do not agree with their premise that Sikhs are discriminated against in Punjab. Sikhs are a majority in Punjab just as Hindus are majority in other states of India and how can the majority be discriminated against by the minorities?

However, the primary fight of Khalistanis was against the Indian state. In my opinion, anyone who is engaging in a struggle against the oppressive state, even if their ideology and practice is very different from ours, cannot be our direct enemy. We may not be fraternal with them due to conflicting ideologies but as there is a common enemy, there is a possibility of some sort of coordination.

And with this in mind, I should say that communists in Punjab have also made mistakes in that period of '70s and early '80s. We should never forget that the primary enemy of people is the Indian state and imperialism. If we consider the state to be a secondary enemy and Khalistanis as primary enemies then that is an erroneous understanding in my opinion.

There were some organisations which considered Khalistanis to be the primary enemy and concentrated their efforts in opposing the Khalistan Movement even if it came at the expense of collaboration with the state.

WU: *Do you think during this movement, this antagonism between communists and Khalistanis has softened somewhat?*

Surjit Singh: I think so. I cannot speak for all communist organisations but at least BKU (Krantikari) has come to an understanding that the primary enemy of Punjabi farmers is the central government and not Khalistanis. Let me again emphasise that we have very different ideologies, our practices and modes of struggle and resistance are very different. But we believe an understanding can be reached with them as we have a common enemy.

WU: *The influence of WTO, World Economic Forum and IMF in formulation of these farm laws is very clear. Do you view the farmers' struggle as a fight against imperialist forces?*

Surjit Singh: Even now India is part of the WTO (World Trade Organisation), so this type of anti-people policies and Acts will continue to be forced upon the people. It was due to this protracted movement that for now the laws have been repealed but till the time India remains part of WTO, it will have to keep forcing these types of policies in one form or another on the people. So, our struggle will continue till India leaves the WTO. In this sense, I agree that the farmers' struggle was against the imperialist forces.

WU: *Should SKM highlight the role of WTO and raise the demand that India should get out of WTO?*

Surjit Singh: Certainly. In the initial phases of the movement, constant propaganda to highlight where these laws are coming from was done. In fact, from the stages at the protest sites, various farmers' leaders have again and again emphasised that till India remains part of WTO, such policies and laws will continue to be enforced and implemented.

WU: In future, *can this movement be turned into a struggle around issues of forceful capture of land which will bring together farmers, Adivasis and people facing displacement on a common platform? Or do you think this movement will stay confined to the issue of MSP and more broadly to the issues of landed farmers only.*

SURJIT SINGH: Right to MSP is simply one aspect of the anti-imperialist struggle. Even if we win this right, the fight against imperialism will not be over. In our understanding India still remains colonial. In the past, the colonial powers ruled directly and now they rule via WTO, IMF and World Economic Forum. So the character of India as a colonised country has not really changed.

The Adivasis have a clear slogan *"jal, jangal aur zameen"* (water, forest and land) which summarises their fight against multinationals and big Indian corporates. This has a rather direct overlap with the core demands of the peasantry which is also a demand for *jal* and *zameen*. So, as far as this fight against big corporates and imperialism is concerned there is a lot of commonality between these struggles.

WU: *Now I want to ask you about what many felt was a sectarian approach of SKM towards people's issues. They confined themselves mainly to the repeal of the three laws. For example, in Bastar 10,000 Adivasis have been fighting for six months against CRPF camps on their lands. But SKM did not release any statement on that struggle.*

SURJIT SINGH: This movement was primarily confined to three states as you know and so issues that arose in other states such as the historic struggle by Adivasis in Chhattisgarh against CRPF camps, in which protesters have also been shot, was not addressed. However, there is a coalition of BKU unions, a federation of 35 unions in which this issue was discussed and there was even a preliminary discussion that representatives from various BKUs should go to Chhattisgarh to show solidarity with the Adivasis. However, due to various constraints this did not materialise.

WU: *But we did not hear any statement from SKM when atrocities on Dalits occurred or Muslims were lynched and killed even in the three states participating in the movement. So how can this movement transform into a larger political movement which will resist the fascist onslaught?*

Surjit Singh: I totally agree with you. In fact, in Haryana, as we speak, a boycott of Dalit agricultural labourers by landed farmers is going on in many villages. There are attacks on Muslims too, as you said. We hope that these limitations in SKM's approach will change as we go forward.

WU: *When Nodeep Kaur[4] and Shiv Kumar were arrested and abused in prison, initially SKM was hesitant to release any solidarity statement. But later they did come around and tried to engage with labour unions, highlighting the issues surrounding the labour codes from their stages. However, I feel that they did not make enough efforts to take this forward...*

Surjit Singh: Absolutely. I must say BKU (Krantikari) did openly support the demand for the release of Nodeep Kaur and Shiv Kumar. We did a press conference immediately and gave a written complaint at the police station against the abuse of both of them in police custody. SKM initially did not openly support their cause but neither did they make any negative statements. So, I agree that in these instances SKM's limitations did come out. However, I can also say that many organisations which were highly confined to farmers' issues have now realised that farmers' issues and demands cannot be seen in isolation. For example, Haryana's biggest farmer organisation explicitly raised the issue that caste atrocities on Dalit farmers is a reality, and we have to coordinate with Dalit organisations. This is a huge change.

We also kept political parties far away throughout the movement. We never allowed any political party leader to speak from our stages. In my opinion, this also gives a chance to go to villages and convince the villagers that just as we kept politicians far away from this struggle, let us also keep them away from our villages and our lives.

Endnotes

1. Chaired by Professor M. S. Swaminathan, National Commission on Farmers (NCF) was formed in 2004 and submitted five reports between the years 2004 and 2006, sug-

gesting ways to enhance productivity, profitability and sustainability of the major farming systems in India. In common terms, the reports are known as the Swaminathan report.

2. Deep Sidhu was a Punjabi actor and activist, who shot into the limelight following the Red Fort violence during the farmers' tractor rally on Republic Day in 2021. Sidhu was twice arrested after being accused of playing a part in the conspiracy to hoist a Sikh religious flag at Red Fort during that program. He died in a road accident in February 2022.

3. Lakha Siddhana a gangster-turned-activist from Punjab was also one of the accused in the Republic Day violence that happened in Delhi on 26 January 2021. Sanyukt Samaj Morcha (SSM) nominated Lakha as one of its candidates in the Punjab assembly elections (2022).

4. Nodeep Kaur is a Dalit labour activist engaged in organising contractual workers in the Kundli industrial belt, in Sonipat, Haryana. On January 12, 2021, while leading a demonstration demanding wages due to the workers, Nodeep and her fellow comrades were brutally attacked by goons hired by the company management and Haryana Police. She, along with Shiv Kumar, another Dalit activist of Mazdoor Adhikar Sangathan (MAS), were arrested, Nodeep was beaten and sexually harassed while in police custody, and released on bail after nearly a month in prison.

The Struggle for Legalising MSP will Continue at the National Level

Joginder Singh Ugrahan, Bharatiya Kisan Union (Ekta-Ugrahan)

Joginder Singh Ugrahan is the President of Bharatiya Kisan Union (Ekta-Ugrahan), one of the largest farmer unions in Punjab. An ex-army man and a farmer himself, 77-year old Joginder Singh led one of the largest contingents of farmers at Tikri border during the year-long farmers' movement. Active among small and marginal farmers, BKU (Ekta-Ugrahan) has a huge following in Punjab, for its relentless campaign to highlight the havoc caused by the agrarian crisis. It has played a significant role in raising the demand of compensation to families of farmers, who succumbed to suicide and loan waivers. It is also known for its opposition to state repression, communal violence and violence on all minority groups.

This interview was conducted by Manjit Sharma for GroundXero on April 2, 2022. Manjit Sharma teaches Economics at DAV College, Chandigarh.

GroundXero: *Joginderji, you were in the undivided Bharatiya Kisan Union (BKU). Tell us why you joined BKU and later separated from it to form your own independent faction of BKU (Ekta-Ugrahan)?*

Joginder Singh: We read the programme and constitution of Bharatiya Kisan Union before we joined it. BKU in Punjab upheld itself as a non-partisan farmers' representative organisation. The stated objective of BKU was to act as a pressure group from outside of electoral politics. The BKU held the position that agriculture should be excluded from the ambit of the WTO (World Trade Organisation), which serves the interests of corporates and facilitates uneven competition by victimising Indian farmers. We concurred with its constitution and political positions, particularly the position that BKU will be non-political, it will not associate itself with any political party. My comrades and I strongly shared BKU's opinion that the peasant movement should be fought separately without allying with any political party.

Balbir Singh Rajewal, Ajmer Singh Lakhowal, Pishora Singh Sidhupur, Bhupinder Singh Mann were our leaders at that time. But soon we realised that our leadership was not committed to the stated position of BKU. They were tilting towards political parties. At one point, Lakhowal formed a political party known as Lok Hith Party. Our leaders started talking about Khalistan, a separate religious state for Sikhs outside the Indian Union. Under such circumstances, we had to break up with them. After parting with them, we worked under the leadership of Pishora Singh Sidhupur. Sidhupur led us for many years. But soon he also got close with Jathedar Gurcharan Singh Tohra (who remained president of the Shiromani Gurudwara Parbandhak Committee in Punjab for 26 years), and we had to part ways with him also. Then, in 2002, we formed our own *jathebandi* (union)—BKU (Ekta-Ugrahan). Even today, we are committed to those principles on which we separated from those BKU leaders to form our separate *jathebandi*. We believe that the main reason for the success of the farmers' movement was that the movement did not belong to any political party, religion, to any one caste, to any one state; the struggle was across religions, regions and cultures. The *Dilli Morcha* (sit-in at Delhi borders) did not allow political party leaders to take the stage; rather, they were excluded. This was an important reason for the success of the farmers.

GX: *BKU (Ekta-Ugrahan) is at present the largest farmer union in Punjab. Share with us the historic struggles that the union has led in Punjab.*

JOGINDER SINGH: By the way, there is a lot to be shared in this respect, but I will mention only the historic struggles which have become a part of our achievements.

In 2002, Captain Amarinder Singh (then Chief Minister of Punjab) introduced electricity bills on irrigation motors used to pump water in the fields. We told the farmers not to pay the electricity bill. We called for a boycott of bills only when we were sure that the farmers would respond to our call in large numbers. Two organisations in Punjab, one was Majha's Kisan Sangharsh Committee and the other was ours, we both fought till the end. The government insisted but the farmers did not pay the bills. At last, the government had to waive off electricity bills amounting to Rs 57,000 crore.

In 2012, we asked our leaders and cadres to make a list of farmers who had committed suicide due to debt. When we got the district-wise list of farmers' suicides, we organised a seminar-type programme in Bathinda's Haji Rattan Gurudwara to which intellectuals and economists were invited. The women and other members from families in which two to three men had committed suicide also attended the programme. During the seminar, reasons for suicide of farmers were discussed. It became clear that the government and its policies were responsible for the suicide of a large number of farmers; we concluded that these were cases of murder, not suicide, and raised the demand that the government should compensate the suicide victim families with financial assistance.

When this demand for compensation was raised, at that time, no one could imagine getting compensation for suicide. Farmers and even our own leaders had apprehensions whether the government would give any compensation to such families. Earlier, the family members were shocked and scared if an incident of suicide happened in their house. They used to go to the village sarpanch or police and plead with them to save them from legal harassment. But today, if a farmer commits suicide in Punjab, his family would ensure that the postmortem is done, the FIR is registered with the police. They would go to the police station and argue that this person committed suicide because he was under debt. Now they are not afraid to say so. They charge the government with suicide. Due to our efforts, in 2014, the Punjab government announced compensation of Rs 2 lakh to each family impacted by a farmer-suicide. Our demand was for Rs 5 lakh compensation, besides employment for a family member and debt-waiver for the surviving family. Our *jathebandi* in Punjab has been relentless in its struggle to get compensation for the families of farmers who have committed suicide.

Before the 2014 parliamentary elections, we included some of the demands of agricultural workers like allotment of residential plots to them in our agenda. To press for the joint demands of farmers and labourers, the Secretariat at Bathinda was cordoned off, its four gates were blocked, and finally Rs 96 crore was sanctioned by the government. It can be called another historic victory.

Our organisation has also been at the forefront of several other movements, including that against grabbing of farmers' land by the corporates under the guise of land acquisition for industrialisation. We opposed the acquisition of 376 acres of land in three villages in Barnala district by the Trident Group. We also organised the farmers against land acquisition for a proposed thermal power plant by India Bulls in Govindpur village in Mansa. We opposed the state government's decision to privatise the power board, and joined the movement against attacks on landless Dalit agricultural workers in Sangrur. In 2015, the cotton crop was extensively damaged due to white fly; we held a protest for over a month by blocking one side of the road outside the Bathinda district administrative complex. The government was compelled to disburse Rs 640 crore compensation to farmers at Rs 8,000 per acre.

GX: *At present, what are the main issues that BKU (Ekta-Ugrahan) has taken up, particularly after the victory of the farmers' movement?*

JOGINDER SINGH: The struggle for legalising MSP (Minimum Support Price) will continue at the national level. Our understanding is that this struggle is going to be a long and protracted one. This is not a fight with any individual ruler, it is a fight over policy matters. This is a war against the economic policies of the ruling classes, a war against the WTO, a war against imperialism. Therefore, this battle will not be won by any single organisation or class. Agricultural workers, factory workers, students, women, small shopkeepers, small industrialists—a large section of them will have to be taken along in this struggle. We have started the process of engaging in their struggle, supporting them and seeking their support in our struggle.

Our immediate objective is to formulate a pro-farmer loan and credit policy and an agricultural policy. Farmers' debt and unemployment of youth are two major issues on which we are working. We have to deal with the issue of unemployment of youth in Punjab. Then, we have the issue of eradication of drugs. We are also saying that damage of crops due to natural disasters is the responsibility of the government. These are our immediate or short-term concerns.

The long-term issues that we deal with include the struggle for implementation of the Land Ceiling Act, i.e., to ensure distribution of surplus land among the landless farmers. Landless farmers, often called agricultural workers, should be given cultivable land so that they can support their families.

GX: *Agriculture is a state subject; the central government by enacting laws on agriculture is violating the federal structure. Why are you not raising this issue?*

JOGINDER SINGH: I agree that agriculture is a state subject, but the state governments too are following the dictates of the WTO. Even the states are bringing agriculture under the control of the corporate sector. No single political party ruling in any state at present has a model with which it could combat the policies of the central government. So, there is no point in just talking of more powers to the states until we have an alternative policy model at hand.

GX: *You talked about the Land Ceiling Act, i.e., distribution of surplus land among landless farmers. What in your opinion is the relevance of the slogan 'land to the tillers' in Punjab?*

JOGINDER SINGH: *Land to the tillers*—this could be the slogan of other political parties. We have not given any such slogan. In our understanding, there is an unequal distribution of agricultural land in Punjab. Some don't have land to support their families, while some landlords even have railway stations on their land and some have thousands of acres of horse-farms. The government should put an end to this unequal distribution of land. It should implement its own land ceiling of 17.5 acres. But, as I said earlier, it is a long-term struggle.

GX: *Peasantry is not a homogenous category. There are many sections, often antagonistic to each other within it. What is the understanding of your organisation regarding the contradictions that exist among different sections of the peasantry in Punjab? How did these contradictions impact the farmers' movement?*

JOGINDER SINGH: See, we are aware of these contradictions from the beginning of this movement. We have continuously harped on the point that this struggle is a larger struggle, it is neither a struggle of a particular caste, nor a particular segment of farmers or workers. We have to point out continuously that this is a much bigger movement, where our enemy, the Indian state backed by imperialist forces, is much more powerful. We have been able to convince the various forces participating in the movement, be they small farmers or agricultural workers or small shopkeepers or students, that the policies of this government are also against their interests. So, we all have to stay united and oppose it. People understood this and remained united despite many internal contradictions. And we succeeded in forcing the government to take back the three black laws.

GX: *Your organisation played a leading role in the farmers' movement. When and how did you start the protests in Punjab before the* morcha *(front) was shifted to the Delhi borders?*

JOGINDER SINGH: The movement in Punjab started from July. When the ordinances came in June, we read them minutely, viewing all aspects. Then we held meetings with our cadres to educate them about the ordinances and decided to take the matter to the masses. We held a five-day *morcha* in the villages [25-29 August 2020]. We decided not to allow Akali Dal and BJP leaders to enter villages, and questioned the leaders of other political parties about their stand on the ordinances. For five days people from different sections—farmers, labourers, women and youth—came together to stage demonstrations to take the issue to the people, telling them how these laws would impact them. Then we set up two *morchas*, one at Badal village and another one at Patiala city, both home-turfs of ex-CMs of Punjab. In both these *morchas*, a large number of youth participated. Harsimrat Badal, who was a Cabinet Minister in the Modi government, had to resign due to the protests. We realised that the matter had reached the people and they were responding.

We were not in favour of the call for indefinite *rail roko* (rail blockade), keeping in mind the interests of the people of Punjab. We had suggested the gherao of corporate establishments and the houses of BJP leaders. We led a dharna outside the residences of Punjab CM Amarinder Singh and the Badal family for five days [15-22 September 2020].

We felt that other organisations of Punjab should be united and we should fight this battle together. Our view was that, if there was an agreement, then we would fight together, but if there was no agreement even then we would fight in a coordinated manner on the basis of a minimum programme. Then the movement reached Delhi.

GX: *It has now been over three months that the contentious farm laws have been withdrawn. Farmers have triumphed over pro-corporate agricultural reforms of the Delhi rulers. What is your organisation's overall review of the movement?*

JOGINDER SINGH: The positive thing in our review is that it is the first struggle in which so many organisations from all over the country fought together on a common minimum agenda and won. There is not a single farmer organisation, apart from the BJP-RSS controlled ones, that didn't participate in the struggle. It can be said that this was not a movement of the farmers alone; it became a people's movement—the people of India vs. the Modi government at Delhi.

The second most important aspect is that the Modi government has been acting in a fascist way, like the way they had brought in the three ordinances and then made them into Acts in parliament through a brute majority. There are so many instances of this government having acted like this, but it remained unchallenged. The farmers' movement, for the first time, posed a challenge to them. They tried in so many ways to break our unity, but in the end Modi had to bow down. This resistance of the farmers has indeed become an example, not only to Indians, but to the whole world.

Thirdly, the struggle also made people understand that it is not Modi, an individual, who is bringing such laws. The corporate sector is behind this. The people identified this. This is the first movement that directly targeted the corporates; till now, they have remained behind the scene. Today words like Adani-Ambani, WTO, corporate are on the lips of even children in Punjab. The political significance of this is that a large section of people has come to realise that the fight is against the corporates, and that our rulers are working in favour of the corporates, they are just pretending to have concern for the masses.

These are some of the positive aspects. The negative is that due to a large number of organisations coming together for the first time on the basis of common minimum demands, it has not been possible to come up with a solid criterion as to what would be the way of our functioning. How do we deal with one another? How do we properly recognise one another's rights, coordinate and at the same time maintain the independent status of each organisation? These were the things which created a lot of confusion, misunderstandings and difficulties during the movement.

We think achieving this much was no mean thing. Of course, some of the demands associated with the movement still stand. But the big thing is that the arrogant Delhi government and Modi had to bow down.

GX: *You talked about differences and misunderstandings. One such difference which came out was the allegation against BKU (Ekta-Ugrahan) that you were unwilling to go to the Delhi morcha and even had to face opposition from the youth. Would you like to clear the confusion? What actually happened?*

JOGINDER SINGH: It is wrong to say that we were not willing to go to the Delhi *morcha*. In October 2020, a meeting of the farmer organisations was held at Delhi's Gurudwara Rakab Ganj Sahib. We all agreed that we would work together. We accepted the joint decision to take the protests to Delhi.

Then a meeting of the unions of Punjab was held and it was decided that on 26 November, a march toward Delhi would be started. There was a BJP government in Haryana and it was clear that it would stop us at the Punjab-Haryana border. It was decided that we would sit on the road at the point where Haryana police would put barricades to stop us. We would spend the night there, inspect the situation and move further according to the situation. This was not our decision; it was the joint decision of all the unions. However other unions and organisations followed the youth, broke the barricades and reached Delhi, but we remained firm on the joint decision and stopped at the border and withstood the pressure of the youth. Even after receiving their abuses, we spent the night at Khanauri and Dabwali border. Only when all the organisations breached the decision, we too decided that we would move towards Delhi by breaking all the roadblocks, and we reached the Tikri border on 27 November with thousands of our members. It is wrong to allege that we were reluctant to go to Delhi. The point was whether to clash with Haryana police or not. If we were not ready to go to Delhi, we would not have campaigned in hundreds of villages for days mobilising people for the march to Delhi.

GX: *Another difference which came out in the open and created a lot of controversy was when your organisation raised the demand for the release of political prisoners on International Human Rights Day on 10 December from the protest site at Tikri border. How do you look at that incident now?*

JOGINDER SINGH: The symbolic protests were done to remember and acknowledge those who had been put behind bars for criticising the government. And, it wasn't the first time we have done such a protest. We have been doing so since 2018, soon after the arrest of human rights activists in the Bhima Koregaon case. We firmly believe that these activists should be freed immediately. The issue of their release was on our charter of demands. Just because various unions representing different ideologies came together for a common cause, they don't need to shelve their individual programmes. In fact, the demand for the release of the activists was also mentioned in a memorandum handed over to Narendra Tomar (Union Agriculture Minister) by over a dozen farmer unions [14 October 2020].

GX: *Were these differences or confusions due to the fact that BKU (Ekta-Ugrahan) was formally not a constituent of SKM? What were the political differences behind that stand?*

JOGINDER SINGH: We worked in coordination with Samyukta Kisan Morcha (SKM). Our major difference is regarding how decisions in SKM are taken on the basis of majority vs. minority opinion. Our position is that this principle should not be applied in a coordination platform. It can be implemented within a single organisation but in a platform of various organisations, like SKM, it undermines the independent existence of organisations. It is unjust and unfair with organisations having a minority opinion. So we never joined the SKM but always coordinated with them during the struggle and carried out all collective decisions.

We are still in coordination with SKM though we don't agree with its majority vs. minority policy of decision making, but we do agree on the common minimum programme decided by SKM. At the same time, we want to maintain our own organisational and political independence; we are free to take any action which will not affect the programmes of SKM. In our view, SKM should formulate new criteria on how it will function. We have shared our opinion with SKM in this regard.

GX: *One of the major crisis moments for the movement were the incidents that happened on 26 January 2021, when the Kisan Tractor Parade spiralled into chaos, violence and the Red Fort incident took place. How do you see that incident?*

JOGINDER SINGH: It was collectively decided in SKM that a Kisan Tractor Parade would be organised by the farmers to celebrate Republic Day on 26 January. There was no talk of going to the Red Fort or parliament. The ring-road around Delhi was chosen for the tractor parade by us but the government didn't give permission for it. The unions decided that we should not insist and agree to the route the administration permits us. But there were certain forces, including religious ones, that wanted to spoil the struggle. Some forces wished to escalate the struggle towards conflict and violence. They created havoc and the police helped them so that the BJP-RSS may play their game. Most of our people who came from the villages had never visited Delhi before and so they were unaware of the roads in Delhi. The farmers had no plans to march on undesignated routes. Police kept directing them towards the Red Fort. Thus, according to our understanding, the decision of SKM was right and the forces which went to the Red Fort were wrong. What happened on that day did not occur all of a sudden. It was a conspiracy hatched in advance. The act of unfurling the Sikh religious flag at the Red Fort provided the government an opportunity to give the movement a religious and separatist tag and begin a propaganda war against us. But people understood that it was a conspiracy.

GX: *But Sikh religious nationalism played an important role in this struggle. There are many who consider this as a struggle between the Sikhs and the rulers in Delhi. There were also talks in the media about the 'Sikhs vs. comrades' debate within the SKM and at protest sites. What is your opinion about this?*

JOGINDER SINGH: It is in the nature of Punjabis that whenever they take part in any struggle, they do it from the heart. Punjab fought openly and wholeheartedly when it fought against the British and they took part in this movement also with an open heart. Sikhs have inherited a great tradition of *sewa* (service) and sacrifice. It's an integral part of Sikh culture. Sikhs set up langars not for the first time during this movement. They are always on the ground serving people whenever there is a crisis in any region of India. Sikhs helped the migrant workers during the Corona epidemic; even now they are helping people in war-ravaged Ukraine. Punjab has just one and a half percent of the total land in India but we produce grains that fill the entire stock of the nation. On the battlefield, in the armies, in the police, in athletics, wherever they go, the Punjabis fight with sincerity.

The battle against the farm laws was neither of the Sikhs nor of the 'comrades' (communists or leftists). It was a battle of the peasants, of the workers, of the people of this country who were to be affected by the laws. Those who occupied the protest stage on 26 January, wanting to raise the issue of Khalistan in the name of federalism, cursed the SKM leadership as weak and corrupt, it is they who tried to create the 'Sikhs vs. Comrades' narrative, but the majority of the farmers understood their intentions. We wanted to keep the movement secular and peaceful by isolating such forces. For us it was a battle between the people of India vs. the rulers in Delhi.

GX: *So the struggle faced challenges both from within and outside...*

JOGINDER SINGH: Yes, there have been many ups and downs, as the Modi government was hell bent on harming the *andolan* (movement). But it gradually grew from being a kisan *andolan* to a people's movement. The government intended to suppress us the way it had earlier repressed the anti-CAA (Citizenship (Amendment) Act, 2019) movement by inciting communal violence [referring to the riots in Delhi in February 2020 that followed the anti-CAA protests]. They wanted to do the same thing here by hatching a conspiracy on 26 January, by labelling us as separatist Sikhs. But we remained alert, united and focused.

The Lakhimpur killings and then the brutal killing of a poor Dalit man at Singhu border at the hands of a Nihang leader was also a BJP plan. But we never got derailed and remained focused on our struggle. We worked very hard and reached out to the people and got massive support from them across the country. We lost over 700 lives of our farmers in this agitation.

GX: *Punjab and the country have witnessed many farmers' movements after the Green Revolution. How was this movement different from those other movements? What was unique about it that it touched the imagination of the entire nation?*

JOGINDER SINGH: The most important feature of this movement was sustaining such a long struggle and yet remaining peaceful even in the face of so many provocations. It was something remarkable and unparalleled. Secondly, many farmer organisations of different ideologies fought together on a minimum programme, i.e., to repeal the three agricultural laws. This has never happened before. The major feature this time was that people of different castes and religions, of different regions, of different states, for the first time came together to protest, and they won. This has not happened before. Another important feature is that this movement was not of the land owning farmers only, it was supported by small shop-owners, middle-men in the *mandis* (agricultural produce markets—APMCs), truck unions, agricultural workers, factory workers, women, students and unemployed youth. In this respect, this struggle was different and unique from all other farmers' movements in the recent past.

GX: *How much of the decision of repealing the laws by the Modi government was influenced by the assembly elections scheduled in UP and other states, as compared to how much of it was influenced by the pressure of the movement?*

JOGINDER SINGH: You are right that the government's decision and the timing to withdraw the laws may have had a connection with the assembly elections in the five states. The biggest weakness of a ruler is the chair. When his chair is in danger, when his power begins to falter, he starts trembling. This struggle brought Modi's graph down both inside the country and also abroad. Children were burning effigies of Modi, masses were abusing and cursing him. Modi's image was tattered. His pet cronies Ambani and Adani also became targets of the masses. Modi felt that if he did not step back, his political graph would come down more, an internal revolt within BJP might brew up, already Maneka Gandhi, Varun Gandhi, the Governor of Meghalaya Satyapal Malik were opposing the BJP openly.

Modi was in a fix, he was not able to find a way on how to act, the government tried to break our unity through negotiations but there were many organisations and they couldn't convince all of them. When the by-elections took place, BJP faced defeat.

What was the situation in Punjab? The BJP leaders could not go out in public. They had their own government in Haryana. But, even in Haryana, they couldn't enter the villages. When we started the movement, the government was adamant in its position. They ignored us and laughed at us. As the movement grew stronger over time, BJP realised that they had failed to judge our strength of unity. They became scared of the growing number of people participating in the movement; they could see how the movement, instead of fizzling out, was growing stronger day by day. This was posing a threat to them. The risk of electoral loss in assembly elections, particularly in UP, worried Modi. The only way for him was to announce that the laws would be withdrawn completely.

GX: *Even though all the demands were not met, why did SKM and your organisation agree to end the Delhi Morcha?*

JOGINDER SINGH: The *morcha* is not over. It was only suspended. We came back knowing that we had not been given a legal guarantee on MSP, that those responsible for the Lakhimpur Kheri massacre of farmers still remain unpunished. So we cannot say we have won completely.

But with the government withdrawing the laws in parliament, one phase of the movement was completed and the farmers won, as the primary demand of repeal of the farm laws was achieved. The battle for the legal guarantee of MSP for all crops is a far bigger battle. It is a long-term battle. So, SKM decided to lift the Delhi *morcha* after the initial victory and prepare for the long battle ahead. The movement still continues. We marched together to Delhi and we also came back together.

GX: *Police cases against protesters are still to be withdrawn; no committee has been formed regarding MSP. With BJP comfortably winning the elections in UP and other states do you think that the Modi government will keep its promises?*

JOGINDER SINGH: See, we can't say that cases have not been withdrawn against the protesters. In Punjab, most of the cases have been withdrawn. There is news that even in Haryana cases against protesting farmers have been withdrawn. Almost all tractors of the farmers that were seized by the police have been returned.

We twice got a call from the government regarding formation of a committee on MSP, we wrote back to the agriculture secretary asking him to send us the names of who are the other persons in the committee and what will be the power of the committee. We will look into it and discuss it after getting a reply.

Yes, it is an old tactic of the government to accept people's demands without implementing them. There is a need to keep the pressure on for enforcing the demands and we are doing that. Recently, we protested, demanding punishment for the culprits of the incident in Lakhimpur Kheri. From 11 to 17 April 2022, we have announced an action plan for MSP in all states. We are also planning for a programme in Lucknow, UP, on the Lakhimpur Kheri incident. So, we will continue our protest for the rest of the demands.

GX: *The SKM led the Delhi morcha. All the organisations were united throughout the struggle. But after the repeal of the laws and announcement of assembly elections in Punjab, SKM split on the question of participation in elections. How do you see the future of SKM?*

JOGINDER SINGH: See, SKM is still intact, but no doubt it will be affected by the split. But the split was inevitable as some unions merged into a political party to contest in the assembly elections. Fighting elections is not a sin, we don't mind contesting in elections. The party wing is always separate from the mass wing. The farmer organisations of the CPI and CPI(M) are also in the SKM. They don't fight elections, their party does. We have no issue with this. The mass organisations have their own separate existence.

In this case, twenty-two farmer unions merged into the Sanyukt Samaj Morcha (SSM)[1]. They made a political party by dissolving the unions. We objected to this. It's their democratic right to contest elections and we do not have an issue with that. Even if they want to convert their entire organisation (kisan union) into a political party, they can do that. Our point is that when it is clearly decided that no political party can be a part of SKM and this movement, then how can SSM—the party they formed after dissolving the unions—be a part of SKM? Their decision has hurt us. Still, our friends are not understanding. We are ready to hear them. The process is going on. Talks and discussions with those unions are taking place, especially with unions from Punjab. We hope most of them will return.

GX: *BKU (Ekta-Ugrahan)'s stand was that it would not support any party in the election, but it didn't give any call for a poll boycott either. Don't you think your election stand was politically ambiguous?*

JOGINDER SINGH: There was no ambiguity in our stand. We consider electoral politics as a derailing and misleading activity. The farmers' struggle has proved that the rights and interests of the farmers cannot be saved and ensured by sitting in parliament or assemblies; this can be achieved only through mass struggle. So, we took the opportunity to explain to the people of Punjab why we do not support the idea of farmers unions contesting elections. We raised the slogan *Vote di jhak chaddo, sangarsh de jhande gaddo* (Stop depending on vote politics, plant the flags of rebellion), urging people to strengthen mass struggle. On 5 January 2022, thousands of farmers and labourers rallied in Sangrur to oppose Narendra Modi's visit to Punjab. SKM gave a call to observe 31 January as the 'Day of Betrayal' to highlight the non-fulfilment of promises made by the government to the farmers. We burned effigies of the Union government and Modi outside the district collector's office in Sangrur. On 17 February, we held a massive rally in Barnala to remind the people about the importance of mass struggle. BKU (Ekta-Ugrahan) has been standing true to its belief that no real change comes through electoral politics.

The impact of the movement and our campaign during elections drastically raised the level of political discourse in Punjab. In the villages, people including women confronted politicians who came seeking votes and questioned them over their agenda and how they planned to solve their real problems relating to agriculture, health, employment, etc. The kisan *andolan* ignited a feeling and awareness among people that Punjab needs a change.

GX: *You are talking about the impact of the movement on raising people's political consciousness in Punjab. Yet the Aam Aadmi Party (AAP), which never stood firmly in support of the farmers' movement, won overwhelmingly in the assembly elections in Punjab. How do you explain this?*

JOGINDER SINGH: The people of Punjab in particular felt that a big change was needed, a non-corrupt political party was needed for governance. Any party that can save them, eradicate drugs, solve the problem of debt and unemployment in Punjab, end corruption and make agriculture a profitable business. And to bring this change they decided to get rid of the traditional parties—Congress and Akalis. The elections in Punjab were politically significant in the sense that all the big leaders of these two parties were defeated by the masses. It is not that AAP has won, it is actually a defeat of the other traditional parties. It is a lesson for AAP also that if they act in the same way as earlier parties, they will also be punished by the people.

We accept that the SKM couldn't emerge as a strong alternative political force to channelise the peoples' urge for change in the direction of mass struggle. People had no other option but to vote for AAP as the only political alternative available to them. If our friends who formed the SSM wouldn't have taken this step to contest elections, then the entire politics in Punjab would have centred around peoples' issues, and

SKM would have emerged as an alternative centre of people's political power. It's unfortunate that we couldn't achieve this.

Endnote

1. Cracks appeared in the Samyukta Kisan Morcha (SKM), after 22 Punjab based farmer unions (all constituents of the SKM) floated a new political party, the Sanyukt Samaj Morcha (SSM), and announced it will contest the assembly elections in Punjab. Balbir Singh Rajewal, one of the leading farmer leaders and the face of this new political front announced its formation to the press on 25 December 2021. The 22 unions and their leaders were suspended from the SKM. The SSM failed to win even a single seat in the assembly elections.

If We Unite and Fight Together, then We Have the Power to Change the Policies of the Government

JASBIR KAUR NATT, PUNJAB KISAN UNION

> JASBIR KAUR NATT, a state committee member of the Punjab Kisan Union (PKU), is from Mansa district in Punjab. After graduation, she took up a job in the Punjab Electricity Board. She started working with the Bharatiya Kisan Union in 1996 and became part of Punjab Kisan Union (PKU) when it was formed in 2007. She has worked extensively on farmers' indebtedness and suicide in Mansa region of Punjab. She was one of the most prominent women leaders of the farmers' movement at Delhi borders.
>
> HARSHITA BHASIN and SAHIL MEHRA from South Asian University conducted this interview in early January 2022 on behalf of GROUNDXERO.

GROUNDXERO: *You had a government job that was outside of the agriculture sector. What pushed you to work in a farmer organisation?*

JASBIR KAUR: Prior to the Green Revolution, farming used to comprise of natural and indigenous practices. I still have memories of those days from my childhood. The manure made from cattle-dung would be used in the fields. Wheat and cotton were the key crops. Paddy came in much later. It was introduced in our region only after 1985-86. In Amritsar, Hoshiarpur and Gurdaspur district, paddy used to be cultivated. In the Malwa region, paddy was rarely grown as it required a large amount of water. Gradually, the use of pesticides and fertilisers also increased. The problem of weeds wasn't that high in those days. But weeds became a huge problem after the introduction of pesticides and fertilisers. In those days, the labourers used to pluck weeds from wheat or cotton fields using manual techniques. These days, the weeds are killed by spraying chemicals. However, all these new practices have had an adverse impact on our health and ecology. So, while our yields increased, it wasn't accompanied with our wellbeing and happiness. Our farmers got indebted and reports of farmers' suicide on account of debt started coming during the '90s. Economic troubles and conflicts within households also rose, as the family members started blaming each other for the debt.

In Mansa, my home district, we would hear about many cases wherein farmers' lands were being auctioned off as they failed to repay their loans. Court cases would be registered against them, or they would be harassed by the police. So, we began raising the question: what made the farmers indebted in the first place? Over time, we began to study these issues and realised that it was the anti-farmer policies of the government that created these problems. These policies were biased towards the big companies which wanted to sell their products—seeds, pesticides, fertilisers etc. to the farmers. Earlier, every house had a bullock cart, which got replaced with a tractor. Banks started giving loans to farmers to buy tractors if they owned 10 acres or above of land. It depended on the land-value in different areas. Later, they reduced this collateral to just 2.5 acres of land. So even small farmers would avail such loans and use the money for other necessities and wouldn't be able to repay the instalments. Banks would, of course, try to recover their loans. There are tractor *mandis* (agriculture produce market) which continue to be held in Punjab wherein indebted farmers come to sell their tractors. Since other consumer loans were not easily accessible for farmers, the farmers were trapped in a vicious circle of indebtedness under tractor loans.

I was a government employee; so, I never worked for the party directly. But I used to work amongst government employees, women, farmers and labourers. We would raise issues concerning the farmers which slowly expanded to issues of agricultural workers as well. That's how I got close to the farmer organisation. We used to take up whatever issues would crop up, such as the issue of farmers' suicide, debt or compensation to families of farmers who had committed suicide.

GX: *What were the issues concerning the farmers that PKU took up during those days?*

JASBIR KAUR: Initially in your political journey you may have different queries. But when you see the issues on ground, the queries change. All the *sangathans* (organisations) continued to raise questions around government policies and organised struggles around them. For instance, there was the question of Bt cotton seeds[1]. I remember that the farmers used to store a part of their produce as seed for the next sowing season. But the Bt seeds would germinate in such a way that it wasn't possible to prepare seeds at home from the crop. If you would attempt to do so, the weedicides wouldn't work properly on crops grown from those seeds, or the yield would be too poor. We knew that these changes would come about in agriculture as our leaders had warned us about them when the New Economic Policy was adopted in the '90s. When there was an agreement with the World Trade Organization (WTO) in 1995, we heard and read about the implications of such policies—how the government would pave the way for transferring the *jal, jangal, zameen* (water, forest, land) to the corporates. We used to explain the implications of such policies to the people through rallies, meetings etc. in one village or the other, almost every day.

But people did not understand our criticism. When we used to raise slogans like *Inquilab Zindabad* (Long Live Revolution) or *Samrajyavad Murdabaad* (Down with Imperialism) or *Punjivaad Murdabad* (Down with Capitalism), they inferred that we are communists, but the meaning of such slogans was beyond their comprehension. Since this farmers' movement has happened, if you now ask anyone what *punjivaad* is, they will explain to you that corporate houses which have come to steal our lands comprise *punjivaad* (capitalism) as well as *samrajyavad* (imperialism). When these laws were brought in June 2020 as ordinances, people came to know about them through newspapers, TV and social media. At that time, there was a lockdown and restrictions on movement of people were quite stringent. Also, at that time, there was an agitation underway in Punjab against the atrocities of microfinance companies. That agitation had spread across all districts of Punjab within a very short span of time. Punjab Kisan Union as well as a labour union called Mazdoor Mukti Morcha had come together for the agitation against microfinance companies. Many agricultural workers as well as small farmers or poor families' incomes dried up during the lockdown. But the microfinance companies kept pressuring them to pay their loan instalments. There were also some incidences of suicide after recovery agents of these companies had come to the borrowers' houses. The agents would pick up household assets such as a gas stove and cylinder or a bike if there was one around. We campaigned on this issue from village to village.

GX: *We do not see many women organisers and leaders in the farmer unions or the agricultural worker unions. What do you think can be done by the unions to change this situation?*

JASBIR KAUR: This is true that there are only a few women leaders. However, we cannot say that their involvement and contribution are any less in protest movements. Women's participation is strong in farming activities as well as their membership in the farmer unions. There is a saying in our Gurbani—*"Jabe baan laage tabe ros jaage,"* meaning that only when someone is attacked, and when an issue impacts their family, they recognise the need to understand it and get involved in it. Now that the farmers and farming are under attack, women are actively participating in the protests, but they are not in leadership.

However, I can say that in the future, whether in farmer unions or worker unions, there will be significant women membership and representation. It is because now they have become conscious. Earlier the environment was such that women were under a lot of restrictions from the family, they were not allowed to go anywhere, which have reduced in recent times. Earlier, even the farmer unions couldn't realise the importance of women members. Male dominated society exists everywhere, even in Punjab, and the dominating idea is that men will take things forward. As we can see, for some time now, there has been a demand that there should be reservation for women in legislative bodies. We have for long been demanding 33 percent reservation for women, and this we have been doing for a long time, since the era of Prime Minister I.K. Gujral [1996-97]. We also protested in front of the parliament house raising the demand for 33 percent reservation for women in parliament and state assemblies, and we even had to face a lathi-charge for that. Now this question and demand will also be raised in various farmer unions. People are much more aware and conscious that women constitute 50 percent of the total population and they should be equally represented. We believe that in the future, women's representation in both organisation and leadership positions will surely improve.

In my family, my husband, my children, my brother-in law, all work with the union. So, almost all of my family is willingly associated with the union. I got to know my husband through our shared political ideology. We used to work together in the union and later got married. There were no restrictions on me and wherever I was required I used to go for union work. Even if I hesitate to go anywhere, my husband always motivates me and encourages me to go for it. It is because of his support that I am in the leadership. I travel to places, and I am much more confident now.

GX: *Images of the farmers' movement in the media reflected the presence of women in the protests. But women farmers are still invisible in Indian official statistics. The media and the state also portrayed them as daughters, wives and mothers of the protesting male farmers, not as independent stakeholders. What are your views on this?*

JASBIR KAUR: Yes, usually the land is in the name of the male head of the household. Ownership gets transferred to a woman heir after the demise of her husband. If the father dies and his children have not been named in the will, then legally the ownership of land should go to all the children—both male and female. However, usually the ownership is transferred in the name of the men of the household and not in the name of the women. Women do not usually engage directly in cultivation activities like ploughing the field, so society does not consider them as farmers. The Samyukta Kisan Morcha (SKM) has given recognition to women farmers and also has decided to observe 18 January [2020] as the Women Farmers' Day. It is just the beginning. People will become aware that even women are farmers. This movement has raised consciousness and awareness among many women, making them recognise their true potential and power. They are realising, "we can also form an organisation and we can also fight." So, in the future, things will change for the better.

GX: *Do you feel that a leftist farmer union which also fights for broader social and political issues must have a separate women's wing?*

JASBIR KAUR: There are certain issues that both men and women need to fight together, for example, the three farm laws, unemployment, the economic situation of the country, etc. These are common issues. There are also some issues that pertain only to women and for which they must raise their voices, for example, the question of their equality in the society or their fight against drug abuse and domestic violence which men are not willing to join as they may feel it is directed against them. Having a separate wing for women is important to organise women, to make them aware of their power and encourage them to participate in the movement. If women stay inside their homes and do not participate in this movement, then the movement will not become powerful enough. Hence, for these reasons, we must form separate women's wings.

For example, sometime ago, we raised this question—there is a high incidence of suicide in Punjab, both amongst farmers and agricultural labourers. There are many families who did not receive the compensation and the government kept postponing it. Even in this movement against the three farm laws, the families of the martyrs have not received any sort of compensation so far. In 2017 or 2018, we mobilised a lot of women and went to meet those women who had a suicide in their family but didn't receive any compensation. We raised the issue that when the head of the household commits suicide, the family continues to be in debt as they lack any alternate sources of income. The government refuses to take any responsibility. They would only receive a widow pension which was Rs 250 per month in Punjab. Later it was increased to Rs 500, then to Rs 750, and now, just before the elections, to Rs 1500 per month. A household cannot survive on these paltry amounts. We raised the demand that something should be done to help these families survive—either guarantee employment to the women, or announce measures so that these families can meet their basic needs.

If there is heavy dependence on drugs in the society, where men and boys indulge in drug addiction, the women are forced to bear the brunt of the consequent unhappiness. When men are under a lot of stress, they find refuge in alcohol and drugs. "I am very sad due to all this debt," they say. But the women cannot alleviate their sadness by drinking alcohol. If that man commits suicide now, then all the burden of raising the children falls on the woman in the family. She must remain alive to take care of the children and for that she needs a source of income.

GX: *Indian society (both rural and urban) is extremely patriarchal. As a member of a left union, does the women's wing in your union take up issues related to patriarchy, such as dowry, exploitation of women farmers in their households, domestic abuse etc.?*

JASBIR KAUR: Yes, we deal with all this. There is a also a different organisation—All India Progressive Women Association (AIPWA) for this. However, many farmer unions still do not have a separate women's wing. If there are cases related to domestic abuse due to dowry, rape or murder, the unions come forward to fight. Many unions have fought long battles to help the victims get justice.

GX: *Do you see any gender issue arising within the farmer union? And if it does, how does the women's wing and the union deal with it?*

JASBIR KAUR: So far, we have not experienced many such cases in our union. If any such case arises, we ask the victim to submit a written complaint, on the basis of which a committee is formed and an enquiry team investigates after hearing both sides. After investigation, action against the culprit is taken, and he may be removed or dismissed from the organisation. The crime is made public and even reportSed to the media explaining the person's offence. Such cases are handled very strictly and there is no leniency.

GX: *We saw that during the protests at the borders, most of the cooking and cleaning was shared by men. Has that continued?*

JASBIR KAUR: It was only during the protest that men partook in cooking and cleaning. In their homes, men never used to do these things before, nor do they do any of it now. Hopefully, this change will come over time, where men will volunteer to share the household chores like cleaning clothes or washing utensils. This will take time. In a working family, where both the husband and the wife work, both go out for their job, they do have to share the responsibility of household work. Here, the husbands feel that since the wife stays at home, she should do all the household chores.

GX: *Women agricultural labourers do not own any land, and even women belonging to most of the small farmer families do not own land. Do you think that this "landless" status can be a rallying and unifying point for women from families of small farmers and agricultural labourers? In general, how do women activists view the question of land redistribution and what is their view on the demand for land by landless women farmers?*

JASBIR KAUR: There are some fundamental differences in the fight between the two classes. In Punjab, the Land Ceiling Act placed a ceiling of 17.5 acres on land ownership. We have been demanding for a long time to reduce the ceiling to 10 acres. Many large farmers own hundreds of acres of land and that land should be redistributed among marginal farmers and landless agricultural labourers. Some time back, the new Chief Minister of Punjab (Charanjit Singh Channi) agreed to this demand. But due to pressure from the big land-owners, he retracted his decision. There are other issues at play as well, like caste. For example, the Jat Sikhs are the dominant caste in Punjab. Even if they are landless, they have their caste pride. Many Dalit women from landless families work in the fields of Jat farmers, but women from landless Jat families would never work as a labourer in any other farmer's field. The Jat women might engage in stitching, or put up a small shop, but she will never work as a labourer. So, the class and caste positions and their inherent contradictions are obstacles to uniting and rallying landless women based only on gender.

GX: *Dalit women activists have spoken on how caste, patriarchy and the state collude to oppress Dalit landless women. "No liberation can be imagined without putting at the centre stage Dalit landless women's oppression," said one Dalit woman. What, in your opinion, is the condition of Dalit women in Punjab? What are your programs to address their issues of oppression—caste, patriarchy, and equal wages and landlessness?*

JASBIR KAUR: Our organisation is associated with a Communist party [CPI-ML Liberation]. We have always fought for the rights of the Dalits. In 2009 we fought for the allocation of residential plots to them and even went to jail for it. The government—both the Congress and Akali Dal in Punjab—had promised Dalit families will be allotted a 5 *mar-*

la (1 *marla* = 0.013 hectare) plot, but later they backtracked on their promise. We helped in capturing and redistributing the vacant panchayati lands to the Dalit families. Given the high rates of inflation and their meagre incomes, it is very difficult for them to purchase land and build houses. Because of our struggle, police cases were filed against us. We have been demanding an increase in the employment days under MGNREGA for Dalit workers to at least 200 days and a daily wage of Rs 700. Wherever women labourers work, we have always demanded that they should be given the same wages as men. We keep fighting for issues like their employment, children's education, health etc. As mentioned earlier, we have been fighting to reduce the land ceiling from 17.5 acres to 10 acres so that land can be redistributed to Dalits and also other landless general caste labourers.

GX: *The massive participation of women was clearly visible in this struggle. How was this mobilisation of women achieved? Was it spontaneous?*

JASBIR KAUR: Efforts were made to campaign from village to village and we also encouraged women to join the protest. Initially, we had to campaign and make people, particularly women, aware of the issues of the movement, to make them conscious of their rights and power. They started realising that they were 50 percent of the population and that they should also join the protest and fight. Once the movement picked up and protests became strong, women started joining on their own.

GX: *Tell us about the difficulties that women farmers faced when they were away from their families and children to be at the protest sites for long periods of time. How did they deal with it?*

JASBIR KAUR: The women who had children back at home used to travel back and forth between their respective village and the protest sites. They used to spend a week here at the protest site and travel back home for the next week. The children were left either under the care of their grandparents, or one of the parents used to stay back in the village to take care of them. Those having grown-up children did not face so many problems, but those with small children had to make such adjustments. As I have mentioned, my own family is not engaged in farming, but those families that depend upon farming had to go back time to time to look after their crops. If the husband was sitting at the protest site, then it was the responsibility of the wife to look after the crops. It was relatively easier for the people not engaged in farming to be on the borders.

GX: *The Supreme Court (SC) said that the women and the elders should be sent back home from the dharnas at the borders. How did women react to this suggestion of the SC? How do you view this questioning of women's agency in the movement by the SC?*

JASBIR KAUR: When the SC suggested this, there was a strong opposition from the women protestors: "We are not coaxed into joining the protest, rather we have come on our own will and this is our fight too," they said. After that the number of women protestors did not decline; in fact, it increased. People realised, that if the SC was giving such suggestions, it meant that the government was behind this. We also realised that there could be a possibility of a physical attack after sending women, elders and children back home. Therefore, taking into consideration all these factors, more women joined the protests and openly challenged them by standing their ground.

GX: *In your opinion, did women have any significant role in decision-making in this movement?*

JASBIR KAUR: As I mentioned earlier, women leaders are very few in number. There were about two or three women leaders at the Singhu border. I was at the Tikri border. Whatever small number of women leaders were present, they were always a part of the meetings and contributed equally in the decision making process.

GX: *The struggle was successful in forcing the government to withdraw the three farm laws. Do you believe the committee on MSP (Minimum Support Price) will deliver its promises, or was it just a face-saving step both for the SKM and the government? Apart from MSP, what are the other issues that you think need urgent attention?*

Jasbir Kaur: Even if there is a resolution on MSP, the problems will not get resolved. The situation of the farmers will not improve on its own after the revocation of these laws. For that, there are additional demands. There should be an agricultural policy through which farmers are able to reap benefits, there should be a guarantee of employment, education and health facilities for farmers' children. The state should provide all this. It has basically washed its hands of all responsibilities. Employment guarantee is important, as small and marginal farmers having less than 2 to 2.5 acres of land are not able to survive. We are constantly speaking about these issues and fighting for them.

GX: *I have one last question. What lessons have you learnt from this historic farmers' movement?*

Jasbir Kaur: I experienced such a movement for the first time in my life. A movement which was so massive in its scale and so long in its duration. Also, for the first time, I have experienced unity of this scale where 32 farmer unions from Punjab, Haryana and almost 500 unions across the entire country representing different ideologies came together. This whole movement has taught me one important lesson—if we unite and fight together, then we have the power to change the policies of the government. I find it a valuable and a very important lesson. I have also learnt another important lesson that if we all live in peace and harmony with one another, ignoring the small differences in our ideologies, then we can unite on common issues.

Endnote

1. Bt cotton is a genetically modified cotton variety containing a pesticide which ought to protect the plant from bollworm. In 2002, a joint venture between Monsanto and Mahyco introduced Bt cotton to India. Its introduction created a huge controversy and many consider it as being the main reason for a resurgence of farmer suicides in India.

This Movement will be Forever Remembered as a Foundation of all People's Movements in the Coming Future
Hannan Mollah, Akhil Bharatiya Kisan Sabha

> Hannan Mollah is the General Secretary of All India Kisan Sabha (AIKS), one of the constituent organisations of the SKM. He is also a member of the working committee of the All India Kisan Sangharsh Coordination Committee (AIKSCC). He has played a pivotal role in bringing together farmer' unions from different parts of the country on a common platform.
>
> This interview by GroundXero was conducted in Kolkata, a week before the Prime Minister announced that all the three farm laws would be withdrawn.

GroundXero: *26 November 2021 would be the first anniversary of the ongoing farmers' movement. At this point of time, how do you evaluate this movement?*

Hannan Mollah: My evaluation is that the farmers' movement led by the Samyukta Kisan Morcha (SKM)—a joint platform of farmer unions opposed to the three farm laws—has a few unique characteristics. First of all, in the history of India, a mass movement as widespread and prolonged as this one, based on the issues impacting the lives and livelihoods of almost 90 crore Indians, has never been organised before. One can perhaps speak of agitations organised within specific states, but a protest movement of this scale encompassing nearly the entire country, has never been organised before.

Secondly, almost all farmer unions in Punjab and about 500 organisations from all over the country are involved in this movement. All sorts of ideologies have come together with a common understanding primarily based on four common demands. Each of these organisations has its own set of demands and programs. They have all come together under the SKM umbrella while keeping their own politics intact, and are unitedly agitating in support of the four common demands. Even after almost a year these organisations have not had any significant differences of opinion amongst themselves. Generally, even in a very small movement, we see that even five or ten organisations fail to work together. But this time, all organisations within the SKM have so far remained united, and have stood firm on their common demands.

Thirdly, even after so many attacks and provocations by the government and its agents, the movement has remained non-violent. This is the first non-violent mass movement that is going on for such a long time in the post-independence era. We had stated that our protest will be peaceful because violence would ensure BJP's victory, whereas non-violence, ours. It would have been easy for them to crush the movement if we had indulged in violence during the agitation, and we are not going to give them that chance. The farmers understand this. This is the reason why the movement has remained absolutely peaceful and resolute in its determination to compel the central government to repeal the anti-farmer laws.

The fourth characteristic is, the movement has received support from a very, very large number of people. This kind of wide-ranging support from across the country does not have many precedents. The various workers' federations and the ten Central Trade Unions have been supporting us since the very beginning of the movement. Besides, the students, youth and women, citizens of many nations and the Indian residents in those countries have given us a lot of support. Almost five to six countries have raised the topic of this movement in their parliament. But, in our own parliament they have failed to resolve anything at all.

An important thing to note in these characteristics is that the movement has never been only for the protection of the interests of the farmers. The specific demands of the farmers also address the interests of all sections of the society. Take for example, the ration system (PDS). The three farm laws would hand over the present system of public distribution of food grains entirely to the speculators and black marketers. This will lead to precarious living conditions for a large section of the population. Our movement is keeping the public distribution system of food grains alive.

Also, we can see that people opposing this government are being attacked, their democratic rights are being throttled—democracy itself is under siege. The primary goal of this movement has been to save the democratic and constitutional rights of the farmers. However, saving those rights for everyone else in the country is also amongst our demands. Thus the movement has many dimensions, which is precisely why we are so keen on taking it forward. Over 700 people have died in the course of this movement, or rather, I should say that they have been martyred. The farmers have sat through 0 to 45 degree celsius of temperature and in pouring rain for days at a stretch. This is where our strength lies—in the tenacity of the farmers. Without that, we would have been nowhere. The farmers have been saying, 700 of us have died so far and let another thousand die, but we will not move until the three farm laws are repealed. This is precisely the kind of fighting spirit that has helped in keeping the leaders of so many organisations together. The significance of this movement lies in all of these aspects. Many people have commented, "India's farmers' movement will show the path for many democratic movements all across the world." And that is in my opinion no exaggeration. This is how this movement has kept itself alive and kicking.

When a movement takes place in any democratic country, the elected government speaks to the protesters and tries to resolve the issues. Not this government of Narendra Modi though. We were ready to discuss our demands with the government since the very beginning of the protest. It is true that we have problems with the laws and we wanted to have direct discussions with the government on them. Initially, the government made some attempts but all negotiations failed as they refused to discuss the repeal of the three pro-corporate laws. Since then, for the last seven to eight months, the Union government hasn't responded at all. What the government actually hoped was that the farmers would get exhausted and frustrated sitting on roads and their unity would break. There were many conspiracies on their part to derail the movement. Our farmers understood this and doubled their efforts to keep the movement united and alive.

There is another reason why the people of India are supporting this longest democratic movement in the history of this country. They understand that if this farmers' movement fails, no other people's movement will survive in the near future. So, the people have identified with the positive sides of the movement and are continuing to support the farmers. We are setting an example for ourselves—how to keep a movement alive for such a long time, identifying where the problems lie, which issues should be emphasised and discussed—we are still learning and gathering experience. We have also been planning action programs each and every day so that we can continue to exert pressure on the government. This is how we are continuing our struggle.

GX: *We have seen how a large section of the Indian farmers has been organised through this movement. But, till now, the farmers from the eastern and southern parts of the country are not actively supporting and participating in this movement like those from Punjab, Haryana and UP. Is it because they could not be reached or are there other reasons for their passivity?*

HANNAN MOLLAH: How we evaluate a movement also depends on our perspective. There are two dominant streams in this movement. One consists of six states of northern India from which the farmers have mostly come to Delhi and are at present camping at the borders encircling the national capital city. This is the principal feature of the movement. It is not like there are thousands of people sitting out there all the time. People are coming and going, some are staying for a few days, followed by others. This is how it has been going on. Their number is sometimes ten thousand, sometimes twenty thousand or even fifty thousand. This is what constitutes the primary thrust for the movement.

However, there are also 15 to 16 other states, which have also been responding to each of SKM's call of action. These two streams of the movement have been flowing simultaneously. There are some other issues as well. The trains are not running due to Covid restrictions. Thousands of people are unable to travel all the way to the borders of Delhi, so they have organised protests in their respective states. Almost 40 crore people participated in the Bharat Bandh.[1] The bandh did not happen only in Punjab and Haryana. Those two states are indeed the epicentre of the movement—in the front rows—as they say. But to say that the movement belongs to only the farmers from Punjab and Haryana is a calculated malicious campaign. It is a pan-India movement. A historical movement supported by the majority of the farmers in India.

You see, in the thousand years' history of India, no movement ever had a uniform people's participation in every part of the country. After all, it depends on the nature of the overall assault. Who is affected more intensely through these farm laws, and who is not affected as much? If today the MSP (Minimum Support Price) is abolished, and the three laws are implemented, the farmers in Punjab, Haryana and western UP will suffer the maximum, as they will be forced to sell crops in the private *mandis* (agricultural produce markets) for a lesser price than they do at present in state government notified *mandis*. So, it is obvious that they are facing an immediate attack. Those in other parts of the country know that the laws would not affect them immediately in the same way, since they do not have access to public *mandis* anyway, and hence are forced to sell food grains at prices far below the MSP. MSP is practically available to the farmers of these three northern states only.

MSP for paddy is Rs 1,868 per quintal. Even this price is not fair. It is much less than the total expense incurred. Nevertheless, this is the price announced by the government. When both the seller and the buyer are registered, this is the price to be paid for purchasing paddy in the government *mandis*. But, nowhere in private markets in India are farmers getting a price of more than Rs 1,200 to Rs 1,500 per quintal for paddy. Almost 80 percent of Indian farmers are not able to avail the MSP fixed by the Union government.

Therefore those who were getting this support price, mainly the farmers of Punjab, Haryana and western UP—as they began to fear the risk of losing it, their reaction obviously had much more intensity as compared to other farmers who were not getting MSP and had no access to government *mandis*. But one should not assume that there is no reaction among farmers in states other than north India. When the farmers were being attacked while marching towards Delhi, and the bandh was called across the entire country, almost 40 to 50 crore people participated in it. The media is spreading malicious campaigns by parroting and amplifying the government's narrative that the movement is limited to the surplus-producing rich farmers from Punjab.

GX: *We have seen that the attempts to implement neoliberal economic policies have led to massive attacks on the rights of the working class. But* *the workers do not seem to be taking to the streets in protest. The four labour codes, privatisation of PSUs (Public Sector Undertakings)—despite such draconian measures, the trade union response has been limited to calling ritualistic annual strikes. While the farmers are out on the streets challenging the government, the workers aren't. What is your opinion on this?*

HANNAN MOLLAH: Due to the implementation of neoliberal policies for the last 25 years, the trade unions have become dysfunctional. Neoliberalism operates through a system of abolition of permanent jobs. 90 percent of the workers are now temporary or casual workers. These casual workers are not able to build up an organised movement. They might lose their job at any moment. A casual worker doesn't have any labour rights and the few that they had earlier, have now been taken away through these four labour codes. So even if a trade union tries to organise protests, the casual workers are unable to participate. They also do not have faith in the unions, who they view as representing the interests of only the permanent workers.

Secondly, the way farmers can leave their work for months and stay put at protests, the workers cannot do that. They cannot leave their work in the companies or factories to sustain such a long movement. So, the nature and form of the two movements are bound to be different. Problems do exist. Trade union movements have lost their intensity throughout the world. The goal of neoliberal policy is to abolish the very existence of the organised working class in the industries. They want the entire workforce to be turned into a huge pool of contractual labour. Once that happens, there will be no guarantee of anything—no permanent jobs, no labour rights, no fixed working hours, no holidays, no breaks, and on top of that, the constant threat of retrenchment. This is the mantra of neoliberal policy. For the last thirty years, this has been implemented all over the world. The trade unions have lost the power to retaliate. Perhaps, the working class will rebel if at some point they feel their backs against the wall as they keep facing repeated attacks. Perhaps then, the working class movement will emerge and assume different forms. But organising workers to resist has become very difficult at this point of time. Besides, the government is following the policy of selling all public sector enterprises to private companies. If everything gets owned by the corporates, then even the few rights that the permanent workers have now will also not be guaranteed anymore. This atmosphere of uncertainty is making it even more difficult for the workers to organise a strong movement. Not that they are not making any efforts, but the trade union movement at present is not going to take the form of farmers' rebellion.

This farmers' movement is actually the first anti-corporate mass movement in India. Before this, slogans used to be raised against the corporates like *Tata murdabad, Birla murdabad* (Down with Tata, Down with Birla). But the corporates have never been directly attacked. These farmers, through blacklisting Reliance Jio sim-cards or closing down Reliance retail stores and petrol pumps and Adani agri-logistic hubs, have directly attacked the corporate for the first time. No other section has been able to do this till now.

GX: *You said that left, centrist and even right-wing feudal organisations are part of this joint movement against corporate attack on farming. Is it the pressure of the farmers from below that has kept such politically divergent groups together? What are you telling the farmers sitting on the borders?*

HANNAN MOLLAH: From the very first day we have tried to convey one thing to the farmers, that is, if the three laws are implemented, then the farmers will lose all chances of survival. And, that the government is trying to create a farming system compatible with corporate needs, instead of one that is responsive to the needs of the farmers. The farmers will lose all leverage in the new system. Everything around farming—production, distribution, transportation, marketing, storage—will be taken over by the big companies. The farmers will lose control over everything.

Contract farming very much exists even now, but that is limited predominantly to the small farmers. Say, for example, you have 5 *bighas* (1 *bigha* = 0.1338 hectare) of land, and you work and reside in Kolkata. Now, you give the land on rent to someone in your village to cultivate. But the law on contract farming that the government has been proposing, presents us with a new model, where the contract will be between the farmer and a company. If such a contract is signed with a company for 5 *bigha* of land, the farmers' own interests would not be taken into consideration. Those with economic power will have the ultimate say in all the negotiations. The farmers would be forced to agree to the conditions imposed by the likes of Ambanis and Adanis.

Every year the farmers suffer from drought, flood, excessive rain, and incur losses. But, eventually, they survive and even recover. If they sign corporate contracts, the Ambanis and the Adanis will end up buying their lands for a pittance. Slowly, the farmers' land will come to be owned by the corporates. Haven't you seen what happened in Gujarat? What did companies such as Pepsi and Coca Cola do to the farmers? The companies might impose a condition that you can grow tomatoes but cannot sell it to anyone else. If the tomato's colour is slightly changed due to rain, or if it gets stained, they may reject the entire lot. It means a year of complete loss for the farmer—the whole year's production going to waste. All such conditions are for the profit of the companies only. The ordinary farmer will have no say.

We started explaining to the farmers that this corporate entry is going to have long-lasting effects, and the farmers grasped the gist of the situation in their own ways. The farmers are now aware of these three laws. They might not be able to articulate it with the language I am using right now, but they clearly understand that there are a lot of things in these laws that would harm them. It is the pressure from these farmers which has kept the unions united so far.

GX: *What is the lesson of this farmers' movement for the Left political parties?*

HANNAN MOLLAH: You see, the lesson to learn for the Left movement is that we will be able to prevent this neoliberal onslaught if the corporates can be forced to go on the back foot. The big farmers' participation in this movement is significant in this context. In general we understand that if we can make the corporate houses uncomfortable, the rich land-owners amongst the farmers, who are usually the local exploiters, will also get weaker. They usually live by allying with the corporates, so they do not really want the corporates to disappear. Despite that, the big farmers or the rich land-owners participated in this movement as they realised that the farm laws would harm their interests as well. Of course the middle farmers, marginal and small farmers rightly realised the great peril they were facing and joined the protests in large numbers. So the Left should realise that a united struggle of all sections is needed to take on the neoliberal policies.

GX: *Of course, not all the agrarian contradictions will be resolved at this moment by this movement. But what are your thoughts on the future for farmers in the coming days?*

HANNAN MOLLAH: We think that if we can force the government to guarantee procurement of crops at MSP, only then can the farmers be saved. Otherwise they will not survive. It is for this very reason that the farmers have become so desperate. It is a do or die struggle for them. The farmers cannot do without the Minimum Support Price. The price that they get today in the market, is not even close to the expenses they incur. It is much less than that. Moreover, all the things needed for farming such as seed, fertiliser, electricity etc. have become costlier than before. In this situation, the farmers' crisis cannot be resolved without ensuring the purchase of their produce at a fair price.

We are not telling the government that it must by itself buy all the crops. We are just saying that you must make a law which does not allow anyone to purchase crops at any random price. When you are buying crops in a *mandi* for a fixed price, let the other 80 percent of the places follow that same price. And the violation of this law should be made punishable—that is our only demand regarding this issue. What is happening is that the crops are being bought from the open market for Rs 1,200 per quintal and then sold to the government for Rs 1,800 per quintal. But the money is not going to the farmers—all of it is going to the middlemen. The farmers are being cheated. This needs to be stopped.

GX: *This movement is reaching its first anniversary. If the Modi government still refuses to negotiate, what are your plans?*

HANNAN MOLLAH: The lies spread by the Modi government have by now been exposed before the people. They do not believe in the government's campaign anymore. Modi is deliberately lying when he says his government has approved and is implementing the Swaminathan Committee formula of MSP. It's a blatant lie! What they are giving is 1.5 times of A2+FL costs and what we are demanding is C2+50 percent. The price as per 1.5 times of A2+FL costs is 15 to 20 percent less than if calculated on the basis of C2+50 percent formula. The government is basically trying to make things easy for the companies.

See, we are organising a farmers' movement. We are not a political party. However, we have realised that elections indeed plays a role even in terms of our movement. This government won't be stopped unless they are threatened electorally. Though no farmer leader, from our side, will fight the elections, we have decided that whenever there will be an election in any state, we will organise farmers' *mahapanchayats* (massive gathering of farmers) and explain to the local farmers and the people, that BJP is your number one enemy, and so don't vote for them. Given that, who else you want to vote for is up to you. SKM has never campaigned supporting any candidate of any party. We will just explain to the farmers not to vote for the BJP.

GX: *What are your thoughts on countering the role that the mainstream media has played towards vilifying this movement?*

HANNAN MOLLAH: The media has consistently attacked us and continues to do so. They are calling us Khalistanis[2], Pakistanis, China's agents, and what not. Using criminal elements, they designed the entire plan of vilifying the farmers on 26 January. But even then, they couldn't succeed. No one believed them. When we went to the farmers, and told them the government and the media were lying, the farmers believed us. We told them that those who created all the violence inside the Red Fort have photos with Modi, Shah and the Minister of Agriculture, they understood that all the media propaganda is part of a conspiracy against the farmers and the movement.

Now the government has become more desperate. When nothing worked, they resorted to physical attacks. First the incident of lathi-charge in Haryana, then the shooting in Assam, and then, in broad daylight, the Union minister's son mowed the farmers with his car in Lakhimpur.[3] How many farmers will you kill? There are 80 to 90 crore people who are behind us. You cannot kill every one of them.

We are saying this time and again that this farmers' movement is one of the longest mass movements in India, and this movement will be forever remembered as a foundation of all people's movements in the coming future.

Endnotes

1. Farmer unions called a Bharat Bandh on 8 December 2020 after several rounds of talks with the government over the farm laws remained inconclusive. SKM decided to intensify the agitation against the laws by calling for Bharat Bandh, expressed their dissatisfaction with amendments to the laws proposed by the government, and reiterated the demand for repeal of the laws and a legally guaranteed MSP on all crops.

2. The Khalistan movement's goal is to create a homeland for Sikhs by seceding the State of Punjab from India and establishing a sovereign, ethno-religious Sikh state called Khalistan ('Land of the Khalsa').

3. On 3 October, 2021, four farmers returning from a protest were killed in Lakhimpur Kheri (UP), after a car in the convoy of Ashish Mishra, the son of Union Minister of State for Home Affairs, ran over them. A journalist also died in the incident.

Top: Woman Farmers' Day being observed at Tikri border. **Below:** Farmers protesting at Singhu border. **Photo credit:** Workers Unity.

The Democratisation of the Man-Woman Relationship is a Part of the Struggle to Democratise Society

SUKHWINDER KAUR, BHARATIYA KISAN UNION (KRANTIKARI)

> SUKHWINDER KAUR is a state committee member of BKU (Krantikari), which was formed in 2004 and has been working among marginal, small and middle farmers in around 10 districts of Punjab, mainly in the Malwa region of the state. She has worked as a Lab Technician in the Health department. Sukhwinder Kaur was a founding member of Aurat Mukti Morcha formed in 1995. She joined BKU-Krantikari when it was formed in 2004.
>
> On the eve of 8 March 2021, Sukhwinder Kaur spoke to BAMA, a feminist magazine published in Bengali. A year later in March 2022, GROUNDXERO interviewed her.

PART I

BAMA: *Tell us about your personal and political journey. How did you come into this movement? How did you get involved with BKU (Krantikari)?*

SUKHWINDER KAUR: I have been in the movement for a long time. I had been involved in student politics, later I got involved in peasant movements in Punjab...

BAMA: *Could you tell us about the participation of women in the movement?*

SUKHWINDER KAUR: There was a time when it was very difficult for us to bring women into the movement. The situation has changed now. Many women are now in the struggle, leading the movement, voicing their opinions. Especially in this [farmers'] movement, a lot of women have joined, many women have come to the forefront of the struggle. They are building women's committees in their villages, and many women have come to Delhi Morcha (farmers' protest sites at borders of

Delhi). Many women are actively participating in occupying toll plazas, malls and in blocking the highways in Punjab.

BAMA: *How did this change come about?*

SUKHWINDER KAUR: I feel two or three factors played a huge role. Firstly, there has been a long history of mass movements in Punjab. Many unions have consistently worked for years in building consciousness amongst the people. Furthermore, the agrarian crisis has a deep impact on people in Punjab. Women started moving out more, many went into higher education, many migrated taking their family along with them. It was women who had to take things into their hands, sustain families, put food on the plate... women always did that, but the crisis made their contributions more visible. Previously, women's mobility was restricted, they were not allowed to travel alone... these regulations got relaxed because of the crisis. Women had to venture out... work, study, take charge of the family. The agrarian crisis helped recognise women's work, their role in society, their labour. Working class women had to work day and night to survive. The crisis made women's labour visible, made women's role in agrarian society visible, and this further opened roads for women's education. Although, in some cases, women's education still remains a means to marry them off, yet, the recognition that women could play a significant role got established during this time.

BAMA: *What is the position of women in these organisations? How would you describe their participation?*

SUKHWINDER KAUR: You see, this is a male dominated society. If you look at Punjab's history, it is dominated by men. Women's role is hardly talked about, discussed, and acknowledged. So even in organisations, we have to fight to make our place. It is a difficult fight, as women have to first come out of the shackles of family, home, motherhood... still women are joining the struggle. Women studying in universities are playing a significant role in organising. The Pinjra Tod movement[1] played a significant role in Punjabi University in Chandigarh and Patiala. There have been attacks on them [activists of Pinjra Tod movement] too. When these women became vocal, when they began writing in newspapers, there were cases registered against them... again these repressive measures brought more people on the streets in support of them... all in all, as the agrarian crisis intensifies, so does people's will to fight. Women have come to realise that, they are fighting for dignity and their fight is being recognised.

In 1991 when the Dunkel Draft was being signed, we already knew that this would be dangerous for agriculture. We knew we would have to resist this. However, there was not much response from people. a few educated people would debate with us, they said we are overreacting. They felt that since the government has failed to deliver, private companies would be able to make things better. Now we know what happens when public sectors get privatised. We have seen what has happened with BSNL, we have seen what has happened with education and healthcare services getting privatised. People are more aware of what can happen if agriculture gets privatised. They know if private companies get full control over agriculture, none of us will survive. Let me give you an example. When people had jobs, even those in clerical jobs would get a salary of Rs 30,000 to Rs 35,000 per month. Those with permanent jobs would get periodic raises in salary. These days even those with PhD degrees who get jobs as faculty in universities, hardly get a monthly salary of around Rs 21,000. Most jobs are contractual. People have seen these changes; people have been through enough. This is what made the peasant community enter the struggle. They know this is our last chance. With everything getting privatised, land is all that we have left. Since this is the site of the Green Revolution, there is a concept of MSP (Minimum Support Price). With the MSP being lifted, prices at which farmers sell grains will fall. Farming would be impossible to sustain. With farmers' suicides, debts, unemployment being on the rise, if the prices fall, we will lose control over cultivation. This is why we have all come together to fight. Our culture is intimately woven with agriculture, our songs are about villages and villages are in danger, all our singers have now come together to sing about the peasants' struggle. Almost 200 songs have been composed so far. These songs play a significant role in organising. Singers who previously sold their songs for lakhs are now coming and performing on their own at the protest sites.

Since land is at stake, the entire community has risen in struggle.

Punjab has had an old rivalry with Delhi. It is ingrained in our culture. There have been many songs regarding Delhi even before this movement. The movement has awakened all sections of society, and women cannot stay outside it. Everyone is in this together.

BAMA: *Can you elaborate a bit more on the land question? A few days back we read the Supreme Court asking unions why women have been 'kept' in the movement... The state does not recognise women as farmers. We know 75 percent women work in the fields, but only 12 percent have land ownership. Are these issues discussed in this movement?*

SUKHWINDER KAUR: People are quite angry. You should look at our history. Women fought the Mughals alongside men. There was severe repression, their children were killed, yet the women never gave up.

It is true that women are not recognised as farmers, we call them landless farmers. Women are an integral part of farming in Punjab. Many families would have had to give up farming, if women did not work in the field. Men can't work on the land alone... home, hearth, field, cattle... there is a total system in place. One can't separate one from the other. Women play an important role in this. They are landless farmers. Women are defying the Supreme Court's order. We have come here to fight; we will not go back.

Although land ownership mostly belongs to men, one can't separate women from land. Our next struggle is to ensure property rights for women. Now we say in our speeches, women's sacrifice needs to be acknowledged. They do not own land, yet they are fighting, they are sacrificing more than men... people listen to what we say.

BAMA: *You were talking about farmers' suicides and...*

SUKHWINDER KAUR: Yes, it is a huge issue. If you talk to the families, their stories are heart-rending to hear. When the debts become too much, men often commit suicide leaving behind women and children. The situation of women in these families is really precarious. They often work as tailors to sustain themselves. They have to keep going. How much does one earn from tailoring? It is never enough to sustain families. Many women have come here [Delhi borders] with pictures of men in their families who have committed suicide. They are in the movement as well as working to sustain their family, taking care of the children. The society too is hostile. These women are constantly surveilled upon, always asked where they are going, why they are going out every day. They have to put up with so much sacrifice, so much to be in the movement...

BAMA: *Punjab has had a rich history of struggle against corporate land acquisition...*

SUKHWINDER KAUR: Yes. The important aspect of this movement is that we have identified whom the fight is against. We have directly declared war against those who are trying to take away our land. There is a permanent dharna going on here [in Delhi]; along with that, people are also agitating at the gates of corporate businesses in Punjab. Everything has been shut down. Toll plazas have been closed. People have occupied Ambani's retail stores and Adani's silos (hi-tech grain warehouses). In my city, we occupied Easy Day (a multi-chain store) for two months. We forced it to close. There was a call to boycott Ambani. There was not much space there even for ten people to sit, yet people were at it. Small shopkeepers benefitted from this... this is why the peasants were able to garner a lot of support in the city...

BAMA: *So many women have come to this movement, there is so much discussion about women's participation in the struggle. Is this having any impact on the families back home? Are the old equations changing? Will this play any role in challenging patriarchy at home?*

SUKHWINDER KAUR: Yes, absolutely. There was a lot of resistance at first. Men felt insecure about women coming out, voicing their opinions, asserting themselves. But things are changing now. Petty fights in the family have lessened. Women have found an opportunity to live for themselves, to be part of something big, their world is becoming bigger. The equations at home are also changing. The relationship is no longer that of employer and employee. Relationships are becoming more equal. Spaces at home are getting democratised. This will benefit everyone.

BAMA: *Has this changed traditional gender roles in the family and movement space?*

SUKHWINDER KAUR: We often make jokes about this. Here, men are running the langars. We tell them, "It is good that you've learnt how to cook." They joke, "Yes, we have learnt to cook now, so if you get annoyed, we won't have to coax you..." When we go to the langars, men serve us with respect. They don't expect us to cook there. It is good that men are in the kitchen here. This will have a huge impact. Punjab has been struggling with the drug problem for long. The youth are into drugs, many die of overdose. At one time the situation was very hopeless. This movement is changing things. It has changed the youth. Young people are at the heart of the movement. They are the life of the resistance. They are its strength. Who knew they had so much discipline in them! Not everyone is with our organisations. There are many who have just come for the march to Delhi, yet they are so disciplined. The youth are cooking, cleaning. They have brought in washing machines to clean our clothes.

This movement has offered a possibility for the young generation to do something, to change. They are asserting themselves, organising. They voice their opinions, tell us if we are wrong. They are getting up on the stage to speak, they are handling the media, they are standing with posters. We never knew there was so much possibility in Punjab! Somehow, they were not able to connect with us. The movement has made that connection; it has created that space. We were not able to attract them before, and the movement has done that.

One of the slogans on our tractors reads, "This is not just a fight for this harvest, it is a fight for the future." Organisations have not dictated this, people have themselves realised this. People are writing slogans on their own. Some are bringing photographs of Bhagat Singh with them, some are bringing photographs of Guru Gobind Singh, some are carrying banners with quotations. There has been a significant change amongst the youth. Previously, they would spend time taking drugs, listening to obscene music, and lazing away. Now they have a purpose. This is a huge victory in itself. We would often discuss with concern that our future generations would either move away to Canada or give in to drugs... we would be concerned about the future of Punjab! The movement has changed all of that. It has ushered in new morality, new values.

I should also add that we have been here for 3 months now, there have not been any complaints of harassment. I am mostly at the Singhu border. I have not heard of any complaints. This is an important thing. There has been a change in the value system. It is not that these things do not happen in Punjab but it has not happened here yet. We do not know how long the movement would go on, but it will bring in a significant change in the society in Punjab. It has made a shift in people's mindsets, in thought... that will remain.

BAMA: *You are at present in Singhu. Singhu, Tikri, Ghazipur—the protest sites—each have their own characteristics. Can you tell us more about women's participation in all these sites?*

SUKHWINDER KAUR: The protest sites at Singhu and Tikri are huge. In both places, women are participating in large numbers. Tikri has a huge participation of women. This is primarily because BKU (Ekta-Ugrahan) has worked among women a lot. Women protesters are more there. Singhu is different. Here there are organisations, but there are also many people who have joined as individuals. There are people who have come from villages in their own trolleys. Women have also come. Organisations have brought in women, but many have come on their own too. Tikri is more organised. But here there are various kinds of people. If one wants to see Punjab, it is in Singhu. There are people from all sections of Punjab, people across spectrums, across ideologies.

BAMA: *It has become quite a festival...*

SUKHWINDER KAUR: Yes, it has become like a festival. Everyone has to participate. One needs to note that right from the beginning there has been a deep sentiment for this struggle. It is not just superficial. There is discipline, there is an organised resistance.

This is what happens when people are pushed to the brink. I never imagined people would stay put for so long. The organisations have instilled this in people. The idea that one has to keep patience, one has to keep focused. We had mentally prepared ourselves for a long haul, we would have to sit patiently for days. Now we have built village committees. All the organisations from the villages are in those committees. They collect funds in accordance with the land one has. Every week there are vehicles that go to the villages to drop off people and bring in a new set of people. People come and sit here in rotation. This has become a part of their daily lives. Previously we had to plan how one could bring in more people. Now people are doing it themselves, we do not have to worry about that. We have committees in every village that are taking charge. This is because of the movement. This is the work of the committees. They collect funds, organise people, arrange travel, oversee the details.

BAMA: *Even farm work back at home in Punjab is being done accordingly...*

SUKHWINDER KAUR: Yes. When some people are sitting here in dharna, others are working in their land at that time. The harvest season is near. This is the time to harvest maize and to sow paddy. So, arrangements have been made. Those who will stay here, their land and crops will be looked after by others. I think this culture has always been there in the peasant community.

BAMA: *Different organisations have joined the movement. Khaps from Haryana too have joined... we know khaps have a patriarchal and casteist history. How do you view their role?*

SUKHWINDER KAUR: You see, even *khap* panchayats[2] have taken a new role here. There are women who are driving tractors and joining the movement. We are all working together now. We had a negative view of *khap* panchayats before. The movement has made them play a positive role. If you look into the *mahapanchayats* (massive gathering of farmers) being organised by the *khaps*, a large number of women participate in them. They remove their veils, give speeches, and assert themselves. A large number of women from Haryana participated in the tractor rally [26 January, 2021]. They came from Haryana driving tractors. People from Punjab and Haryana are in this movement together. There is an exchange of ideas, culture... we women go and eat together... Sometimes we go to the Haryana langars, sometimes they come. So somewhere patriarchy is also getting challenged. There will be some positive changes. The *Khap* is very organised and rigid. We really don't know how much of a dent this movement will make, but there will be some impact. We had such a negative impression of *khap*, but they have so far played such a significant role in this movement.

BAMA: *Repression of the movement is also intensifying... They are cutting off electricity, water, and the internet connection at the protest sites...*

SUKHWINDER KAUR: People have been bearing it all with utmost patience. There was a complete blackout. The internet was off. We had to call everywhere to get news. On 26 January, newspaper offices were closed, there was no news in the next day's newspapers. Electronic media was attacking us. People back home were concerned about what will happen to us. There were threats. We would say we are fine, that there would be no attack. Even if they do attack, we will defend ourselves. We are not afraid. There is food in the langars. We will be okay. For two to three nights young people kept vigil outside the camps. Haryana played a historical role. People came in trolleys. They stood guard and said, "If anyone attacks Punjab, they would have to go over our dead bodies." This changed the entire scenario. The movement has tested our patience. It has also shown our strength. It has shown that people are intelligent enough to know what is what. They [the government and media] have vilified the movement. They called us Khalistanis, they called us Maoists. But the people were unwavering in their support. We said "Yes, we are all that. Now please repeal the three farm laws."

The other day a BJP leader was supposed to address a meeting at Shamli. He went to one village. But no one listened to him. Everyone said, "First go and repeal the laws to ensure our MSP." The BJP has been sidelined for now. We don't know what will happen later. This is a big country. There are many forces. So far we have been able to challenge BJP in a big way. Now, you people in Bengal can say how much of a challenge you are putting up there. We are all looking forward to the [assembly] elections in Bengal.

BAMA: *The movement has been able to weave in various struggles. There* *has been a demand for release of political prisoners. There has been a call for struggle against imperialism. Perhaps this coming together of various struggles has also worked in challenging the government...*

SUKHWINDER KAUR: Absolutely. People were not able to talk about a lot of issues. This movement created that space. Furthermore, Punjabi people are all over the world and they are very connected to their roots. When we held tractor rallies here, there were rallies in Canada and the UK as well. This helped boost the morale of the movement. Several organisations abroad came out in support. I was just reading yesterday that 27 farmer organisations in America had expressed solidarity with our movement. They broadcasted scenes from the Singhu border in the Super league for 30 seconds. A message has been sent across the world that what Modi is doing is wrong, that the demands of the farmers are just, that our movement is correct. We have already won the moral battle. We have been able to establish to the world that we are right.

BAMA: *How has women's participation historically been in Punjab's peasant movements? We have seen women in Bengal coming to the forefront of struggles in Tebhaga, Naxalbari, or even during the recent Singur-Nandigram movement...*

SUKHWINDER KAUR: You see, there has not been enough documentation or recognition of women. There are names of only a few women leaders in history. Even in Sikh history, one will find names of only a few women. But there is not much information about what role they played, what they had done. We know about the men who were in the movement. When there was the Tebhaga movement in Bengal, in Punjab we had the Muzara, that is, the tenant or sharecropper farmers' movement. Women took part in it in huge numbers. Women occupied lands. But their names find no place in history. This is a problem. Punjab is quite progressive, it has a rich culture, yet there is no recognition of women's contribution. We raise these questions in our interaction with students in universities. We keep saying women's contributions need to be written about.

There is something about Punjab. There is a history of resistance movements here. Yet very little has been written about it. There is also a dearth of intellectuals who would take some time out and write about these struggles. Even our Sikh history has been written by the British. In general, there is very little written material about the struggles here and women's narratives have been written about even less. But women participated. Very few rose to leadership positions. Women took part in occupying land...

BAMA: *Can you tell us some stories about the women who have been in those struggles? If you remember some women's names... If they have been erased out of history, we need to write about them.*

SUKHWINDER KAUR: There were two or three women in the Naxalbari movement—Mahinder Kaur, Kebal Kaur... sometimes one finds a Facebook post with some old photographs... There was one Durga *bhabi* in Bhagat Singh's group. She made arrangements for meetings. She was the one who arranged the meetings before the Assembly attack. Durga *bhabi* led from the front; she took part in armed action. If we look further back there was Bhago. When Guru Gobind Singh had to leave Anandpur fort during the Mughal attack, many became martyrs, many were arrested. People were giving up and returning to their villages as they did not want to die. Bhago was a woman leader in that village. She inspired people to fight back. She rode a horse and went to the battlefield to fight.

There was Bibi Gulab Kaur in the Ghadar movement[3]. She was going off to America when she came across members from the Ghadar party. They were campaigning on their way to liberate India from British rule. Gulab Kaur heard about their campaign and wanted to return too. Her husband refused. Gulab Kaur left her husband and joined the Ghadar movement. She arranged shelters for them. She would often disguise herself and work for the party. She is known as Ghadri Gulab Kaur. This is what I remember... one may find names of some women leaders in history, but we do not know anything about the other women who were in the various struggles. We need to look for stories of those other women. Gulab Kaur was not from any rich background nor was she from any political family, she was from a poor family... but she was in the struggle till the end.

I keep telling university students that I have to go around in villages talking to women... holding meetings, building committees, organising dharnas, giving speeches... I can't find time to sit and read. I have to be out every day so I don't get much time to study. But I really want this work to be done. So I tell scholars to do this. Someday someone will write. These days educated women think this is important work. They feel the need to establish women's contributions. Women in student organisations engage on this issue, they call us for talks and we share our experiences. I have to go here and there... if there is a quarrel in the village, I have to intervene... if there is any marital dispute, I have to intervene... then we have to organise movements against the state. I hardly get time.

BAMA: *Your vast experience in the movement too needs to be shared with younger generations...*

SUKHWINDER KAUR: Yes. I have heard so many stories from women in the villages... women who come in the movement tell their stories. Many had not stepped out of their homes before and now they have become involved with the committees. We will be organising 8 March (International Working Women's Day) here at Singhu. We have plans to hold programs with women in Punjab too. This is a good moment to organise women. Even the men would not resist now. This is the time to focus on bringing women out of the four walls of their homes. We are looking at this as a great opportunity. Once women come out in large numbers, it acts as a magnet. We need to create the magnet.

BAMA: *Yes, stories like that of Gulab Kaur will inspire more women...*

SUKHWINDER KAUR: Yes. I tell women these stories. People like hearing such stories. There is this woman in Singhu—her son passed away due to Covid. She feels, it is the hospital that killed him. She was staying alone at home. When the movement began, she organised women from her village and came here. She has been staying here since then. She feels we are all her children now. Once she got up on the stage and gave a speech... then it started raining, people began to leave and disperse. She stood in the rain and began sloganeering. Everyone stopped and joined her. She is not from any organisation, she has her own troubles. But she turned those troubles into her will to fight, to be in the struggle. Now she gives speeches, sits in the dharna, works for the movement, gives her input. None of us taught her these things, life trained her.

It's about to be summer... we will be tested again, how to survive the movement in the sweltering heat...

BAMA: *How are you preparing for the months ahead?*

SUKHWINDER KAUR: We are changing tents keeping in mind the summer heat. We are thinking of bringing in coolers. We will manage. We are all workers; we are all struggling people. We are used to staying in the field. We will survive on the streets too. There will be some problems. Food might get stale. We will think of something... Maybe bring in refrigerators... In Punjab there is a culture of raising funds, we have been surviving on that. It is not possible for the organisations to arrange all this. But arrangements are being made. Someone or the other has been coming forward to help. We have no idea how so much is being arranged. Someone posts on Facebook about a shortage of wheat, immediately someone or the other comes with a truck full of wheat.

PART II

GROUNDXERO: *You have been involved with women's organisations for a long time. You were one of the founders of Aurat Mukti Morcha in the 90s. Tell us about the kind of work Aurat Mukti Morcha was doing. Did you take up issues related to women's problems within the household and community while also addressing issues related to agriculture and livelihoods?*

SUKHWINDER KAUR: I have always been active. In 1995, we founded Aurat Mukti Morcha (Women's Liberation Front). Some of the core members left as they grew old and we could not continue the organisation. I kept myself actively involved in working for women, I was addressed as a *'unionwali.'*

Aurat Mukti Morcha continued till almost 2005. We addressed a range of issues related to agriculture since our work was mostly among women of peasant families. And we addressed issues specifically related to women, especially around 8 March when we would campaign around women's issues. Sometimes it would be about violence and how the state uses rape as a tool for repression, or on issues like the discriminations women face at home, or domestic violence. Women members would campaign in villages and organise the programs entirely on their own.

We had to challenge the patriarchal and feudal outlook among our own people, in each of us in fact! For example, we once decided that only women would put up 8 March posters. It was also decided that men can help only if their help is requested by women. The idea was that if women did postering in the village, they would also interact and have discussions with villagers and discuss with them about women's issues. The experience will help them learn. But some of the male comrades took their daughters with them, asked them to stand aside and put up the posters themselves! They did not believe that girls could or should put up posters. The feudal outlook that is found in society also exists within the organisation.

We had very few women members and they were not educated, most even didn't know how to read or write. Neither were they able to develop critical thinking as women, nor did our male comrades understand this problem faced by the women's organisation. Those at the cadre level were given more household responsibilities and could not participate fully in our activities. The family directly could not stop women members from participating in the *aurat morcha* (women's front) because the peasant union was involved. So, women were indirectly stopped by putting more household workload on them, such as suddenly buying two more milking cows at home. Increasing her responsibilities at home would automatically stop her from going out. I remember two women activists, who were gradually assuming leadership roles, got imprisoned at home.

The *morcha* showed us the kind of problems women face within the family, organisation, and society. Now we are able to take up issues of domestic violence, both physical and mental. We try to negotiate and create mutual understanding to resolve the issue. When that is not possible, we help the woman file an FIR in the local police station. Today, that is the faith people put in our women's organisation, which is the women's wing of BKU (Krantikari).

GX: *Can you take us through your involvement with BKU (Krantikari)?*

SUKHWINDER KAUR: BKU (Krantikari) was formed in 2004 around the time our *aurat morcha* affiliated to the earlier formation was winding up. It has been very challenging to work on women's issues in the women's wing of BKU (Krantikari) because the organisation's main focus is addressing farmers' issues related to agriculture.

When the current struggle began in 2020, the women's wing of BKU (Krantikari) was formed. We are enrolling members, as well as building units in the villages. The challenge is to make it function as an independent women's organisation. We want it to be independent so that women agricultural workers can also join along with women from other sections of the peasantry. This is not easy because caste is a central issue. The women agricultural workers being mostly Dalit, and farmers being from land-owning dominant castes, it is tough. But whether you are a worker or from a farmer's family—domestic violence, the custom of dowry, and discrimination are faced by all women. These issues are common to us all, whether farmers or workers.

We need to create awareness of what the right to property means for women. Right to property makes sense if women can use what they get in any way they want. We supported a woman for several years, she finally won her case against her brother and got her share of her father's property. She wanted to give some of the property to her daughters, but her husband declined. There is no point then in fighting such cases unless women are also prepared to make independent decisions.

The social transformation that we are seeking will take years. Women's right to property has to become accepted by the society. She cannot be tossed between brother and husband. We have to work more to establish that society as a whole can benefit when women get their due. Society has to understand and accept that it is wrong how simply being male makes the brother or the husband the sole heirs of property.

This *andolan* (movement) has made one thing clear—male comrades have understood the importance of women's participation. This is one of the biggest achievements of this *andolan*.

GX: *How does patriarchy impact life and culture in Punjabi society? What are the forms of control in women's life? How do you deal with those issues?*

SUKHWINDER KAUR: We have to understand Punjab and the deep rooted patriarchy in Punjabi culture, where just as in most other states and rural communities, a son-bearing mother is celebrated to the extent that phrases to this effect become part of day to day life.

From birth, to every stage of life, a woman is controlled. They are not allowed to go anywhere without an escort even if it means going up to the school van. For women to have the freedom to roam freely, we have to fight society and not tie up women. When women are controlled tightly, we suppress their confidence and make them nervous beings. After her marriage, she has to take permission from her in-laws even to visit her parents and she is told how long she can stay there. If she takes a job, her salary is never her own. Even what is given to her as gifts in a marriage are taken away from her.

Feudal and patriarchal thinking is internalised in the society. Nowadays, if a son is born, only a few families go for a second child. But if it is a daughter, there has to be another child. It has been more than thirty years that sex-determination tests are being done to plan a male child. The adverse effects are being felt now. Youth are unable to find a bride. But it is worse when the son goes into addiction or leaves the country to go abroad. Parents do not have anyone to look after them in their old age. Even then, a girl is viewed as a liability. You have to spend again on her education and upbringing and then spend on her wedding and dowry. So, no one wants a girl child. There is also total control of women's sexuality in marital life.

Parents choose the groom. But when there is a conflict or the husband misbehaves, she has nowhere to go. Women tolerate abuse and violence and do not tell their parents; they feel obliged due to the money the parents had spent on the marriage. The number of cases of depression is high and the number of married women committing suicide is not small. Parents insist she has to adjust because the dignity of the family is at stake. We counsel parents. We tell parents their responsibility doesn't end with marrying off daughters.

What are the options for a woman to get out of a violent and abusive marriage, especially when she is unwanted by her parents or brothers? How will she feed the children and herself? Any woman who faces a breakdown in marriage must be supported by the state. In our opinion, the state must ensure a safe place and also provide money or work that can help the woman earn. Only then will she be able to face the situation with confidence and can put an end to an oppressive marital relationship. She needs social security to live independently and resume life.

Patriarchal and feudal thinking goes against us women but also against men. Male domination has to be discussed with men. It is a simple truth that if you give her a scooter, she can do so much more outdoor work of the household and the men could be free from some responsibilities. Why lock her up? Why view a woman as a burden?

There is another phenomenon that shows the levels of control faced by even educated girls. There are those who have passed 10+2 and are sent abroad to Canada or Australia so that their earnings will bring prosperity to the family and slowly the whole family will also be able to migrate. These girls who were never allowed to go out of the home are sent alone to a foreign country! Often, their marriages are fixed back home and in many cases the prospective in-laws too have financed her foreign journey, hoping that after marriage she will help in the migration of their good-for-nothing son. When the girl refuses, she is accused by both the families.

Here, I would like to talk about control of women's sexuality, since it is seldom discussed. Sexual lives are complex. Husbands have no awareness that the sexual act needs the consent of both persons. Women are not able to tolerate force and coercion beyond a point. Violence happens when she does not oblige. Women become passive, and men aggressive. Women find themselves trapped in such situations even in their 40s and 50s. Men expect to be pleased and cannot take rejection. The husband-wife relationship is a vexed one and what happens in the bedroom is seldom known. Women have no one to talk to, not even their grown-up children. We tell women to clearly say "No" and not give in to pressure. If there is force or misbehaviour by men, we talk to the men. They feel exposed. It is only when they feel their misbehaviour is getting exposed to others, that it works in our favour. The threat of her speaking up to others helps in controlling men's behaviour. Women also feel confident when they are able to break the silence.

But after that how we address the issue, how we persuade the man to see from our point of view and the language we use becomes a matter of tactics and skill. In most cases, relations have improved. The democratisation of the man-woman relationship is a part of the struggle to democratise society. If there is no transformation within men, how can society be democratised?

GX: *Do you see Left-affiliated farmers' and agricultural worker unions responding to women's specific problems just as they respond to issues related to agriculture? Is it more effective for women's wings to be independent or as part of a party organisation?*

SUKHWINDER KAUR: At the moment it is only BKU (Ekta-Ugrahan) that has a large women's wing and they address women as well as agricultural issues.

In any case, women are organising for the farmers' movement. If we have a women's wing, we have to address both sets of issues, even if women-specific issues get less attention. But if women are aware, they can do both. What I mean is that while forming a women's wing we should foster consciousness in women as women. Then only can a women's wing of a farmer union play the role of a women's organisation.

Even on farmers' issues, what should our role be? Not just to listen and come back. We have to see the world around us as women. We have to bring to their attention issues of discrimination and control of women's lives in every aspect, even in the movement space. Women participants welcome such discussions and become more involved because these issues are about their lives.

Mass organisations do come together to give a fight if it is a specific issue of oppression like the one in Faridkot that BKU (Ekta-Ugrahan) had taken up or the one in Mehal Kalan that led to a sustained joint struggle. If women want to work on their issues, it can happen from within mass organisations. Our struggle is like a double-edged sword. We have to fight the state and we have to fight within organisations and communities. It is an ideological war and we have to fight patriarchal thinking and patriarchal control everywhere.

GX: *Landless women are getting entangled in debt more and more. Tell us about the campaigns of BKU (Krantikari) in organising landless women workers against the harassment of microfinance companies.*

SUKHWINDER KAUR: This came to our notice during the pandemic. We were doing relief work because the economic distress was acute. We came across many cases where people simply could not return loan money because of zero earning during the lockdown period. Then we found out that almost 90 percent of working class women were in debt. Largely private companies run microcredit schemes in villages. The agents of these companies were intimidating and threatening these families. We first convinced the villagers that if one or two women are unable to repay the loans, others should not go and harass them for extracting money. That is the responsibility of the company and other women are not to extract repayment on behalf of the company.

Initially some women were scared. We told them that if a company insists on putting the responsibility of extracting repayment from the defaulters on you, then the organisation will deal with it. Soon women gathered courage and we would gherao the recovery agent. The next thing we did was to negotiate with the agents and explain that while demanding repayment they cannot harass borrowers because there was no work during the lockdown. The agents agreed. Then we went to the administration and brought to their notice that when no one is allowed to enter villages because of the lockdown restrictions, why are company agents entering villages? The administration was forced to give orders to the police to prevent agents from entering villages.

The women are scared, if they do not make loan repayments they become ineligible for getting loans. Their Aadhar [identity] card numbers are on the database of the companies and it is easy to check if someone is a defaulter when she approaches another company for loans. So, women sell anything they have, even utensils, to repay loans.

Earlier men used to get loans but now women have also been brought into the scene in the name of empowerment. Loans are given in the names of women for self-employment but they are used mainly for household expenses. The family gets money for its daily needs and the loan is in the name of the woman—that is her empowerment! These are debt traps as they can seldom get out of it. The microfinance companies and banks make profit and the government collaborates. This leads to mental distress and suicide.

The peasant unions are organising Karz Mukti Abhiyan (loan waiver movement). There has to be a nationwide movement to curb the increasing indebtedness of the peasantry. In Punjab alone, there is a debt of about Rs 4,000 crore held by agricultural workers alone. Why can't it be waived off entirely? A movement demanding freedom from debts can unite small farmers with labourers, including women. They are all in debt. It is a problem of huge magnitude. All progressive organisations and unions must be part of such a movement.

GX: *Entire villages and communities sustained the struggle, endured extreme hardships for more than a year. To what extent can we attribute this perseverance and discipline of the people to the historical, cultural, and religious ethos of Sikhism?*

SUKHWINDER KAUR: This *andolan* was possible because of our Sikh history. The langar is a significant practice of the Sikh faith. When we were mobilising and bringing such huge numbers of people to the Delhi borders, we did not have any worries about where the food would come from. We had informed people to carry their own ration. But our ration kept lying in the trolleys, langars were set up by gurudwara committees and various Sikh institutions. We expected langars to be set up, but we did not expect it at the scale at which it happened. There were langars from Anandpur Sahib, Amritsar, and Kurukshetra. The Delhi Gurudwara Prabandhak Committee was there. There was a separate one from Bangla Sahib Gurudwara. The Amritsar Prabandhak Committee had set up several langars. Khalsa Aid was there. A langar was even set up by people from British Columbia.

The Sikh religion is itself born out of struggle. Serving food and fighting against oppression is ingrained into our community, culture and practices. Each gurudwara is like a community centre. In any struggle, the gurudwara becomes the place for meetings and gatherings. Doing voluntary work or *sewa* (service) is part of Sikh ethos. People go to gurudwara simply to give service. It is part of our identity and culture. Donating 10 percent of our income to the gurudwara is a tenet of our religion.

The larger unity for a community cause like the farmers' movement is a question of Sikh identity. Sikhs across the world are also supporting it because the Punjab peasantry is under attack and it is leading the resistance. Sikhs who are not farmers are also supporting because there is concern for Punjab and its people. Sikh faith is about *mazloomo ki raksha karna, ondi ladai ladna aur onnanu khana khilana* (To protect the oppressed, to fight for them and to serve them food). The ideological influence of the first Guru—Guru Nanak—has been internalised by the followers of the faith. His preaching was revolutionary. As the religion evolved, we learned to defend ourselves with the sword too. This began after the martyrdom of Guru Arjan, our fifth Guru. The sixth Guru taught *meeri* and *peeri,* which means both *talwar* (sword) and *vichardhara* (thinking) are required to protect and establish our faith.

We have historically been against Delhi governments. History is being replayed. Awareness has spread widely about how the Delhi government and the companies are out to establish control over grain and land. The laws have been taken back for the time being but this struggle has a long way to go.

Endnotes

1. Pinjra Tod is a women's collective, which was established in 2015 in campuses of Delhi universities. The collective was built around the demand of female students to challenge the patriarchal and regressive moral codes and rules that existed in girls' hostels.

2. *Khap* panchayats are quasi-judicial bodies, especially among Jats in villages of Haryana and Uttar Pradesh. *Khap* panchayats have gained notoriety owing mainly for issuing certain controversial and regressive diktats (honour killings) against love marriages between couples in the same gotra (clan) or inter-caste marriages.

3. Ghadar—also written as Ghadr in English—is an Urdu word for rebellion. The Ghadar party was formed in 1913, by Indian immigrants, mainly Sikhs and Hindu Punjabis, settled in North America. It was founded by Sohan Singh Bhakna, Lala Hardayal, Pandit Kanshi Ram. The aim of the Ghadar movement was to get rid of colonial British rule in India by means of an armed struggle. Ghadar leaders like Kartar Singh Saraba, Bibi Gulab Kaur, Durga Bhabi and their 'spontaneous acts of bravery' became a part of Punjab's

folklore and continue to be so even today.

A farmer in a protest gathering. **Photo:** Rithik Jawla.

A farmer waiting to collect milk at Pakora Chowk (Tikri border). **Photo:** Rithik Jawla.

The Farmers' Struggle Successfully Exposed the Imperialists and Corporates as the Enemies of the Indian Masses

MANJIT SINGH DHANER, BHARATIYA KISAN UNION (EKTA-DAKAUNDA)

> MANJIT SINGH DHANER, a 65-year-old farmer leader from Barnala district of Punjab, is the senior Vice President of Bharatiya Kisan Union (Ekta-Dakaunda). Dhaner was falsely implicated and sentenced to life imprisonment when he was leading a people's movement against the rape and murder of a young girl in the village of Mehal Kalan in 1997. A concerted campaign by peasant unions led to his release in 2019. Despite the Supreme Court upholding his life sentence, the state government was compelled to seek remission from the Punjab Governor twice. He was one of the leading figures in the farmers' protests at Tikri border.
>
> HARSHITA BHASIN and SAHIL MEHRA on behalf of GROUNDXERO, interviewed Manjit Singh Dhaner in early December 2021 after the three farm laws were repealed.

GROUNDXERO: *When was BKU (Ekta-Dakaunda) formed? Also, what in your opinion is the main crisis in agriculture in Punjab? In other words, what are the main issues concerning the peasantry in Punjab?*

MANJIT SINGH: BKU (Ekta-Dakaunda) was formed in 2007. At first, I worked with the undivided Bharatiya Kisan Union (BKU) which was formed in the '80s to represent mainly the large land-owning farmers. Then in 1994, BKU entered electoral politics and we separated ourselves from it to form BKU (Ekta). I continued working in it. Then in 2005 I was wrongfully framed in a murder case and was given life-sentence. People fought for my release, and after a year and a half, they got me out of jail along with two of my other comrades. In 2007 we decided that we should form a separate faction of the kisan union, and hence, BKU (Ekta-Dakaunda) came into existence. Today, our union works in fifteen districts of Punjab and is among the biggest farmer unions in the state.

As regarding the main concerns of the peasantry in Punjab, the first thing is that the cost of cultivation has become too high and the prices for the crops the farmers get leave them with very little or no profit. There are also a lot of other problems. Agriculture is the major sector of Punjab's economy, yet there are not enough agricultural output based processing units in the state. Whatever small number of state-owned processing units there were like cotton and sugarcane mills, have closed down due to their neglect by the state government. This too has contributed to the aggravation of the agrarian crisis. The farmers do not get fair prices for their produce nor for their labour.

The present agrarian crisis should be seen in its historical context. The agricultural sector in India was controlled by the British during the colonial period. Indian agriculture was developed only to cater to the needs of the world market, as a supplier of raw materials. After Independence in 1947, the Indian government decided to boost productivity in the agricultural sector by introducing the Green Revolution, which was largely dominated by domestic and international corporates. The supply of inputs like seeds, fertilisers, machinery etc. were provided by these corporates, through which they earned huge profits. The financial sector, including the banks that provided loans to the farmers were also a part of this program. For example, in the Malwa region, banks provided huge loans to the farmers for cultivation of grapes and kinnows. Later when the farmers could not get adequate price for their produce, they became indebted and had to sell their land to clear the debt. There were many problems that emerged with the Green Revolution model. For example the issue of soil quality degradation came up, the produce became poisonous, the groundwater level fell, along with the spread of many diseases. Earlier we could extract water at low costs, but now withdrawing groundwater has become very expensive. Farmers have to invest heavily in buying machinery [pumps] to extract water for irrigation.

So, farmers were already facing problems of high cost of cultivation and indebtedness. Then, in the early '90s, came the New Economic Policy (NEP), propagated by the International Monetary Fund (IMF) and World Bank (WB), consisting of liberalisation, privatisation and globalisation of the Indian economy. These policies put a restriction on the amount of subsidies that were provided to the agricultural sector. This further deepened the crisis in agriculture even as the farmers had no alternate livelihood opportunities. A large number of agricultural workers and small farmers got pushed out of agriculture and this led to a massive increase in unemployment. The absence of any alternate opportunities of livelihood for the farmers and indebtedness led to a rise in the incidence of farmers' suicide. No government ever tried to alleviate the problems. Then, in 2008, global capitalism faced the worst financial crisis, and it happened for the first time that the corporates started purchasing agricultural land on a wide and large scale. The corporates wanted to acquire control over the agri-industry. This is because they realised that other businesses can go into crisis but agriculture is one sector whose produce will always have a rising demand due to increasing population.

The current policy reforms in agriculture in the form of the three farm laws enacted by the Narendra Modi government should be seen as a part of a larger global imperialist institutions induced policy. We believe that agriculture as an economic activity is now no more profitable for farmers, even for big farmers. That is how we see the present agrarian crisis.

BKU (Ekta-Dakaunda) has taken up these issues on its own and has also united with other unions to fight on these issues. This is because, in our understanding, all comrades should join forces in order to defeat our common enemy. In Punjab, almost all the major struggles have donned a united face, where many unions have come together to fight against the common enemy.

GX: *What have been your organisation's programs and actions to address these issues ?*

MANJIT SINGH: The issues exist on such a large scale that no single organisation can tackle the problems on their own. Our organisation has held farmers' demonstrations and rallies and fought against the high electricity bills. We are now getting subsidies on electricity usage. Our irrigation pumps run on free electricity. The electricity bill waiver was one important concession that the farmer unions have achieved through united struggle. Agricultural workers also get 200 units of electricity free per month. Twenty unions of both farmers and agricultural workers came together to fight for this. We also fought against land acquisition for a private thermal power plant at Gobindpura, a small village in Mansa district. There was once a crisis in the cotton-belt of Punjab. The cotton crop got infested with *chitti sundi* (white fly pest). Many unions came together to demand compensation for the loss to the farmers. The government was providing a compensation of only Rs 800 per acre; after a month-long agitation we won a compensation of Rs 8,000 per acre for the farmers and Rs 800 per acre for the agricultural workers who had lost employment because of the pest-attack.

We should not look at this crisis as a local problem, rather this crisis in agriculture exists at a national as well as global level. However, the crisis in our country started deepening in the regions that belong to the Green Revolution belt. It is true that in this region there are many farmer unions who tried to stop the imperialist onslaught. However, the attack continued and we also continued our struggle and won small victories through which the unions kept gaining experience and became stronger. If there were no unions and no struggle, the conditions would have been far worse, and even the struggle against the pro-corporate farm laws would not have been this strong.

We have focused our efforts on issues such as farmers having access to markets where the produce can be sold in a timely manner and farmers can get a good price, the availability of cheap inputs and against forceful acquisition of agricultural land. Further, we tackle various environmental issues that come up. In addition, we also continue with our struggle on many social issues. The point is that our focus has not been limited to only the economic aspects but also covers various social and political dimensions of the agrarian crisis.

GX: *'Land to the tillers'—how relevant is this slogan in present day Punjab? What are your views on the issue of land redistribution? What are your organisation's programs in this regard?*

MANJIT SINGH: The slogan of *land to the tillers* has been important both before and after Independence for the entire country as well as Punjab. However, after the Green Revolution, due to the spread and penetration of capitalism in agriculture especially in Punjab, the slogan no longer holds its earlier relevance. There exists the question of redistributing the surplus land, but redistribution of land should be directed towards forming collective farms rather than individual ownership of small lands. Though it is important to provide land to the ones who are still landless, the most important point is that we have to challenge the exploitative model of agriculture being pushed by imperialism and capitalism by placing forth the model of collective farming as an alternative. In our discussions with farmers, this idea of developing a new model of collective farming is being given more importance, and farmers are thinking about challenging the current model that destroys the environment, causes indebtedness, suicide and distress sale of land, creates unemployment, talks of dumping excess food grains in the high seas, etc. We agree that the panchayati common land should be distributed among the Dalit agricultural workers in the villages. Their demands are fair and we also support them in their struggle for land. But our demands mainly focus on a proper *mandi* (agricultural produce market) system and the issue of farmers' getting an MSP (Minimum Support Price) for their produce. The demand to reduce cost of agricultural inputs and guaranteed MSP for all crops at *mandis* are more relevant in the present circumstances. The slogan of *land to the tillers* does not give primacy to such demands.

GX: *There is a common view that whatever farmers' produce in Punjab is bought by the government at MSP? What is the real picture regarding MSP in Punjab?*

MANJIT SINGH: In Punjab MSP is available to the farmers for only wheat and paddy, and to some extent for cotton. The government announces MSP for as many as 23 crops every year but apart from wheat and paddy there is no assured government procurement for any other crop This leaves the farmers at the mercy of market forces. The other crops are purchased by private traders often below the MSP announced by the government. For instance, MSP for maize was Rs 1,850 per quintal in July 2020 but it was sold by the farmers for only Rs 1,000 per quintal in the market. Similarly, MSP for moong (a variety of pulse) is around Rs 7,000 per quintal but farmers get only Rs 5,000 per quintal in the market. The government's procurement policy has been targeted to purchase only wheat and paddy, and for that too we have to fight and struggle as they plan to further limit the quantity of procurement.

We think that in addition to a 50 percent return on the comprehensive cost of production, the farmer's labour should be categorised as skilled-labour and quantified accordingly while calculating the cost of production. Also, for us the demand of guaranteed MSP on all crops is not limited to Punjab alone. We have to think of the farmers in the entire country, for example, the dismal situation of farmers in Bihar and Uttar Pradesh; hence, our demand for MSP is for all of India.

GX: *You mentioned being sentenced to life imprisonment in 2005? Will you share with us some details about what happened? Was it related to the Mehal Kalan incident?*

MANJIT SINGH: Yes. I, along with two of my comrades, was accused of murdering an 85 year old man. We were actually framed in the case for leading a movement seeking justice for a girl, who was brutally gang raped and murdered by powerful goons in Mehal Kalan village in 1997. The incident, in which I was framed, took place during a court hearing of that rape and murder case in March 2001. I along with Narain Dutt and Prem Kumar were convicted by the Sessions Court and sentenced to life imprisonment. It was a conspiracy hatched by the goons and the police to crush the people's movement that had erupted following the rape and murder of a young girl in Mehal Kalan village.

GX: *Tell us in detail about the people's movement following that heinous incident in Mehal Kalan? How did you organise the struggle to ensure punishment to the perpetrators of the crime and get justice for the girl?*

MANJIT SINGH: It happened about 25 years ago on 29 July 1997. An 18 year old girl, Kiranjit Kaur, from Mehal Kalan village in Barnala district, went missing while returning home from college. A few hours later, her clothes, books and bicycle were found at a farm in the village. Her family and the villagers suspected the owners of the farm of abducting her. But since there was a nexus between the police, politicians and these owners, even an FIR was not filed. They were well-connected and used to rule over the entire area.

I am from the same village. At that time I was the block president of BKU (Ekta). When all the facts were brought before us, we pointed the police towards that farm. The goons' house was right next to the police station, where they had that big 40 *kila* (1 *kila* = 3 acres) farm. All the proof was staring us in the face. But we also realised the difficulty involved in bringing them to justice.

The police instead of arresting and questioning the goons picked up about twenty youths and tortured them. So we first raised the slogan, "Release the innocent youths and punish the real culprits." We took out a rally that passed through the village with this slogan, and by the time we arrived at the centre of the village near the police station, thousands of people had joined us. People knew who had committed the crime. This is how the protest started.

In a couple of days, we gave a call for another action. We declared a blockade of the big road that goes from Ludhiana to Bathinda. People participated in huge numbers—particularly the women. We formed a 14 member committee—Mehal Kalan Action Committee—to seek justice for "Punjab's daughter." The people really put forward a very big struggle. There were demonstrations every five to seven days until the accused were arrested. After their interrogation, the body of the girl was found 14 days after the interrogation in that same farm belonging to those goons. I saw the body and it's difficult to think about it even now. What they had done to her cannot be described in words. They had been monstrous.

The post mortem report revealed that the girl was raped and murdered. A DNA test report of hair strands found on her hand also matched with the culprits.' We testified against the goons in the court. We gave an open call for struggle, and various farmer and worker organisations, students and teachers, joined the struggle. We had a two pronged strategy; waging a legal battle and also mobilising more and more people on the ground to put pressure on the administration. These continued parallel to each other. Hundreds of people would throng the court on every date of hearing and raise slogans demanding justice for the girl. At last, after four years of legal battle and mass struggle, on 16 August 2001, four of the six accused were convicted and sentenced to life imprisonment by the Sessions Court. The High Court (HC) and the Supreme court (SC) also upheld the Sessions Court's verdict. People's struggle for justice won.

GX: *When and how were you implicated in the murder case?*

MANJIT SINGH: The incident in which I was framed happened in March 2001, a few months before the four goons accused in the Mehal Kalan incident were convicted and sentenced by the Sessions Court. During one of the court-hearing dates of the case [1 March 2002], a squabble broke out between the supporters of the accused and the protestors in the Barnala court complex. An 85 year old man named Dilip Singh, who was a member of the family of the accused, got injured in the clash, and he died ten days later.

The police, politicians and goons got together to implicate the leadership of the movement. An FIR was lodged targeting me as the main accused as I was leading and organising the struggle. Along with me Narain Dutt and Prem Kumar, two other leading activists of the movement, were booked as well. They alleged that I had a knife in my hand and I stabbed the man, while Narain Dutt and Prem Kumar were holding his hands. In fact, nothing like this had happened. The reality was that during the clash, a local farmer hit the old man with an axe. Later, he died.

GX: *How did people respond to you being falsely implicated in that murder case?*

MANJIT SINGH: We came to know about the murder charges on us from our lawyer. The police conducted raids in the village to arrest us. However the villagers were resolute about not letting the police enter our house. They gheraoed the police station stating that we were innocent. After the public outrage, the government asked the PP (Public Prosecutor) to withdraw the case against us in the court, but the court dismissed the plea. I had to stay in Barnala jail for 42 days before getting bail.

All three of us were sentenced for life imprisonment on 30 March, 2005, and were again sent to jail. Thousands of people marched from the court to the statue of Bhagat Singh, raising slogans *Gundagardi nahi chalegi* (hooliganism can't go on) and kept the struggle alive. Ironically, for one and half years, three of us and the four goons convicted of rape and murder of the girl, were serving life sentences in Bathinda Jail. Two months before we went to jail, we had handed over the movement to the second rung of the leadership, telling them that they should not panic and should continue the struggle in good spirits.

Outrage against our imprisonment snowballed into a people's movement in Punjab. Not only farmer unions, but teachers, students, youth, women came together to demand our release. They launched massive protests, forcing the Punjab government to recommend to the Governor to pardon us. But this decision to pardon us [July 2007] was challenged by the accused in the rape case in the HC, which set aside the Governor's pardon order. The two Action committee members, Narain Dutt and Prem Kumar were acquitted by the HC but my life sentence was upheld. The matter went to the SC which too upheld the HC's order and gave me four weeks time to surrender before the Sessions court.

GX: *But you were pardoned again for a second time...*

MANJIT SINGH: Yes. When the SC upheld the HC's decision of my life imprisonment [3 September 2019], entire Punjab erupted in protest. In a span of a day, effigies of the SC were burnt in more than 500 villages. A united struggle by the youth, students, workers, farmers, employees, women, anganwadi workers and others exploded. Activists from 42 organisations got together to seek my release.

First they held a *morcha* (demonstration) in Patiala. For seven days people held demonstrations to put pressure on the then CM Amarinder Singh to take the case back and quash the sentence. We kept mobilising with full force, the government was observing our strength, so we showed them how strong the public opinion was against the court order. We decided that we would celebrate Bhagat Singh's birth anniversary on September 28 in Barnala. Since September 27 was the Shahadat Divas (Martyrs' Day) of Gurusharan Singh (famous playwright and theatre activist), we decided to celebrate that too.

On September 30, I was to surrender at the Sessions Court. Over 30,000 people came out on the roads in Barnala on that day demanding my acquittal. I was sent to Barnala jail. For 47 days, over 3,000 people sat in a dharna outside the Barnala jail during the day, and about 500 of them slept outside in tents at night. About 42 farmer unions, including BKU Dakaunda, BKU Ugrahan, Kirti Kisan Union, Krantikari Kisan Union, Kisan Sangharsh Committee Azad, and more than three dozen organisations of agricultural labourers, employees and students united under the umbrella of Sangharsh Committee for Manjit Dhaner to secure my release.

Bowing to people's pressure, the Punjab government finally sent a file to the Governor recommending remission of my sentence. On November 15, the Governor gave his consent, making me the first person in Punjab to be pardoned twice in the same case. Thousands of activists, including a large number of women wearing green and saffron *dupattas* (scarves), greeted me as I walked out of the Barnala jail, a free man.

GX: *So you were once again a free man and within a few months in the forefront leading another battle—this time against the Modi government's farm laws...*

MANJIT SINGH: To me, the farmers' movement at Delhi was a reminder of the protests that rocked the Malwa region of Punjab for my release. However this time, the fight was harsher and longer. In 2019, we were fighting against the Punjab government, but this time the fight was against the central government and the big capitalists. This time too, people's united struggle forced Narendra Modi to withdraw the anti-farmer laws.

GX: *Did you expect that Modi would withdraw the farm laws? What was your reaction to the sudden announcement to repeal the three laws? Was it right to end the protest without fulfilment of all the demands?*

MANJIT SINGH: When the withdrawal of the three farm laws was announced by Narendra Modi, it felt like a daydream. It was a people's victory. People's struggle had won. The farmers consider their land to be their mother that provides them with food. When we started the protests in June 2020, there were 10 farmer unions from Punjab. Then it was increasingly realised that in order to defeat the enemy everyone had to set aside their small differences and come together to form a joint committee. We jointly organised protests in Punjab for two to three months and then decided to move the protest to Delhi. There, our farmer comrades from Haryana, UP, Rajasthan, MP and other states joined us, and we continued our struggle to repeal the laws.

Even before the central government decided to repeal the laws, we had already won many battles in this struggle. Firstly, we were able to establish among the people of the country that our demands are morally right. We could justify our demands even at the global level. The farmers' movement won the solidarity of the people and communities who were being repressed by the pro-corporate economic policies and fascism of the Modi government. There was also the question of privatisation of public sector enterprises and the legislation of the Labour Codes, which brought the worker and employee unions out in our support. The attack on our Muslim brothers and sisters, Adivasis and Dalits and arrest of many public intellectuals had pushed a large section of democratic and secular forces against the government. So, not only peasants, but people from all sections, expressed support for our movement and stood against the Modi government. The BJP lost badly in West Bengal assembly elections. The incident at Lakhimpur Kheri also made them realise that the situation might impact them negatively in the upcoming elections in five states, especially in Uttar Pradesh. The huge rally called by the farmers at Muzaffarnagar[1] made the BJP especially nervous.

But still we didn't anticipate that Narendra Modi would repeal the laws. We had indeed understood that he was no longer invincible. So, when repeal of the laws was announced, we had the option of continuing our agitation till all our demands, many of which had originated during the course of protests, were met. However, there was a sentiment building up against us, where people had started questioning why we were not leaving even after the laws had been repealed. He [Modi] was also creating disputes among the unions so as to destroy our unity. We were of the view that we should end the protest on a strong and positive note, so that we can unite again in the future and stand a better chance at winning our other demands, most importantly, the demand for legal guarantee of MSP for all crops.

GX: *What in your opinion is the significance of this movement in taking forward the anti-capitalist struggle of the masses in this country?*

MANJIT SINGH: The farmers' struggle successfully exposed the imperialists and corporates as the enemies of the Indian masses. Though we have been campaigning against them for years, it has become clear to the people now.

Never in the history of India, not even during the 1857 mutiny, have people been united to such a large and wide extent, as was witnessed during these protests. The protests inspired unity among all sections of the oppressed masses. The major challenge that lies ahead for us is how to preserve this unity. It has happened for the first time that all the mainstream political parties were sidelined and this movement brought to the forefront the farmers and workers of the country. To preserve and strengthen this unity, to keep the idea of a united struggle alive, to correctly identify our enemy and especially to find a model of agriculture in contrast to the one imposed by the corporates, are the most important tasks ahead. The movement's achievements should not be limited to just the repeal of the three laws.

GX: *What are your views on farmer unions participating in the election? In particular, what are your views on the Sanyukt Samaj Morcha (SSM)—a political front contesting the Punjab assembly elections—floated by many farmer unions who were part of the Samyukta Kisan Morcha (SKM)?*

MANJIT SINGH: See, our organisation does not participate in elections. We have campaigned among the people that only through unity and struggle can we achieve our goals. The real purpose of elections is to cheat the people. The political parties vying for power try to hide the main problems and the actual causes of the people's problems. Protests and agitations are important ways for people to fight for their rights. Moreover, we think that these elections are a conspiracy to divert people from the achievements of this historic struggle—the unity that was established, the understanding regarding the real issues, the importance of struggle that was developed in people's mind and the way the truth about the character of political parties was unveiled. Through election campaigns, the ruling classes are trying to divide the people again on the basis of caste and religion. Further, they are trying to morally corrupt the people by giving them money, alcohol, drugs, etc., while portraying goons as their saviours.

The farmer unions which have formed the SSM should have instead tried to provide guidance to the people on how to take forward the struggle against the WTO and how to unite farmers and workers in this struggle. The kind and scale of unity that was established by the farmer's movement has aroused the political consciousness of the masses. They have started surrounding and questioning political leaders about their issues. So it was more important to carry forward the mass struggle rather than waste energy and resources in elections and weaken the unity of the SKM in the process.

Endnote

1. On 5 September, 2021, a massive Kisan Mazdoor Maha Panchayat of over 10 lakh people cutting across caste, religion, state and language was held at Muzaffarnagar in UP. Mission Uttar Pradesh—SKM's campaign to defeat BJP in the state—was launched. The conspicuous presence of thousands of Muslim farmers alongside Jat Hindu farmers in several farmers' protest gatherings across western UP, and in the Muzaffarnagar MahaPanchayat, was an unprecedented sight, more so after the 2013 Muzaffarnagar riots that divided rural Western UP along Hindu-Muslim religious lines. At the time of the Muzaffarnagar riots, it seemed that Jats had suddenly abandoned the 'farmer' identity and instead, embraced a Hindu fundamentalist identity. With the farmers' protests that started in 2020, however, the farmer identity appeared resurgent across the region once again.

This Movement has put Farmers Squarely Back into the Nation's Political Canvas
Kavitha Kuruganti, Alliance for Sustainable and Holistic Agriculture

>Kavitha Kuruganti has years of experience of working on farmers' rights and sustainable farm livelihoods. She is the founder-convener of the Alliance for Sustainable and Holistic Agriculture (ASHA), a pan-Indian alliance of more than four hundred organisations working toward food sovereignty and sustainability. Kavitha is a leading member of the All India Kisan Sangharsh Coordination Committee (AIKSCC) that played a crucial role in initiating the movement against the repeal of the three farm laws.
>
>GroundXero conducted this interview in March 2022.

GroundXer: *Today as we reflect on the farmers' rebellion against the farm laws, we see events that led to it. AIKSCC was formed after the Mandsaur police firing. Then AIKSSC played an important role in the formation of the SKM in formulating and articulating the opposition to the ordinances. Tell us about this period till the formation of SKM to lead this movement.*

Kavitha Kuruganti: Credit goes to All India Kisan Sangharsh Co-ordination Committee (AIKSCC) for being one of the largest farmers' joint platforms through the years of 2017, 2018, 2019 and 2020. It was in October 2020 that AIKSCC put out an unconditional proposal and sent out an invitation to other farmer unions and alliances, asking them to join hands in fighting against the three central laws and also to demand for MSP as a legal right. Remember that in 2018 itself AIKSCC had drafted a final statute with widespread consultations across India for farmers' legal right to freedom from indebtedness and for guaranteed remunerative prices. Many political parties were also mobilised to support the farmers in their demands. So, in a sense, a good foundation was laid by AIKSCC for the formation of SKM and the subsequent historical agitation.

GX: *Do you think the farmers' protests that erupted in Punjab in 2020 after the farm ordinances were promulgated had a pre-history of peasant struggles in the state and should be seen in connection to them?*

KAVITHA KURUGANTI: The protests in Punjab certainly have deep connections with the historical, religious and political movements in the state. The Sikh religious ethos around justice as well as *sewa* (service) are what stood the SKM-led movement in good stead. Farmers from other states drew great inspiration from the Sikh protesters (mind you, I am not calling it Punjab protesters, and am specifically pinning it down to one religion and the ethos that it promotes in all its followers) and this inspiration will stay with them for a long time to come.

GX: *After more than a year of struggle and sacrifices, the farmers' agitation ultimately forced the government to repeal the three laws. What stands out in your memory about this movement, as an activist who looks at the agitation in the context of farmers' struggle against the corporate assault on farming and livelihoods?*

KAVITHA KURUGANTI: What are the sharpest memories? To me, some of the core values that the so-called "ordinary protestor" or the so-called "ordinary farmer" brought to this movement are the outstanding aspects of the last one year. Those core values are really personified and embodied in almost every person who participated in this movement. You can't miss these because they stand out. The notion of unity, for instance: this is one movement which has taught India's farmer unions as well as the farmers themselves that if they are united they can actually assert their identity as citizens, which allows them to be back squarely and firmly in the public debate on nation-building. This sort of emphasis on unity, and experiencing the strength that comes with it, is something that every protester would talk about, and I experienced it myself! Peace is the other value. There was never a single moment when the protesters who were being led by the SKM ever gave up on this value. And, this is actually pretty interesting because most of the protesters looked up to revolutionary heroes like Bhagat Singh, Sukhdev and others, but what they adopted in their actions were Gandhian principles of *satyagraha* (non-violent resistance, and assertion of truth). Another outstanding value embodied in each person was that of hope, which of course comes from being a peasant. You are really into a risky enterprise, and you are not going to go into the next sowing season unless you hope to be able to harvest something at the end of the season.

Two other values that the protesters brought to the movement emanate from the Sikh religious precepts—*sewa* and *shahadat* (sacrifice/martyrdom). The movement imbibed these two values from their Sikh comrades from Punjab. *Sewa* was everywhere—everyone was actively exploring ways in which they could do something for the larger cause: it could be sweeping the streets of the protest township, and making sure that the place was clean; or feeding someone a meal. There was a woman farmer from Punjab, who would stitch clothes for the protesters free of cost: people had to bring their own pieces of cloth and she would stitch *kurta-pajamas* for them. In a certain sense, there was a gift economy running at the protest venues. As for *shahadat*, being ready to become a martyr and sacrifice one's life for the cause, that was something unique about this movement. In other *andolans* (movements) people are ready to go to jail, but here they were willing to give up their lives—and more than seven hundred protesters did die due to various reasons in the *andolan*.

Finally, there is the striking memory of people's resistance against corporate control and crony capitalism—the protesters physically occupied a mall at the Singhu border (one of the entry points into the capital city). There was a physical structure there, from which KFC operated. It had a large parking lot. People pitched their tents in there, turned it into an encampment, and started living there. They also went to the top floor and hung huge pictures of heroes of the independence movement and warriors of the Sikh faith. This was the most iconic image from the last twelve months—that of our resistance against the brazen attempt to hand over control of our food and farming systems to corporations. There are many such memories but these really stand out.

GX: *When the negotiation with the Union government started, you were part of the negotiating team from the SKM side. What happened during the talks? There were allegations by the media of farmer leaders changing goal posts and being absolutely rigid. Why did the unions not accept amendments to the laws as was suggested by the government?*

KAVITHA KURUGANTI: If one looks at the negotiations (which were all incidentally video-recorded with the footage being with the government), it is clear that four demands were put forward by us right from the beginning. There is no question of changing goal posts. As for why farmers were "rigid" about their demand for full repeal of the three laws as the only way forward, there are concrete reasons.

Farmers demanded the repeal of these laws because they understood that these three laws sought to alter the legal architecture of Indian agriculture to the detriment of the farmers and that they would also work in tandem with each other. The government also knew that these three laws work together and therefore, brought them together as a package. The core message of these three Acts as a whole was that the government of India does not care for, or respect, the federal polity of the country, or the welfare provisions enshrined in the Constitution, and is happy to let the small and marginal farmers as well as poor consumers fend for themselves. These would result in unregulated power to corporates and agri-businesses at the expense of crores of small and marginal farmers of India. Farmers wished to save the future of farming and farmers in the country.

Farmers demanded the repeal of these laws also because they were never asked for by the farmers or their organisations, the government did not organise any pre or post legislative consultations with the principal stake-holders with no draft Bills circulated for public comments and so on, which is an important part of any democratic law-making process. These were rushed through parliament in violation of parliamentary procedure, and were illegitimate right from the beginning in terms of the processes adopted.

In fact, it is important to note that for several years now, farmers in the country have been fighting for a legal entitlement for guaranteed realisation of a remunerative MSP (Minimum Support Price) for all farmers and all agricultural produce. But the government chose to ignore this demand despite lakhs of farmers coming into Delhi in 2017 and 2018. On the other hand, it chose to bring in legislation which went in the exact opposite direction!

Farmers demanded the repeal of these laws because 'Agriculture' and 'Markets' are State subjects under the Constitution, and through these laws, the Centre was blatantly encroaching into the domain of the State governments. The Centre used the item "Trade and Commerce" under the Union List to justify these Central laws, but farmers contended that it is 'Markets' that are being directly and drastically affected by the laws. Further, for farmers, the state government and its agencies are not only more accessible, but they are also more accountable. When regulation is with the state government, the entire administration from the village agriculture and revenue officials to *taluka*, division and district level officials have the duty to intervene on behalf of the farmers when required, and the farmers have an opportunity to use the administration as well as local elected representatives to address their issues. These avenues become ineffective for farmers when the agriculture markets and contracts are brought under a Central legislation.

As to why farmers did not agree to amendments but were only demanding a full repeal—it was clear that a little tinkering here and there in the name of amendments was not going to improve things, because the very objectives of these laws went against farmers' interests. When the objectives are wrong, it follows that the rest of the clauses in a statute will be wrong too.

Why did the farmers not agree to the offer from the government that they will suspend the implementation of the laws for around two years, until a joint committee looks into all issues? The answer is simple. The protesting farmers did not trust the government not to revoke the suspension as soon as they ended the agitation. Towards the end of the agitation, more demands were certainly added, essentially because the agitation itself threw up issues of false cases being foisted, justice in the Lakhimpur Kheri massacre, justice for martyrs of the movement etc. However, during the negotiations, no goal posts were changed.

GX: *The Supreme Court had suspended the operation of the laws and constituted a Committee with experts to go into the laws. It was sort of a victory. Why didn't SKM suspend the movement then?*

KAVITHA KURUGANTI: This question is similar to the one above. For one thing, the protesting farmers and SKM were seeking a political redressal to the issues they were raising and not a judicial redressal. It is an elected government's policy direction that affected citizens were challenging, and this was not in the domain of a Court of Law to resolve it in any case. Yes, the constitutional validity of the three Central government laws was probably to be resolved by the Supreme Court. But the implications of these laws on livelihoods of the poor in India, of the power wielded by corporations on our food and farming supply chains, and sovereignty issues emerging, were issues that a Court could not have settled.

The Committee constituted by the Supreme Court was another issue, though it was a minor matter—it was ridden with conflicts of interest, so to speak. Advocates of the three laws were made members of the Committee. How could the Supreme Court itself have been guided in its decision-making by such a biased Committee?

GX: *What explains the total silence of the government after the talks broke down till the sudden announcement of repeal of the laws in November? Was it only because of the upcoming assembly elections, particularly elections in Uttar Pradesh?*

KAVITA KURUGANTI: Throughout the agitation, BJP, especially in certain states, was under tremendous pressure from local farmers' protests. This was then translating itself into pressure on the central government constantly and cumulatively. The first setback was in assembly elections in five states, where BJP did not perform as well as it expected. Poll surveys by credible organisations like CSDS Lokniti showed that even in distant states like Tamil Nadu, the farm laws were certainly a factor in voting behaviour. From October 2021 and the Lakhimpur Kheri massacre incident, led by its own Minister and his son, BJP was on the backfoot.

It was a cumulative outcome of the entire agitation, and the ground was slipping from under its feet that BJP and PM Modi announced the repeal of the three laws. The upcoming Assembly elections in 2022 could have been a trigger, but to give the protesting farmers credit, it should be acknowledged that they also knew that ultimately, in a democracy like India, elections are a powerful weapon that ordinary citizens have. That is why they announced Mission UP and Uttarakhand as a key strategy of the Samyukta Kisan Morcha (SKM) in July 2021 for putting pressure on the BJP and its central government.

GX: *Farmer unions have fought for loan waivers, compensation to families of those who have committed suicide. But these are mere symptoms of the agrarian crisis. Don't then these demands bypass the need to address the basic structural issues causing the agrarian distress in the first place?*

KAVITHA KURUGANTI: Farmer unions indeed picked up environmentally unsustainable agendas as well as agendas that actually provide greater markets for certain kinds of corporations to thrive and prevail. Further, they have also not always picked up structural issues related to agrarian distress. Social justice and environmental sustainability have not always been issues of importance for all farmer unions. Farmer unions have also allowed themselves to be split into commodity groups (potato farmer union, sugarcane farmer union etc.), little realising that this itself is unsustainable. Women farmers or tenant farmers or Adivasi farmers don't find space in the 'mainstream' farmer unions, neither in terms of agendas or membership or leadership.

However, just to pick up on the example of loan waivers, and also compensation to farm suicide families, I would like to think that the past decade or slightly more than that did see a shift in the discourse. From mere loan waivers, the attempt in AIKSCC has been on "Freedom from Indebtedness," which is a far larger concept and a significantly different approach than earlier demands. This approach asked for a bankruptcy code, similar to what is available for other sectors, in agriculture too, which is full of risks. Similarly, there have been attempts at looking at triggers and factors that cause this complex phenomenon called farm suicides. Through efforts of platforms like MAKAAM (Mahila Kisan Adhikaar Manch), the shift has also been away from the ones who committed suicides to the women farmers left behind in the families, who need to be rehabilitated in an alternate paradigm of farming.

I would also like to point out that the resistance against liberalised trade in agriculture has in fact nailed a particular structural issue in our globalised capitalist economies of big capital leading to erosion of autonomy and impoverishment. So it would be unfair to say that farmers' movements did not always pick up structural matters. I would like to conclude that the shift in discourse is happening, while the shift in agitation-based demands is not yet happening.

GX: *Your contribution through campaigning for sustainable agriculture for years has been significant. What are your views on bringing in such positive demands in the struggle? What can be the direction of this movement in future if we were to go beyond the repeal of the farm laws? Do you see any possibility of SKM going forward to address the systematic crisis which produced the symptoms—indebtedness and suicide?*

KAVITHA KURUGANTI: Farmer unions are most often seen responding to the immediate issues of their constituencies. It is not clear that they have a clear long-term vision for farming in India. The ones driven by leftist political ideologies also do not have this in my opinion. There is a dire need for raising "constructivist" agendas into farmers' movements. Whether SKM will be that platform which will incorporate these agendas is to be seen, because even on something like MSP legal guarantee, SKM was not able to stand firm on its demand at the time of ending the agitation. We should remember that in all such movements and campaigns, fighting against something is often easier than fighting FOR something.

In the SKM, during the year-long agitation, there was no opportunity to add new agendas or even discuss them. Even now, the pending issue of legal guarantee to MSP is something that is already on the platter along with other pending demands. It is not clear when SKM might be able to discuss other issues. I say this with a clear recognition that the MSP guarantee demand contains within itself several paradigm-altering aspects and can address indebtedness and distress quite well, if framed properly. If MSP is legally guaranteed, then farmers growing many crops will have equal entitlement to remunerative prices, and diverse crops will be grown, leading to sustainability. It will also reduce disparities in price regimes in different regions of the country for the same commodity. Such a price guarantee regime will stabilise farm incomes and possibly shift farmers to low-cost farming (since farmers will try to increase margins between costs and guaranteed prices), reducing debt and distress.

GX: *What are your views on the Green Revolution model being unsustainable even if the issues of easy availability of credit, procurement of produce at remunerative prices, crop insurance are addressed? Free electricity to farmers has meant more use and wastage of groundwater. How can these adverse ecological practices be addressed? Do you see SKM playing a role in this? What are the possibilities?*

Kavitha Kuruganti: There is more than ample evidence out there about the ecological unsustainability of the Green Revolution model. About 15-20 years ago in the official establishment, whenever we talked about the Green Revolution and its environmental and corporate footprints, there would be a severe adversarial reaction and great defence of the model. Now things have changed. There are many official documents that highlight the limitations of the model. So that debate that is over, and the verdict is already out. Unfortunately the fallouts are being experienced by farmers as well as consumers all over the country.

What you are asking as the second question is interesting—can SKM play a role in addressing issues that a Green Revolution paradigm presents? Can SKM play a constructive role in promoting alternatives? I doubt it. I find that most farmer unions know how to take up agitations against something successfully, but do not know how to promote something successfully. In South India, there are farmer unions like Karnataka Rajya Raitha Sangha (KRRS) which have promoted the natural farming paradigm, and remember, it is not only part of their environmental consciousness but also part of their political ideology around farmers' autonomy and sovereignty too. The north Indian farmer unions are yet to catch up on this and we have quite some way to go on this path.

GX: *The massive participation of women has been a hallmark of this agitation. Yet, the question of ownership of agricultural land by women, an issue which is marked by enormous inequities and gender discrimination, never come to the forefront. We would like to know your views and also if SKM is trying to address the problem?*

Kavitha Kuruganti: Well, because of the hold of patriarchy in India, women who are involved in agriculture are not even considered farmers, because farmers are understood to be land-owners, and women largely don't own land in India. Our view is that women need to be given land entitlements, and treated on par with male farmers, with or without land ownership. On the other hand, to promote their empowerment and for radical change in rural women's lives they do need to have equal land rights. Not only are women equal partners in agriculture, compared to men, they also spend longer hours and more days on farming activities all across the country.

There are two important issues that stand out regarding land ownership. Due to some progressive amendments in inheritance rights, even though they apply to specific religious communities, the Indian laws do provide women an equal right in property inheritance on par with their brothers.' But, this provision called the Hindu Succession Act is often not implemented due to the hold of patriarchy—for instance, the dowry paid at the time of her marriage is considered a fair substitute to inheritance of land. A patriarch would tell his daughter, "I have already given your dowry, why do you want to claim a share in property?" And the woman also, in most cases, relinquishes her property rights in favour of her brothers in the hope that if something goes wrong in her marital family, it is the brothers who would take care of her.

But this discussion on inheritance rights of women applies only to those communities which do possess land and where property can be passed on as inheritance. There is a huge section of Dalit households (the lowest strata of Indian society) where inheritance rights for women just don't matter, as neither a man nor a woman gets any access to land ownership. And, in those cases we have to specifically talk about the responsibility of the state to grant land ownership to women. It is a huge pending task for Indian social and political activists, and farmer unions need to pick it up, too.

Has SKM begun addressing these issues? No! They just didn't have the time or the mind space to take on multiple demands simultaneously. It would only have diluted their focus, and the government would have accused them of changing their goal posts. So that was not the right setting for expanding our agenda. Even when it came to the farm laws that SKM fought against and won, the forum did not have a feminist analysis of the adverse implications of the farm laws, even though tens of thousands of women farmers participated actively in the agitation.

GX: *Another related issue to agriculture in the last couple of decades is that of debt driven suicides by farmers. Is the SKM thinking of proposing credit lending and banking reforms in the agricultural sector so that a farmer is not driven towards private money lenders who charge exorbitantly high interest rates?*

Kavitha Kuruganti: SKM has not picked up on that issue, yet. The joint platform is merely an infant, only a year old, even though it has gained much success in its infancy. But in the AIKSSC, the issue of debt driven suicides has been taken up with definite purpose. AIKSCC formulated the Farmers' Freedom From Indebtedness Bill, 2018, a draft legislation to establish a national legal framework to free the Indian farmer from the burden of debt. It was based on a legislation which the Kerala legislative assembly had passed in 2006, and which led to a dramatic reduction in debt driven suicides in Kerala.

The Kerala law stated that any indebted or bankrupt farmer or agricultural worker could put in an application to the State Debt Relief Commission saying that they were bankrupt, and were unable to repay their loan, which would prevent a creditor or lender from taking up legal proceedings against that person. They could not take any action that could typically trigger suicides. Which means, the lenders could not auction or seize the property, or paste a notice outside the farmer's home saying that the house belonged to a defaulter, or dishonor a farmer in front of his/her entire community. Even though suicide is a complex phenomenon, the loss of social honor often pushes farmers toward suicide.

The Farmers' Freedom From Indebtedness Bill, 2018, was introduced as a private member's bill in India's parliament. But private members' bills are difficult to pass, and this too was never taken up for consideration by the Lok Sabha. Soon it was time for the 2019 elections. The government showed no interest in bringing this bill for discussion. The bill had some important features—it introduced the concept of limited liability for farmers, which is taken for granted for the biggest capitalists all over the world, who have limited liability regarding the risk faced by their enterprise, making their own personal properties and assets safe in case of the failure of the business. Limited liability does not apply in agriculture, which is one of the riskiest enterprises out there. In India, a banker would still demand payment for a loan irrespective of crop failure, natural disasters, even if there was a government notification declaring a season to be a drought. You are forced to repay your loan at the end of the season.

Provision of limited liability in the Farmers' Freedom From Indebtedness Bill, 2018 could address many risk factors related to farmers' indebtedness, and my colleague Kiran Vissa and I drafted it. The Bills were improved based on very elaborate, widespread processes of consultation across the country before it was made into a private member's bill. It is a good piece of legislation, and we need something like that for farmers all over the country.

GX: *Coming back to the farmers' movement. The demand for a legal guarantee of MSP was not met. How important is this demand to the farmers and do you think SKM's should have continued with the agitation till this demand was met? What are the SKM's future action plans to achieve it?*

KAVITHA KURUGANTI: This has indeed been a great disappointment personally for me. I believe that repeal of the laws only took farmers back to where they were in June 2020, in dire straits. It has not given them any additional rights and entitlements, given that the MSP demand could not be secured by this powerful agitation. I certainly believe that SKM should have continued with its agitation till this demand was met. Having said that, I also feel that having lost more than 700 farmers as martyrs in the movement was a heavy price that the movement paid. So any further continuation of the agitation had to weigh all the gains and losses objectively, and based on such an assessment, the agitation concluded. However after the Assembly elections are over, and after some equilibrium is restored in the joint platform, an agitation around MSP has to be launched in a well planned manner, and secured for all farmers of India.

GX: *What does this victory, though partial, means for the Indian farmers and people's movements in this country?*

KAVITHA KURUGANTI: This movement and its success in repealing the three laws offer very important lessons for all people's movements in the country. For one thing, the movement put farmers squarely back into the nation's political canvass. It taught farmers a valuable lesson about strength in unity. It also gave them organisational insights into working together, putting aside real differences in ideologies and differences in styles of functioning.

Other people's movements can draw inspiration from the persistence, determination, peace, solidarity and cooperation that this movement showcased.

Importantly, it showed the nation and the world that a Prime Minister, who was projected as invincible, had to ultimately bend to citizen pressure and people's power. This itself is a strong inspiration to pick up other matters of justice and entitlements of citizens.

Editorial Note

Some portions of the above interview have been taken from another interview of Kavitha done by Pallav Das. The link to that interview is:

https://radicalecologicaldemocracy.org/indian-farmers-prevail-a-conversation-with-kavitha-kuruganti-a-farmers-rights-activist/.

We have also used the following link:

http://www.kisanswaraj.in/2021/06/24/why-farmers-are-insisting-on-a-repeal-of-the-3-central-farm-laws/

SECTION II

CONVERSATIONS WITH LEADERS OF AGRICULTURAL AND RURAL WORKERS' UNIONS

Protesting farmers displaying a placard requesting media to tell the truth. **Photo credit:** Workers Unity.

Martyrs of the farmers' movement. **Photo credit:** Workers Unity.

The Solution to the Caste Question will Only Come through the Acquisition and Distribution of Land
PARGAT SINGH KALAJHAR, KRANTIKARI PENDU MAZDOOR UNION

> PARGAT SINGH KALAJHAR is a leader of Krantikari Pendu Mazdoor Union (KPMU). The union works among agricultural workers, landless peasants, rural workers and garment workers. Since 1998, KPMU has been fighting for land rights of agricultural workers and other demands such as employment under MGNREGA, minimum fair wages and social security. KPMU had spearheaded the struggle of Dalit agricultural workers in Punjab to acquire one-third of panchayati common land on lease. It is also a part of Sanjha Mazdoor Morcha, a joint front of seven agricultural and rural worker organisations in Punjab.
>
> WORKERS UNITY interviewed Pargat Singh in Bhawanigarh, in Sangrur district, on 8 September 2021.

WORKERS UNITY: *Tell us first about your union—when did it start and what are the issues KPMU has fought for since its inception?*

PARGAT SINGH: KPMU was formed way back in 1998, and since then we have been continuously working on the issues of the landless peasants and agricultural workers, the majority of whom are Dalit.

In 2008, we raised the issue of rights of the landless Dalits to the panchayati common land in Benra village, in Sangrur district. As per law, a third of panchayati land (land belonging to village council) should go to Dalit landless peasants on an annual lease. We went to the village and talked to the Dalit labourers, told them about the law and their rights. Initially, they did not want to join any struggle on this issue because they could not believe that agricultural land could ever belong to them. They had been historically oppressed and did not have any hope that they could also become landed farmers. They believed that the right to land was only for the dominant castes and not for the Dalits.

We held multiple meetings in the village. People told us "No, this is not possible here, we can't get land here." But everyone knows that the village auctions which award panchayati lands on lease are fraudulent. The rich farmers and zamindars belonging to the dominant Jat caste capture the land in auction by putting up 'dummy' Dalit candidates. This has been going on since 1964 when the law was passed.

After a lot of efforts, eventually, we were successful in convincing and organising the Dalit landless labourers in Benra village. Behal Singh, our comrade, mobilised 250 Dalit families of the village under the banner of KPMU. A Dalit collective was formed in the village. The Dalits started organising meetings and rallies in the village asserting their claim over panchayat land. This, of course, was not acceptable to the dominant caste Jat farmers. They began to feel threatened. There were confrontations in the village because of this, pamphlets were distributed accusing us of instigating the Dalits. But the resolve of the Dalits in Benra village was strong and we were successful in taking eight acres of panchayat land on lease. Earlier, during the auction, the annual price [rent] for the same size of land used to go up to Rs 8 to 10 lakh. We brought it down to Rs 18,000 to 20,000 per acre.

This success gave an unimaginable level of happiness and confidence to the landless Dalits, since it seemed so unbelievable that this could actually happen—Dalits can own and cultivate land. It was a historic moment for the Dalits in Punjab. Benra became an experimental model of a Dalit Collective gaining control of land in auction. The size of the acquired land (eight acres) was too small for cultivation of food grains. So, in a conscious departure from the traditional rice-wheat cycle, the Dalit Collective in Benra cultivates fodder crops—Chari (sorghum) and Berseem (clover). Even today, in Benra, our Dalit comrades are farming collectively on that land. And they divide the yield amongst themselves equally.

The idea of a Dalit collective spread all over the state, particularly in the Malwa region, creating a panic amongst the rich farmers, who had been deceitfully acquiring and cultivating the land earmarked for Dalits. From 2008 until today, we have been waging struggles like these in villages. The solution to the caste oppression in villages will only come through acquisition and distribution of land. That is why we explain to people that they need to organise on the question of land. We are seeing some very encouraging responses in various villages in Patiala, and many landless farmers have got land in that area.

But, direct conflict takes place in villages where the *chaudharis* (generally upper-caste village chiefs), who have occupied the land for ages, want to hold onto it. They get troubled when there is a shift in the power dynamics, when they feel that power is slipping from their hands. Generally, when Dalits raise the land question and fight for the land which is rightfully theirs, we see a direct confrontation between the big farmers, landlords and the landless. In many villages, small and marginal farmers support us and so the conflict in Punjab is directly with the big farmers. Of course, as we all know, the police, the administration and the MLAs (members of the State Legislative Assembly) are all from their class and caste, and take their side.

There is a village nearby named Jhaloor. The struggle for land has been going on there since 2014. Around 522 *bigha* (1 *bigha* = 27,000 square feet) of land there belonged to the Dalits. We were lathi-charged there, as dummy auctions were going on in Bhawanigarh and we were protesting along with comrades of the Zameen Prapti Sangharsh Committee (ZPSC). Cases were filed against 41 people, and I also stayed in jail for eight days. Collectives led by ZPSC and KPMU are raising the land question and have been successful in creating awareness about it among the landless Dalit peasantry of Punjab.

WU: *What has been the role of the farmer union during this struggle by the Dalits to claim their legal share of panchayat land in the villages?*

Pargat Singh: BKU (Ekta-Ugrahan), a big farmers' mass front in Punjab, gave immense support to us during the Jhaloor struggle. Dr. Darshan Pal and others in the Krantikari Kisan Union (KKU) similarly provided support in another struggle that happened recently. In fact, KKU even lost one of its units in a village when their leadership stood with us during a land struggle. There are certain collectives who are inspired by these leaders and their ideologies—they too provide support to us. But in the villages, when a Dalit collective is formed, issues arise. The caste contradictions are still very deep-rooted in rural society and the worm of casteism is present in the mindset of many landed farmers even though they are members of radical and progressive farmer unions, and in some cases, this includes even the union leaders. We repeatedly try to explain to them how one-third of panchayati land is a legal right of the Dalits. But most of them refuse to listen to any reason, as control over land and keeping landless peasants as bonded agricultural labourers are key to their power and wealth.

WU: *While travelling through different districts of Punjab, such as Ludhiana, Malwa, Mansa, Moga, and Patiala, we spoke to a large number of agricultural labourers, who said they couldn't find work this year, as migrant labourers from Bihar are back, and they work at lower wages. So, for agricultural workers, the issue in Punjab is not only land but also a decent living wage—how does your union view this?*

PARGAT SINGH: Our union is of the view that in accordance with the increasing cost of all aspects of living in not only urban but also rural areas, the wages of workers should also increase proportionately. A complaint rose this time as well that the outsider Bihari workers took away the jobs of the local Punjabi labourers. There are certain villages, near Patiala, where the *zamindars* employed only the migrant workers, not even a single local labourer was employed.

We firmly believe that a fair wage is a worker's fundamental right. The labourers should get a fixed minimum wage, Rs 700 to 800 per day. Sometimes, the village panchayats decide and fix the daily wage, but it has no legal basis to do so. Under the MGNREGA scheme, for example, the daily wage is Rs 221. A huge amount of work is extracted from the workers. Rural workers are demanding Rs 500 to 600 per day as wages under MGNREGA as well.

Modi has now brought a new labour law that has removed the eight-hours work per day limit. One can now extract 12 to 13 hours of labour from a worker, if one wants. This makes the situation even worse.

Before and during Covid-19, we saw the devastation that was brought on rural workers. The agricultural labourers, rural workers—their work stopped completely. There's a town called Bhawanigarh. Every morning, people gather there at the labour *chowk* (junction). The labourers are assessed: who is strong, who can work how much, etc. And yet, the wage is the same for the strong and for the not-so-strong ones. If 50 people gather every day, maybe 30 get work, and the rest sit there for the whole day and then return home.

Like the farmers are demanding guaranteed MSP (Minimum Support Price), shouldn't there also be a guaranteed minimum wage for a worker?

WU: *Farmers are, for more than eight months, camping on the Delhi borders demanding repeal of the farm laws. They are saying that the farm laws will harm not only the farmers but also the agricultural workers. Slogans of farmer-worker unity are being raised. You have often been to the borders in solidarity of the farmers' struggle. How do you think conversations can take place between farmer and labour unions so that the unity slogan can become a reality on the ground?*

Pargat Singh: We have always tried to speak to farmers' groups including the ones sitting at Singhu and Tikri borders. We have organised agricultural workers and gone there to support their struggle. But firstly, the demonstrations which are going on there are primarily against Modi and the ruling class. Secondly, the slogans raised during their protests might be about farmer-worker unity, but the agricultural workers do not really connect with their slogans or feel that the farmers' protest is theirs too—and this is a bitter truth in my opinion.

As we discussed during the last question, even today, if you go to the villages, the ruling class there consists of the big farmers and landlords and everything works just as it used to earlier. Of course, I should mention that there is one visible change, thanks to this movement. Earlier, the *chaudhari*s and landlords used to put up flags of the Congress party or some other bourgeois party which looked after their interests. But now, they had raised the flags of farmers' collectives like Samyukta Kisan Morcha (SKM) at the roof of their houses. So, even they are becoming aware of whose interests parties like Akali, BJP, and Congress represent. But when it comes to the landless Dalits and the agricultural workers, their mindset continues to be the same.

The other noteworthy aspect which you have raised is how the protests talk about worker-farmer unity. I feel that the core demands raised by SKM do not at all cater to the issues directly impacting the labourers. Of course, the three farm laws attempting to bypass the *mandis* (agricultural produce markets) are bad for the labourers. But this is more incidental as closing of *mandis* will impact the entire peasantry. The issues that impact the labourers directly, like the PDS, are not in the charter of demands of the farmers.

We understand that the leadership at the Singhu border comes from a rich and dominant caste farmer background. They have easy access to food, shelter, and all that they need. There are only a very few farmers' collectives and organisations in SKM that take into consideration the demands and issues of the agricultural labourers.

When the SC/ST (Prevention of Atrocities) Act, 1989, was diluted in March 2020, and President Ram Nath Kovind signed it, India saw so many Dalit organisations coming out on the streets in protest. A Bharat Bandh was called on 2 April on that issue, buses were burnt, many people died, so many cases were registered and many people are still in jail. At that time, the farmer unions were silent.

In the villages, the Dalits complain that when the SC/ST Act was diluted, most of the farmer unions did not utter a word. Only one or two farmer unions spoke about it. The agricultural labour unions and other Dalit collectives came to the forefront at that time. It was only after the successful Bharat Bandh that the Modi government backtracked and withdrew the amendments. Similarly, in many districts in Punjab, the workers have reported that the big farmers oppress them. Although, this does not happen in places which have strong Left farmer unions functioning. In such places, they arrange mutual talks on issues pertaining to wages and other things. But such villages are very few in number.

Also, at the Singhu border, the labourers' leadership barely gets any space to speak. I myself stayed at the Singhu border for one and a half months and witnessed firsthand a lot of what is going on there. The land question and the issues facing agricultural labourers are being ignored even today.

WU: *The agricultural workers' unions have not only been supporting the farmers' movement, but are now building a movement of their own in Punjab. What are the demands of the joint front of the agricultural and rural workers that has been formed recently?*

PARGAT SINGH: In Punjab, there are seven agricultural/rural worker unions that have come together on a single platform recently to raise common demands. The main demand that has emerged from this joint initiative is the acquisition of one-third of the panchayati land by the Dalits on a contract basis and at the cheap rate.

The second demand is that the Dalit landless labourers should be allowed to become members of the cooperative societies, and cheap loans that the farmers get from there should be made available to the landless also. We have already started writing official letters, for example in Bhawanigarh, demanding membership for the landless Dalits in cooperative societies.

The third demand pertains to debts and loans. For example, there are villagers where houses of workers are on unregistered lands; so they do not get loans from either the government or the banks. They have to resort to private microfinance companies to avail loans at about 36 percent interest per annum. They are, in many cases, unable to repay the loans. They take another loan to repay the earlier one. People get trapped in a vicious cycle. We are demanding that all governmental and private debts of the agricultural workers should be waived off completely.

The fourth demand is related to the allocation of land for building houses. You have seen how small the plots are on which the houses of the rural workers are built. Generations of landless workers end up spending their entire lives in a single tiny room on a tiny plot, with a broken toilet with not even a door, with just a piece of cloth hanging in front of it. In such a small space, they also have to keep their cattle, and a small gas stove in a corner which is supposed to be the kitchen. One small room contains all of this. So we demand that bigger plots be given to the landless farmers and agricultural workers, and additionally a loan of five lakh rupees be given to these families for the construction of houses on those plots.

The fifth demand is concerning the violence on Dalits. In Punjab, the Dalits face a lot of caste violence. For example, recently, a young Dalit boy had stolen something and he was caught and dragged to the village *chowk* (village square). Four people held his legs and hands, and others thrashed him with sticks in full public view. We protested. Then a complaint was lodged against our union, alleging that we protect thieves over. On the contrary, it is us who believe that you should hand the thieves to the police and file a case if you have any evidence. To beat someone up in the centre of the village—no one has the right to do something like this. So we demanded that a case be filed under the SC/ST Atrocity Act against such violence. Of course, no one was arrested in that incident, even though, legally, the accused persons should have been immediately arrested. But in Punjab, such accused persons from upper castes enjoy high status and power. Even if they are booked, they call the ministers and save themselves from the provisions of the SC/ST Act. So, we demand strict actions to stop casteist violence.

Additionally, we demand that all anti-labour laws proposed by the RSS/BJP government be repealed, including the one on the relaxation of the eight-hour workday limit. The NREGA scheme should be implemented more extensively and work under it should be given for the whole year.

We have also placed a demand regarding employment. Captain Amarinder Singh, the then CM of Punjab, had promised to provide one job to each household. The promise has not been fulfilled and it should now be met by the Congress government. These are the demands that we have raised in our charter.

Now that elections in Punjab are due early next year, if we don't build pressure from now, nobody is going to even look at us for the next four to five years. On the other hand, if we are able to put pressure on the politicians now, we can surely make them fulfil at least some of our demands; at the least, we will popularise these demands amongst the workers. There are so many workers who don't even know what our demands are.

WU: *How successful has the joint platform been so far and what is its future in your opinion?*

Pargat Singh: The success of the joint *morcha* (front) can be seen in the fact that probably for the first time, such a huge number of labourers have come together on an organised platform, even though they don't have the resources and organisational strength of the farmer unions. The *morcha*'s success can also be seen in the workers' passion in making their demands. District-level meetings were held from 10 to 14 July [2021], village-level protest marches were organised from 15 to 25 July and a demand charter was submitted to state ministers and Congress MPs from July 27 to 29. These protests culminated in a three-day continuous sit-in demonstration in Patiala from August 9 to 11. It was historic in the sense that thousands of agricultural and rural workers assembled and held demonstrations for three days.

An important aspect of the Patiala *morcha* was that ration and other necessities were collected from the villages. The food grains, the utensils, the provisions for cooking—everything was brought by the workers collectively from their houses. Besides, the KPMU set up a langar for all the participants in the Patiala dharna. We did not want to be dependent on anyone for food. We wanted to see for how long we could continue our struggle on our own resources and strength.

We placed our charter of demands to the administration and got an appointment on 18 September (2021) with Minister Brahm Mohindra (Minister of Local Government and Parliamentary Affairs, Elections and Removal of Public Grievances). If a solution is not reached during the discussion with him, our joint morcha will launch further actions like protesting in front of or marching to the houses of the ministers. There is a possibility of holding a bigger rally of workers in Chandigarh or once again in Patiala.

WU: *In the present anti-Delhi atmosphere in Punjab, the demand of Khalistan has also begun to gain some relevance. When people are talking about issues like corporate control over imperialism, causes of farmers committing suicide, right of Dalits to own agricultural land and get fair wages, this separatist religious-political issue is being brought to the forefront as well. How do you view this development?*

Pargat Singh: Frankly, in KPMU's opinion, we do not at all believe that Khalistani politics is a dominant force right now in rural Punjab. Even at a time when it was in the forefront, it just ended up causing more harm to the people's movement and the toiling masses. The Khalistani bogeyman is merely a propaganda, and exaggerations of its influence on the farmers' movement is part of the ruling class's tactics to malign the movement. At present, in Punjab, the Khalistanis do not enjoy that much power and status. Of course, they exist, but they do not have the power or capacity to lead or control a massive or prolonged movement. In fact, the Khalistanis highlighted by the media have turned out to be close to the BJP. I think this is simply an RSS tactic to create a religious divide in the movement. RSS is a fascist organisation which is against the religions of the minorities—be it Islam, Sikhism, Buddhism or Jainism.

Politics should be of the people—the landless peasants and workers. Caste oppression and Hindutva needs to be annihilated. Annihilation of caste and eradication of communalism have been the teachings of our gurus also. Our gurus fought against communal and caste divides. Baba Banda Singh Bahadur's struggle was directed towards equal distribution of land. It is the people who will create the socialist society imagined by Bhagat Singh, Baba Ravidas, Guru Nanak and the martyrs of the Ghadar Movement. This is what politics by the masses and for the masses really means. The revolutionary path that has been given to us by our Gurus—the path of Baba Banda Singh Bahadur (a Sikh warrior who waged war against the Mughals) and his revolutionary ideas—will lead us towards a truly democratic society.

Under the Farm Laws, with the Entry of Corporates, the Farmers will Lose their Land and the Agricultural Workers, their PDS

LACHHMAN SINGH SEWEWALA, PUNJAB KHET MAZDOOR UNION

> LACHHMAN SINGH SEWEWALA is the General Secretary of the Punjab Khet Mazdoor Union (PKMU) that works among agricultural labourers, who are mostly Dalit. Formed in 1993, PKMU is active in Muktsar, Bhatinda, Sangrur, Jalandhar, Faridkot and Moga districts of Punjab.
>
> Lachhman Singh was born in 1972 in Sewewala village of Faridkot district. He was a college student when a group of armed Khalistani militants attacked a cultural program in his village, killing 18 people. This incident triggered his decision to become a social activist. Lachhman Singh campaigned widely to make agricultural workers in Punjab aware of the disastrous impact of the farm laws and highlighted the significance of Kisan-Mazdoor Ekta.
>
> WORKERS UNITY interviewed Lachhman Singh in early April 2022.

WORKERS UNITY: *In Punjab, what are the main issues and demands of the agricultural workers?*

LACHHMAN SINGH: The biggest issue among the agricultural workers is that of landlessness. Their main demand is land ownership. Land is a natural resource and everyone should have an equal right to it in the same way as over air, water and sunlight. Landless agricultural workers have the strongest right to own land because it is they who toil and cultivate the land. Even the Swaminathan Commission had in its report, pitched for land reforms and said that the issue of unequal land ownership is deeply entangled with political and social issues. Since 2013-14, agricultural workers unions in Punjab have raised the demand to implement in spirit, not just in word, the law on auctioning 33 percent of the pachayati cultivable land to Dalit agricultural workers. The landlords, however, engaged in a propaganda that today Dalits are demanding the panchayati land; tomorrow they would want to snatch our land. Their propaganda was aimed at fanning fear, particularly among small farmers belonging to the Jat Sikh community.

The second biggest issue is unemployment. After the Green Revolution, mechanisation of farming with the introduction of harvester combines, chaff-making machines etc., has left agricultural workers with only a few months of work in the fields. The use of weedicides displaced manual rooting out of weeds. The wheat chaff machines replaced the work of women workers engaged in gleaning the fallen ears of wheat. The overall harvesting season was reduced to a few months. This means that the agricultural worker has to either take up other jobs outside farming or remain unemployed in the remaining months of the year. These workers take up various jobs like working as porters in the *mandis* (agricultural produce markets), as hawkers on streets and railway stations, as rag pickers, in MGNREGA or as construction workers in towns and cities. But they still rely on the income generated from farming. Agricultural workers search for other jobs only when they can't find a job on farms. That is also why they leave other jobs during the sowing and harvesting seasons.

The question of a minimum living wage is also a major issue and demand of the agricultural workers. Most of them have no house of their own. This is also a big problem for them. Apart from these, as majority of agricultural workers are Dalit, there is the problem of caste oppression, even if it is not as barbaric as in UP, Bihar and other states. The Green Revolution has not only snatched away the employment of agricultural workers but has also spread killer diseases like cancer on a large scale. Ground water level has depleted alarmingly and has become contaminated due to indiscriminate use of pesticides. Cancer has reached epidemic proportions in many districts. A train running between Punjab and Bikaner [in Rajasthan] has come to be known as the "cancer train." Although the disease is widespread among the farmers as well, they have land as a resource and can avail loans for treatment, but agricultural workers being landless, don't even get loans. Our union conducted a survey in which it was found that in Punjab, 19 percent of the total debt incurred by the agricultural workers is spent on medical expenses.

WU: *Typically, how many days of work in a year is available to* khet mazdoors *(agricultural workers) in farming?*

LACHHMAN SINGH: In our survey, we found that various regions in Punjab differ in this regard. For example, cotton cultivation is done in the Malwa [the area south of Sutlej river] region. There, they get work for two and a half months to six months, while in fruit growing areas like Muktsar and Fazilka, agricultural workers get work for only one and a half months in a year. Even in the paddy season, work is available for only one and a half months. But in areas like Doaba [the region between Sutlej and Beas rivers], where apart from the Rabi and Kharif crops, potato and other vegetables are also grown, work is available for three to four months. In villages that are close to cities, these agricultural workers drive rickshaws or go to the *labour chowk* (a place in the city where daily wage workers gather every morning in search of work) in search of odd jobs as masons, cleaners etc. An agricultural worker actually does different types of work at different times of the year.

WU: *There are reports that agricultural workers too are succumbing to suicide in Punjab. What are suicide rates like among the agricultural workers as compared to the farmers?*

LACHHMAN SINGH: One of the biggest reasons for suicide among agricultural workers is debt. Often, they reach a situation in which the economic condition of the agricultural worker becomes so bad that they don't even get a loan, even if it is for an emergency medical treatment or for a wedding in the family. Severe financial crisis is the main reason for committing suicide[2]. Of the 16,000 suicides in Punjab, as documented in a Punjab Agricultural University coordinated report, 7,000 were that of agricultural workers. So, the number of suicides by agricultural workers is at par with that of the farmers in the state. But they are mostly not reported. To certify a death as suicide, documents showing proof of loans given must be shown, which are seldom found with agricultural workers.

WU: *Agricultural wages are high in Punjab when compared with other states. Why, then, are agricultural workers in debt? What is the nature and extent of their debts that forces them to succumb to suicide?*

LACHHMAN SINGH: Whenever there is a discussion about debt, suicide and loan waivers, it is only done in the context of the land-owning farmers. Farmers in Punjab are organised. Their unions are strong. They can bargain for loan waiver schemes. But even in their case, it is electoral politics that decides whether a loan waiver is given or not.

To understand the conditions of the agricultural workers, we did two surveys in 2017, one on the extent of debt among agricultural workers and the other on their amenities. Our survey involved more than 1,618 families spread over 12 villages in six districts of the Malwa region and two villages in Jalandhar district of the Doaba region. It was a random survey. We found 84 percent, or 1,364 families, were under heavy debt. Each agricultural worker family, on an average, owed Rs 91,000. The remaining 16 percent or 234 were "debt free," not because they did not need loans but because no one was prepared to lend any money to them.

Our survey revealed that agricultural workers owed the maximum to microfinance companies and the least amount to government banks. Private banks had lent more at higher rates of interest, almost comparable to that charged by private moneylenders. Interest rates were as high as 50 percent in case of loans from microfinance companies. The total loan given by these companies accounted for nearly 23.16 percent of the total debt, which is almost the same as that lent by private moneylenders. Loans by big farmers to agricultural workers accounted for 15.46 percent of the total debt, while loans given by the small farmers accounted for 6.88 percent of the total debt.

So, essentially, the agricultural worker is indebted to everyone— banks, moneylenders, land-owning farmers, microfinance companies. We found that construction of homes and medical expenses are the two major reasons for taking loans. Agricultural workers also incurred debts for cultivating land taken on rent.

Agricultural wages are high in Punjab when compared to other states but as most of the workers are indebted to farmers, the wages are never paid in full. To meet loan obligations, women agricultural workers also do a lot of non-farm work for free. A large part of the wage earning is spent on paying interest on loans from private money lenders.

WU: *More than half of the agricultural workers are women. Women from agricultural workers' families also go into debt. What is their condition?*

LACHHMAN SINGH: The women coming from families of agricultural workers, landless farmers, small farmers or families who have been pushed out of their land are falling into the trap of private microfinance companies. The interest rate charged by these companies is generally 26 percent per annum but it often goes up to 40 to 60 percent by adding various other charges. The companies argue that the interest rates are high because they are providing loans to high risk categories. They provide loans just on the basis of an Aadhar [identity] card. Women often take loans from multiple microfinance companies. When they are unable to pay loan instalments, the companies give them more loans for repayment of previous loans. Soon they are entangled in a debt trap. The duress of the women agricultural workers is that they do not get loans from anywhere else.

Apart from this, a novel way of debt recovery has also been figured out by these companies. For example, loans are given by forming a group of say 20 women. If two women in the group are unable to repay the loan, the remaining 18 women are asked to either pay those instalments together or make the defaulting women repay, if need be, by confiscating the defaulters' household items. This is totally illegal because the process for loan retrieval by attaching household assets and seizing them requires an order from the court. Many other coercive methods are also adopted and all this is done in the pretext of providing loans by forming self-help women groups. Only the profits of microfinance companies are increasing day by day, while women workers are being fleeced in the name of women empowerment. Yet no government wants to curb this practice.

WU: *You also talked about a second survey on the living conditions of the agricultural workers. What were the findings?*

LACHHMAN SINGH: Our second survey was on the amenities and living conditions of agricultural workers. A huge section of workers do not even have their own houses. We had surveyed 1,640 families. We found that 440 families, or 27.5 percent of the families did not have their own houses and 643 families had only an one-room house with no separate kitchen area. The survey found that 493, or 30 percent of the families did not have any toilet facility and 457 families had no facilities for bathing. When women wanted to take a bath, male family members were told to step out or a cot covered with a bed-sheet was propped up to act as a curtain.

The condition of agricultural workers is already bad. The new farm laws, if they were implemented, would have made it worse. Landlessness is one of the major reasons for the present plight of the agricultural workers. They are looking for jobs outside agriculture, which are too few to meet the demand. The farm laws were meant to create more landless farmers by consolidating land in the hands of big farmers and agro-business houses.

WU: *In the Malwa region, where your union is strong, the agricultural workers and even their children go to neighbouring states to pluck cotton. These children skip school for months and it is locally called "cotton break."*

LACHHMAN SINGH: Malwa was the region where cotton was traditionally grown in Punjab. But after the Green Revolution, cotton has gradually been replaced by paddy. Cotton cultivation needed a lot of manual labour. Paddy cultivation needs less labour. There would be just 25 to 30 days of work in a year. There are few avenues to get earnings for labour for the rest of the year. Now, the biggest challenge in front of the agricultural labourers here is to provide two square meals a day for their families including their children. They have to compromise on education and many other basic necessities. The agricultural worker families in Malwa region not only go to the neighbouring states of Haryana and Rajasthan for cotton plucking, but they go as far as Gujarat. So, the children miss two to three months of school. Since the teachers in schools are also aware of this, they adjust to the situation and do not strike off the names of those children. In government schools, 95 percent of the students are from Dalit agricultural workers' families. Even during summer vacation, when it gets too hot, these children work in paddy fields. That is, in addition to women, there are a large number of children among agricultural workers and obviously their wages are very low. In fact, it is direct child labour, but it does not become an issue given the economic condition of these families. To address this custom of employing child labour, our union has demanded that the agricultural workers should be given cultivable land, round the year employment, and the government should provide nutritious food to their children in school.

WU: *Your union also went to the Delhi borders with agricultural workers in support of the agitating farmers. The agricultural workers participated in the protests but their numbers were low. Why?*

LACHHMAN SINGH: Since the agricultural workers associated with our union have been in constant struggle, their level of political awareness has increased, and it was not difficult to explain to them the importance of supporting the farmers' protest. They were quick to realise the disastrous impact the farm laws will have on their own lives. Even the agricultural workers who only participate in our programmes but do not fully endorse the policies of our union, went to the Delhi borders. We had been part of the agitation from the very beginning; many of us joined the protest on 26 November, the day the *Dilli Chalo* march began. We again went to the borders on 7 January (2021), along with women and children; we joined both the BKU (Ekta-Ugrahan) and the Kisan Mazdoor Sangharsh Committee protest sites at Tikri, Bahadurgarh and Singhu. We stayed there till 10 January. We went back to Punjab and began mobilising agricultural workers to counter the false propaganda by the RSS-BJP in the villages.

In Punjab, other agricultural worker unions had also taken up the issue of opposing the farm laws. So, agricultural workers were participating in protests, yes, but their numbers were low. The reason is that agricultural workers are daily-wage earners and cannot afford to stay away from work even for a single day. Also, when the *Dilli Chalo* call was given, it was the paddy and cotton harvesting season. Many workers were engaged in cotton plucking in Rajasthan and Gujarat and many were working in the *mandis* (agricultural produce markets). It was not possible for them to join in protests far away from where they lived. Also, it was beyond the capacity of the agricultural worker union to meet the travel expenses of taking hundreds of workers to Delhi.

WU: *What was the role of BJP in creating confusion among the agricultural workers, particularly Dalits? PKMU campaigned to combat BJP's propaganda. How successful were you?*

LACHHMAN SINGH: In Punjab, the BJP spread canards against the farmers' protests among the Dalit agricultural workers and created confusion among them. They said the farmers' agitation is over MSP (Minimum Support Price) and the land issue. Neither has anything to do with the agricultural workers. BJP campaigned that Modiji wants to snatch land from rich Jat farmers and give it to Dalits, so there is no need for them to go to the farmers' protest. The BJP tried to pit Dalits against Jats, even Jats against non-Jats. Initially, their propaganda infiltrated to some extent among the general Dalit population. Caste oppression is a reality in Punjab, and is one of the main reasons for the estrangement of Dalit agricultural workers from the farmers. So when the BJP campaigned against the farmers' protest, the ordinary Dalit agricultural workers also felt that it would be good if the Jat farmers lose their land and their families too are forced to work in others' fields. Only then would the Jat farmers understand the plight of Dalit agricultural workers.

Our union launched an awareness campaign, in which we went from village to village, and tried to explain that this is not just a question of MSP and land of the farmers, it is a direct attack on the PDS (Public Distribution System) in our country. We explained to them how the implementation of the Essential Commodities Act will affect everyone, how the control of prices of food grains will go into the hands of the big companies. We told them drinking water was once free, but now it costs Rs 20 per litre after the companies started bottling and selling packaged water. The same thing will happen with food and vegetables, once big companies gain control over their production and distribution. Efforts were made to convince people with these arguments.

In our campaign, we highlighted that when big companies like Adani, Ambani or WalMart get into agriculture, it would become impossible for the agricultural workers to get work; at the scale these big companies do fully mechanised farming, they will need only a few manual labourers. The Green Revolution has already shrunk farm jobs, entry of big companies would not only take away more jobs, agricultural workers will also lose access to the fodder that they now take from the fields for their cattle. We told them how the issue of MSP is also directly related to the PDS. At present, only rice and wheat are available in the ration shops, while other cereals should also be given. If these 'black' farm laws are implemented, then in the long run only private players will procure food grains; when the government will not buy grains for PDS from the *mandis*, then how will they receive subsidised ration? Under the farm laws, with the entry of corporates, the farmers will lose their land and agricultural workers their PDS along with rising food prices in the market.

We told them about a big silo (hi-tech grain storage facility) already being operated by Adani group in a grain market in Moga district. It has a capacity to stock two lakh tons of food grain, but since packing, loading, unloading, everything is highly mechanised, only a small number of skilled workers are employed there. Computerised quality checks are done and the grains are cleaned by machines. So, in future, if the *mandis* are gradually taken over by private players, machinery will naturally replace human hands. Thousands of porters, those who sew sacks, those who clean the grains, or those who set up shops selling tea and food outside the *mandis*—all would lose their work. Agricultural workers understood this well because outside the farming season, they depend on similar jobs for their livelihood.

These arguments had an impact on them; and at least one thing became clear to them that the new agricultural laws were not what was being told to them by the BJP.

WU: *PKMU also organised two rallies—one in Bathinda and a huge one in Barnala grain market. What was the impact?*

LACHHMAN SINGH: The Mazdoor-Kisan Ekta Maha Rally was held in the grain market of Barnala on 21 February 2021. It was a massive gathering. More than two lakh farmers and agricultural workers gathered on that day. The rally was called by BKU (Ekta-Ugrahan) and PKMU when the movement was in a crisis following the events around 26 January in Delhi. It was of historic importance as the farmer union and agricultural labourers' union came together to agitate against the Delhi regime. It expanded the magnitude of the struggle and showcased the unity between farmers and labourers in opposing the farm laws. Along with the demand to repeal the three 'black laws,' the rally highlighted the impact of these laws on agricultural labourers. The issue of farmers being labelled as Khalistani was also addressed. The non-religious and non-party character of the struggle was emphasised.

PKMU also gave an independent call for a state-level rally of agricultural workers in Bathinda on 15 March 2021. It was the first big rally of agricultural workers in Punjab against the farm laws. Some five thousand agricultural workers—both men and women—from across Punjab took part in that rally in Bathinda. The idea was to make agricultural workers aware of the impact of the farm laws on their lives, and also to highlight their role in the farmers' movement.

WU: *But despite these efforts, agricultural workers did not spontaneously participate in large numbers in the protests? Yes, they were taken to the borders and even in protests inside Punjab by the unions. Is it true that one of the reasons behind this was that the Samuykta Kisan Morcha (SKM) excluded the demands of the agricultural workers from their agenda?*

LACHHMAN SINGH: No doubt, agricultural workers could not participate in large numbers. One of the reasons for that, as I just mentioned, is their economic condition. Farmers had an advantage, they could plant crops and go and participate in the protests, leaving behind one or two family members to look after the crops. The problem with workers is that they have to work every day at the farms, or they have to go to the city in search of work. They would not have been able to be present at protest sites regularly, even if protests had been on their own issues.

Another big problem was that many unions that were part of the SKM were not successful in reaching out to the agricultural workers in the villages. Perhaps they were too busy mobilising the farmers. We were continuously raising the demand in the SKM meetings [through BKU (Ekta-Ugrahan)] that PDS should be one of the central demands of the farmers' agitation, but at that time this was not only excluded from the agenda but also neglected. Later this demand was pushed by many other agricultural worker unions. But, as compared to the farmer unions, the agricultural worker unions are weak, therefore, this demand could not be effectively brought to the forefront.

An important fact was that this movement belonged mainly to the farmers. Though the three farm laws affected, apart from the land owning farmers, the agricultural workers, rural non-agricultural workers, hawkers, small shopkeepers and even small businessmen, a common front of all these sections could not be formed. If the demands of these sections, apart from those of the farmers, could have been included in the movement's core agenda, then there could have been a common front. There was full support from all the other groups to the movement. This was evident in the way the entire state closed down when the Bharat Bandh was called. This happened multiple times. But a common front couldn't be formed.

WU: *So you are saying that developing the struggle on common demands of farmers and workers was ignored? Did it happen because of the antagonistic relation that historically exists between Jat farmers and Dalit agricultural workers?*

LACHHMAN SINGH: Hopefully, this will happen in future. If we could combine the demands of all sections, a much stronger movement can be built. Many demands of an agricultural worker and a farmer are the same, for example, the issue of land. There has been a demand that agricultural land in excess of the Land Ceiling Act should be identified and distributed among the agricultural workers, landless and small peasantry. In Punjab, only a small percent of wealthy farmers oppose this. Small farmers with less than five acres of land find it difficult to sustain. In Punjab, 17 percent of farmers have lost their land and have become landless. The demand to give land to small and landless farmers matches the demands of agricultural workers. The second biggest demand common to both is the availability of loans. What I mean is not only loan-waiver schemes by the government but access to avenues to get easy loans at low interest rates because both the agricultural workers and the small peasantry face difficulty in getting loans. There are many other common issues affecting small farmers and agricultural workers such as suicide and inflation.

Also, it's not true that farmers and workers unions have not fought together. BKU (Ekta-Ugrahan) and PKMU have fought many battles together. In 2015, when the issue of losses incurred by the white fly epidemic was raised by 12 organisations, eight of them were farmer unions and four of them were worker unions. And for the first time, compensation was not only given to farmers but was also given to wage labourers. Now we are faced with the problem of pink bollworms infecting the cotton crop. The government, in its attempt to divide farmers and workers, often gives compensation to farmers but not to agricultural workers. The issue of compensation due to loss of crops is a common demand for farmers and workers because in such an event, the agricultural worker also loses his wages and work. Hence both should be compensated.

In the year 2012, for the installation of a power plant in a village in Mansa, 1,200 acres of land were acquired by the government. Farmer and worker unions held joint protests and demanded that the agricultural workers also be compensated for their loss of earnings. And for the first time in Punjab, in the context of land acquisition, 133 agricultural workers' families got compensation of three lakh rupees each.

PKMU's leadership is from the landless Dalit community and many of them who went to Tikri along with the workers were from villages of Punjab, where Dalits had once clashed with other Jat farmers over village common land, one-third of which is meant to be reserved for Dalits. But these conflicts did not prevent us from joining the movement.

WU: *Do you see any possibility in the near future of a rise in wages of agricultural workers as a result of your support to the farmers' movement?*

LACHHMAN SINGH: In the last paddy season, when the farmers' protest was going on at the Delhi border, there was a small dispute between agricultural workers and farmers regarding wage rate for sowing of paddy. Certain farmers fixed the wage rate by themselves and announced through gurudwaras that agricultural workers demanding higher wages than what was fixed would be socially boycotted. SKM categorically stated it was wrong and the farmers and workers should fix the wage that is mutually agreed upon. As a result, mainly big farmers, who were putting pressure on the workers, had to back down. In a village in Sangrur, farmers boycotted the agricultural workers; in fact, local leaders of BKU (Ekta-Ugrahan) were also involved in the boycott. Senior leaders went there and reasoned with the farmers that if the demand for MSP by farmers is justified then higher wage is also the workers' right. Most of the farmers calmed down. BKU (Ekta-Ugrahan) dismissed from the union those farmers, who were not willing to change their mind. The daily wage of the workers increased. The rate of sowing one acre of land that was Rs 3,500 increased to Rs 4,000, although local agricultural workers were demanding Rs 5000 to 6,000 per acre.

The movement has made farmers understand that the government is not going to bend without agricultural workers' support of their movement. However the change in attitude is not as big as if some revolution had happened. But the courage of agricultural workers to raise their demands has increased. They have realised that if farmer unions can build a protest and win against Modi, then workers can also do the same. And when workers supported the farmers in their battle against Modi, they too expected that farmer unions would also support their struggle. This is the reason why the platform of seven agricultural worker unions held a *rail roko*[3] (rail blockade) protest in December 2021, when farmer unions returned from the Delhi borders. Many farmer unions actively supported the agricultural workers' struggle.

WU: *What is the view of PKMU regarding the Punjab assembly elections? How successful was the call for boycotting the elections and putting land distribution on the agenda?*

LACHHMAN SINGH: For a long time, Punjab's agricultural workers and *pendu mazdoors* (rural workers) unions have come together and fought for their demands. This time when the farmers' protest was going on, seven agricultural and rural worker unions also revived their *sanjha morcha* (united front). Actually, after the new farm laws were announced and the farmer unions launched a united struggle, the agricultural worker unions also had a discussion, and a united front of seven unions was formed. We prepared an eight point charter of demands[4]. We started protests outside the houses of MPs and MLAs. We mobilised workers in huge numbers and protested outside the house of the then chief minister Capt. Amarinder in Patiala for three days from 9 to 11 August 2021.

Before the announcement of the elections, the seven worker unions very enthusiastically pushed forward these demands. In December, we organised a *rail roko*. It was for the first time in the history of Punjab that agricultural workers had held *rail roko* protests. But the situation of the worker unions is the same as that of farmer unions. The united front broke down during the elections. Some of our comrades from other unions became candidates in the assembly elections.

We decided to move forward with our own agenda. We sought opinions of our village leaders about land, debt, electricity and employment. How will a worker get a dignified job? How can the issue of indebtedness of agricultural workers be solved? We reached out to the people with these issues during the election. We believe that it does not matter which party wins in an election. Nothing is going to change until the economic policies dictated to the rulers by the imperialist countries and corporates are not challenged. On 17 Feb 2022, BKU (Ekta-Ugrahan) organised a big rally on this issue. We participated in that rally.

Today, the courage to question leaders of political parties has increased among the common people. People are asking politicians for answers to their issues. Of course, there was never any hope from these leaders. Nor do we expect that AAP (Aam Aadmi Party) will raise slogans against imperialism or take land from big landlords and distribute it among the Dalit agricultural workers or oppose the economic policies. But our campaigns and struggles help us expose them. The vote for AAP in Punjab is not for them but for breaking the hegemony of the existing big parties—the Congress and Akalis.

WU: *AAP has now formed the government in Punjab. How do the farmer and agricultural worker unions plan to move ahead with their demands?*

LACHHMAN SINGH: It was always tough to go against high-statured leaders like Capt. Amarinder or those from the Badal family who ruled us for decades. People were therefore more satisfied defeating these powerful leaders than electing AAP. People think that if AAP does not fulfil its promises, then they can mobilise people and force it to accept their demands. I think AAP will perform better on issues like electricity, schools and hospitals, but they will not be able to make much progress with real issues because those are linked with the country's overall pro-corporate economic policies.

Endnotes

1. Naujawan Bharat Sabha is an outfit that was formed by the revolutionary leader Bhagat Singh. It was revived in the 1970s in Punjab by Meghraj Bhagtuana, a social activist.

2. For details on suicide of agricultural workers, see interview of Prof. Sukhpal Singh, p-367-388 in this volume.

3. A *rail roko* protest was held on 12 December, 2021, by several agricultural and rural worker unions in Punjab. They were demanding repeal of amendments to labour laws, daily wage of Rs 700, 200 days work in a year under MGNREGA, waiver of pending electricity bills and free residential plots to workers.

4. For details on the eight-point charter of demands of the agricultural and rural workers in Punjab, see Appendix III, p-493.

In Order for our Demands to be Accepted, We have to Organise and Fight First; We have to Unite the Rural Workers

DARSHAN NAHAR, GURNAM SINGH AND MAHIPAL, DEHATI MAZDOOR SABHA

> DEHATI MAZDOOR SABHA is a union which works among the daily wage labourers, agricultural labourers and vegetable vendors in the villages of Punjab. It has played a significant role in the formation of Sanjha Mazdoor Morcha, a joint front of seven agricultural and rural workers organisations in Punjab.
>
> A team from WORKERS UNITY had travelled to Punjab to cover the three-day Patiala morcha from 9 to 11 August 2021 called by several agricultural and rural workers organisations in Punjab. The team spoke to a number of activists present at the protest site. This is an interview of Darshan Nahar, Gurnam Singh and Mahipal, the leaders of Dehati Mazdoor Sabha (DMS).

WU: *Please tell us about your organisation, what kind of work your organisation has undertaken and in which districts of Punjab.*

DARSHAN NAHAR: Dehati Mazdoor Sabha is a *jathebandi* (union) of people who work as daily wage labourers, agricultural labourers and vegetable vendors in the villages of Punjab. Dehati means rural. Ours is a *jathebandi* of rural workers.

WU: *Tell us about the history of your organisation. When did you start this organisation and what were the issues of your struggles?*

DARSHAN NAHAR: Actually, this is a very old organisation. It was formed around 1955-56, later its name was changed to Khet Mazdoor Union. In 2001, we again started using the old name—Dehati Mazdoor Sabha. We work among the rural workers. We have complete empathy with the urban workers but rural workers suffer more from poverty, starvation, and face many other problems. We organise them, we help them form committees. Like, we make one committee of seven villages. Then these committees form a *tehsil* (a local unit of administrative division) committee and the *tehsil* committees form a district committee. In this way, we connect the whole of Punjab by forming a state committee.

WU: *How did the seven organisations of rural and agri-workers in Punjab come together to form a united front and what are your primary demands?*

DARSHAN NAHAR: The *sanjha morcha* (united front) was a necessity for us. Punjab's farmer unions took the initiative, formed a united platform named Samyukta Kisan Morcha (SKM) and launched a struggle to repeal the three farm laws. They are sitting in protest in Delhi at Singhu Border, Tikri Border, and in other areas. It has been eight months now, and during these eight months, around 600 comrades have been martyred, including landless workers and women, who own no land but went there only in solidarity with the farmers' cause. Along with supporting the farmers' demand for repeal of the three 'black' laws, we also have our own demands regarding the Public Distribution System (PDS), repeal of the Electricity Amendment Bill 2020.

Our organisation fully supports the farmers' protests. We have formed our own *morcha* of rural and agricultural workers for our own demands that we want to raise before the Punjab state government. Our organisation took the initiative in this regard, our leader Gurnam Singh Dauji [General Secretary of DMS] initiated the process to bring the seven organisations together. Three months ago, we held a meeting in Jalandhar after which we reorganised this joint *morcha*. We had formed it earlier, but it had disintegrated.

First, we demand that the 'black' farm laws which Modi has introduced be wholly repealed. Along with that, we demand that the anti-labour amendments to the labour laws be revoked immediately. Moreover, Punjab's rural workers have a collective debt of Rs 6,000 crore. We want this debt to be waived off fully by the state government. Further, the procedure and rules of giving us loans by the government in future should be made easy. The loans should be for long term so that instead of having to repay them within three years as we have to do currently, the workers can repay the loans in 10-15 years. Besides, no interest should be charged on such loans.

Second, electricity bills have increased drastically. The state of Haryana buys electricity from Punjab but sells one unit of electricity at the price of Rs 2.50. While electricity is produced in Punjab, we still have to pay about Rs 12 per unit. They provide us with 200 units [per month] of free electricity. But by inflating the price, they recover a much higher amount from us. Our demand is that irrespective of religion or caste, previously pending electricity bills of all needy people be waived completely, whether they are Brahmin, Jat, or SC.

Next, the government should give 5 to 10 *marla* (1 *marla* = 0.013 hectare) plots to every rural worker's family for building houses. Captain Amarinder Singh [the then CM of Punjab] had promised that he would give 10-*marla* plots along with grants to build houses. But he has not fulfilled any of his promises, including this one. So our third demand is that 10-*marla* plots should be given to the rural workers along with a minimum grant of Rs 5 lakh to build houses on the plots. Rural workers should have a place to live like humans.

Our fourth demand is concerning pension. Both the states of Haryana and Himachal Pradesh pay a higher amount of pension than Punjab. In Haryana, the amount of pension is Rs 2,500 per month. It is not about the party in power, it may be any party. But in Punjab, the pension amount was initially Rs 250, which was increased to Rs 400. Then again that amount was increased to Rs 700, which also was implemented quite late. Now, finally the government has announced that the pension amount will be Rs 1,500 per month. However, it has been three-four months since the announcement was made but it has not been implemented yet. We do not get Rs 1,500 right now and we do not even know if we'll get it at all or not. Given the realities of Punjab, we demand that old couples should get at least Rs 5,000 as regular monthly pension and continuity of the pension should be maintained. In fact, it is our demand that the pension age for women should be reduced to 55 years and pension age for men should also be reduced to 58 years.

WU: *There has been a continuing narrative stressing farmer-worker unity within the ongoing farmers' protest at Delhi borders. It is being repeatedly said that the farmers and workers should unite in their struggle to achieve success. However, we have been witnessing situations in Punjab where in* many places demand to fix wage of labour is being raised by the farmers. Dalit agricultural labourers are victims of casteist and feudal attacks. In such a scenario, how do you relate with the farmers' protest and its leaders?

[AT THIS POINT, **GURNAM SINGH**, THE SENIOR-MOST LEADER OF DMS, JOINED THE CONVERSATION.]

GURNAM SINGH: *Mazdoors* (workers) and Dalits have been exploited in India for thousands of years. It is still continuing today. Our *mazdoors* have participated in large numbers at the kisan *morcha* (front) currently going on in Delhi and have supported their demands. Apart from that, we thought we should also fight for our own demands and for the recognition of our own problems. So, we united seven organisations into one *morcha* and named it the Pendu aur Khet Mazdoor Jathebandiyon ka Sanjha Morcha (United Front of Rural and Farm Workers' Unions) and at the call of that united *morcha*, we have been sitting here since 9 August [2021] to raise our demands. We too want the unity of farmers and workers to become stronger; both should unite and struggle together. The government wants them to keep fighting amongst themselves so that their strength is reduced. If we strike unitedly, our strength multiplies, and it will be difficult for the government to ignore us. The government supports big land-owning farmers who employ different tactics to exploit us, including issuing calls for social boycott of agricultural workers. When the season to sow paddy comes, they announce a certain amount of wage and declare that any farmer who pays more than that fixed wage to the workers will be fined and any agricultural worker who demands a higher wage than that will be socially boycotted. This has happened in the previous sowing seasons as well. When the time to sow paddy came, the rich farmers fixed the wage of the agricultural workers and our organisation and other organisations as well fought against this illegal practice. We want farmers and workers to unite and fight against Delhi but that unity can't come at the cost of the workers' interests. We stand by the workers' demands and we will help the farmers in their agitation against the central government as much as they help us in our struggle for our rightful demands. But in order for our demands to be accepted, we have to organise and fight first; we have to unite the rural workers. Only then can others lend their support to us. If we ourselves are feeble or unwilling to fight, no one else can come to our aid. They can only help us when we start our own struggle.

WU: *One more thing is that other than the problems of local agricultural workers in Punjab, migrant workers from Bihar and UP who come to Punjab in different seasons have their own problems. They are paid less wages as compared to the local workers. Does your fight for rural workers include the demands of the migrant workers?*

GURNAM SINGH: Yes. When migrant workers come, we not only make efforts so that they join our organisation but also help them to recover their wage from those big landlords who unfairly deprive them. No matter where a worker is from, no matter where he is born, whoever is a worker is our comrade. No matter which state a worker migrates to Punjab from, we will help them. We request them to come and meet the local rural worker organisation. We also request them to not accept lower wages so that local workers are not compelled to work for a lower wage as well.

[AT THIS POINT, **COMRADE MAHIPAL**, ANOTHER LEADER OF THE UNION, JOINED THE CONVERSATION.]

WU: *Mahipalji, the issue of land is very important in rural India. Historically, in Punjab, we see that land is largely concentrated in the hands of the Jat farmers. Dalits are largely landless. There's a law in Punjab that one-third of the panchayati common land should be given to landless Dalit families. However, this law is regularly violated, and big landlords and wealthy farmers take hold of the land through proxy or dummy Dalit candidates. How does your organisation handle this?*

MAHIPAL: First of all, we have included this issue in our charter of demands. Secondly, we do not want to keep this struggle confined to only Sangrur and Patiala districts. We want to spread it to the whole of Punjab. The level to which this law [allowing one-third panchayati land to be given to Dalit agricultural labourers] has been violated in Punjab, perhaps, it has not been done anywhere else. We want to bring this to the forefront. Thirdly, as Comrade Gurnam said, for this, we need to raise the consciousness level and also the fighting spirit of those who face this issue. When we achieve this and our strength is properly established, we will make it a priority issue of struggle too. However, right now, the demands that Darshan*ji* and Gurnam*ji* mentioned are the ones that rural workers are most agitated about.

We have not ignored the issue of land ownership by Dalit rural workers. However, let me tell you that this issue [of panchayati land] is in a sense a trivial one. The basic question is of land reforms—distribution of surplus land in excess of the ceiling, among the landless peasantry. The Swaminathan Commission had talked not only about MSP (Minimum Support Price), it had also raised the issue of land reforms. Even before that, the Mandal Commission, which was defamed as only dealing with job reservation, has also emphasised that the ultimate solution to address poverty in rural areas is land reforms. That suggestion has completely been ignored and overlooked. So, the basic question is of land reforms. Everyone should possess land. The social repression and discrimination you talked about—land reform will also be a significant solution to that problem.

When we talk about workers in the context of the Indian subcontinent, we cannot ignore patriarchy and *Manusmriti*. How can you expect that the landlords in the villages will not be driven by these two things? I'll give you an excellent example. In the village of Katiyal, our workers began a demonstration in front of a police station against an illegal resolution passed by certain farmers which stated that farmers should pay low wages fixed by them and that if anyone asks for higher wage or if anyone pays higher wage then they will be boycotted. Workers demanded either legal action against these people or a public apology from them. We backed the workers in this fight. Some local leaders of the farmer organisation were involved in this boycott call. The effect of our struggle was that the farmer organisation snatched its flag from those local leaders. If we do not fight for our issues, if we do not raise our problems boldly, then, even if we keep begging others to stop the social atrocities or caste discrimination, it will not happen. Our *morcha* is currently prioritising and highlighting the issues in the eight-point charter of demands. We want to spread our message that we need to fight against the government, we need to fight against the corporate. We will fight shoulder to shoulder with the farmers. But when the same farmers exploit us or discriminate against us on the basis of caste, we will fight against that also with the same intensity as is our capacity. Even if only one of us is left on the ground, we will keep fighting. This is our organisation's basic idea.

And we do not spare patriarchy either. For us, social injustice is not limited to caste alone. Women's issues are an important aspect of it. Without combining the two, the matter cannot be satisfactorily addressed. Our demands to address this are few and simple. If we have to explain in one line, we are demanding social security. Social security means, the society provides for those who do not have means of survival. The government does not have to spend from its own pocket. The government is already collecting taxes from the masses. Unfortunately, it is not spending that on the objectives and purposes for which it is collecting taxes. Corporate loans are being waived. Rs 5 lakh crores of corporate loans have already been waived till now. Even during the pandemic, corporate loans have been waived and new loans have been granted to them. Our loans are insignificant in comparison. There is a difference between our loans and their loans. Corporate loans are for earning profit whereas ours are for survival. If a daily wage earner does not get work in the morning, by that very evening that worker is compelled to take a loan in order to save his children from hunger. This is the basic difference between their [corporate] loans and ours. They are wasting the national wealth whereas the money we spend will boost the economy. No matter how many drums 'Modi and Company' or the corporates or the intellectuals who support them beat, until the time workers have sufficient money, the economy of India will not revive. And what are we demanding? We are asking for MGNREGA [a government scheme that ensures 100 days per year of paid employment in rural areas]. Where MGNREGA work is not available like in the urban areas, we want something similar. In MGNREGA, we demand minimum wages as per the recommendations of ILO (International Labour Organisation). This is not such a big demand.

WU: *It has been found through official government data that in Punjab, MGNREGA workers get work for not more than eight or nine days in a year instead of the guaranteed 100 days.*

MAHIPAL: The maximum number of days is 38 in some districts like Muktsar. In other districts workers get work for a lesser number of days. Nowhere in Punjab do workers get employment for 100 days in a year, at times they do not get wage for the work they do under MGNREGA. Punjab has not even passed a notification under the provision which states that if a worker does not get payment for work done by him within 15 days, he will get one-fourth extra payment. We are demanding 100 days of work under MGNREGA and we are also demanding its extension so that it includes urban workers as well. Each adult member of each family should be given work for the entire year with minimum wage per day as recommended by the ILO.

We also demand social security. I am sorry to say, social security does not mean only pension. Education, health facilities, shelter, sanitation, potable water—not the kind of polluted water that gives us cancer but drinkable water that saves lives, all of these constitute social security. Social security is the method to ensure that each person has equal access to the basic facilities which secure survival.

Even during the Corona wave, our people could not access medicines, even cheap ones, in the hospitals. There was no new recruitment of nurses and pharmacists. The Corona warriors who were recruited were kicked out as soon as the wave subsided a bit. They came here today and narrated their story. This is the level of insensitivity of the governments—of Modi, of Captain Amarinder. We have another issue with Captain. In order to win the 2017 election, he had made big promises to us. We will not let him sit in peace at least till 2022. After the 2022 election, no matter who comes to power, we will see him also.

WU: *First the farm laws were introduced and immediately thereafter the labour codes which are no less dangerous. However, the voices of opposition from the workers—both industrial and informal—trade unions, employees' federations etc. are not as forceful as that of the farmers. Similarly, it is not just the farmers who are committing suicide, agricultural workers* *are its victims too. So, why is it that farmers' issues get highlighted and farmers can unite to launch intense struggle but when it comes to workers, irrespective of whether they are agricultural workers or industrial workers or rural workers, their issues are not highlighted, not discussed among the intellectuals, not even spoken about.*

MAHIPAL: First of all, it is just as we see in case of patriarchy; there is a mindset moulded by *Manusmriti* and no one is free from it. The next thing to remember is that the deficit of consciousness and awareness that we have inherited through thousands of years cannot be regained in mere days. For the past 4,000 years, we [Dalits] have been pushed behind, education has been snatched from us. It was declared that we cannot go to school, we cannot listen to sermons, we cannot acquire the knowledge or learn the language of the sages. The most important thing is that no one will help us make up for this deficit. We, the rural and agricultural workers, the Dalits, have to do that ourselves. It has already started. The stronger our voice gets, the more firm will be the support we receive. No one had thought that *arhtiyas* (commission agents in agri-markets) would come in support of Punjab's farmers. But when the farmers began their struggle, it became so broad and grew so intense that even the *arhtiyas*, with whom the small and even middle farmers have a basic conflict of interest, came to their support. People will come in our support too, if we too can develop a united struggle.

More than 95 percent of the labour force is in the unorganised sector. They have no organisation. Nor are they themselves organised. Secondly, among the organised sector, one section is constituted of white-collar workers who are only concerned with their own salaries. The person who is drawing a salary of Rs 70,000 a month will not speak up for the contractual workers of their own department, even if that person is a union leader. Rural agricultural labourers like us also fall under the unorganised workers' category. So, the need of the time is a united *morcha* of rural workers and urban unorganised workers. The number of white-collar workers is declining anyway. There are so many departments where only one percent of workers are regular workers, while 99 percent of workers are unorganised.

We think that the agricultural workers are the link between peasants and urban workers. We participated in the farmers' movement as per our capability. We are not under any false impression that our demands are the same as theirs. How many of the top leaders at the farmers' protest are landless? It is not enough to just declare *"Mazdoor-Kisan Ekta."* How many of our representatives are there in their collective leadership body? How many women are there? This friend of mine [points to a person sitting beside him] went to the Delhi border on 26 December, he returned home after staying for 66 days at protest camps, stayed at home for only one day, and then went back again to the protests. He is currently here for our *morcha*. If he is told to go there again, he will immediately go. He does not own even one yard of land anywhere in India. This is our sincerity of support to the farmers' movement. But where is our representation in their leadership or our issues in their charter of demands? We want to ask them what our position is there. Just saying that they are fighting against the labour code is not enough. Even after eight months, we still do not have any *sanjha* (joint) committee of worker and farmer unions at the national level. These are things that need to be urgently addressed.

A militant struggle has been launched by ZPSC in Punjab to establish land-ownership rights of Dalit landless farmers. **Photos credit:** ZPSC.

SECTION III

CONVERSATIONS WITH LEADERS OF ZAMEEN PRAPTI SANGHARSH COMMITTEE

A Pan-India Movement for Land Redistribution Among Landless Peasantry is a Must
Gurmukh Singh, Zameen Prapti Sangharsh Committee

> Gurmukh Singh, 44, is one of the co-founders of the Zameen Prapti Sangharsh Committee (ZPSC) and is the Zonal Secretary from Sangrur. Hailing from a Dalit community, Gurmukh joined the Punjab Students Union (PSU) while studying MA in Economics. He dropped out of a PhD programme and became a fulltime political worker. Since 2014, Gurmukh has been a leading organiser of the militant struggles launched by ZPSC to establish land-ownership rights of Dalit landless farmers. In the course of the confrontation with administration and landed peasantry, Gurmukh has many criminal charges filed against him, including attempt to murder.
>
> Workers Unity had a long conversation with Gurmukh Singh on March 2022.

Workers Unity: *To begin with, tell us when and under what circumstances ZPSC was formed. What were its primary demands?*

Gurmukh Singh: One could say that ZPSC was formed, and our struggle began in 2014. Actually, the formation of ZPSC was not planned from above. It originated from the struggles based on the ground realities in the villages.

When the Green Revolution began in Punjab, due to the mechanisation of the farm processes, agricultural workers lost their jobs. They were of course free to leave their villages and work in the industries. But back then in Punjab, industries weren't developed enough to provide jobs to such a large number of people who were pushed out of agriculture. Those evicted from land settled for jobs in the non-farm sectors, in the *mandis* (agriculture produce markets) and the grain warehouses.

The fact remains that the Dalits, who in rural areas are mainly agricultural workers, live in precarious conditions. They occasionally get work—during sowing and harvesting of wheat, paddy and potato. More than 32 percent of the state's population is Dalit. But they have never owned any agricultural land in Punjab, nor have they had many job opportunities outside agriculture.

At that time, we were working amongst the Dalit agricultural workers on issues related to food security and irregularities in the supply of food items through ration shops. We had a comrade in Sekha village in Sangrur district, who was from a Dalit family. He brought to our attention a land dispute in his village. We visited his village and came to know about *nazool*[1] lands that should be given to Dalits as per the law. The struggle started with the objective of restoring the possession of that *nazool* land to the Dalits of that village. We organised them, captured the seven acres of *nazool* land in Sekha village from the upper-caste farmers who had been occupying it and introduced collective farming on it by the Dalit families. The villagers told us that the same issue existed not only in their village, but in a neighbouring village as well. We went there too. We realised that this was a far wider phenomenon. Even though the Dalits were legally entitled to have a share in *nazool* land, the actual possession of these lands had remained with the landlords and the rich farmers.

In Sekha village, after acquiring land the Dalit families began *sanjha kheti* (collective farming). The success in Sekha greatly enthused the landless Dalit peasants in different villages, and they approached us to help them get possession of land in their respective villages. We kept going from one village to another. Meanwhile, we also began to talk about the fact that apart from the *nazool* land, one-third of the common panchayati land in villages meant for Dalits was also in possession of upper-caste rich peasants and landlords. Dalits en masse had been denied possession of this land by the rich Jat farmers.

We decided to call a meeting of the villagers. But in Punjab nobody can simply go to a village and say openly, "This land belongs to the Dalits. It has been forcefully taken away by the upper castes and now we want it back." The Dalits were scared to even call a meeting in their own villages. They said, "We will attend the meeting if it is arranged in a different village." We got in touch with many villagers on an individual basis, and then called a meeting in a small *kasba* (hamlet). Dalit peasants from about 21 villages attended that meeting. We began to feel that the people had started gathering courage.

At this point, we decided to form an organisation. First, we felt that we should form a farmer organisation, because the Dalit agri-labourers were actually landless farmers and they wanted to organise themselves to own land which they are legally entitled to. But how the Dalit farmers perceive a farmer organisation is different from the others. They said they did not want to form a farmer organisation. We asked, "Why not?" They said, "The farmer organisations exploit and use us. They take us to their rallies, but do not address our issues...." But, they themselves were farmers working on others' lands, they were not workers per se. So forming a worker union did not make any sense either. Finally, it was decided that the organisation will be called Zameen Prapti Sangharsh Committee, since our main purpose was to acquire land. They liked the idea and in our next meeting people came from about 60 villages.

Then we had a conference in Badrukhan village in Sangrur district, where we discussed issues facing the landless Dalits and released our charter of demands. We raised the issues of *nazool* land, panchayati land, land for their housing and land to dispose of animal excreta. We also raised the issue of implementing the Punjab Land Ceiling Act, 1972.

This is how ZPSC was formed, and the first phase of our struggle was initiated. It was in 2014. At present, our organisation has around 10,000 members, and we are active in the Sangrur, Barnala, Patiala, Malerkotla and Mansa districts of Punjab.

WU: *How did the struggle spread from Sekha to other villages?*

GURMUKH SINGH: As I just said, our movement began with a struggle for the right to *nazool* land in Sekha village, and then we moved to the struggle for the panchayati land, one-third of which the Dalits can take on yearly lease under the Punjab Village Common Lands (Regulation) Act, 1961.[2] In the same year [2014], there was also another struggle in a village called Balad Kalan in Bhawanigarh *tehsil* (administrative unit) in Sangrur district. It emerged as the biggest centre for this struggle. This is owing to the fact that the village panchayat in Balad Kalan had a huge 375 acres of land and thereby the Dalit share also added up to a substantial 125 acres. When we visited the landless Dalit families there, they told us, "There is some panchayati land in our village, in which we have one-third share, and we are trying to get it for a long time. But, neither the village chief nor the administration has been allowing us to do so."

The Dalits of Balad Kalan organised themselves into a unit of ZPSC, and held protests and launched an agitation for their rights. We announced that we would not allow the upcoming auction to take place. In fact, they held an auction under police protection, and as always, kept the Dalits out of it. We went directly to the auction centre. They wouldn't let us enter. But we were also adamant. The police lathi-charged us and arrested about 40 of us, including women. The female comrades were released relatively soon after. But the rest of us were charged under several sections including IPC 307 (attempt to murder). We were offered bail, but we refused. We said, "Instead of eating at home, we are eating in jail, it doesn't make a difference to us! We won't appeal for bail."

We took a decision of not applying for bail, so that we can put pressure on the government to withdraw the false cases through agitations. There were protests for our release all over Punjab. An indefinite dharna was called by ZPSC with a clear demand that "our people must be released." The dharna went on for 51 days, at the end of which the police and the administration had to release all of us—the political workers and the villagers.

However, we did not let our struggle wane. After the release, we decided that we would take over the same land, even though a farce *boli* (auction) had already been conducted. Finally, as the protests broke out throughout the state and continued, the state administration and the panchayat agreed to surrender control of the land. The Dalit representatives of the local ZPSC committee bid for the entire 125 acres of land and got it at a price of Rs 24,000 an acre. That was our first significant victory through an uncompromising struggle. The Dalits of Balad Kalan have been doing *sanjha kheti* on that land since then. Their united struggle foiled the earlier practice of usurpation of the panchayati land by the rich Jat farmers.

Next year again, the *sarpanch* (village head) in collusion with the revenue and development officials tried to capture the land by putting up dummy Dalit candidates during the auction. We fought back. When we were denied entry into the auction hall, we blocked the highway outside it. The police brutally lathi-charged us and many of our people were arrested. We didn't give up, and forced them to call a fresh auction where we got the land at Rs 23,000 per acre.

Meanwhile, news of the struggle in Balad Kalan had spread through many districts, and it inspired other landless Dalits to rise in protest. In March 2015, we organised a Dalit *mahapanchayat* (massive gathering of Dalits) ahead of the auctions in May. It was attended by delegates from 80 villages of five districts. We acquired land that rightfully belonged to the landless Dalits in 15 villages, including Badoh, Jhaneri and Grachon. The villages where Dalit collectives under ZPSC were formed included Bijda, Namod, Kalara, Chandeli, Bavpur and others. In March 2016, a ZPSC convention was held in Grachon village, where we had won the lease of the reserved land. The convention was attended by over 400 Dalit delegates from over 100 villages.

WU: *We have heard that ZPSC also started the 'Boli Boycott Movement' as part of the struggle during this phase. Tell us about that.*

GURMUKH SINGH: You see, even an open *boli* is essentially a gathering of rich and powerful Jat farmers. They pick some random man from the landless Dalit community, bribe him with some money or alcohol, make him bid for the reserved land and acquire the land in his name. Also, the bid amount was raised so high by the rich Jat farmers that our Dalit collectives couldn't match them. Even though the Dalits needed to pay half of the market rent for such land, it was still a big sum for the Dalits, who were largely landless peasants. The only option then left was to take loans from private moneylenders at heavy interest. There was also no surety of being able to get the lease in the following year. In Balad Kalan, the size of the land was big, the Dalit peasants could produce surplus for selling in market as well and thereby pay the yearly lease amount; but in most villages, with the land on offer being very small, it was also uneconomical to pay the huge yearly lease amount.

Earlier that year, the administration had allowed lease of 30 acres of panchayati land in Jhaneri village for a *gaushala* (cow shelter) at the rate of Rs 7,000 an acre and that too, for a 30 year lease period. We said that land should also be leased to us on similar terms. The majority of Dalit families in Balad Kalan, and in other villages where ZPSC was active, decided to boycott the bidding process that year unless the administration was willing to lower the bid price.

We decided that we would not allow any more of such fraud *boli*s to take place. Direct action was the only way and we went and occupied the lands and staged a continuous dharna on them to ensure that no one else was able to take control of that land through fraudulent auctions. But police repression started immediately, and many of our comrades were arrested. Multiple criminal cases were slapped on our members, but finally there was a compromise. We forced them to lease the land to the Dalit collectives at concessional price. The yearly rent for panchayati land auctioned to the general category used to be 60,000 to 70,000 rupees per acre. But for the land that is reserved for us, we paid only Rs 20,000 per acre. This happened, thanks to the *boli* boycott movement.

WU: *The struggle faced intense repression from the rich dominant caste farmers and the police. We heard about the atrocities on Dalits at Jhaloor. An old Dalit woman was even hacked to death. In Punjab militant protests by farmer unions are a regular affair, so why do groups like ZPSC face such state repression and violence?*

GURMUKH SINGH: Farmer unions in Punjab regularly organise protests, gheraos and roadblocks. But we had to face repression from day one. It is because we have raised the question of land for the Dalits. People think that Punjab is a developed state; they assume that there are no caste atrocities in Punjabi society. But it is simply a matter of lifting the curtain. A superficial glance might make one feel that there is no real caste hierarchy and all Punjabis are brethren. However, the simplest way to expose the ground reality is to raise the issue of land for the landless peasants. When Dalits raised the issue of land, the real oppressive and casteist face of the dominant caste farmers and the state came to the surface.

Actually after a point, the state administration began to feel that this movement was spreading in Punjab, and the Jat farmers in particular were alerted about the possible rise of the landless Dalits in their own villages. They joined forces with the ruling-class politicians, police and local administration to crush this struggle.

I told you about police repression on us at Balad Kalan. In Bhadohi, where the Dalits acquired 22.5 acres of land, the story of police and Jat farmers' brutality was the same as at Balad Kalan. At Jhaner, too, we were attacked by the goons of the *jagirdars* (landlords). A series of FIRs were slapped and arbitrary arrests were made in several villages to break the struggle. By 2016, Dalits in about 44 villages had launched protests to obtain their share of panchayati land. We were successful in most cases.

We faced the stiffest challenge by the landlords at Jhaloor village in Sangrur. That was where our movement faced the most intense repression. The landed upper-caste farmers hired goons and attacked us. There, the issue was the Dalits' claim over six acres of cultivable land that was fraudulently auctioned off to a 'dummy' Dalit person who bid on behalf of the local *jagirdar*—Gurdeep Babban. We protested and occupied that land. The police forcefully evicted us. The Dalit villagers uprooted the rice seedlings, and later also destroyed the unripe paddy on that land.

ZPSC organised a rally outside the office of the SDM in Lehra, a town near Jhaloor, demanding that the land be handed over to the Dalits in the village. On 5 October 2016, when the protesters including those from other villages returned to Jhaloor from Lehra, Jat men, armed with stones, bricks, scythes and iron rods, along with hired goons, attacked the protesters. As we had prior information of the attack, we were prepared. So we resisted, but were outnumbered.

They broke open the doors and windows, entered Dalit homes and beat up whoever they could lay their hands on. The Dalit women were abused, groped, molested and thrashed. Our village president's home was attacked. They tried to set it on fire. However, as we already had prior information, we had managed to shift him to another safe house. But his 72-year-old mother, Gurdev Kaur, was in the house. The Jat attackers chopped off her leg. She suffered severe injuries and died soon after in the hospital. The police arrived hours later. Our people were attacked by the Jats and goons, yet we were slapped with various charges by the police. The police took 50 to 60 Dalit men into custody.

When Gurdev Kaur died, her family members decided they would not allow a post-mortem, until the Jats who killed her were arrested. Dalit villagers, along with the ZPSC, held daily protests outside the district collector's office. Students, writers, intellectuals, and ordinary citizens joined the protests. The body of Gurdev Kaur was cremated with full honour. Thousands attended her funeral procession. Our protest compelled the administration to announce compensation, they asked us to vacate the land and accept compensation for the victim. But we refused. Instead we demanded that the 32 Jat men named in connection with the murder come to the Dalit *mohalla* (neighbourhood) and apologise. They didn't, and the court case in the matter is still going on.

A number of farmer unions like Kirti Kisan Union, BKU (Ekta-Ugrahan) and BKU (Ekta-Dakaunda), along with many Left-affiliated unions stood with us. But those aligned with the CPI and CPI(M) stayed away, saying that we were disturbing peace in the area. The right-wing farmer unions openly sided with the Jats.

WU: *Why did you then support the farmers' movement given these ground realities? It was a movement led by the landed Jat farmers who regularly commit such atrocities on the Dalit labourers.*

GURMUKH SINGH: It is a mistake to think of the farmers' movement as that of landed farmers only. The three farm laws would have impacted the entire peasantry, including the landless rural working class. This is the reason landless farmers, agricultural and rural worker unions also supported the movement at Delhi borders and actively engaged in the struggle against the three laws.

It was clear to us that if the laws were implemented, the PDS (Public Distribution System) would have been the first casualty in Punjab. The state government-run *mandis* (agricultural produce markets) would have been gradually dismantled. As I said earlier, during the Green Revolution, the agricultural workers lost their work, as machinery replaced human labour. Many took jobs in the *mandis*. Earlier, it was mostly the migrant workers from Bihar and UP who used to work in Punjab's *mandis* during specific seasons [season of harvesting paddy and wheat].

But gradually the Dalits from Punjab began to work there as well. So, closing down of the *mandis* would have meant thousands of Dalit labourers losing their jobs. Besides the *mandis*, agricultural workers evicted from land found jobs in the grain warehouses run by government agencies, like FCI (Food Corporation of India). Such workers are called *palledars*. There are lakhs of *palledars* in Punjab, and they are primarily Dalit. They would have lost their jobs as well if the farm laws were implemented. At present, in Punjab, every Dalit household and backward caste family, who hold a BPL (below poverty line) card get 200 units of electricity free. The Electricity Amendment Bill would have taken away this subsidy. The proposed amendments in the Essential Commodities Act would have made the prices of food to be dictated solely by market forces. The government was to interfere only if the prices were increased by 100 percent in case of perishable food or 50 percent in other items. Food inflation hurts the working class the most. It means that we will have unemployment and higher prices for food at the same time. So these laws were a direct attack on the landless farmers as well, and hence the repeal of the laws was also our demand, and ZPSC supported the farmers' movement from its inception to its eventual victory.

WU: *You have said in many discussions and interviews that while the Dalit organisations in Punjab supported the farmers' movement, the ordinary Dalits didn't. What were the objective reasons that the Dalit agricultural workers didn't identify themselves with the farmers' movement?*

GURMUKH SINGH: Yes, nearly all the Dalit organisations in Punjab opposed the new farm laws and supported the farmers' movement at Delhi borders. But the ordinary Punjabi Dalit did not support this movement at a mass level. Both have their own reasons for this.

The farmers' movement was primarily against the RSS-BJP. The RSS-BJP want to bring back the *Manuvadi*[3] system of governance in our country. Our political priority is to defeat these reactionary fascist forces at any cost. They work far more viciously against the Dalits than the Jat farmers. Those who are aware of this larger political situation, including the various Dalit organisations in Punjab, opposed the laws and campaigned against Modi and RSS as much as they could. The RSS and BJP tried to instigate the Dalit workers by playing on the contradictions between them and the Jat farmers, but they were not successful.

One slogan was floated around in villages during the first phase of the movement: *Daliton ko zameen sirf Modi de sakta hain, aur koi nahi de sakta!* (The only person who can give land to the Dalits is Modi, no one else can give land!) As if Narendra Modi was going to take away land from the upper-caste farmers and hand them over to the Dalits! Obviously, this was spread by the RSS and BJP. But all the Dalit and revolutionary organisations which fight for the landless peasantry know these age-old propaganda tricks of the far-Right groups. No one was going to pay any attention to them in Punjab at that point.

We tried to organise agricultural workers and take them to the *Delhi Morcha* (farmers' agitation front at Delhi borders), more so after the incidents there on January 26. We organised rallies, street plays and meetings in villages to mobilise Dalit agricultural workers to join the struggle at the borders. It is true we didn't receive the support we had anticipated.

There was also an immediate reason for this. Just months before the farmers' agitation began there was a lockdown in the entire country including Punjab on account of the Covid pandemic. It was the sowing season for paddy in Punjab. There was a scarcity of migrant labourers from Bihar and Uttar Pradesh who normally come to work in the fields during the sowing season. Due to the lockdown, they could not reach Punjab and those who were already there had left for their homes. The local agricultural workers' wage is always higher than that of the migrants, who often work on subsistence wage. But the Jat farmers were not ready to pay higher wages to the local Dalit labourers. They too stood their ground and refused to work. The Jat farmers held meetings amongst themselves and announced through the village gurudwara that Dalit labourers demanding higher wages than the fixed rate would be socially boycotted.[4]

The social boycott of Dalits by the Jat farmers was implemented in several villages. The Dalits in rural Punjab were angry at these developments. Such incidents sharpened their antagonism with the Jat farmers, and so, when the farmers' movement began, the participation of the landless peasants and agricultural workers was naturally far less. Many Dalits said, "Why should we back the farmers? Let them keep our demands at the centre of their movement." But we pointed out, "How can we say that? How can we say that we will support it only when our demands are included?" We argued with them, "Suppose railway workers are engaged in a struggle. Can we tell them that we will support you only if you include the demands of the agricultural workers in your agenda?"

There were also practical problems. The agricultural workers don't own tractors and trolleys. Hence unlike the land-owning farmers, they can't travel to the borders. Tickets are expensive. Most of the agricultural workers are daily-wage earners. They can't afford to stay at the protest sites for long periods.

During the movement, we spoke to the farmer unions about these issues and developments. But not all the 32 organisations within the Samyukta Kisan Morcha (SKM) are the same. There are revolutionary organisations with a strong commitment to annihilation of caste, but there are also rich farmer unions dominated by Jats as well. We feel the SKM should have taken the agricultural workers and landless farmers along with it in this movement. They should have addressed the issues of the Dalits labourers and the lack of their representation in the movement. Only then might the Dalits have felt that this movement is theirs too.

But in spite of all these antagonisms, and regressive views that many farmer unions hold towards the issue of land ownership by the Dalits and caste atrocities, ZPSC didn't stand aloof from this movement. We joined in large numbers and stayed at the protest sites on the borders. Various Ambedkarite groups in Punjab also went to Delhi. Even the BSP in Punjab announced that they were against the RSS-BJP and supported the movement.

WU: *Coming back to the ZPSC's struggle in Punjab, undoubtedly landless Dalits constitute the most oppressed section in the rural society. The bulk of the peasantry in Punjab are the small farmers owning less than five acres of land. They live in precarious conditions. They were also the primary pillars of the farmers' movement. What are the impediments to forging an alliance between the landless peasants and small farmers in Punjab? Or does ZPSC see itself as an organisation exclusively for the landless Dalits?*

GURMUKH SINGH: The roots of our organisation are in the villages of Punjab. Our cadres and support base are amongst the landless peasants. Historically, landless peasants in Punjab have been Dalits. But there is also a misconception about us. It is not that ZPSC is exclusively for the Dalits or the landless farmers. In our understanding, all farmers are not the same. There are *jagirdars* (landlords) and *dhani* kisans (rich farmers); then there are the middle farmers; finally there are small farmers and the landless farmers or agricultural workers. Let us consider the case of panchayati land. We demand that one-third of the common land must be leased to the landless Dalits. But at the same time, we also say that the remaining two-third of that land should be given to the small and marginal farmers, because that part of the land has also been captured by the big farmers and landlords.

Recently we took up the issue of loans given to the landless peasants by microfinance companies which have pushed them into huge debts. Just like the small farmers, the Dalit agricultural workers are also under huge debt. Incidence of suicide amongst agricultural workers in Punjab,[5] because of debt traps, is no less than what it is amongst the landed farmers. Since Dalits don't own land, they are denied loans by the banks. They are not made members of the village cooperatives which give loans on low interests. Hence they have no option but to depend on private microfinance companies for taking loans at exorbitant rates of interest. This issue snowballed into a huge controversy during the lockdown. With no work available and zero income, the Dalit agricultural workers were not able to pay installments of earlier loans. They also incurred a lot of extra debt in those days. A lot of small farmers' families were also affected. We launched a struggle against these loan companies. We prevented them from entering the villages and organised protests demanding that the government announce loan waivers for landless peasants also. In this struggle, a section of the small and marginal farmers, especially the women from their families, joined our struggle. A few even became members of ZPSC.

Our struggle is for both the landless and small farmers, and we want an alliance of these two classes in rural Punjab. It is predominantly the caste factor which prevents small farmers who are Jat from joining us. But our relationship with small farmers is slowly improving.

WU: *What have been the role of the students and other progressive Left and democratic forces in terms of extending solidarity and support to your struggle?*

GURMUKH SINGH: Students and youths from the villages help us regularly. At various places, they have organised strikes and burnt effigies in protest demonstrations in our support. They participate in our rallies and dharnas too. They also invite us to their universities, so that we can take our views to the larger student community. In fact, many of the leaders of ZPSC come from a background in student politics. We get regular support from them.

We try to maintain good relationships with Left and democratic forces, including human rights organisations. But, the problem is that nobody is ready to raise the issue of land for Dalits in Punjab. Many, if not all of them, are of the opinion that capitalism has arrived in India, or at least in Punjab, and hence the land-question is no more that important. But this is a completely wrong understanding of the ground situation in Punjab. The land-question is still of central importance here. In Punjab, Dalits, who are only 32 percent of the population, own only 3.5 percent of private agricultural land. In fact, only about 20 percent of Punjab's population own any agricultural land. And, they are mostly Jats. So, the issue of land redistribution is extremely relevant in Punjab even today.

WU: *You talked about 'sanjha kheti.' Your organisation has experimented with cooperative farming. Now, many people are saying that the road ahead in agriculture has to be through such collective farming efforts. Can you tell us about your experience with cooperative farming?*

GURMUKH SINGH: In the villages where we have been able to claim ownership of the panchayati land, the Dalits work on it collectively in small groups. Sometimes, even the entire village community works on the land together. This is the only way forward, as farming individually on small pieces of land is not profitable. For example, the green fodder for buffaloes is distributed equally to everyone. Commercial crops like wheat or *dhan* (paddy) are also farmed collectively.

We form village-level committees. These committees have elections and they hold meetings every six months to discuss all debits and credits. The committees that fail to do this are dismantled. The Dalit community in the village collects money beforehand for paying the auction prices. Then we all decide together whether to farm individually or collectively. Many do it collectively, especially in small lands, where you cannot use tractors. In Balad Kalan, since the land was large, we also collectively bought a tractor.

Initially, in most villages, we tried to make people farm together. But soon people had disagreements and the village-level cooperatives broke up. So, we told them to divide up the land. In other villages, where the people are in agreement with us, we told them to do cooperative farming. Neither of these two solutions worked.

The best formula is to go neither totally individual nor totally collective. For example in Balad Kalan, where this initiative began, two people decided to leave us because we wanted to build one large group. When we let the people decide the way they wanted to cultivate the land acquired, it worked out well. People formed their own small groups. We told them that it was fine to form their own groups if they did not get along with others. So there is just one committee, but there are different groups under it and they farm together. All costs are shared equally amongst everyone involved. In a sense, this is still cooperative farming. It is just that it is not done at the level of the entire village, but cooperatives of smaller sub-groups. This approach has been the most successful. In almost every village, this is the method by which cooperative farming is now being carried out.

At the ground level we are promoting cooperatives. But the state suppresses such initiatives from above. It is important to remember that this model is only sustainable when the peasantry is in control of the agrarian policies. The state only promotes the capitalist model of cultivation favourable to landlordism and big farmers.

Also, in a village, there are many groups supporting the Akali, the Congress, the Aam Aadmi party and other political parties. These different groups exist amongst the Dalits as well. So, they often try to break these cooperatives. In Gharachon, the entire village had in fact run away from us. They thought that now that they had obtained land, they had no need for ZPSC anymore. The panchayat there told the people that if they wanted land at low rates, they would give it to them. They scared them by saying that we would force people to become members of ZPSC, make them join other protests and it could lead to having FIRs lodged against them. The people listened to the panchayat and left us. Our unity broke. But we had confidence in ourselves. The panchayat leaders divided the people and subsequently captured the land all over again. So all the people of the village once again came to us. We told them to accept the mistake they made and not repeat it. We had to fight all over again, but eventually they won back their land.

Actually, most of these people do not join us out of a political ideology. This is still not a political movement. This is, first and foremost, a struggle based on the issue of livelihood and dignity of the Dalit agricultural labourers. So, they join our struggle for land, but ideologically most of them are still not with us. For them to join us ideologically as well, other strategies have to be devised. We are still working on that.

WU: *All over India, Dalits work primarily as labourers—be it in the farms, or under MGNREGA in the villages, or as informal workers in the construction sector or other industries in towns and cities. Why didn't you think of forming an agricultural worker union? And could you also talk about the relationship between ZPSC and other agricultural worker organisations in Punjab?*

GURMUKH SINGH: Agricultural worker organisations take up issues pertaining to agricultural workers' wage, PDS, pensions, etc. While we work with Dalit landless farmers in their struggle to acquire land which is rightfully theirs, we hold that the landless farmers are not agricultural workers and we do not want to dissolve their identity into that of agricultural workers. That will not bring about their emancipation in any form. Hence, ZPSC wants to work as an organisation of landless peasantry. It is an organisation belonging to the Dalit landless farmers. The land-owning farmer unions in Punjab today do not have Dalit members. Even Dalits who have some land cannot be a part of such unions. As for the landless, they are not even considered farmers in Punjab. In other states, there are farmers who own land and who don't. But here in Punjab, there is only one kind of farmer—those who own land.

There are some rural worker unions who focus on the PDS issue, the MGNREGA issue and other issues pertaining to rural workers including agricultural workers. But our primary issue is land ownership. We want to take our movement forward based on this basic demand.

We have some targets now. The *niji zameen* (private land) in possession of the rich upper-caste farmers do not follow the Land Ceiling Act limits. The rich and the influential own a large amount of land—100 to 200 acres in many cases. The amount of land that the Captains or the Badals possess on paper alone is more than 5,000 acres each. The onset of capitalism has not eradicated the principal contradiction in Punjab's agriculture sector. The demand for redistribution of land is still a core issue.

WU: *In September 2021, seven agricultural and rural worker organisations in Punjab had formed a* sanjha morcha *(joint front) to press for their charter of demands. Why didn't ZPSC become a part of that united front?*

GURMUKH SINGH: A meeting of those organisations was held in Moga [in Punjab]. We were also invited and we did go there. A lot of issues were discussed in that meeting. But they did not agree to make the demand of land-ownership for the Dalit labourers one of the main demands of the *morcha*.

The second reason is, in the case of panchayati land, instead of annual auctions, we are demanding 33 years of lease—the way companies are given land on long-term lease. When we placed this demand during the discussion, some of the unions said that they did not agree with us. If the worker organisations oppose Dalits getting land on long-term lease, how can we join their *morcha*? A lot of their demands are about getting government concessions, such as getting *atta* (flour), *dal* (lentil) and other items through PDS, more days of work under MGNREGA, etc. These are reformist demands which are used by the state as part of their carrot and stick policy towards protesting masses. Even then, since we believe in a joint struggle, we have been supporting them from outside; we have also been to their protest programs because they are our comrades. If these unions agree that the right to land is one of the primary demands of the landless peasants and include it in their charter, then we will certainly join the *sanjha morcha*.

WU: *Do you think that the land struggles for Dalit labourers should only be limited to what they are legally entitled to get on rent in auctions? What about extending the struggle beyond legal boundaries, like forceful occupation of land in excess of the prescribed ceiling?*

GURMUKH SINGH: We describe the current phase of our movement as *militant mass struggle*. At present, we are fighting to ensure the rights given under the laws and guaranteed by the Constitution to the Dalits. There is a need to extend the struggle beyond the legal rights. In the case of panchayati lands, we are demanding that the land be leased for 33 years on a cooperative basis, instead of the annual auction system. Now we are raising the issue of the Land Ceiling Act. Our demand is that the land above the ceiling should be identified and distributed amongst the landless. We also demand a reduction of the land ceiling in Punjab. The reason being, when the land ceiling was fixed at 17.5 acres, the productivity of land was less than what it is now. But now a farmer with 10 acres of land can sustain his life comfortably. Hence, we are demanding that the ceiling should be brought down to 10 acres.

However the Land Ceiling Act has a lot of loopholes. Sometime back we published a list of names of people having more than 100 acres of land in and around the Sangrur area. Some have fruit gardens or farms with different kinds of trees in these lands. Some said that they had animal farms. People have figured out different methods to keep their land far beyond the ceiling.

Also, even if excess land is distributed, the law has a lot of defects. The Act says, land should be distributed to the landless—but the tenant farmers are also counted amongst the landless. So, under the Act, surplus land will be given to the tenant farmers. But then where will the labourer go? Because of this confusion, we don't raise the slogan *land to the tillers*; we demand redistribution of land amongst the landless agricultural workers, small and marginal farmers.

In Punjab, when the Act was made and land reforms were introduced, the Jats were the tillers. While they got the land, the Dalit labourers remained landless. The Jats are 27 percent of the population and Dalits are 32 percent, yet Dalits do not have any land whereas Jats own most of the cultivable land. So even on this issue, we have a lot of obstacles to tackle.

WU: *When the news of the Modi government taking back the three farm laws was announced, what was ZPSC's primary reaction? Was SKM right in suspending the agitation? How has this movement inspired your struggle and your organisation?*

GURMUKH SINGH: When the three laws were withdrawn by Modi, we felt happy. It was a great victory for the historic movement. Now, as to whether they should have ended the protest or not, it was their decision. Whatever they decided, I think it was alright, as it was decided collectively. Some people thought that the *morcha* at the borders should have continued till the MSP (Minimum Support Price) demand was met. They accuse SKM of abandoning the MSP struggle. I think it is not true that SKM does not want to fight for MSP. There are serious logistical and practical issues in any protest movement, especially for a movement that had already extended for over a year.

The impact of the farmers' movement and its victory is deep in Punjab. Now, when we go to the villages, a lot of people talk to us, thanks to this movement. We tell them, "See how strong the farmer organisations are; they held a *morcha* (demonstration) in Delhi for so long, and you don't even come to the meetings!" Now there is a feeling that if we come together, and organise our struggles, we too can succeed. People now have increased faith in the mass struggle to achieve their demands.

WU: *Now that it is election time in Punjab, what position is ZPSC taking during the assembly elections?*

GURMUKH SINGH: ZPSC does not support anyone in these elections. We do not support any candidate or any of these political parties including AAP. Nobody has raised the landless peasants' or rural workers' demands in their campaigns. How can we support them? We have told everyone not to vote in the upcoming assembly election. If some people insist on going, we urge them to vote for NOTA (None of the Above).

We are campaigning among the Dalits, encouraging them to concentrate on the struggle.

WU: *What are the recent struggles that ZPSC has led or engaged with after the victory of the farmers' movement?*

GURMUKH SINGH: We have been engaged in various struggles over the past few months. One of them is in a village called Fatehgarh. The central issue there is about 300 acres of panchayati land. Dalits wanted to build a *dharamshala* (hospice) on this land. The upper-castes in the village—especially those belonging to the Bharatiya Kisan Union (Sidhupur)—organised themselves and said that they would not let Dalits build a *dharamshala*. Usually when a *dharamshala* is built in a village, nobody really objects. But the Jat farmers thought that the demand was an excuse for ZPSC to capture the 300 acres of panchayati land in the village. They feared that the Dalits in the name of building a *dharamshala* would organise themselves and acquire the panchayati land that the Jat farmers belonging to BKU (Sidhupur) had in their possession. We are continuing our protests in Fatehgarh.

We have another ongoing struggle in the village of Shadi Hari on the issue of *nazool* land. It is an obstacle that we always face. It concerns membership of Dalits in the village cooperative society. The rich farmers do not want Dalits to become members of these societies. In Shadi Hari, Dalits raised this issue and we organised protests. In many villages, where we have an organisation, we forced them [rich farmers] to make Dalits members of the cooperative societies. But there are still many villages left. The farmers get loans through cooperatives paying merely a 4 percent interest, whereas Dalits have to pay 14 percent interest.

WU: *The farmers' movement won and the three laws were withdrawn. Do you see any significant change in the attitude of the farmer unions within the SKM towards the agricultural workers on the ground?*

GURMUKH SINGH: The SKM is not an organisation based on one ideology. It is a platform of all kinds of people and unions. All the farmer unions within the SKM should be looked at separately. There are quite a few unions who clearly talk about worker-farmer unity and also stand with the agricultural workers. But there are other unions within the SKM that are opposed to the workers' demands. We cannot put all of them in the same bracket. These unions represent different sections of the farmers.

Whenever we faced repression from the landlords or the police, unions like Kirti Kisan Union (KKU), BKU (Ekta-Ugrahan) and BKU (Dakaunda) stood with us in solidarity. In the Jhaloor incident that I was speaking about earlier, BKU (Ekta-Ugrahan) went beyond symbolic solidarity and actually turned up in significant numbers at our protests. But what happened as a result is that their unit in that village soon got disbanded. The Jat farmers drifted to right-wing unions.

On the other hand, there are unions like BKU (Sidhupur) who hold dharnas and go on strikes to oppose us. Recently, as I mentioned earlier, BKU (Sidhupur) organised themselves and said that they would not let Dalits build a *dharamshala* in a village. Such attitudes can't be changed suddenly.

During the farmers' movement at Delhi borders, all these unions were jointly participating in the struggle to repeal the three laws against a common enemy. We supported their struggle. But, our relationship with a platform like SKM, a coalition which includes unions like BKU (Sidhupur) and many other such unions of rich farmers, will depend upon what demands SKM raises in the future. Their demands will determine how much we can work with them.

WU: *The SKM is indeed a front of many unions representing interests of different sections of farmers. But, as we have discussed, there is no representation of agricultural workers or landless peasants' organisations in SKM. Do you see any such possibility in the future? Has there been any progress towards this end in the last one year?*

Gurmukh Singh: In my opinion, it seems very unlikely that SKM will include agricultural worker unions or a formation like ZPSC even in the next phase of their movement to ensure legal guarantee of MSP for all crops. I think if SKM leadership pushes for such a decision it will split. There cannot be any progress on this issue. Organisations like ZPSC cannot exist within platforms like SKM.

Even during the farmers' movement, before the incidents of 26 January [2021] leaders of agricultural worker unions were not allotted time to speak on the protest stages at the borders. Even when I myself spoke, I spoke during the time allotted to KKU, a revolutionary left peasants' union. I was not allowed to mention the name of ZPSC during my speech. Some farmer unions within the SKM had proposed that they should call agricultural worker unions, discuss their issues and include them in the struggle. At that time, BKU (Sidhupur) and some other rich farmer unions opposed the proposal saying *"Jat ki marge!,"* meaning, "Are the Jats dead!"

After the violence on Republic Day, when the state repression peaked and the movement was in danger, and people were leaving the protest sites in fear, only then they said that everybody including Dalit labourers could come and support them. It was only after the events on 26 January that put the farmer unions in the backseat that some of them started raising the slogan of *kisan-mazdoor ekta* (farmer-worker unity). They even celebrated Babasaheb's (B.R. Ambedkar) and Gurdasji's (Sant Ravidas) birth anniversary at the protest sites. Suddenly, they remembered the Dalit icons and heroes!

WU: *Last question. What are ZPSC's future plans?*

GURMUKH SINGH: Apart from expanding our struggle in Punjab, we think a united platform needs to be formed on an all-India basis, where landless farmers and Dalit organisations which are ready to struggle for the demand of land can come together. We had tried in the past, but so far, we have not succeeded. For example, we went to Gujarat during the Una Movement,[6] where Jignesh Mevani coined and raised the famous slogan—"You catch the cow's tail, just give us our land." We went there hoping that the movement would seriously take up the land issue of Dalits. We stayed there and interacted with Jignesh. But we felt he had become more interested in being an MLA. The slogan was merely an election gimmick. Then there are many NGOs that work amongst the Dalits. But they work mostly for their own profit. Even Chandrasekhar Azad of Bhim Army[7] has drifted towards electoral politics.

If a movement raises the demand of land for the landless Dalits, we would support it wholeheartedly. If through this interview, our words reach out to comrades in other states who are thinking along these lines, we would like to join forces with them without any hesitation. A pan-India movement for land redistribution amongst landless Dalit peasantry is a must.

Endnotes

1. The Nazool Lands (Transfer) Rules, 1956, Punjab, define "Nazool" lands as "land situated beyond two miles of the Municipal limits, which has escheated to the State Government and has not already been appropriated by the State Government for any purpose"; or it is "such other land as the State Government may make available for being transferred under these rules" (Govt. of Punjab, 1956).

2. The Punjab Village Common Lands Regulation Act, 1961 has a provision that out of the total cultivable land available with the village panchayat and which is proposed to be leased, "thirty percent, ten percent and ten percent, respectively shall be reserved for giving on lease by auction, to members of the Scheduled Caste; Backward Classes; and dependants of defence personnel killed in any war after the independence of India" (Government of Punjab, 1961).

3. The term *Manuvad* denotes the ethos of a society governed by *Manusmriti* or Laws of Manu, believed to be the first ancient legal text amongst the *Dharmasastras* of Hinduism. Dr B.R. Ambedkar held *Manusmriti* as responsible for the caste system in India and, in protest, he burnt the text publicly on 25 December 1927.

4. Based on a door-to-door survey of 2,400 villages in six districts of Punjab, a study revealed that 7,303 agricultural labourers died by suicide in the state of Punjab during 2000-18. Out of these suicide cases, around 79 percent happened because of the heavy debt burden on the labourer families, while the remaining 21 percent suicides occurred due to other socio-economic factors. 83 percent of suicide victims belonged to SC category and 8.76 percent belonged to the backward castes (BC). For further details see interview with Dr Sukhpal Singh, p-367-388 in this volume.

5. Panchayats in several districts of Punjab passed resolutions fixing wages for agricultural workers for the paddy-sowing season in June 2020, as the demand for local labourers had increased in the wake of the scarcity of migrant workers due to the nationwide lockdown because of the pandemic. The local labourers, who are predominantly Dalits, were threatened with social boycott and fines ranging between Rs 5,000 and Rs 25,000 if they refused to work at the fixed wage rate. As per the resolutions passed by the panchayats, agricultural workers would be paid anywhere between Rs 2,500 and Rs 3,200 for sowing rice on one acre of land. On the other hand, labourers were demanding Rs 4,000 to Rs 4,500 per acre.

6. In July 2016, seven members of a Dalit family were assaulted by a group of cow-pro-

tection vigilantes for skinning a dead cow in Una in Gujarat. Thousands of Dalits in Gujarat started a 10-day march from Ahmedabad to Una to protest against atrocities on the Dalit communities in the state. The foot-march, named Aazadi Kooch (Freedom march), ended on August 15 in Una, where thousands of Dalits had converged to observe 'independence.' This assertion of Dalits following the Una incident has often been referred to as Una Movement.

7. The Bhim Army is a Dalit organisation named after B.R. Ambedkar. It was founded in 2015. Chandra Shekhar Aazad is its most well-known leader. The organisation is based in Saharanpur district of Uttar Pradesh. It runs free coaching classes for Dalit and Bahujan students. In March 2020, Bhim Army entered electoral politics and Chandra Shekhar officially announced his new political party named Azad Samaj Party.

In the Villages where the Struggle is Strong, the Hold of Patriarchy is Slowly Breaking
Paramjit Kaur Longowal, Zameen Prapti Sangharsh Committee

> Paramjit Kaur Longowal is the Zonal Secretary of the Zameen Prapti Sangharsh Committee (ZPSC). She is one of the founding members of ZPSC and an organiser of the struggle for Dalit ownership of agricultural land in the villages of Punjab since 2014. Paramjit Kaur's work also focuses on various issues faced by Dalit women agricultural workers and organising them in the struggle for land rights.
>
> This interview is a consolidated outcome of many conversations Workers Unity and GroundXero had with Paramjit Kaur during the one and a half years of the farmers' movement, including one long interview on 13 August 2021 at Patiala.

Workers Unity: *You have been one of the leaders of the Zameen Prapti Sangharsh Committee (ZPSC) almost since its inception. When and how did you join the ZPSC?*

Paramjit Kaur: After completing MA and my marriage, I joined the ZPSC in 2014. Since then, I have been working for it. While in college, I got in touch with Punjab Students Union (PSU), a revolutionary left student organisation. In 2014, when we formed this organisation of Dalit agricultural workers, we based it on the issue of ownership of agricultural land by the Dalits. Today, I'm the Zonal Secretary of ZPSC.

WU: *Like many others, you too joined the ZPSC after being engaged in student politics. How and why did you join the PSU and later on the ZPSC?*

Paramjit Kaur: I am from Patiala district. I was married here in Sangrur in the Longowal family. I did my graduation in Patiala. I was born in a Dalit family and my father was a daily-wage labourer. My problem in those days was that I had to travel by bus from home to college, and

I did not have the bus fare. I came to know that a student bus pass was available, but the private buses refused to accept that pass. I used to fight daily with the bus conductor. It was around this time that I came to know about PSU. At that time, PSU was organising students over the issue of college tuition fees and bus fares. So, I became a member. I thought this cannot be only my issue. There must be other girls who faced the same problem. During those days, government buses didn't go to our village, only private buses operated there.

We thought of organising a strike over this. I convinced the other girls that we should organise and fight. We bought the bus pass at a concession, but the government buses did not go to our village, so what was the point? I would urge other students not to pay the bus fare, I would fight with them regularly, arguing that it is because of the fact that they pay, it has become normal. I myself never paid, and always fought with the conductors and drivers. I actually didn't have the money, how could I have paid even if I wanted to?

We put up a fight on this issue. We were able to negotiate half-ticket fare for our trips to college. I emerged as a leader within this movement. Then, I completed my graduation and got admission in an MA course at Govt. Ripudaman College at Nabha. My organisation (PSU) supported me. We rented a room in Patiala. I shared the room with three to four other girls. We were able to use the bus pass now, as there was a government bus available there. But then, there was the issue of tuition fees. Once, our scholarship money had not come through, but we were asked to pay the tuition fee anyway. I organised a protest. We refused to pay the fee. We won that fight. This is how my MA was also completed.

Then I got married and I came here [Sangrur]. In our area near Jalandhar, Pendu Mazdoor Union (a Left rural worker union) had some organisation. I tried to form a branch of Pendu Mazdoor Union, but we were not successful. At that time, a front on the issue of land for the Dalits was formed. Mukesh, Gurmukh and others, my comrades from youth and student movement days, were already working in that front. They suggested that since there were no women members in the ZPSC committee, I should join it. I agreed, and from 2014, I have been a part of the ZPSC. It has been about eight years now that I have been working with ZPSC. I have realised that our material and social conditions have nothing to do with God writing our fate; it is the system and policies which do not allow equality to be achieved in society.

WU: *How different was your experience while working with Dalit labourers over the issue of land from that of organising the students? What were the initial struggles that ZPSC launched?*

PARAMJIT KAUR: I had a very different and enriching experience after joining this front. I used to work in the students' front on the issue of tuition fees, bus fares, etc. After college, we used to go to meet students and their parents in the villages, in order to organise Dalit students who studied in government colleges. We were organising on the issue of securing a concessional bus pass, and other issues of relevance to the students, such as tuition fees. These issues affected us the most. But, we did not get a very positive response from them. We would spend so much time just trying to convince them. At times, we felt they just didn't want to fight for their rights.

But, after joining ZPSC, when we started raising the issue of land—the legal right of the Dalits to own village common land—there was a wave of enthusiastic responses. The same Dalit villagers reacted spontaneously. We did not have to do a lot to convince them. They started connecting with us on their own, particularly the Dalit women.

There are different kinds of *shamlat* land[1] in Punjab. *Shamlat* land is owned by the village panchayat. There is panchayati land, of which the Scheduled Castes (SCs) have a 33 percent quota. Then there is *nazool* land. The SCs can access *nazool* land by forming a society and doing collective farming. We raised the question regarding the share of the SC or Dalit community in all these types of land.

In Barnala [erstwhile Sangrur] district, there is a village called Sekha, where there was an ongoing dispute over land. The *nazool* land in the village was taken from its legitimate owners [Dalits], and illegally occupied by upper-caste people. So, we went there and were able to get the land back to its Dalit owners, and they still use that land for farming. When this news spread through campaigns, people came to know about us. They heard that an organisation called Zameen Prapti Sangharsh Committee had been formed and that they were fighting to gain back the ownership of the illegally occupied land belonging to the Dalits.

People from a village called Balad Kalan near Bhawanigarh contacted us; their issue was related to panchayati land. They had filed a legal complaint to get one-third of the common panchayati land. The land was captured by the Jat farmers through a bogus auction and people from Dalit community were made to work on this land. The Dalit labourers were demanding that this land be given to them. They contacted us and we fought on this issue. It was a tough fight. We held a protest at the district headquarters for days during the summer. There was a huge participation by women in this protest. Our struggle at Balad Kalan and its victory was a milestone.

Our fight started with Sekha village, and since then it has been growing every day. It has spread across a number of villages. Rural Dalits are becoming conscious of the fact that a one-third share of panchayati land belongs to them and they are forming Dalit collectives and taking this land on lease. They are bolstered by the fact that there is an organisation fighting on this issue.

Panchayati land is spread in unequal amounts across villages, and in some villages it is too small, though Dalit labourers are successfully taking control of it. We are now getting ourselves involved in a new issue, the issue of implementing the Land Ceiling Act, 1972[2]. The proper implementation of this Act, i.e., the seizure of land in excess of the limit and its redistribution amongst the landless peasants has not been done. The Act exists only on paper. We will now take our struggle in this direction.

WU: *In the beginning, when you visited the villages and especially when you were organising Dalit women, it must have been challenging because the issue of land is always seen as a masculine one. What problems did you face initially, when you were trying to mobilise women? What were your experiences?*

PARAMJIT KAUR: Actually, we did not face a lot of difficulties regarding this particular issue, because it is Dalit women who work in other farmers' fields. They have an organic relation to agricultural land as labourers, and depend on it for livelihood. Initially, our meetings were attended largely by men. But as we continued conducting regular meetings in the villages, we could soon reach out to the women, and most of them responded positively to what we were saying. Although we had to conduct several meetings to acquire adequate participation from women, once they realised that we were talking about how they could get respite from working on someone else's land they understood it. They would say, if it is really written in the law that one-third share of the common panchayati land belongs to us then we will fight for it, tell us what we should do. Hence, wherever we went, we could catch the attention of the women easily, and they would also understand our point quite easily; we did not face any serious difficulties.

The Dalit women actually enhanced our understanding of their problems. Dalit women do all the household work, and at the same time, most of them are also daily-wage agricultural workers. They won't have food at their home in the evening if they don't work that day in the fields, as it is their only earning. They told us about how they were harassed and at times even sexually abused while working in the fields owned by the upper-caste farmers. The land-owners would keep a watch on which woman had newly arrived in the village after getting married, and she would be especially targeted and harassed. The land-owners ogled them as if they had a right over the bodies of these women as well.

Many agricultural worker families rear cattle to supplement their meagre income. They need *hara-chara* (green fodder) to feed the cattle. Owing to the use of herbicides, weeds for fodder had become scarce. It could be found only on the forage along the canals and on the edges of agricultural lands. The Dalit women going to collect fodder from the fields of Jat farmers were routinely insulted and harassed with physical and verbal abuse and casteist slurs.

This is the environment within which the Dalit women had to work and live. Naturally, the women connected more deeply with the issues of land and their legal rights to own land. So, wherever we organised struggle demanding their ownership rights over village commons land under the occupation of the upper-caste big farmers, these women were always in the forefront; they stayed with us in the protests, in the sit-ins, even during the night. They would go home, finish their household work in an hour and return to the protest sites. I learnt that access to even a small piece of land was not merely an economic gain for them, for the Dalit women it was a kind of emancipation from daily humiliations and insults.

WU: *You talked about Dalit women's response to acquire land. Tell us in detail about some specific struggles and the role of Dalit women in them.*

PARAMJIT KAUR: As I told you, women participated equally in the struggle for land and the number of women participants kept increasing over time. But the struggle to acquire land was not easy and it often took a violent turn. In rural Punjab, land means power and prestige. The upper-caste big farmers and *jagirdars* (landlords) were not going to give up land in their possession to the Dalits so easily. We had to forcibly occupy those lands and guard them for days. Like men, the Dalit women, too, had to face the wrath of the *jagirdars*, police and the state.

Our fight in 2015 at Balad Kalan was a milestone. There was a brutal lathi-charge on the protesters; at least half of them were women. A lot of people were injured, someone broke their leg, some got stitches on the head; women also suffered a lot of injuries. They, too, were arrested. But they were determined that it was their land and they wouldn't let it go. This was a good experience in our movement, and ultimately through a struggle that spanned several months, the Dalit families in Balad Kalan village succeeded in claiming their right over the 121 acres of panchayat land. In Bhadohi village too, many including three women were injured. But they occupied their share of the panchayat land. We were in disbelief. These were the women who were not ready to get out of their houses to talk, but today they are even ready to fight the police, the upper-caste Jat farmers!

The most severe challenge we faced was in Jhaloor village. There, the Dalit families were attacked by Jat men and armed goons hired by them. Dalit houses were vandalised, Dalit women were groped, molested, and beaten up. Over 40 Dalits were severely wounded. Gurdev Kaur, a 72-year-old Dalit woman died as a result of injuries sustained during the attack. Thousands attended her cremation and swore to continue the movement.

In Matoi village in Sangrur, a few Dalit female students under the leadership of Sandip Kaur started an agitation and finally won the lease of 17 *bighas* of land reserved for Dalits. The Matoi Dalit women's collective grows fodder crops round the year. Now the women of the village no longer need to go to the fields of Jat farmers to collect fodder. The biggest thing that I feel is that, if we have been able to make this *jathebandi* (union) and this movement successful, it is on the strength of these Dalit women.

WU: *No doubt, one of the features of this land struggle has been the participation of women in significant numbers. How difficult was it for Dalit women to come out and assume leadership within the struggle? What difficulties did they face both at home and within society at large?*

PARAMJIT KAUR: As you say, one of the special features of this movement has been the participation of women in significant numbers. Even though they are illiterate, they have the experience of everyday struggle and are playing a leading role in occupying the land in the villages. Today, when a journalist like you comes from far off to record their struggle, they feel happy that someone has come to talk to them, talk about them. They have the feeling of being a human being; they feel that they are also being respected.

But, they do face many difficulties in leading the struggle, particularly the women organisers. They don't work only in a single village, they have to travel to other villages; they also have to participate in the district-level meetings. The common problem, even today, is money—the expenses. Some of our women members are highly capable organisers, but they have backed down as it is not possible for them to spend so much money. We support them, but at times that is insufficient. Another factor is that sometimes they have to face sexual harassment. There are always sections in society who are interested in pulling women back. They pass comments like "she is marching with the flag because she does not have a man to stop her," or "your family has given up on you and hence you are doing this." The women often feel that others think of them as being characterless. Sometimes these things force some women to back down. But there are also examples where some of the women have gained political understanding of this situation, and they have realised that they will have to face these things. But given the social backwardness in rural societies, it is difficult for Dalit women to participate in the role of a leader. Though their number in our organisation is the same as that of men, it is mostly men who become the leading organisers at the district level. But at the block level, like in Sherpur block, Sangrur block, Bhawanigarh block, Nabha block, there are many women leaders. One of our leaders is Shindal Kaur, who does organisational work in 12 villages. There are many like her who have come forward. These were ordinary landless Dalit women, who rose up during the course of the struggle and became block-level leaders.

WU: *How has this struggle affected the power dynamics between men and women within the family? Have Dalit women been able to assert their power and dignity gained through struggle in their homes?*

PARAMJIT KAUR: Some women who joined us by themselves have husbands who regularly drink. That is the only escape Dalit men have, and they also use physical abuse upon women in their own families. If you go to the villages today, you will find many cases of domestic abuse—husbands who are fighting with their wives, hurting them physically, throwing kids out of the house. This issue is prevalent within the Dalit community. But, in the villages in which land has been given to Dalits after a struggle, this problem has reduced. Men who are thoughtful have realised that the women have fought alongside them for land, and that the land struggle has become a success only because of the participation of women. The abusive behaviour actually stems from the pressure that these men are under, and when they gain some land of their own, this pressure reduces and they become hopeful that their conditions can change. Earlier, they did not have any faith in any struggle; they would stop women in their own families from participating in the struggle.

Also, a lot of women stood up against their husbands. They participated in the struggle even when their family is unhappy with that participation. For example, during a protest in Patiala, there was a lathi-charge on us and it was almost 9 to 10 pm before we could return. Many of these women were not allowed back in the house, their husbands were saying, "Go, go and stay at the protest site!" But they never complained to us by saying that they wouldn't come because their husbands would fight with them. They still joined our movement, they had faith that their conditions would change with this struggle and a lot of these women participated in the struggle despite their families or husbands being unhappy.

In many villages, we have supportive men who encourage women in their families to participate in our organisation. They know that we have their interests at heart. This was not the case initially, but now they understand. Also, we have given leadership roles to women, so their husbands don't try to stop them at all. Now we go and tell the men "Today you will be working at home, as she is coming with us for a demonstration."

Often the women request us to talk to their husbands or family elders in order to convince them to allow them to go for protests, saying, they will agree if you will talk to them once, but we object to this saying, "What is this? You have to take your stand and face the family." So, in a way, in the villages where the struggle is strong, the hold of patriarchy is slowly breaking. I feel, compared to the educated and urban working classes, patriarchy is being challenged more by these Dalit women in the villages.

WU: *We have been visiting different regions of Sangrur and have observed that the male daily-wage labourers are getting at least 300 to 350 rupees per day, whereas the women are getting about Rs 200 only. What is your opinion on this gender-based difference in wages?*

PARAMJIT KAUR: On top of being discriminated against as Dalit women, these women have to struggle against the notion that women cannot work as much as men. This makes it difficult for them to even get work in the first place. The labour laws talk about equal wages for both men and women, but it is not implemented anywhere—not just in Punjab, but anywhere in India. Dalit women are forced to do whatever work comes their way. The discrimination is happening thanks to the *chaudharis* (village heads) and the government. The government doesn't implement its own laws. If it penalises the discriminators, only then can this issue get resolved. We try to address such issues in the areas of our struggle.

WU: *What has been the role of women in the collective farming on acquired land that the ZPSC has tried to promote? Do Dalit women get land in their names?*

Paramjit Kaur: Women have been playing an equal role in collective farming on lands acquired on lease. There are several villages in which men are the ones primarily active in the collectives, but in the district of Sangrur, in villages like Kalra, Badrukhan and Jhuneri, women participate substantially in collective farming on the acquired land. In fact, in some villages, for example in Kalra, men do not participate at all. Women gather in groups of four and five and go to water the fields even at 1 am in the night. The duties are distributed. If some families are not at home for some reason, or are having some difficulties, the women would water their fields as well. This sort of common exchange of chores is natural especially amongst women.

As for whether the lands taken on lease are in the woman's name, it is up to the village committee to decide whom the land is given to and to whom it is not. Mostly, it is men who are given the land. But in many villages, women do take land in their names. For example, in Badrukhan, five women have taken *patta* (land deed) in their names. Similarly, in Kalra, two *pattas* were allotted in women's names, and two were allotted to men. In Kalra it has been happening like this since 2014.

When we started the ZPSC, we had nearly equal women participants because it is the women who are humiliated and oppressed the most. As we take this struggle forward, creating Dalit women land-owners is one of our primary agenda. We have implemented this in several villages. We absolutely stand by this agenda. Women's names must be on the land deeds, as they are more deeply engaged with the land and also the most adversely impacted by landlessness.

WU: *You talked about the struggle over taking on lease the panchayati and* nazool *land in the villages. Apart from the land issue, what are the other issues concerning the landless Dalits that are being raised by the ZPSC?*

Paramjit Kaur: Apart from our main demands regarding *nazool ki zameen* and panchayati *zameen*, we took up the issue of loans taken from private microfinance companies and membership of Dalits in the village cooperative societies. We have raised the issue of compensation in the case of suicide by agricultural workers. We have demanded long-term fixed tenure of the lands auctioned to the Dalits instead of the present one-year tenure. We are demanding that priority must be given to Dalits who bid collectively for panchayati land, instead of allocating land to individual Dalits, who in most cases are 'dummy' candidates bidding on behalf of the landlords. We are now demanding implementation of the Land Ceiling Act and redistribution of land in excess of the ceiling amongst the landless peasants. Besides these things, we have to address many social issues that arise in the villages.

WU: *ZPSC has raised the issue of compensation in case of the suicide by landless farmers. While studying the state of rural Punjab, I ran into two studies. One said that there were 12 lakh women trapped in debt to microfinance companies. And the other, a study by Prof. Sukhpal Singh, found that not only land-owning farmers, but agricultural labourers were also committing suicide. What is your experience on the ground?*

PARAMJIT KAUR: It is true that the number of agricultural workers committing suicide is large and most of them are Dalits, but this never comes up in discussions on agrarian distress in Punjab or elsewhere. Whenever there is such a case, for example, there was an incident in a village near Dhuri, another one in Haryao Khurd in Patiala, it was casually accepted that the victim in the first case had three daughters and therefore, he killed himself. In the latter case, the suicide was attributed to family issues. The basic reason behind these suicides is poverty and debt. In the case of farmers, suicide becomes news. So, when they commit suicide, in most cases, the family receives monetary compensation, and some concessions on the loans incurred. The farmer unions fight for them. But there are no such provisions for Dalit agricultural workers when they commit suicide, it is said "he had problems in the house" or "he died because of a drinking problem." The suicides of the labourers never come up on the agenda, though the reasons are always the same—they are poor, they are hungry, they are in debt, they don't get any government loans.

Mostly, it is the male labourers, who also happen to be the heads of the families, who commit suicide. They often do not disclose their debt liabilities to other family members. In some cases, the women agricultural labourers also succumb to suicide[3]. Most of them are from Dalit families.

There is a government scheme for getting compensation, but it is too difficult for Dalit workers to take advantage of this scheme. Sometimes, if the victim's family is connected to us, we try to put pressure on the officers concerned and help them in getting compensation. If you go to a village, except for four to five families, you will find that most of the Dalit families face similar conditions. How many cases can we take up? The Dalits lose faith, accept defeat and think that this is their fate.

WU: *The last time I met you, it was at a protest dharna in Patiala organised by ZPSC. ZPSC had then raised the issue of waivers of all kinds of loans for indebted landless labourers and also small farmers...*

PARAMJIT KAUR: Yes. About 90 percent of rural Dalit women in Punjab have taken loans from private microfinance companies. Before the lockdown was declared in April [2020], many of these women, who work as daily-wage labourers, used to pay back the loans from their earnings. But after the lockdown, they lost work. So, they became loan defaulters. The agents of the microfinance companies harassed them almost every day. They would come and stand at the doorstep of their houses at seven in the morning, asking them to pay the loan EMI (Equated Monthly Instalment). The women were abused and shamed for their inability to pay the EMI on time.

We organised local agitations against this issue. The coronavirus had not been brought by these labourers. Then, why should they be the ones suffering the most from it? Moreover, the government waived the loans of the land-owning farmers and the big corporate companies. So, we demanded that the loan that these women took from the microfinance companies should also be waived. We held demonstrations, and only then did Captain Amarinder's government (Amarinder Singh was the Congress Chief Minister of Punjab at that time) announced a Rs 590 crore loan waiver scheme for the agricultural workers. However, his decision was merely a way of fooling people. He said that only the loans up to Rs 50,000 taken from registered Primary Agriculture Cooperative Societies (PACS)[4] would be waived. But our women are not even allowed to get membership in these cooperative societies in the first place! Without membership how can they take loans from such societies? Most of their loans are from private microfinance companies and the government scheme was silent on this aspect. So, we demanded that all kinds of loans, including loans taken from private microfinance companies, should be waived.

WU: *Not only agricultural labourers, women from the small farmer families are also under debt. What was their response to your demand and protest in this regard? Also, are there any government schemes under which Dalit women can avail of low-interest loans? Why can't they access those loans?*

PARAMJIT KAUR: This issue was first brought to our attention by some of the affected women who were from our own organisation. They were unable to repay their loans anymore and the people from the loan company were harassing them. When we raised this issue, we got a good response from landless women, but they were not all Dalit women. The women from upper-caste landless and small farmers' families were also affected.

Today, even farmers with five acres of land in Punjab are poor farmers and the number of landless farmers is also increasing. When we started the struggle on this issue, these women also responded positively. People may say that ZPSC is only for the Dalits, but we don't think of ourselves in that way. It is true that the majority of our members are Dalit, and we do speak and struggle against caste oppression and exploitation, but we say that like the Dalit community, the condition of upper-caste landless and small farmers is also precarious. However, the Jat landlords keep instigating them by saying—*tussi hun chude-chamaran naal jana e aa* (will you now join ranks with these lower-caste people?)

Whenever agents of these microfinance companies would come to a village, the women would gather with a red flag and *gherao* (surround) them shouting slogans. They stopped coming, but soon then they found another way. These loans are group loans and the groups have leaders, so the companies would give concessions to the leaders and make them repay the loan. Then, they would tell others in the group that their leader has repaid her loan, so now they would also have to pay their share. The way these group loans work is that, if one person in a group doesn't pay one's debts, the rest of the women in the group aren't given loans either. We also had to fight against these dishonest leaders. But because of lack of access to other avenues for taking loans, 90 percent of rural women are compelled to take loans from these private companies at high interest rates. These loans are not for daily sustenance. Most of these loans are spent on medical emergencies or in giving gifts like a sewing machine or a washing machine for dowry during their daughters' wedding. This is what we found out when we did a survey.

WU: *Generally, from what we have seen across India, farmers take loans for education of the children or for medical expenses or, in many cases, for dowry. Could you describe to us in detail the reasons that you found during the survey? What compelled these poor women to take loans from private sources?*

PARAMJIT KAUR: We found that most of the loans were to meet urgent medical expenses and for giving dowry during marriages. Many of them have houses which are in bad condition, so they took loans, say to replace the leaking roof, many to build latrine and bathroom. Only a few loans were for the education of their children.

The loan amount was somewhere between Rs 20,000 and Rs 1,00,000. No more than that. The loan amount varied from Rs 30,000 for some to 50,000 or 60,000 for others. Another problem was that the total loan amount was not borrowed from just one company. Suppose, the house needs to be repaired, they would borrow Rs 20,000 from one lender, Rs 20,000 from another, and so on. We found that on an average they were indebted to four or five companies. The problem was that when they paid one of them, the EMI of another loan would be due, and so on. Their whole month would be spent trying to pay back the EMIs.

There was also another problem the women faced. The issue of loans is connected to the issue of ownership of land. If Dalits had owned land, they would not be forced to take loans from microfinance companies in the first place. They could then access loans from government banks and village co-operative societies, just like land-owning farmers. As I said, they are also not allowed to become members in the village cooperative societies. So, they are scared and thought that it would be better to somehow repay these high-interest loans. Otherwise, no one would lend them in future during an emergency. They are under immense pressure to pay back these loans, and a lot of women suffer from depression. Under this pressure, especially in the areas near the cities, many have even turned to prostitution.

Whenever we hold protests against these private loan companies, we also demand, at the same time, that the cooperative societies in the village should accept landless Dalits as their members. It should not be the case that only landed farmers can become members. We fought for this. We *gheraoed* the government officers raising this issue. We made the state government publish a notification that any woman, any man— basically anybody from the village irrespective of caste or land-ownership status—can become a member of the village cooperative society. We have helped a lot of Dalit agricultural labourers become members of such societies.

We have also raised the issue of representation of the Dalits in the running of such cooperatives. It is legally required that when a committee of the Agriculture Cooperative Societies is elected, there shall be one-third representation of Dalits in the committee. The usual practice in this case is also similar to the bogus auctions held in the case of panchayati land. The rich and powerful Jats will obtain a signature from some Dalit persons and show on paper that there is Dalit representation. We raised this issue. If it's a public cooperative society, and farmers from the upper-castes can take loans from it, then why can't we? There are government welfare schemes under which if we [Dalit women] want to start small business in the village, we can avail loans from the Agriculture Cooperative Societies on low interest. You don't even have to pay the interest if you repay the loan amount within 40 days. We can't just ask women to boycott the microfinance companies, because we know they don't have any other option. In times of need they look towards these companies as their only hope. The microfinance companies also quickly give loan to them just on the basis of an Aadhaar (identity) card. The interest rates are high, but when someone in your family is dying, you don't have an option. Hence, we also fight to ensure that Dalit men and women are allowed membership in the Agriculture Cooperative Societies.

WU: *You pointed out that the loans incurred by Dalit agricultural worker families are not for education of the children. What is the general scenario of education amongst the Dalit families in the villages? How much education do the girls in particular get?*

PARAMJIT KAUR: For girls, in most cases, it is until graduation. A large section of the girls gets married off after +2 (12th grade). Even if the family is in a somewhat better condition, their daughters, too, have to work on the farms. Only then is it possible for them to study up to BA or MA. This was true even for me when I was growing up. It is not possible for a Dalit student, both boys and girls, to go for higher education without working. Our children don't want to place an extra financial burden on their parents. Scholarships and reservations do help a lot. It is only because of reservations that a lot of us are able to continue with our education today.

The attitude towards educating girls is changing among the people who have joined us. But dowry during marriage is still a big problem. Also, in many cases, married girls are dropped off at their maternal homes within three months [after marriage], the in-laws and husbands don't come to take them back. Many families now come to us and ask us to find a suitable match for their daughters. They trust us because they know how our mindset is, and they believe that we will be able to find a good match with similar values for their daughters. Especially the families who are in our committees, those who work with us, come to us seeking help. We try to help them; we have to engage in such social activities as well.

WU: *How do the women members of ZPSC, who after such intense struggle have acquired some land on lease, even though the size is very small, see their own and their children's future? Farming is not profitable anymore, and especially on such small pieces of land. As agricultural workers, they* hardly get work for more than 30 days in a year. Rural workers never get 100 days of work under the MGNREGA scheme, and the construction sector which employs most of the rural youth is also stagnating. What future do they see for young children and youth?

PARAMJIT KAUR: It is true that farming is no longer profitable, but our struggle for land is not just for profit, it's not merely an economic issue but a social struggle for human dignity. The issue of ownership of land for Dalit women is linked to safeguarding her izzat and *atma-sammaan* (self-respect). It is because Dalits are landless that they face extreme oppression and exploitation; they are not even considered human beings. The access to ownership of land is a form of emancipation.

As for the problem of unemployment in rural Punjab, it exists for both the general castes and the Dalits. To create jobs, we need agriculture-based industries. If there are no agro-industries here, then even if the Land Ceiling Act is implemented and the Dalits get some land and grow crops, there will be no market for it and it won't benefit anybody.

We need government *mandis* (agricultural produce markets). That is why we support the farmers' struggle against the new farm laws which will dismantle such *mandis*. It is an important issue, but all the sown crops do not get *mandi* rates, only wheat and rice are sold at MSP (Minimum Support Price). The rice-wheat cropping pattern has also caused the groundwater levels in Punjab to go down; there was news that only 17 years of water is left underground.[5] This is a serious issue; Punjab will face ecological disaster soon if we don't change the cropping pattern. To shift from the current wheat-rice model, we need MSP for all crops, not just for wheat and rice. We are with the farmers who are fighting on the issue of MSP, but it will be beneficial only if it is given on all the crops. The ZPSC will fight on this issue, even if the farmers' front does not.

So, we need agriculture-based industries, we need to change the cropping pattern and we need MSP for all crops. The current farming model that we have here will destroy the whole farming community. We are raising these issues even now and when we all have land we will be able to focus more on them. Future generations will find employment only through an ecologically sustainable model of agriculture and local industries based on its output. Otherwise, how many will get a government job?

WU: *The final question—the farmers' movement erupted a few months after the lockdown. We are now hearing stories of how, during the lockdown, the Dalit agricultural workers were socially boycotted over the issue of wage. We heard from you how the struggle for agricultural land of the Dalits is suppressed by the Jat farmers. You have been to the farmers' movement at Delhi borders, where the farmer unions raised the slogan of mazdoor-kisan ekta (worker-farmer unity). How far have such slogans of solidarity been translated into reality on the ground?*

PARAMJIT KAUR: During the farmers' movement, there definitely was a feeling of solidarity between the farmers and the labourers, and people hoped that something new would come out of this. But in practice, this did not happen. On the ground, labourers are still being treated very badly. The labourers are therefore not in support of the farmers in general; they are in support of certain Left farmer organisations. These organisations are making efforts to include the labourers in their struggle, to take up their issues, and to address the common issues that affect the labourers as well as the small farmers.

If we want to raise slogans of farmer-worker unity, first of all we have to pick issues common to both small farmers and labourers. Secondly, we cannot ignore caste issues. Whenever there is a call for a social boycott of Dalit labourers, the farmer unions must take a stand against this and acknowledge that this is wrong. When they do not talk about these things, when they do not involve themselves in the problems of the labourers, then how can they expect Dalits or labourers to join them in their struggle! The farmers will have to talk about caste-based oppression. They will have to remove the bias from their minds that Dalit agricultural workers are slaves, that Scheduled Caste people are inferior; that they do not have any ownership right over village land. Until they do this, I do not think that any solidarity with upper-caste land-owning farmers is possible. In this, we can only rely on radical Left organisations, not on rich farmer unions. Those unions will not allow the Land Ceiling Act to be implemented. They simply want to protect their interest while keeping the exploitative feudal system intact. These farmer leaders had split the Samyukta Kisan Morcha (SKM) into two parts; they are busy fighting elections in Punjab, while the revolutionary unions are working to advance the movement.

It is only through movements that the caste barrier can break, but only if the movement is a common one, a shared one. Take for example the farmers' movement against the three laws. Agricultural workers do not own any land at all, so they did not join the farmers' struggle in large numbers at the borders. After the laws were repealed and the farmers came back, they now taunt the agricultural workers, saying—you [agricultural workers] didn't come to Delhi; you did not join us; you did not turn up in large numbers; we [farmers] have defeated Modi by ourselves.

The things they say are not nice. They are intended to hurt the Dalit labourers. How can you fight the WTO, the imperialist forces, if the *mazdoors* (workers) are not with you? The slogans of solidarity are nice, they will continue to be raised and heard, but nothing is changing on the ground.

Endnotes

1. In Punjab, there are two categories of *Shamlat* or commons land belonging to panchayats—*nazool* land and panchayati commons land. *Shamlat* land is mainly used for cultivation, and is allotted through an open auction every year. One-third of *shamlat* lands in Punjab are reserved for Dalits.

2. Under the Punjab Land Reforms Act, 1972, a family unit (husband, wife and children) cannot own more than 17.5 acres of fertile agricultural land with access to good irrigation facilities. However, a family can hold up to 52 acres, if the land is barren and without irrigation facilities.

3. 7,303 agricultural labourers died by suicide in Punjab during 2000-18. Although as much as 87.57 percent of the victims were men, 12.43 percent were women. This shows that women labourers are under more stress as the proportion of women labourers amongst suicide victims is much higher than that of women from farmers families (8.2 percent). For further details see the interview of Dr Sukhpal Singh, p-367-388 of this volume.

4. A Primary Agricultural Credit Society (PACS) is a co-operative credit institution at the gram panchayat and village level in India. The main function of the PACS is to provide short and medium-term purpose loans to its members. Farmers are provided seeds, fertilisers, agricultural equipment along with short term loans.

5. A block-wise assessment of groundwater resources in 2020 by the Central Ground Water Board (CGWB) found that most of the districts in Punjab had over-exploited the groundwater levels. Groundwater extraction has already reached 150-200 metres in most places in central Punjab. If the present rate of depletion continues, Punjab's groundwater is expected to drop to below 300 metres by 2039, as per CGWB.

A tractor displaying the protesting farmers' demands. **Photo Credit:** Workers Unity.

SECTION IV

CONVERSATIONS WITH JOURNALISTS, ECONOMISTS, POLITICAL AND CULTURAL ACTIVISTS

The Evolution of the Left in Punjab has not Happened Independent of Sikh Ethos

HARTOSH SINGH BAL, POLITICAL EDITOR, *THE CARAVAN*

> HARTOSH SINGH BAL is the political editor of the magazine *The Caravan*. He has 20 years of experience as a journalist and maintains a keen eye on developments in Punjab. The Caravan magazine has a rich trajectory of insightful coverage on politics, art and culture. In recent years, the magazine has surpassed in its critique of ruling class politics and ethos from a people's standpoint that is eerily absent in mainstream media.
>
> WORKERS UNITY interviewed Hartosh Bal on 1 March 2021 on how the history of Punjab and the Sikh community is related to the farmers' protests along with some other pertinent issues.

WORKERS UNITY: *In the ongoing struggle we see constant references being made to history, whether they be references to the Pagdi Sambhal Jatta Movement or the Praja Mandal Movement or other anti-feudal, anti-colonial struggles that have taken place in the past. But when we see Punjab from the vantage point of Delhi, there is a gap between how Punjab ought to be seen and how it is seen. How do you see Punjab from a historical point of view?*

HARTOSH BAL: The term—north India—if you think about it then this term dates back before the Sikh wars that took place in Punjab that led to its conquest around 1847. If you look at India's map, what we call Uttar Pradesh (UP) isn't really a land in the north; apart from western UP, most of it is really eastern India. What is really in the north is Punjab and Haryana… once Pakistan was South-Western Punjab, and up north you had Jammu and Kashmir. So this was the region that was once the Sikh Empire. Or before that it was ruled by the Misls.[1] Or, at other times, it was a state administered from Delhi.

This area has its own history, its own sub-nationalism, its own culture and language. Without understanding this, it is not possible to understand these protests, or the specific characteristics of Punjab: its agriculture, or its history of protest. This is because we have an insufficient understanding and knowledge of history before 1947. The attempt to build a national history, which started from Ashoka and went on to Akbar and from there all the way until 1947, and so on, the big mistake this narrative makes is that it ignores these sub-national histories, which are very important in themselves; an understanding and information about them is lacking. This is what has happened with Punjab as well.

WU: *In Punjab's history, Delhi comes up frequently as a point of reference, especially as the locus of conflict and political struggle. In this agitation too, when Punjabi popular singers have made mention of Delhi, it is this conflict and distance between Delhi and Punjab that is referenced. What is the historical origin of this?*

HARTOSH BAL: In the Mughal Empire, Punjab was a province that was controlled from Delhi. The capital city was Sirhind. Following this there was the Sikh emergence when the Sikh community assumed power that culminated in the empire of Ranjit Singh. This empire carved itself out from the Mughal Empire. It was established by breaking away from the control of Delhi. The breaking of this control took a hundred years, from the time of Guru Gobind Singh to the time of Aurangzeb and Bahadur Shah Zafar, followed by the Misl period, during which the fight was with Delhi. And when Punjab ultimately broke off it did so as a sub-national entity that defined itself in opposition to Delhi.

Finally, when one views this against the backdrop of the subcontinent's subsequent history, we see the imposition of British laws in Punjab during the period of British colonial rule which was once again centred in Delhi. So when Punjab reorganises itself, this reorganisation takes the form of a fight against Delhi. This is an integral part of Punjab's history.

The invocation of this history, of Baghel Singh (a warrior and military general celebrated in Sikh history as the vanquisher of Mughal Delhi) during the Misl period and his attack on Delhi and the subsequent setting up and funding of gurudwaras such as Bangla Sahib, Sis Ganj and Rakab Ganj, all this is tied to the history of that time. People are not aware of this history in Delhi, that the neighbourhood of Tis Hazari in Delhi is named after the 30,000 men led by Baghel Singh, but in Punjab this is a well-known fact.

So when talk of marching towards Delhi happens, this historical imagery is naturally invoked. When we talk of protest now, there is also talk of the past hundred years of agrarian protests, or even non-agrarian anti-colonial protests; these protests have also been directed against Delhi.

WU: *The Sikh ethos in Punjab and the iconography of this ongoing agitation draws significantly from the Sikh/Punjabi tradition, especially the history of the Sikh Gurus. In this sort of agitation, is it a contradiction that religious iconography is as strongly present as are the symbols and iconography of progressive movements?*

HARTOSH BAL: Whether this is a contradiction or not depends entirely on your point of view. When there are Sikh people participating in the protests, it is not surprising or outrageous to see Sikh symbolism playing a part in the iconography of the protests. While the leadership of these protests may be from the Left, the motivation behind these protests in Punjab has always been tied together with the Sikh ethos.

Consider the history of the Left in Punjab, the prominent leftists from Punjab, or even before that the Ghadar Movement, which starts from the immigration into Canada and the USA in 1905 to 1910 and their subsequent return, these movements have always been associated to Sikh symbolism—the turban, the beard—these you will see within both the Left movements and the Ghadar movement. The evolution of the Left in Punjab has not happened independent of Sikh ethos.

Bhagat Singh's imagery, for example, appears in two famous forms: one in a hat and the other in a turban. And you can tell who's protesting based on which of these images is most prominent. If you look at Singhu, where the protests are ongoing, when Bhagat Singh is remembered, he is remembered using the image of him in a turban. So there is nothing new in the melding of the Sikh ethos and the Left in Punjab.

WU: *In this protest too, we are witnessing a balance between the Left's* history and the Sikh ethos. Gurudwaras have been important in coordinating logistics and maintaining supply chains, and other Sikh organisations such as Khalsa Aid are openly supporting the movement. After 26 January, we saw a small change in this equation. What is the reason for this? Do you see the balance being disturbed after this?*

HARTOSH BAL: It has made a slight difference, and you can see evidence of this back in Punjab; this has not been reported fully here yet. We know that Nishan Sahib's flag was raised at the Red Fort. The Indian flag was higher up, but Nishan Sahib's flag was raised below it by some passionate protesters.

I think that the Left leaders made a mistake, in that they had not admitted their responsibility for this moment. They have distanced themselves from the events at the Red Fort, but I think that while this was a tactical necessity, on moral and ethical grounds it was wrong. The story that the government span out of this moment was not surprising. Everybody knew one day before that the protest route would be diverted. What happened was to a large extent predictable, I think that the Delhi Police knew it would happen and yet they let it happen anyway—the TV cameras were there at the right time to project this image and to circulate it widely. The effect of this has been predictable too—there was always a fear of this labelling. We all remember the '80s, the early '90s, so this Khalistani label was predictable as well. We saw this with Shaheen Bagh too—how they would break a protest movement by maligning it. At that moment, the leadership completely distanced itself from it.

However, this hasn't meant that the people associated with this movement completely backed off from it. Just the day before yesterday in Bathinda there was a rally and Lakha Sidhana addressed the crowd. There too, there were plenty of people in attendance. The things you mentioned, those remain true. The protest organisations, whether it is the gurudwaras or the langars, their motivation comes from the Sikh ethos. Without it, a protest of this scale would not be possible.

WU: *You had written an article in Caravan titled 'The New Khalistan Conspiracy,' where you spoke about the '80s. GBS Sidhu's new book* The Khalistan Conspiracy: A Former R&AW Official Unravels the Path to 1984 *has come out too. When we were reporting from Punjab, the taboo and fear surrounding this topic was perceptible. Now that there's a Hindutva-based party in power at the Centre, how much backlash is to be expected for using the minority religious iconography and symbolism in a protest? And as you mentioned, this is viewed by many as another Khalistan conspiracy—how do we understand this politically?*

HARTOSH BAL: To expect that this ethos would not be reflected in a protest based in rural Punjab is impossible. The idea of Khalistan, a label that is being used now for the protesters, when compared to the '70s and '80s, is situationally very different. On the one hand, at that time Indira Gandhi had exploited the divide that existed between Punjab and Haryana, because at that time there was an issue of the Sutlej Yamuna Link (SYL) Canal, there were points of conflict between Punjab and Haryana regarding sharing of water. Also, Bhajan Lal's government [in Haryana] had humiliated a number of Sikh officials and ex-army men during the 1982 Asian Games. All these things had a profound effect on the people of Punjab.

This time Punjab and Haryana (especially rural Haryana and the Jat-dominated areas) are standing together. In Punjab too, the Hindus and Sikhs have not separated but are standing together. This movement is not being seen as a rural movement. This farmers' movement is seen as representative of Punjab's cultural and economic future. In Punjab, there is not any big following of Modi, or the Hindutva agenda. If you look at any election since 2014, neither the BJP nor even the BJP-Akali Dal alliance has gotten much support in Punjab. So there is this mindset in Punjab against majoritarian fundamentalism and Hindutva right from the beginning. This is part of the motivation, but the main focus now is the farmers' concrete demands, and in this the Sikh ethos and motivations will naturally come to the fore.

WU: *Punjab is an agrarian society. The canal colonies were built during the time of the British Raj. After that, there was the Green Revolution during which farmers were incentivised to grow crop like paddy to meet the country's food requirements. In this framework, we see the farm laws have caused a lot more anxiety in Punjab and Haryana than other states. Why is that?*

HARTOSH BAL: Punjab primarily grew wheat and cotton, and the production directed at selling in the market began in 1890–1895. Here by Punjab I mean specifically south-eastern Punjab and the canal colonies[2] in Pakistan that we might call south-western Punjab. What we call Punjab today is central Punjab. To believe that the farmers, who have been interacting with the market for around 150 years, don't understand the new laws or market forces or corporate dealings is ridiculous. If they don't understand these things, then who possibly could? The people bringing in these laws—their history with the free market is 20 to 30 years old—while Punjab's relationship with market is much older. The farmer understands this.

Now for the *mandi* system, which came in around 1939 with Sir Chhotu Ram[3]—when did it get included in the procurement system? It was at the time of the Green Revolution. These systems were joined together because of the object of today's focus—paddy and wheat; the government wanted these plantation cycles to be adopted by the farmers. But Punjab is not suited for growing paddy; it has never been grown here historically because there is insufficient water. How do you incentivise a farmer in this area to grow it, then? You assure them returns within the *mandi* system. The effect of this has been that the paddy-wheat cycle became the most remunerative cycle in agriculture. In Punjab, paddy is grown in 80 to 90 percent of the land under cultivation. In the remaining 10 to 15 percent, cotton is grown in areas where there is still a shortage of water.

Here's a fact: in Punjab, from data that is available since 2002, there have been over 16,000 suicides by farmers. Eighty percent of these suicides have been in areas that grow cotton. Now you can figure out for yourself what this means. It means that 10 percent of the land contributes to 80 percent of the farmer suicides! In Punjab, the farmer knows what could happen where the *mandi* procurement system doesn't exist, where they can't get a guaranteed price on their crops, where their crop values are decided solely by market forces. People in Punjab have seen what happens when this system is dismantled.

One more issue which is tied to paddy cultivation, and which people don't think through correctly, is that of basmati. The basmati variety of rice is not covered under the procurement system of the government.

Its price is decided by the free market. It is more remunerative, but still the farmer does not abandon other varieties of rice to grow basmati precisely because in that case they would be under the thumb of open market forces. Just this year, because exporters did not purchase basmati, the earnings from the sale of basmati dropped by Rs 800 to 900 per quintal as compared to last year. Who benefits from this? The middle class here, who buys basmati rice but doesn't pay less for it. The procurer also doesn't lose, only the farmer does. The middlemen and private traders, who buy up most of the basmati, don't lose. Internationally there is some fluctuation in the prices, but that becomes an excuse to depress domestic prices. So the cases of basmati and cotton are very familiar to the farmers of Punjab.

The takeaway from these examples is that when the Punjabi farmer comes up against unregulated market forces, they face losses, which in many cases leads to suicides.

You have travelled through Punjab; you have been to Singhu and Ghazipur. You must have seen that it is wrong to say that the protesting farmers are only rich farmers. Look, the usual earnings from agriculture in Punjab are roughly the same as that of a grade three government employee—around Rs 20,000 to Rs 30,000 per month, if you remove a handful of 'big' farmers. So how can these farmers be called wealthy farmers? But you see that even these meager earnings are today in crisis. The situation is like this: instead of earning say Rs 25,000 per month, you will now be putting farmers in a situation where some months they will earn Rs 5,000, and some months Rs 40,000, and some months they won't make anything at all—they might even lose money! In this situation, planning the future becomes impossible. The burden of expenses and debts increases, the suicide rates increase, and this will inevitably happen because the most significant aspect of these laws is that outside the *mandi* procurement system, it is not just about the private traders, even the Food Corporation of India (FCI) will wash its hands off. In whichever way you spin this, everybody knows that the aim of this government is to destroy the *mandi* system.

WU: *In the national media, this movement is being presented as an anomaly; as if there is no past culture or history of farmers' agitations or* *unions in north India, that it should come as a shock to the people. Those who know Punjab, are aware that in Punjab there is a long history of farmers' resistance and rebellion, a legacy of anti-feudal and anti-colonial struggles. How would you explain this historically?*

HARTOSH BAL: To some extent it is important to understand that Punjab's social organisation is to a large extent (when compared to the rest of north India) different. For one thing, there is no upper-caste dominance in rural Punjab. Thakurs and Brahmins are not dominant castes in the rural areas. There are many Jat castes and some differences between them—some historical, some linguistic—but these groups intermingle considerably. If we look at Sikhism against this social pattern, and compare it to the OBC (Other Backward Classes) protests that we saw around the time of the Mandal Commission, we see that in Punjab a similar event had already happened 400 to 500 years ago. However, that revolution was never completed. After Mandal Commission, Yadavs in UP and Bihar progressed, but it didn't mean that Dalits too were uplifted. This distinction between Dalits and Jats is still very evident in Punjab, and there are still a lot of differences between the two. The mobilisation of Jats is not only the consequence of OBC empowerment over the last 50 years, but it is also a part of the history of Sikhism for the last 300 to 400 years. This rural reorganisation of Sikhs from the time of the Sikh Misls and Baghel Singh and Banda Singh Bahadur [the first Sikh warrior and military leader to wage a war against the Mughal rulers of India] ensured that the land holdings went into the hands of Jats. So another reason that the Green Revolution happened in Punjab and not all over the Indo-Gangetic plain was because in Punjab there wasn't as much tenancy farming—the farmers worked in their own farms with their own hands, not in the lands of zamindars. This situation was amenable to the market, to the adoption of new technologies. Farmers were able to react to the changing situation because their land holdings were directly controlled by them. The farmers here were influenced by Sikhism, the Ghadar movement, and other outside influences, through army recruitment at the time of British colonialism when soldiers left India and then subsequently came back. The Ghadar Party, for example, was significantly influenced by the American Constitution, before the rise of the USSR and the communist revolutions. Talk of socialism had begun in Punjab because of these various influences.

Earlier, you made a reference to the 1907 Pagdi Sambhal Jatta[4] movement. The movement was centred round Jats, but we also have ideas from the Left brought by individuals like Sardar Ajit Singh (Bhagat Singh's uncle), who was also a prominent leader associated with the Ghadar movement. After the Pagdi Sambhal Jatta movement he left India via Iran to go to Europe, and met European revolutionaries. The Pagdi Sambhal movement was, just like today, against agriculture laws that were an effort to change the patterns of land-holding at that time. The Punjab Land Colonisation Act 1906 too had to be repealed by the British government.

In these protests, Jats from what we would today call Haryana and Punjab were involved. The Sikh and Jat peasantry mobilisation has been revisited repeatedly in history since then. The Gurudwara Reform Movement[5], which Mahatma Gandhi called the first victory in the Indian freedom movement, drew its cadres from this very same peasantry, part of whose members included discharged servicemen who fought in World War I and who subsequently returned to India. There was an agrarian crisis, the economy was in decline, and a cause presented itself to them: to retake control of gurudwaras. The Shiromani Gurudwara Parbandhak Committee (SGPC) was formed and after two years of struggle, they too were successful.

After this, there was the Praja Mandal Movement, in which Amarinder Singh's ancestors were involved. The Praja Mandal Movement fought the zamindari system, where land-owners (relatives of Amarinder Singh's ancestors) were extorting Jat peasants. The Praja Mandal Movement stopped payments. Earlier in this movement the Congress and Akalis were present too, but they withdrew support, and the movement was solely in the hands of the Left or the Praja Mandal (people's assembly). Legislation passed after Independence redistributed the land to those who had became *muzaras* (tenant farmers) during the rule of Amarinder Singh's ancestors. This muzara movement started in 1928 and went all the way until 1952. This movement happened especially in this area where today's movement draws its core from, i.e., Malwa, where the majority of the people assembled at Tikri border also come from. The Kirti Kisan Union mobilised on the basis of this history.

The Left has been very strong in Malwa. There are three regions in

Punjab: Malwa is south of the Sutlej, then between Sutlej and Beas there is Doaba, and north of the Beas there is Majha. While the stronghold of the Sikhs is in Majha, because the erstwhile princely court was in Amritsar, the centre of agrarian protests has always been Malwa. In this region, there have been land struggles over the last 20 to 30 years, which haven't really been reported on in Delhi. To some extent, these protest movements have agitated Dalits to have land allotted to them. Some have spoken about agricultural workers' rights. But to a large extent the focus in this region has been on farmers.

WU: *Another important figure in this farmers' movement is Banda Singh Bahadur, who is associated with Sikh history and gave the call for land to the tiller against the zamindari system. So he comes from both the Sikh tradition and the revolutionary land reform tradition. Perhaps he can be called the first person to make land reform a major issue. Maybe the reason why he is constantly referred to is because of this convergence?*

HARTOSH BAL: To some extent, on very broad grounds. When you speak up against caste, when you propagate ideas like langars, when you speak of popular assemblies, where work is done for the community out of commonly collected donations, it is natural that these ideas from the Sikh ethos will find resonance within the Left. On top of this, when Banda Bahadur launched an attack on Saharanpur after the death of Guru Gobind Singh, the Jat kisans were given ownership of the land in that region, and the Mughal zamindari system was demolished. So what you say is true, that land reforms gave Jats ownership of the land. In this whole region, you will see that farmers from Punjab were the first to acquire land ownership. So this 300 to 400 year history that I've mentioned wasn't just a cultural uplift of OBCs. It was an economic empowerment too. We see the effects of this even today.

If you look at it from a different perspective—Kancha Iliah has written an article in *The Caravan* titled 'Where Are India's Shudras?' By Shudra he meant farming communities. Shudra intellectuals in India are very few. Their movement's leadership has always been from other castes. Even Ram Manohar Lohia was a Baniya, he wasn't an OBC. The exceptions to this you will find only in Sikhism, in Punjab. This is because the history of 300 to 400 years of empowerment has meant that the Brahminical influences have completely disappeared. So in Punjab the intellectual requirements are supplied from within the community itself.

You said that there are so many symbols in Punjab; so many ideas are evoked over and over again. Whether the symbolism is of Bhagat Singh or Banda Bahadur, whether the ideas are from Sikhism or the Left, they are ideas that are homegrown, they have come from within the community, they haven't been imported from an external source or ethos. This is an organic ethos.

WU: *As you have just mentioned, in Punjab the Jats are the landed community, and this has historically been their region. Perhaps the British Raj brought in caste-based land and agricultural laws...*

HARTOSH BAL: Yes, The Land Alienation Act of 1900.[6]

WU: *But Punjab also has a large Dalit population, perhaps the largest. The relationship of Dalits with the farmers is as agricultural labourers. In the beginning it seemed like this gap, this contradiction, is massive, it cannot be resolved. When we toured the Malwa region, we encountered a political organisation called the Zameen Prapti Sangharsh Committee (ZPSC), which works among Dalit agricultural labourers. Their leaders and cadres are prominently involved in this present agitation. We visited Barnala, where along with BKU (Ekta-Ugrahan) there was a joint rally by the Punjab Khet Mazdoor Union as well. What we're seeing here is some kind of a convergence between agricultural labourers and farmers, between Dalits and Jat farmers. How did this convergence evolve?*

HARTOSH BAL: There are a number of aspects to this. As I mentioned before, land holdings in Punjab to a large extent—almost entirely, in fact are in the hands of Jats. The caste hierarchy is clearly visible. We can certainly say that if one compares this with the rest of the Indo-Gangetic plain, then the hierarchy is relatively lax and that the situation in Punjab is better. Now, this doesn't mean that the situation in Punjab is good, but when compared to the rest of north India it is better.

The second thing is that the scope and effects of these laws affect the farmer organisations directly. These laws take aim at Punjab's agriculture. The lands of the small farmers will be expropriated; there will be land consolidation, contract farming, mechanised farming, etc. This will force people to exit the rural economy, because this new kind of farming will only give permanent employment to a few. This massive retrenchment is being done at a time when the central government is already unable to generate employment. In the last ten years, the jobs that the government has claimed to produce wouldn't even be enough to employ the farmers who will lose their livelihood as a result of these laws in Punjab, let alone all of India. Thus the rural economy that sustains this labour force is under threat due to these laws. The effort on the part of farmer unions has been to recognise these things and involve themselves in these issues. As a result, the gap has shrunk to some extent. Labour unions are involved here as well. The contradictions will remain too, but this doesn't mean that labourers and farmers are standing against each other, or that anyone is standing with the government. Both these groups are against the government and these laws.

WU: *Along with the farmer unions, there are Left-backed agricultural worker unions as well. A major issue for them is the Essential Commodities Act, and the continuous shrinkage of the Public Distribution System (PDS). This is also a major reason for the two groups to come together. Our observation is that it is often mentioned by farmer and labour union leaders that there may be contradictions in our villages, and they will continue to exist, but the present struggle is against a big corporate system. Do you agree with this articulation?*

HARTOSH BAL: I didn't talk about PDS because PDS is a big issue in itself. It opens up another can of worms. The purpose of the Green Revolution was to achieve self-sufficiency in food grains. If you look at the data, the per capita food grain availability in our country has stayed the same from 1965 until today. The achievement of the agriculture of Punjab and Haryana is that, while the population has grown from 500 million then to 1.3 billion now, the availability of grain per capita hasn't fallen. From the point of view of the whole country, it is a very big failure that between 1965 and 2021 we have not been able to increase the per capita grain availability for ordinary people.

Compare this with Sri Lanka or Bangladesh—I won't even talk about China—there you will see much greater per capita availability of food grains. This is also evident from our undernourished populations. These people constantly say that grains are rotting in the FCI's storage. This is happening at a time when people do not have access to food grains. So these questions—about rotting grains and procurement—must be asked to the government. Instead, we see these questions being thrown at farmers. The government—in a country where there is low availability of food grains—is allowing grain to rot in storage. The responsibility for this lies with the government. It is said that there are difficulties in procurement, that there is a shortage of money. These questions should be asked to the government.

Incidentally, agricultural economist Ashok Gulati has said that if you look at the last 15 to 20 years of the procurement system, it works out effectively as an 'implicit tax' on the farmers, not a subsidy, because the restrictive trade policies drive down profits. They claim that getting rid of the system will benefit farmers, and at the same time there are economists who claim that procurement at MSP is subsidising rich farmers. There's a big game being played with farmers by these economists. I want to say this too, that the economists and commentators that you will see in the media come from one or two upper castes.

WU: *I keep referring to the PDS because in the beginning, when the demand was made to guarantee MSP and to expand its scope, the response was that if MSP was guaranteed, then that would lead to inflation, which would affect purchase of food grains by the urban poor. The government's recommendation is also based on the Shanta Kumar Committee Report, that the PDS system and procurement of foodgrains by FCI be gradually ended. So it seems important that when we talk about the Essential Commodities Act we also talk about the PDS.*

Hartosh Bal: It's also necessary because the government today says that it has not written in the laws that they are removing MSP. They say, it is not written in the laws that they are dismantling the *mandi* system. But we know the background of all this is happening against, and what effect these laws will have. On the one hand you are breaking the *mandi* system. When you do this, parallelly private *mandis* will grow. What will this lead to? The government says that it will lead to people moving away from paddy cultivation and this will lead to crop diversification. This talk about diversification is nonsense. The scale at which Punjab requires diversification implies stopping paddy cultivation in 10 to 15 lakh hectares. This is not a question of diversification. If this diversification needed to happen, it would have happened with the government's involvement, with an extension of the MSP guarantee for other crops. Diversification cannot happen in the hands of private players. So this is another lie that is being spread.

When these private players purchase crops, they will pick up wheat and paddy, after the FCI stops procurement. Everybody knows what will happen to grain availability when things are left to the free market. Everybody understands this significance in the context of essential commodities, where hoarding and price manipulation are real possibilities. This package of laws reflects a desire for a different kind of agriculture, one that is mechanised and based on large land-holding farmers. This will decimate the rural economy. You can create an economy where a few farmers' incomes are increased, but most people will be removed from the rural economy; and agricultural labour will also be affected.

On top of this jobs are not being created, and they want to remove the PDS. So the overall impact will be similar to the effect we have seen on our school and healthcare systems. We are heading towards an American system where public health and public education are missing. The changes to farming will have the following effect: the government will provide a subsidy that is a fraction of what the American government gives its farmers, but even that fraction won't go to the farmers, instead it will go to those doing corporate farming. So the direct benefits are not in purchasing, or in trade; the government's subsidies will only directly benefit the corporations engaged in corporate farming. So this is really a matter of re-organising society. This reorganisation will not only affect farmers, it will also directly affect labour.

WU: *Now let us come to electoral politics. Consider the politics of Mandir, Mandal and Market that the BJP-RSS are constantly driving, the social engineering among different castes and the Rohini Commission report which recommended further fragmentation of OBC quotas. With this 20* *to 30 year long run of identity politics and the economic issues of today (labour law amendments, farm law amendments), we can say that this agitation has filled many of the gaps and fault-lines that existed. We saw in 2013 in western UP the contradictions between Jats and Muslims, or the contradictions between Jats and non-Jats in Haryana and Punjab. With the gaps that this agitation has filled, is there a hope that identity-based politics will shift towards economic and class-based politics?*

HARTOSH BAL: My personal impression, based on reporting on politics for the last 20 years in this country, is that such alliances are temporary. To some extent, we should gather hope from them, but in India the reality of caste eventually comes to the fore. The reality of caste is consolidated to some extent by religious communalism. Without breaking one, the other is difficult to break. In the larger sense, when you talk about political reformulations, this indeed has an effect.

Especially in Punjab, the distance between Hindus and Sikhs is tied to the history and formation of Punjab on the basis of language and the events of the '80s and '90s. Punjab hasn't really owned up to the difficulties faced by Hindus during this period. In Punjab we talk often about Sikh victimisation—you talked about GBS Sidhu and how the Khalistan movement was created. But the effect that has been felt by the Hindu minority—especially the migration in Majha, near Amritsar, from rural to urban areas—has not been documented fully until today. These subjects have not come out in the open.

I do feel, however, that a gap has been bridged by this movement. In the municipal corporation elections, the BJP has suffered its most crushing defeat in the last 50 years. When I say BJP I also include the Jan Sangh, etc. The second gap has been between Punjab and Haryana—an artificial gap which was created in the '80s and '90s based on river water issues. The reason for this is the Centre. These differences have largely been settled. But if we say that in Haryana the division between Jats and non-Jats has healed fully, that will be wrong. The BJP's effort will be to continue this kind of politics.

Today too, you'll see caste-based mobilisations. In Haryana, Rajasthan, and western UP, among the farmers there are a large number of Rajputs. The influence that the BJP has among the Rajputs is considerable, so their involvement in this farmers' struggle is limited. This is despite their numbers being considerable in certain areas where their economic interests should have caused them to join together in this struggle. To some extent, the gap between Punjab and Haryana has reduced. As for the effect on Haryana's internal politics, it is certainly true that the BJP cannot repeatedly win elections by constantly antagonising Jats. In the previous election they were only able to form the government with the help of Dushyant Chautala (of Jannayak Janta Party, also the Deputy CM of Haryana). I don't think any Jat leader can afford to take the risk of supporting a BJP government next time. In western UP there has definitely been such an effect of the movement.

It is also good to pay attention to another aspect that we spoke about earlier, that in Punjab there is a general sentiment against majoritarianism. The Left leaders from Punjab, like Ugrahan and others, have a lot of clarity about this. They are standing against the government on many issues. It's not just about privatisation. They have taken stands against political imprisonment, and in Punjab there is a lot of support for this. These issues are not as big in Haryana and UP. When you talk about Modi or majoritarianism, these things do not play as big a role in these states. So people have come together with different issues. This will have many effects. How long this will take to consolidate, what will happen in the future, these things are difficult to say, but what gains have been won are in my opinion significant.

I think these developments will have an effect on Punjab going forward. There was a despondency in Punjab—despondency about addiction, despondency about debts, or even electoral despondency. Punjab has tried a lot to think past Akali corruption, BJP manipulation and the legacies of the Congress. The Aam Aadmi Party (AAP) gave impetus to this effort. This movement has united Punjab in a remarkable way. Earlier each village would be split into two to three camps, now for the first time we see a movement in the last 40-50 years that has inspired this sort of unity and optimism. The flip side is that if the movement doesn't succeed, or if the government breaks this movement, it will have a deep effect on Punjab.

WU: *Badal and Amarinder Singh, both represent feudal interests of the landed class. It appears there is a vacuum, a gap in Punjab, where other* *political forces can create their space. In between, AAP also arose as an experiment. After this agitation, do you foresee any change in electoral politics in Punjab? Because the farmer unions and Left organisations do not participate in electoral politics. Do you see the emergence of a left-of-centre political party after all this?*

HARTOSH BAL: There is a need for it, and there is the space for its articulation, and there is support, but for now it is unclear whether this will happen. Whether we like it or not, the fight between small and big Jats is a very old fight, which often gets subsumed under the moniker of Jat politics. I frequently refer to this example: at the time of Operation Blue Star[7] at the Golden Temple, on one side we had General Brar leading the Indian army, on the other side we had Bhindranwale. Bhindranwale was a Brar Jat, so was General Brar. Their hometowns were four kilometres apart. Bhindranwale was from a non-affluent family, he was sent to a *taksal* (an educational institution based on the teachings of a *sant* or spiritual leader) where he grew up. General Brar's family, for three generations, studied at Sandhurst and other big colleges. I'm not speaking just of agriculture; even people like me have to some extent gained from the Indian state in many aspects. But in Punjab, there are many small Jat communities that have not benefited from it. This issue has often come to the fore. In the '80s and '90s, the militants came largely from the smaller Jat communities. In politics, the last representation of this was around 1997-98, when Gurucharan Singh Tohra died and after that we had Prakash Singh Badal and Amarinder Singh, whose social class and background were very similar. This has been the time of domination by the *kakaji* culture of big Sikh leaders' sons, who are big farmers and who control politics. We're seeing for the first time a movement where, clearly, there is no influence of Badal, or the Akalis, despite the Sikh ethos. Yes, I think in the last 50 years this is the first time we're seeing a popular movement where the Akalis have no role. Neither the Congress nor Amarinder Singh has the confidence to go and control this movement. And the same is true of the big farmers, the *kakajis*.

The leadership here is of small farmer organisations, led by the Left, which is propelling this movement forward; this kind of leadership has to come to the fore in Punjab in order to change its political future. And it is very important for Punjab. It is clear that Punjab wants change, but where will this change come from? This will be clear only after the movement. I think change will definitely come in Punjab's politics, depending on this movement's failures and successes.

WU: *My last question is regarding the media. A large section of the media has surrendered and submitted to a kind of journalism that takes dictation—a sort of "court" journalism. We see at the same time that via social media and their own IT cell, the farmers have developed parallel channels of communication –Youtubers, Facebook live streamers, etc. Can this sort of alternative media initiatives compete with corporate media, or can they become a viable alternative? Or are these small efforts that have very little meaning?*

HARTOSH BAL: To some extent it has meaning. From the response of the government, it is clear that it indeed affects the government. Whether it is 200 Twitter handles or even our own [*The Caravan*'s] Twitter handle, they want to shut these voices down. They file false cases. Just today, new rules[8] for online regulation have been framed and released where it becomes clear what kinds of actions the government can take in the name of "regulation." So the government does fear these things, because they want a single narrative in this country—their own narrative.

According to this narrative, Navreet Singh's death[9] happened because the tractor flipped over. Whether the people standing there said that he was shot, whether the family is saying something else—these things don't matter. What they want is for neither the family nor the eyewitnesses nor the media to have the right to challenge the narrative of the government. This extends to everything, such as the farm laws and the protests.

The big story is the abdication of the media. What is abdication? Look, India has an English language media, and what is true of the English media is even more true for the Hindi media: both are upper-caste dominated and support the Hindutva agenda. Media and government are working together. It is one thing when you surrender to the government out of fear. And it is entirely a different thing, when you enthusiastically participate in the actions of the government. To a large extent this is the situation of the media: they are participating in the actions of the government. The effect of this is—we know this, and people in Punjab and Haryana know this—that the 9 pm prime time news stories are told by corrupt people. But people listen to them every day, and they have an effect on people, and this effect is visible. The kind of support that Modi has today is because of the help of propaganda and the media. In the face of this support, when we talk about small media houses, or independent media, or social media, they will only have a small effect. However, just because the effect is small, we mustn't say that it is meaningless, this work is important to do.

WU: *Do you have any concluding remarks about the future of this agitation?*

HARTOSH BAL: What has been left out, I think, is what is happening from the government's side. From 2014, this government has only withdrawn one law, that too was a law related to land—RFCTLARR (Amendment) Ordinance, 2014. At that time, there was some strength in the opposition too. This is the first time the government has faced an opposition that they haven't been able to manage, control, or subdue. They haven't been able to put a label on this opposition, despite trying hard.

As far as Narendra Modi or Amit Shah are concerned, they have nothing to do with the country's progress. So they are ready to do anything. The fear is how far these people are willing to go to achieve their ends and the country's ruin. Electorally, they have very little influence in Punjab and Haryana, maybe eight to ten seats in the Lok Sabha. Their fear is related to Uttar Pradesh. Their fear is that there the elections are fought between three to four parties, where 1.5 to 2 percent of the votes make a huge difference. I think the efforts on the government's part has been to break this movement into two to three sections, to emphasise differences between Hindus and Sikhs, to isolate western UP, and to manage Rakesh Tikait. This strategy suits this government well. And after all this, if this doesn't work, then what steps will the government take to have their way? This is difficult to say now because it isn't clear why the government isn't preparing for a repeal of the laws. Talk of suspending these laws for one and a half years is over. Two or two and a half years may pass, but matters are moving towards a complete repeal. The elections are coming, and the government will have to take decision.

I think now this is not simply a matter of Modi's ego; it is about Modi's ability to run an election, based on where his funding comes from. It has become a matter of pleasing his donors as well. The money comes from big corporations. The hold that the BJP has on India today is based on imbalances of electoral funding. In the 2014 election, when Congress was in power, the BJP spent more money than the Congress. Today the situation is such that 90 percent of electoral funding is going straight to the BJP, partly because of the system of electoral bonds. All this money comes from big corporations like Adani and Ambani, without whom it isn't possible to speak of big corporations. Keeping this source of electoral funding alive is very important for BJP, Modi, and Amit Shah. So I see two things: Modi's ego, and this constituency of big corporations that guarantees their electoral success.

Endnotes

1. During the 18th century, Punjab was ruled by the Sikh Confederacy. It was a union of 12 sovereign states called *misl*s.

2. Till the mid-1800s Punjab was an arid area with mostly subsistence farming. To increase tax revenues by commercialising agriculture, the British undertook a massive irrigation project in the region. The land thus irrigated, previously considered wasteland, was allocated in large parcels to peasants to create "canal colonies." Nine such colonies were established between 1885 and 1940.

3. Chhotu Ram was a prominent Jat leader (from Haryana). He is considered as one of the 'architects of kisan politics' in North India.

4. The Pagdi Sambhal Jatta lehar (movement) of 1907 is among the most celebrated historical struggles of the farmers in Punjab. This movement was triggered by the passing of the Punjab Land Colonisation Act 1906 in the Punjab Legislative Council in February 1907.

5. The Gurudwara Reform Movement or the Akali movement was a campaign to bring reform in the gurudwaras in India during the early 1920s. The movement led to the introduction of the Sikh Gurudwara Bill in 1925, which placed all the historical Sikh shrines in India under the control of Shiromani Gurudwara Parbandhak Committee (SGPC).

6. The Land Alienation Act of 1900 classified people as being either "agriculturalist" or "non-agriculturalist" and limited the transfer of land between those two groups. The subsequent Punjab Land Alienation Act of 1907 further restricted the transfer of land

ownership between various groups.

7. Operation Blue Star was a military operation ordered by prime minister Indira Gandhi in June 1984 at the height of the Sikh militant struggle for a separate state of Khalistan to flush out armed militants led by Jarnail Singh Bhindranwale from Harmandir Sahib inside the Golden Temple in Amritsar.

8. The regulations being referred to here are the Information Technology (IT) Rules 2021. Among other things, these rules mandate that news websites, social media sites, etc., take down any information that the government decides to be against national interest. Social media sites are required to provide the government with information regarding their users, the original source of any piece of information, etc.

9. Navreet Singh was participating in the farmers' Tractor Parade on 26 January 2021, when he died. Many eyewitnesses and family members claimed that he was shot by the police, and as a result the tractor he was driving hit police barricades and overturned. The police claimed that he died due to the tractor accident and no shots were fired.

In the Coming Days, the Polarisation Between People Supporting and Opposing the WTO will Get Stronger

PAVEL KUSSA, EDITOR, *SURKH LEEH*

> PAVEL KUSSA is the editor of the Punjabi magazine *Surkh Leeh*. Pavel was one of the organisers of the farmers' agitation and is the coordinator of BKU (Ekta-Ugrahan). He has written many critical articles on various aspects of the farmers' movement against pro-corporate economic policies of the Indian government.
>
> WORKERS UNITY interviewed him on 1 October 2021 at the Tikri border protest site in Bahadurgarh.

WORKERS UNITY: *Let's begin with the farmers' protests which have been going on for over a year now. Just two days ago, protesting farmers were mowed down at Lakhimpur Kheri and the Haryana chief minister made inflammatory statements. It looks like the state and the ruling party are showing signs of desperation in dealing with the agitating farmers. Even the farmers' movement, after a year, is in a stalemate. How do you view the agitation at this point of time, and what do you think is the road ahead?*

PAVEL KUSSA: After over a year of protests, the farmers' movement has actually gained a lot. Of course, the laws haven't been repealed yet; the Modi government's economic reforms are bringing on fresh assaults on different sections of people, but this movement has given all those sections the courage and hope to fight back. It has changed the atmosphere of hopelessness across the nation.

The government took advantage of the Covid crisis and hurriedly implemented various anti-people policies. To deal with the large impending global crisis of capitalism, they brought in labour codes, farm laws, New Education Policy, and many such other programs in various sectors. In the prevailing situation, the farmers' movement has become an example for people to follow. It has shown that you can indeed resist this government, you can indeed fight the attacks on your rights, and this is a huge achievement.

Now we are at a point where BJP has exhausted every weapon in its arsenal. It tried to communalise the protests, but failed. It tried to say that the movement was limited only to Punjab, then only to Punjab and Haryana. All these claims have been proved wrong. They tried to propagate that it was sponsored by foreign forces, but no one took that seriously either. They just could not change the narrative, try as they might. The farmers' movement has been too strong and has so far been able to fight off all the slanderous campaigns. Today, the corporates and the BJP government are on one side and India's farmers and working class on the other side.

The state and the ruling classes have always used violence. Apart from the police and armed forces, the government also indulges in *gundagiri* (hooliganism) to keep dissenting people under control. You know about Bihar, you know what atrocities the Ranvir Sena (a militia formed by the upper-caste Bhumihar landlords to counter the influence of the revolutionary left groups fighting for the rights of the landless peasantry in central Bihar) used to commit there until recently. No doubt, the farmers resisting the policies of the current government will face violence from the state and its agents; the Lakhimpur Kheri massacre[1] is just one such example. We have also heard Haryana CM Khattar's statement that the citizens should pick up sticks and go after the agitating farmers. Even in Lakhimpur Kheri, the killers were connected to a Union minister. The movement is at a stage where farmers need to be prepared against such kinds of violent offences.

But using open violence on the farmers is also proving to be counterproductive. It provokes a lot of response—especially at international level, such as from the UK-based Punjabi population and human rights organisations. So there is a limit that they supposedly cannot afford to cross. But then the BJP and the Modi government do not really care. They might keep using violence despite international outrage, like they did with the anti-CAA/NRC protests. So the farmer leadership and the rank-and-file need to be ready to face this. We need a kind of resistance, where the farmers take charge of their own self-defence. Of course the protests are peaceful and they should stay that way for now. Their [farmers] strength is not enough to go on the offensive at this stage. But they should start thinking about defence against this sort of violence from the BJP and other agents of the state.

I would summarise it in the following way. The main strength of the farmers' movement is in the villages. What is happening on Delhi borders is mainly symbolic. It is big, but still the main strength is not there. The farmers in the villages need to be mobilised, and at the same time they need to organise for self-defence. If they don't start thinking about this now, the BJP might be able to terrorise people into submission.

The other thing is that the assembly elections are going to take place soon in UP and Punjab. In these places, the violent face of the BJP needs to be exposed. It is good that there is such a clear video of the Lakhimpur massacre in the public domain. But even then, the BJP's propaganda machinery, TV channels and other media have started twisting the facts of the incident to create a Sikh vs. Hindu narrative. The violence is so clear in the video that the narrative is not working. Still, it is important that the farmers are able to ensure and highlight that this movement involves people from all religions and regions; only then can BJP be defeated.

WU: *You mentioned that the true strength of the movement is in the villages, so let us talk about that. In the rural plane, we are seeing more and more small and marginal farmers being pushed out from farming and forced to become wage labourers. The labourers do not get more than a month's work in farming, and the wages are also under pressure due to the influx of migrant labourers. How should a farmer union situate its politics in this context?*

PAVEL KUSSA: The first thing to understand is that this struggle that we are seeing has a strong anti-imperialist character. It is a resistance against the attacks of neoliberal imperialist policies. Not all farmer leaders see it this way, but the character of the struggle is anti-imperialist in terms of its objective material interests.

There are two assaults happening on Indian agriculture right now. The first is the adoption of agricultural policies dictated by imperialist interests, which the local corporates also take advantage of. This is mainly in those belts where the Green Revolution model of farming was implemented, where the farmers depend on selling their harvest to the government in the *mandis* (agricultural produce markets) at Minimum Support Price (MSP).

The second type of assault can be found in places where farmers are not tied to the *mandis*. Here, there is feudal exploitation. Feudal exploitation is there in the first type of agrarian belt as well, but that has been combined with imperialist exploitation due to commercialisation of agriculture. In case of areas where there is still feudal expoitation, there is very little surplus produce to sell at *mandis*, major part of production is for self-sustenance or taken by the landlord as rent.

To increase the strength of the ongoing movement, the farmers from this second type of agrarian belt must also be included. Their demands too must be given importance. The MSP issue only matters in the Green Revolution belts. Farmers in other regions don't get MSP. Here, apart from creating awareness about the MSP, the movement must demand building of notified *mandis*. Secondly, feudal exploitation must be dealt with. The land-ownership issue and the issue of debt to banks and *sahukars* (moneylenders) must be brought up. These are the issues that the farmer unions in those regions will have to take up to mobilise the farmers.

I'm not saying that these other demands must become the core demands of this particular movement. This movement will not be changing its core demands: the repeal of farm laws and legal guarantee of MSP for all crops. These demands are the reason why so many farmers have come to the protests. But the leadership also has a second job—unleashing the full potential of the peasantry in the country. For this, the leadership will have to also involve the section of peasants for whom MSP is not the main issue. Everybody must be involved; agricultural workers and landless farmers are mostly concerned about the impact of the Essential Commodities Act and the danger to the Public Distribution System (PDS). These concerns should be given importance.

WU: *When I was talking to various agricultural worker unions, they presented a paradox to me. If the MSP increases, there will be inflation in food prices, and workers will be affected negatively by it. The farmers'* *movement has given a lot more emphasis on MSP and not so much on universal PDS and amendments to Essential Commodity Act. Don't you think that the issues of MSP, PDS, and inflation in food prices are interrelated, and they should be highlighted equally in the movement?*

PAVEL KUSSA: The Essential Commodities Act will definitely affect large sections of people, both in the villages and the urban areas. There needs to be more awareness about this. It is a reality that there is more emphasis on MSP than PDS in the movement. This is not the fault of one person or one organisation. The leadership attempts many things, but they do not always work. Also different leaders are on different planes on these issues. After all there is such a big range of political orientations amongst the unions within the Samyukta Kisan Morcha (SKM)—from the rightist to the far left. And they have different approaches to the PDS issue; some ignore it, some occasionally mention it, some keep raising the issue. Unions, like the BKU (Ekta-Ugrahan), have a long history of agitating on the PDS issue. In Punjab, they went to people's houses, had meetings, mobilised people to educate them that the wheat and *dal* (lentils) they got from ration shops was under attack.

The prominence of any demand in a struggle is mostly decided by whether the relevant sections themselves have a presence and a voice in the struggle—how organised and agitated they are. We should look at this aspect too, apart from what the SKM leadership is doing. No matter what the leadership's attempts are, until the section that is impacted is organised and mobilised to raise their own demands, nothing will happen. Specific issues have come to the forefront of this movement because the landed farmers—the most organised section of the peasantry—have become the main force behind this movement. The leadership must keep trying to raise other demands, educate their rank-and-file to go to the landless labourers, discuss with them about their issues and bring them to the protest. Agricultural worker unions have made attempts, but it has not been enough.

If anyone feels, consciously or unconsciously, that there is a contradiction between the MSP and PDS issues, like you mentioned, the solution is the following. People must be told that all of these policies are interlinked and they come as a single package. However loudly you demand the continuation and increase in MSP, you should equally loudly also demand that the PDS needs to be kept going and expanded. Government also treats them as a single set—either both MSP and PDS should go or neither should. Without PDS, what will the government do with the grain it buys at MSP? Let it rot in their storages! Even the rich peasants owning 15-20 acres of land will have to demand PDS along with MSP because the government will not buy their grains unless PDS is there to distribute the grains.

This raises one more question. What the BJP is saying—actually what the Congress and governments led by other parties also say—how is it economically possible that we pay more money here [buy from farmers at MSP] and sell for less money there [distribute to the public at subsidised price through PDS]? This sounds like a logical economic question, but it is totally a political question. There is a simple solution: abandon these neoliberal policies. The neoliberal idea is that the government stays out of the picture and facilitates what they call "free trade." We should say that to us "free trade" means that the government keeps the corporations out of these things [procurement and distribution of food grains]. We should demand that the government must stay in the picture. Government needs to buy at MSP from the farmers and distribute via PDS to the people. And where will it get the money? From taxing Ambani, from taxing the multinationals. P. Sainath (a noted journalist) keeps saying how in Punjab, there are so many millionaires and billionaires; inheritance tax, wealth tax, profit tax etc. should be imposed on them. Then there will not be a shortage of money in the government treasury. But who will do this!

This is why the farmers' movement must make this demand—give MSP on all crops, tax the rich and use the money to finance schemes like universal PDS. I think that the farmers' movement must very clearly demand all of these things as a set and package it into a single slogan. Also it is equally important to raise the demand to decrease the cost of agriculture inputs. This will help to keep MSP at a reasonable level.

WU: *This entire set of interrelated issues cannot be taken up by the farmers' movement alone. Different sectional movements might raise specific demands. But all these policy measures are part of the corporations-led global economic and political order. The three farm laws are just one part* *of that scheme. This is not visible to the common person in its totality. As a political activist, how do you try to bring to people's awareness the fact that these laws are a part of a whole package and not just anti-people policies of this or that political party?*

PAVEL KUSSA: These farm laws were brought by the Modi government, but the Congress government was also planning to bring such laws in the name of reforms.

Let us go back to the 1960s. Shortly after independence, which was really just a transfer of political power, Indian ruling class politicians were raising slogans of socialism. The ruling classes wanted to build up the public sector and make India self-reliant to some extent. That was also needed to keep the Indian state stable. Even imperialist interests were served through the public sector; the Russians and Americans dealt mainly with the government. This is when the government built the *mandis*, announced MSP and started the PDS as a set of policy measures. They connected these to the Green Revolution. It was necessary for them. The only way to make farmers buy seeds, fertilisers, pesticides, etc. was through making promises about buying their harvest at MSP. All of this had to be done together as a set.

This entire set of policies came under attack in the '90s with the policy shift towards liberalisation, globalisation, and privatisation. It is only because of the strong peasant movements in Punjab and Haryana that MSP and PDS still exist. In 2000, there was a huge agitation in Punjab and Haryana. The farmers blocked the railways for days on these issues. The government tried several times to do away with this system by withdrawing it, but faced stiff resistance every single time. Since the '90s, every government has been taking steps in that direction. The Agricultural Produce & Livestock Market Committee (APMC) Act was amended several times and weakened, they started giving more and more space to private players to enter the sector. For example in 2017, Amarinder Singh's government brought an amendment to the Punjab APMC Act, allowing private players to enter the agri-market. The new farm laws by Modi are much more sweeping, they just want to clean up the entire system speedily, remove all the existing barriers and allow corporations full entry into the sector.

But this plan has been going on since the 1990s. There is an awareness in Punjab that the government is pushing for dismantling of the existing system. People ask, why the Punjabi farmers are leading this movement. The answer is that they were already aware of such policies and were continuously resisting such attempts. The leaderships of the farmer unions have also been campaigning and educating farmers at the village level about the WTO policies such as doing away with subsidies in agriculture and opening it to big corporates. In 1993-94 when I was a kid, the farmer union in my village would make big effigies of the then GATT chief Arthur Dunkel and burn them. At that time, people did not fully grasp the significance of those protests. But they heard what their leaders were talking about.

This continuous campaign and work at the grass root level have been crucial. The leadership has constantly been telling people that companies will come in and take your land and livelihood. In a few years, people started to experience this directly. In 2006, the Trident group[2] acquired agricultural land in Punjab, there was a huge struggle against that. In the Malwa belt, peasants realised that the corporates and industrialists were coming for their land and the government was helping them to capture farmer's land. Then in 2011, Indiabulls tried to acquire land in Mansa, and at the same time, the Land Acquisition Act was also passed. There was a huge struggle, and the government had to amend the Act in 2013. People kept understanding this more and more clearly, as they kept resisting the moves. By now, at least some sections of the people can see things clearly; along with Ambani and Adani, there are also foreign companies—who now want to control the entire agriculture sector.

The idea of imperialism is not new to the people in Punjab. The farmer leaders say that the fact that your fertilisers and pesticides are manufactured and sold by American and German companies is exactly what imperialism is. As far as farmers are concerned, Adanis and Ambanis are also imperialist companies. It is only people like us, who make distinction between imperial capital and comprador bourgeoisie; farmers see them as the same. They don't care who is from where, their concern is how these companies are coming after their land and livelihood. They know that they have to fight against both of them to survive.

There are some farmer leaders, who now get on the stage and urge people not just to fight against the farm laws, but also to get India out of the bondage of the WTO. These are the same farmer leaders who in the 1990s and even in 2000s said that India being under WTO was good for Punjabi farmers! They have now realised, after these farm laws were passed, how even the rich farmers are under the threat of being pushed out from their land by the companies.

WU: *The 1980s saw massive farmers' mobilisation led by Mahendra Singh Tikait in UP, Nandu Gowda in Karnataka, Sharad Joshi in Maharashtra. In these movements, which were mainly organised by the rich peasants, the core demands were also around issues like MSP, debt waivers, etc. But there was always another strand of the peasant movement led by the left, which as you said, was agitating against the WTO, raising the question of land distribution etc.*

In the last five years or so, we've seen both of these strands of the farmers' movement coming together and starting joint protests. The SKM, leading the current farmers' movement against the three farm laws, is constituted by unions from the extreme right to the far left. This process has started since the Maundsar police firing on farmers and the historic peasants' march from Nasik to Mumbai took place. How do you view the coming together of both of these strands?

PAVEL KUSSA: This is a good distinction that you've made. The second stream [farmers' movement in the '80s] was far from the anti-feudal struggle; they mainly involved rich farmers and feudal lords. This strand did not care about PDS and was concerned only with getting higher MSP and debt waivers. But since indebtedness and MSP affect not just the big landlords but also the small and middle peasants, they could also mobilise these sections of the peasantry. The demands which are relevant only to the small and middle peasants such as more land, freedom from *sahukars*, access to cheap loans, other subsidies etc. were never at the top of their agenda. We see that the landlords and the small/middle farmers have common interests as well as contradictions. The anti-feudal left strand has emphasised these contradictions, while the post-1980s strand has stressed on the commonalities.

In this movement, both these strands are involved; however, the shades of commonalities have changed in the last few years. Earlier, the leaders stressing on the MSP demand felt that WTO was advantageous to farmers; they thought that free trade would mean more opportunity to the farmers to sell their produce nationally and globally. But over time they've found that even rich farmers are no match for the big capitalists. The crops they produce on their 15 to 20 acres of land are no match to the sheer volume and power of a Cargill or a Nestle. So now we see that some of the same leaders who were pro-WTO for a long time, are saying very clearly that repealing the laws isn't enough, India has to get out of the WTO as well. And this is increasingly becoming a popular demand. Not as popular as the one about the repeal of the laws, but the consciousness is spreading amongst the farmers, at least in Punjab and Haryana.

Within 30 years we are at the point where no farmer leader can even think of saying that they support the WTO. They've all come around to this side of the line. The support for the anti-imperialist movement and the people who want to build it has increased. The people to whom the issue of imperialism had to be explained with great difficulty, can now see and understand it by observing what is going on. Today an ordinary farmer talks about WTO and companies trying to take their land. This shows the progress of the farmers' movement. In the coming days, the polarisation between people supporting and opposing the WTO will get stronger.

WU: *Punjab is the state with the largest Dalit population. One-third of the population in Punjab are Dalit and in rural areas they are primarily landless labourers. As we were travelling across the Malwa region, where the* pendu mazdoor *(rural worker) unions work, we observed that land had often been captured by the rich peasants in the villages. We also observed caste atrocities and fixing of labour wage. There are instances of definite clashes between the landed Jat peasantry and the Dalit landless labourers. Simultaneously, we also saw some constructive development in the form of a united front with the Punjab landless labourers and the* pendu mazdoor *unions recently during 9-11 August in Patiala. However in the rural areas, the cases of caste atrocities are increasing. Caste is the biggest reality, and without an anti-caste consciousness, no progressive movement can advance in India. What do you think are the challenges* *for a progressive movement, and what are the bases of cooperation and contradiction between the landless labourers and the landed, which is further made complex by the caste angle?*

PAVEL KUSSA: Caste is a big challenge. It requires a huge effort and a lot would depend on organisational approach to address the question. It can only be solved and overcome from a class angle. Primarily, we must take caste, whether it is in Punjab or India, as a 'contradiction within the people.' To take the case of rural Punjab, an area that I have observed closely, it is the landlords who are mainly in need of labour, and they employ labour directly in their farms. The middle and small farmers employ only a few labourers. In their entire expenditure on cultivation, the cost incurred on employing labour is a minor part. What does this mean? It means that there is a direct conflict only between the big landlords and the labourers. This is because the landlords have large land holdings, so they need to hire a large number of labourers and hence to maximise their profit, they will try to pay the least possible wage to the labourers.

What happens is that the big landlords mobilise the middle and poor peasantry in their favour in the name of caste, and together they fix the wage of labour and force the labourers to work at that fixed wage. The agricultural labourers also mobilise their own class against the landlords. A peasant organisation with a revolutionary orientation should consider the agricultural labourers as their allies, on a class basis, and try to resolve their contradiction with the small and middle peasantry by overcoming the caste contradictions between them. At the same time, it should support the labourers' struggle for higher wages against the big landlords.

Conflicts arise mainly during the paddy sowing season, when the demand for agricultural labour is high. During these conflicts, farmers organisations with a revolutionary orientation can prevent such conflicts, they can make the farmers understand that in their total expenditure on cultivation, the amount they pay to the labourers is very low. Instead, they pay large amounts to the multinational companies for buying seeds, pesticides, tractors, etc. They also pay a lot towards loan repayment of the *sahukars*, banks, etc. In fact, the wage they pay to the labourers does not contribute towards increasing their debt at all. Therefore, it is important to make the landed peasantry realise that the reasons for their woes are not the agricultural labourers. I am giving you such a concrete example to demonstrate that if a farmers organisation takes this approach, then they can resolve the conflicts with the labourers.

Often we see both conflict and cooperation between farmer and agricultural worker organisations. Conflicts arise when farmer unions restrict themselves only to the issues of the land-owners and serve the interests of the landlords. Those unions must understand that given the present attack of imperialist forces on the overall peasantry, it is in their own interest, particularly so in the case of small and even middle farmers, that they join forces with the labourers.

I, along with some of the farmer union activists, was part of a survey in our village to understand the class structure. We found that in our village, not a single Jat farmer was landless till the 1980s. But after the New Economic Policy was introduced in the '90s, 16 to 17 percent of the Jat farmers in our village had become landless. In my village, if you take both the agricultural labourers and the Jat farmers, 80 to 85 percent of the population is in need of land. Their issues are the same. They need cheap loans from banks, freedom from exploitation of private moneylenders, cheaper food grains, free and subsidised electricity, and of course land. However, the difference of caste—Jats and Dalits—remains the dividing factor. Their class interests must be brought to the forefront to build a united front and the farmers unions must take the lead to fight against caste atrocities, even when someone from the Jat community is involved. Frankly speaking, the caste question has not been solved in India; communists tried to solve it but have failed. We want to talk from our experience in Punjab, where we try to bring the class question to the forefront and fight against Dalit atrocities in order to resolve the caste question. Certain essential tasks need to be considered in order to build a united front with Dalit labourers, such as, organising the Jat peasantry and developing their revolutionary potential, showing them the true reason behind their own exploitation, discussing with them how to look at issues from their class aspect, and at the same time directing them towards standing against every atrocity that challenges the Dalit assertion.

Dalit consciousness and assertion is growing, and it is a welcome phenomenon, but it needs revolutionary orientation. In Punjab, BKU (Ekta-Ugrahan) has had some experience in this direction. In a village near

Jhaloor, there was an attack on Dalits by landed Jat farmers and BKU (Ekta-Ugrahan) firmly stood their ground in support of Dalits. Some Jat members questioned this position: why should they stand against their Jat brother? The union very clearly stated and educated them about this being a matter of justice. A few Jat farmers left the union on this matter. There was another case in Muktsar in Gandhar village, where a Dalit girl was raped, and the accused were from the land-owning Jat peasantry. We fought unitedly and ensured that the perpetrators were arrested and sent to jail. When such a united struggle of farmers and agricultural labourers starts in an area, it is very hard for anyone to pit them against each other. But this can only come as an outcome of a conscious effort, because a deep contradiction exists within people, which the ruling classes frequently make use of.

The ongoing farmers' struggle has raised the slogan of *kisan-mazdoor ekta* (farmer-worker unity). It is a very positive outcome of this struggle. This slogan mobilised landless labourers to participate in the movement and even encouraged the labourers to consider the farmers' struggle as their own. This led to a breaking down of the caste barrier. Though the caste barrier has not been abolished, it has weakened significantly from before.

A negative narrative was created by many such as on the one hand there are slogans of *ekta*, and on the other, incidents of caste atrocities are happening in the villages. While these atrocities have been happening for a long time, it is a positive thing that despite caste differences, the farmer unions are trying to incorporate Dalit labourers into their struggle. But yes, this unity needs to be strengthened.

WU: *We are seeing a historic movement against the farm laws, but there has hardly been any workers' uprising against the labour codes. When we think on a pan-India level and imagine a mass movement across the nation, how do we incorporate the relationship of the working class/trade unions with the farmers' movement?*

PAVEL KUSSA: Currently, many sections across the nation are fighting for their economic and democratic rights at varying levels. While the farmers' agitation has become huge, others did not. Actually, what is necessary is to make people realise that their fight is against the neoliberal policies and the economic reforms.

The Indian ruling classes are siding with imperialism, and till now we do not have a big enough united resistance against it. Instead, there are multiple fragmented struggles on sectional demands. While these struggles reflect solidarity for each other occasionally, they are not becoming a part of the whole overall struggle against the imperialist attack.

BJP, after their second-term election victory, became confident that they can mobilise majority support in elections through their communal politics and nationalist slogans. So, during the Covid epidemic, they could afford to launch a big economic offensive against the people. Nirmala Sitharaman (Union Minister of Finance and Corporate Affairs) declared large concessions to the corporate sector and at the same time she announced the new farm laws and the labour codes. Further, this set included selling off the public sector companies and introducing the New Education Policy. To counter these attacks, resistance is building up, but not under a united front and a united leadership. There have been many attempts towards forging unity; like when the trade unions called an all-India strike, the farmers supported them and vice versa. But that's not enough.

WU: *The Punjabi youth is facing unemployment and it is also becoming harder for them to go to Canada. At the same time, BJP is pushing its Hindutva agenda, thereby constantly pitting the Hindus against the Sikhs. Historically, since the 1970s–80s, Punjab has seen a phase of Sikh identity movement that inspired the Punjabi youth, also helping them deal with the current neoliberal anxiety. Amidst all this, what is the current status of Punjab and how are the progressive farmer organisations viewing it?*

PAVEL KUSSA: After the Green Revolution, the unrest within the peasantry and youth was used by the ruling classes and that created the ground for the Khalistan movement to flourish. In the current farmers' movement, attempts were made to deviate the struggle by communalising it. For example, during the 26 January [2021] incident, a group displayed a flag of one particular religion at the Red Fort in Delhi. It was done by elements who wanted to drag the movement into religion-based politics. They wanted to use the movement to establish their religious viewpoint, even at the cost of harming the movement. However, one must also acknowledge that the identity of Punjabi nationality has helped the movement and brought people together. But this positive assertion of Punjabi identity should not take a jingoistic form. The farmer organisations have been successful in maintaining the secular and inclusive character of the movement.

WU: *In the past few years, many important movements have been organised such as Dalit identity based movements following the death of Rohit Vemula, anti-CAA-NRC movement led by Muslim women, and now the farmers' movement. Many have stood up against this authoritarian regime and these struggles are in need of having a united front, as you said. But in most cases the struggle takes the form of being against BJP or Congress or limited to economic or identity-based demands against the ruling parties. So, when we imagine a united front of mass struggle, what form do you think it will take?*

PAVEL KUSSA: This is a nationwide concern for people involved in the various movements. Secularism cannot be the only basis of such a united front. Even the Congress claims itself to be secular. A part of the secular, progressive and left section is moving towards the Congress to fight against the Modi government. One has to understand that behind the Modi government's fascist attacks, lie the pro-corporate economic reforms. Using religion and nationalism, they want to fill the pockets of the desi feudal lords and coffers of the corporate sector.

All the electoral parties at national level and in various states are going to implement the same economic reform policies. A truly secular united front against this regime involving adivasis, farmers, youth, students, employees, workers etc. is needed. Yes, sections of the ruling class parties like Akali Dal, Mamata Banerjee, BSP etc. must be used to fight against the Modi government, but to imagine forming a united front for mass struggle with them is an illusion. The electoral parties can be used, but they cannot be provided with a platform within mass movement.

WU: *Congress has made Charanjit Singh Channi the first Dalit Chief*

Minister of Punjab with an eye on the upcoming assembly elections in the state. There is a demand within the farmers' movement to form a political front and contest elections as people are disillusioned with parties like Congress and Akali Dal. Do you think the farmers' movement should form a political party and contest elections?

Pavel Kussa: Currently, this is a burning topic of discussion in Punjab. The people of Punjab are demanding the farmer leaders to enter electoral politics and make laws for themselves. In a way, it is a good thing that the people are relating their issues to politics whereas previously they only used to think in economic terms. However, the limitation is that they are under the illusion that the assembly or parliament can actually make laws in their favour.

The role that the farmer leadership should play is that they should intervene in this political vacuum and bring the basic issues of people around the elections to the forefront such as what the electoral parties' policies are on farmers' debt, their stances on WTO, their policies on providing land to the landless, revoking the 2003 Electricity Act, fighting atrocities on Dalits, improving public health and education, revoking the Private University Act, etc.

Endnotes

1. On 3 October, 2021, four farmers returning from a protest were killed in Lakhimpur Kheri (UP), after a car in the convoy of Ashish Mishra, the son of Union Minister of State for Home Affairs, ran over them. A jounrnalist also died in the incident.

2. In 2006, the Punjab-based textile manufacturer Trident Group acquired 376 acres of agricultural land in Barnala district for a new plant. This sparked a series of agitations by the farmers. Three farmers died and more than 70 were injured. Two years later, a settlement was reached with the Trident Group agreeing to pay 70 percent more than the government rate and the government withdrawing all cases against the farmers.

The Major Focus of the New Laws is to Have Corporate Control over Agricultural Output

Prof. Sukhpal Singh, Economist, Punjab Agricultural University

Prof. Sukhpal Singh is Principal Economist and former Head, Department of Economics and Sociology at Punjab Agricultural University, Ludhiana. He has undertaken landmark research on the agrarian economy of Punjab—unravelling indebtedness, peasant suicides and status of agricultural labour. He has been the coordinator of the farmer suicide study team and member of the committee constituted by the Punjab government to draft a policy for addressing the issue of farmers' and agricultural labourers' suicides and sanctioning compensation to families of suicide victims in the state. He writes frequently in *EPW* and dailies, especially *Punjabi Tribune* and *The Tribune*.

The Workers Unity team interviewed Sukhpal Singh on 30 March, 2021 at Ludhiana. Part II of the interview was conducted by Harshita Bhasin and Sahil Mehra of South Asian University in January 2022 on behalf of GroundXero.

PART I

Workers Unity: *The states of Punjab, Haryana and Western Uttar Pradesh, especially Punjab, are leading the agitation against the three farm laws enacted by the Union government. Punjab is the epicenter of this massive protest. What are the reasons for this?*

Sukhpal Singh: The main reason for Punjab leading the protest is that the state has a well-established regulated agri-market system, which is claimed to be the best regulated market system in the world. Through this system, every village in Punjab has been connected to the market and in every season, the farmers are able to sell their produce in their respective villages at Minimum Support Price (MSP). So, for both wheat and paddy the production and market are assured with minimum risk. In Punjab, Haryana, and Western UP almost all the produce is purchased through the public procurement system at MSP. Although there are some problems with the system, and the MSP system should be improved, it is still better than the rest of India. In other states of India there is targeted procurement whereas in Punjab, Haryana and Western UP there is universal procurement. Within the targeted procurement system, a target quota is fixed by the government, and it does not purchase beyond the targeted quota, the rest has to be sold in the private market. Punjab, Haryana, and Western UP have better infrastructure, better technology, and the benefits of the Green Revolution. Thus, there is naturally an anxiety among the farmers in these states that with the advent of these laws, these benefits will no longer be available, that there will be downgrading of the public procurement system, MSP, regulated markets, etc.

There are also social factors along with economic factors. With these laws there is an anxiety among the farmers that they will lose the ownership of their land and they will have to join the ranks of the labour class.

Another important reason is that in these regions, farmer organisations have been actively working since the Green Revolution. Obviously, it is not that these organisations came up in response to the enactment of these laws! Various aspects of farming like MSP, debts, suicide, power bill, etc.—all these issues have been taken up by these organisations. They immediately organised protests in June, when these ordinances were promulgated. They were later joined by various political parties in September, when the ordinances became laws. Moreover, farming is a central issue in Punjab. Even urban dwellers and NRIs associate themselves with the farming community. However, this is not the case with other states. Some states are not agrarian states. In some others, the Left political organisations are not active among farmers. One of the biggest differences is that many states do not have the benefit of a regulated market system to begin with. The farmers in these states are aware of the problems of debt, suicides, etc. But they are not thinking deeply and seriously about the issues raised by the three farm laws as the people of Punjab, Haryana, and Western UP have been able to do. Still, farmers from different states have been coming to the protest sites at Singhu, Tikri, and Ghazipur borders. In all, the availability of regulated markets, MSP, attachment to land, unavailability of alternate employment opportunities in other sectors of the economy—these are some of the important issues which force the peasantry in Punjab to organise protests.

WU: *Even before the enactment of these laws in September, the situation of farmers and agriculture as a whole has been characterised by severe distress and crisis. There has been news regarding farmer indebtedness and suicides in various states including Punjab, which indicates the severe crisis of the present agrarian model. So even if these laws are repealed, the current agrarian crisis may persist. What are your views on this?*

SUKHPAL SINGH: We can see this in two parts. First is when the Green Revolution was introduced, it led to an increase in production. Later it led to various socio-economic problems, environmental problems and degradation of natural resources. As a result, we are witnessing falling water tables, negative effect on fertility and on our health, and also various other problems like pollution.

A lot of work has already been done to understand the economic problems, which focused on indebtedness, depeasantisation and suicides. Initially the State maintained that there are no suicides in agriculture. Later three universities together planned to technically understand the issue and highlighted the high levels of agriculture related suicides all over India. It was found that in India over 4,50,000 people engaged in agriculture in the capacity of worker or cultivator had committed suicides. Every day, on an average, around 2,500 farmers are leaving agriculture, leading to depeasantisation.

Today, in Punjab there are 10 lakh families engaged in agriculture, and there is a total debt of Rs 1,00,000 crore on the peasantry, which amounts to an average debt of Rs 10,00,000 on each peasant family, while their average monthly income is only Rs 26,700.[1] So, a lot of small farmers are not in a position to even pay back the interest amount on their loans. One-third of the small farmers are not left with any income, and they are on the brink of bankruptcy. Their debt is about 2.5 times their income.

In the last 19 years, 16,600 farmers committed suicide. There is a study by the World Health Organisation (WHO), which finds that for every suicide, on an average there are about 20 suicide attempts. In Punjab, on an average three people commit suicide per day: two farmers and one agricultural labourer. If what the WHO claims is true, then every day in Punjab there are 60 people attempting suicide. So, in this small state that has been hailed as the success story of the Green Revolution and has been modeled to be replicated in other states of India, the situation is so grim that around 60 people are attempting suicide every day.

Now, once a person commits suicide, what happens next? There are many studies that clearly highlight that one-third of peasantry and one-half of agricultural labourers who have committed suicide were the sole bread-earners of the family. You can imagine the plight of those families. Even when that person was alive, the family was not able to manage their economic needs. Whereas now, that person is gone, and there is no one in their family who can earn a living. So, we can only imagine the distressful conditions under which the family must be living.

The Green Revolution enabled the control of corporates over input supply, which has had an important bearing in creating these conditions of distress and suicide. The new laws will not only enable control over inputs, seed, fertiliser, technology, machinery and credit but also on output of agricultural produce. The major focus of the new laws is to have corporate control over agricultural output, through which it will exploit not only the peasantry but also the consumer. It is agreed that even before the enactment of the three laws the situation in agriculture was not good. We also have to accept that the Green Revolution wasn't a good strategy. But these laws will surely further deepen the crisis. Due to these laws, there is going to be depeasantisation which, proving people's anxieties true, will lead to increase in labour supply, which in turn, will lead to fall in real wages, further worsening the economic situation. This is why these laws should be repealed.

WU: *You have written in detail about the impact of the amendments in the Essential Commodities Act on industrial labour and the middle class. In the last 20 years, you have extensively studied the situation of agricultural labourers. A large proportion of the total working force in Punjab's agriculture comprises agricultural labour. Moreover, migrant workers from Bihar and Uttar Pradesh work as agricultural labourers in Punjab. What will be the impact of this amended law on agricultural labourers, and how do you see their role in the ongoing farmers' agitation?*

SUKHPAL SINGH: The Essential Commodities Act will impact all consumers but it will significantly impact agricultural labourers in particular because they already have low incomes to begin with. When this law will be implemented and when it leads to monopoly of agri-business companies in the market, then they will sell the food items at a higher price (which will further reduce the labourers real income), and these people will end up below the poverty line.

Second is that on implementation of these laws, farming on owned land will be affected the most. Depeasantisation will lead to an increase in labour supply. Corporate farming will be dependent upon high-technology and the demand for labour will not keep up with their supply. For these farms there will be a demand for skilled labour, and the agricultural labourers don't have the capital or the skill to adjust to these changes. Since the demand for both mental and manual labour will remain low, this will lead to a fall in the wage rate for these labourers. So, on one hand there will be a tendency of incomes to fall and on the other, due to the presence of monopoly, the prices of food will rise, leading to exploitation at both ends. That is why the ECA in particular will have a negative impact on the agricultural labourers. All three laws together are a package that will pave the way for monopolisation in the agri-business market that will exploit the farmers, remove them from their lands, and in particular, the ECA will exploit the consumers, the working class and agricultural labourers, because their incomes will fall, and they will face rising prices of food items.

In all, the farm laws will exploit the majority of the population and only 8 to 10 percent of the population will not be affected. In the world, the total population is about 750 crores, and of them 200 crore people sleep hungry and are below the poverty line. We have sufficient production in agriculture. Though these laws may lead to an increase in agricultural production, at this stage, the need of the hour is to properly distribute the already existing production. At this time, with the given technology, we can produce and provide a satisfactory standard of living to around 1,100 crore people. Even then, today, 200 crore people go hungry, so what we need is a system that focuses on distribution and addresses the existing income inequality. As of now, we have sufficient resources for the given population. On one hand, sufficient cloth is manufactured, but many people don't have any clothes, a lot of food goes waste, but people don't have anything to eat, many houses are empty and locked, but so many people are homeless. So, the main issue is not that of manufacturing and production, but of distribution. Everyone can be provided with a decent livelihood, however, for that we have to shift our paradigm.

WU: *You have worked extensively on understanding the workforce composition of the agrarian economy. Could you shed some light on the composition of the agrarian economy?*

SUKHPAL SINGH: It is very important to know the population structure of the agrarian economy. For example, according to data from 2011, there are more than 100 crore people in India, out of which 48 crores are working in all the sectors taken together. However, out of them, 26 crores i.e., 55 percent of the total workforce is engaged in agriculture either as a cultivator or worker. In fact, the number of agricultural workers is more than actual cultivators: 55 percent are agricultural labourers and 45 percent are cultivators. The latest numbers highlight that this percentage has been falling and people are moving to the non-farm sector. Actually, the non-farm sector, which could provide employment opportunities to this large segment of population, has not developed much in India, and people usually get casual employment in the non-farm sector. Such is the structure of the agrarian population in India.

When we look at Punjab, out of a total population of 3 crore, one crore is the working population, out of which 35 lakh are engaged in agriculture. Out of that, 20 lakh are cultivators and 15 lakh are agricultural labourers.

Thus, India is still an agrarian economy. So, we should study the issues related to the agrarian economy to understand the constraints and problems faced by the sector in production, marketing, etc., and only after addressing these aspects can we hope to develop a model of agrarian development. Agrarian economy has a different set of problems, and they should be dealt with separately.

WU: *Recently one of your studies came out in* Economic and Political

Weekly, *titled* Agrarian Crisis and Agricultural Labour in Punjab. *It is being widely talked about in leading newspapers and activist circles. Would you please delve into some details of this study?*

SUKHPAL SINGH: Well, since the last one or two decades there have been many cases of suicide in the developed agrarian belt—wherever the model of the Green Revolution was implemented. The entire agrarian belt like Punjab, Haryana, and mainly the cotton belt like Karnataka, Andhra Pradesh, Maharashtra and Tamil Nadu, where the cotton crop had failed and the agrarian economies that got attached to the market, have seen a rise in farmer indebtedness along with rise in the cases of suicide. It is generally understood that there are no incidents of suicide in Punjab because National Crime Records Bureau has maintained that Punjab is the least suicide-prone area. The Punjab government has initiated a study that has been taken up by three universities—Punjab Agricultural University (PAU) (Ludhiana), Punjabi University (Patiala), GNDU (Amritsar), which I coordinated. We did a census that has not been undertaken anywhere in the world. We surveyed each and every household where there was an incidence of suicide instead of collecting data based on sampling.

Closer to the PAU, Ludhiana, there are six districts, having 2,400 villages. In Punjab, there are more than 12,000 villages. In the 2,400 villages that we surveyed, it was seen that in the last 17 years, 16,600 farmers as well as labourers have committed suicide. Out of the total number, over 9,300 are farmers, and 7,300 are labourers. This means that every year 1,000 farmers and labourers commit suicide. This means that every day there are three people who commit suicide, two farmers and one agricultural labourer.

However, the figure of agricultural labourers committing suicide is not actually less. If we look at the total number of farmers in Punjab, it is 20 lakhs, and total number of labourers is 15 lakhs, when we look at the proportion of farmers who committed suicide to the total number of farmers, i.e., 9,300 out of 20 lakh, and the proportion of labourers who committed suicide out of the total number of labourers, i.e., 7,300 out of 15 lakh, then the proportion of both cultivators and labourers who commit suicide out of the total numbers, is almost similar.

In our door-to-door survey we found that the crisis has hit both the cultivators and labourers with equal intensity. When there is a crisis in agriculture, employment gets reduced, affecting the agricultural labourers. We found that districts like Ludhiana, Moga, and certain districts of the cotton belt like Bathinda, Barnala, Sangrur, etc. have relatively higher incidences of suicide than others. For the districts which have low HDI (Human Development Index), based on education, health, and income, there have been higher incidences of suicide. There is a direct relationship between low levels of education, health and income with high incidence of suicide.

It is generally understood that agricultural labourers are mostly people from lower caste categories (scheduled caste and backward caste). However, when we look at the entire data on farmer suicide in Punjab, of the total people in agriculture who committed suicide, about nine percent belonged to the general caste category as agricultural labourers. Earlier they were small farmers who later got transformed into agricultural labourers, and ended up committing suicide. Another nine percent belonged to the backward castes and 82 percent of people belonged to the scheduled castes. In four percent of the households, more than one person had committed suicide.

The major reason behind farmers and labourers resorting to suicide is indebtedness. Around 79 to 80 percent of suicide cases among labourers is due to indebtedness. Economic distress is another important reason. A farmer has land, so they can get a loan by keeping their land as a collateral security against the loan. Labourers don't have land, so they are unable to get loans from institutional sources. They can get loans only from landlords or other non-institutional sources of credit. So, people are dying because of indebtedness and economic hardships. 19 percent (about one-fifth) of the labourers are under severe economic distress and are dying of hunger. Hence, the crisis is much deeper for these people. Earlier it was argued that only those people should get compensation who commit suicide due to debt. As agricultural labourers largely commit suicide under economic distress, the criterion of compensation should be expanded to include this reason as well.

Moreover, it is important to understand the source of credit. The proportion of credit taken from institutional sources is smaller as compared to that from non-institutional sources. Only seven percent of loans have been taken from institutional sources like banks and cooperative societies, the rest 93 percent of the loans are from non-institutional sources. The case is similar for the general population as well, where 80 percent of the general population is under debt, out of which only six percent have taken a loan from an institutional source, while the rest 94 percent had to depend upon non-institutional sources. It has also been seen that the families that have experienced incidences of suicide have a limited access to institutional sources of credit.

Another important and grave issue in agriculture is that of gender in terms of understanding the condition of women, their children, particularly in the families of agricultural labourers. Of the total farmers who committed suicide, eight percent were women. However, this proportion was higher for agricultural labourers—it was around 12.4 percent. This shows that women in families of agricultural labourers are victims of severe economic distress. There is no social structure or support from the government, no relatives who could extend support to their families as everyone around them are also labourers and in a similar economic condition. Comparatively, farmers are able to get such support, while the situation for labourers is quite bad. There is an important book, "Those Who Did Not Die" by Ranjana Padhi, on the state of women workers and small peasantry in agriculture and understanding different aspects of their lives. It presents some heart-wrenching facts on suicides in Punjab that challenges the earlier notion that Punjab has benefitted a lot from the Green Revolution.

Moreover, another important fact is that 60 percent of the farmers and agricultural labourers who commit suicide are youth, i.e., of age 35 and less. Youths are not able to get employment, neither in agriculture nor in the non-farm sector. They are very frustrated. They either go into depression or indulge in drugs and are prone to commit suicide. They face economic distress, lack of employment opportunities, then they suffer from depression and start taking drugs. Their suicide is seen as a case of depression and dependence on drugs, however, more often the economic reasons behind suicide i.e., lack of employment, no source of income, etc., is ignored, which ultimately forces the individual to take refuge in drugs. Hence, our focus should be on these triggering factors. When the youth is committing suicide, it raises question on the entire socio-economic system.

Next, we also tried to understand the condition of the families after they have experienced an incidence of suicide. Out of the total sample of 7,300 agricultural labourers, almost 50 percent of them had only a single earner in the family. The whole family, including the wife, children and his parents, were dependent on the income earned by this single person who committed suicide. On an average, around four people are dependent on the income of this one person. The families were not able to economically sustain themselves, hence they had to take loans, the burden of which then forced that person to commit suicide. The rest of the family continued to live in grave economic conditions with no external help. Half of the families that have lost a member of their family to suicide live under severe economic distress. Suicide does not happen due to a single reason. There are many reasons that force someone to commit suicide, like, they are indebted, being threatened by moneylender, the child is ill, the girl child has some social problem due to economic reasons, etc., which leads to depression. In 44 percent of the families at least one member of the family is suffering from depression. This means that there are economic, social, psychological and physical problems that need to be addressed. It also has adverse effect on education of children, as it has been seen that in 12 percent of the families that have experienced incidences of suicide, the children had to drop out of their education. Now these children are not able to get education, not only due to economic reasons but also because they are psychologically disturbed. Apart from providing economic relief in terms of school fee waiver, mid-day meals, etc., there should be psychological and emotional help too. Further, around 3 percent of the farmer and 12 percent of labourer families experienced disruption of their children's marriage, particularly girl child, due to social and economic stigma attached to suicides. There are children who have dropped out of school, their marriage got cancelled, and they don't have a bread earner in the family, so, we must understand the conditions of these families that are going through such a deep crisis.

WU: *The entire rural and agrarian economy is going through a restructuring for the last two decades. You have a very important study that was also published in Economic and Political Weekly last year on the agrarian* *crisis and the transition of agricultural labourers. Could you talk a little on how this restructuring is happening in the post-Green Revolution period?*

SUKHPAL SINGH: What we wanted to understand was how transformation happened in the post-Green Revolution period. When the Green Revolution was put into practice, area under cultivation and cropping increased, along with mechanisation. When in the mid-1960s, we implemented the Green Revolution model in Punjab, the production, productivity and labour employment increased in the 1970s. High mechanisation started in the 1990s. Earlier in the 1970s and 1980s, a significant proportion of labour was permanently employed and they used to get permanent yearly income in the form of crop share and/or cash payments. They used to get the yearly payment of their labour and didn't have to face unemployment.

When I was doing my M. Phil., we collected data from 100 agricultural labour families in 1991-92 from Ludhiana district. Then last year we again visited those households to see the changes that might have happened. We could not find many of the houses as many of them had been divided into two or three houses. Taking this division into account, we selected 100 families and saw that permanent labour has almost disappeared. Earlier more than one-third of labourers were permanent, now there is no permanent labour. Most of the daily wage labourers are now casual labourers. Some people have been able to find employment in rural and urban non-farm sectors. This means that the transformation and transition of labour in last three decades has converted them from permanent to casual labour and from casual labour they adjusted to the non-farm sector.

Even the non-farm sector has not done very well. In Punjab, between 2007 and 2015, 18,700 small scale industrial units have closed down. This means that every day six industrial units have been closing down. Labour is not able to find employment in agriculture and not even in industry. Hence, in this age of neoliberalism, the introduction of capitalism in agriculture has reduced employment opportunities in agriculture as well as in industry, leading to high unemployment.

There is also this aspect that labour of Punjab cannot migrate to other states for employment. This is because of the logic of capitalism—

it leads to uneven development, i.e., it leads to greater development in certain areas while less development in others. For example, the difference between city and village—centre and periphery, respectively. In Punjab the wage rate is higher, hence, labour from UP and Bihar (where the wage rate is relatively low) come to Punjab for jobs, similarly, people from Punjab migrate to Canada and Australia as the wage rates are comparatively higher there. So migration is caused by unequal development. This is a common phenomenon in capitalism where people migrate from villages to cities, from city to city across states, and to other developed nations, also known as emigration.

In 1991, there were five lakh small farmer families in Punjab, who owned less than five acres of land. In 2001, there were only three lakh small farmers, and the remaining two lakh farmers disappeared. 26 percent of them joined the labour force, and out of these 26 percent, six percent became agricultural labourers. As I have mentioned earlier, 15 lakh already existing agricultural labourers find it difficult to get employment, then how will these new entrants into the labour force find employment? Even now, when we categorise them as agricultural labourers, we are in doubt whether we should call them agricultural labourers or not. Rather they should be categorised as rural labourers because a major part of their employment and income does not come from the agricultural sector. Usually in order to categorise, we see how much time a person devotes in a particular job and how much income one earns from that job. In agriculture, there are only two peak seasons, April-May is the harvesting season for wheat. People get employment in this harvesting season, and when sowing of paddy happens. So in both seasons combined there is 70 to 80 days of work available in agriculture. For the rest of the 280 to 300 days there is no work for labour in agriculture, and they have to work somewhere else.

WU: *Do they get work in MGNREGA or shift to non-farm jobs like in the construction sector in towns and cities?*

SUKHPAL SINGH: They do find work through MGNREGA. MGNREGA aims to provide 100 days of work in a year, however, most people get only 30 to 40 days of work in a year. The MGNREGA's wage and number of employment days are limited. Why employ only one person in a family for 100 days? All the workers should be provided employment for all the 365 days, which we call full employment, but that is not happening. There is no employment opportunity in the non-farm sector, there are no agro-processing units, no labour-intensive manufacturing units, no employment opportunities in the rural areas. The only sector where labour gets employed is the construction sector, which is now completely shut down due to the pandemic. Last year, there was no work available in the construction sector. This has added to the misery of the labourers. So we see that with this kind of transition—and there is a greater possibility for this kind of transition to continue with the implementation of the new laws—they will not be able to find employment anywhere. Industry is in crisis and agriculture is also in crisis, so the new laws will only worsen the condition of labourers and small peasantry, as they will not be able to find employment anywhere.

PART II

GroundXero: *Now that the government has repealed the laws and the movement has ended with success, what are the likely implications of this movement that you foresee?*

Sukhpal Singh: There have been many implications of the farmers' movement. For instance, every household in Punjab held the opinion that these laws should be repealed. We have never seen anything like this before—every person in the state irrespective of their profession supported the cause in their hearts. When these laws were brought in, people felt that their land, crop and livelihood would be lost—the peasant would end up as a wage worker, thus lowering wages for even the existing labourers. So, they fought against all of this. And the people who fought are being showered with immense gratitude and honour. People come down to the roads to catch a glimpse of these people who fought for their justice.

An impact of this movement is that if any laws now come about against the people, people will struggle against it as they feel now that it is possible to achieve anything if they struggle over it. A lot of people feel lucky to have been born in this age to have witnessed this historic movement. So many people mentioned to me that they felt unlucky as they couldn't go to the Singhu border.

There is a need to organise such sentiments to channelise efforts towards betterment of society. There is a need for people on the Right as well as the Left to think about the common man. People fought; in fact, they were ahead of the leadership—people used to say that we won't come back home until the laws are taken back. They would claim that either they would come back with the laws repealed or their dead bodies would come back. And many dead bodies indeed arrived.

The leadership must now critically think about the way forward. I can only say that the economic issues need to be resolved and MSP needs to be there. All farmers of India should fight for MSP. The government talks about zero budget natural farming. What we really need is that we estimate our demand for various crops—food grains, oilseeds, fruits, vegetables etc. and then see where all this can be grown. Based on this exercise, we should make regional plans. Once our domestic needs are taken care of, we can cater to the foreign markets.

It is possible to grow a variety of pulses in Punjab, but nothing is being done for their production as well as marketing. In fact, we import pulses as well as oilseeds from other countries. While very few people eat rice in Punjab, we cultivate so much of it as against pulses and oilseeds. In the process, we are harming the water table, environment as well as causing air pollution. Pulses will fix nitrogen, use less chemicals, suit our environment as well as substitute our imports. But farmers can go for diversified crops only once MSP on all crops is guaranteed.

GX: *The government has agreed to set up a committee to deliberate over the demand for legal guarantee of MSP to the farmers. But many experts and even unions harbour concerns over the feasibility of government guaranteed MSP for all crops. What are your thoughts on this?*

SUKHPAL SINGH: There is indeed a need for MSP as farming is not a profitable venture. Unless we have assured marketing, farmers cannot make any income out of farming. MSP is not something very high; it is a 'Minimum' support price fixed by the government itself. The Swaminathan Committee Report recommended that MSP should provide C2 cost plus 50 percent returns. A 2005-06 report by the National Commission on Farmers also recommended that MSP equivalent to C2 cost plus 50 percent returns would make farming profitable. Subsequently, the Ramesh Chand Committee report in 2013-14 recommended that C2 cost needs to be revised to include cost of technical labour, rate of interest on entire capital, rent for land, marketing cost, etc. and 10 percent over the revised C2 cost must be given as MSP. The Swaminathan and Ramesh Chand calculations arrive at similar figures—Swaminathan's C2 plus 50 percent returns or Ramesh Chand's revised C2 cost plus 10 or 15 percent returns would come out to be almost similar. Often, people ask how profits can be as high as 50 percent but the true figure isn't really 50 percent as Swaminathan's MSP calculation underestimated costs by about 35 percent. The Ramesh Chand Committee which came up later suggested a more accurate methodology to measure costs.

It's being argued that it is not possible to give MSP for all crops. The government declares MSP for 23 crops but neither all public nor private procurement takes place at this MSP. There is no purpose of such an MSP at which no actual procurement takes place. All these cost concepts—A1, A2, B1, B2, C1, C2 and C3—don't exist beyond agriculture, as you just have a final cost for any product which includes all expenses incurred in its production. All these cost concepts are being used only in agriculture just to create a lack of clarity over final costs.

The government claims that giving MSP on all crops to farmers would require an enormous amount of funds i.e. about Rs 17 lakh crore for 23 crops. As per my estimates, if we calculate the value of the total production of these 23 crops at current MSP, the figure comes out to be approximately 10 lakh crore. The government argues that besides procurement, they incur costs over transportation and storage which involve a lot of inefficiencies. These inefficiencies include spoilage or theft on account of lack of storage facilities, corruption, etc. If the government manages to correct these inefficiencies, then it may be possible to assure MSP at the cost of 11 to 12 lakh crores.

Let's note that the entire production of crops is not meant to be sold in the market. A part of it is retained for self-consumption, livestock, or seed. The production that comes to the market, i.e. marketed surplus for wheat and rice, is about 74 and 90 percent respectively. It is even less for some other crops. So, the value of the marketed surplus at MSP comes out to be less than about 8 lakh crores. And, if we include storage and transportation costs of about 10 to 20 percent, the total sum does not exceed 12 lakh crores. In fact, this entire sum is also not required all at once. The procurement of Rabi is disbursed via Public Distribution System (PDS) or market before the Kharif crop arrives. There are three-four agricultural seasons in India, which means you just need about Rs 4 lakh crores for a particular season. In fact, there are sub-seasons as well. So, this expense is not a big deal. After all, the government is not buying dirt. It is buying grain which has demand all over the world.

If the government would spend on storage, then it can be seen as an opportunity for investment. After all, we also need to provide livelihoods to people. For instance, there are about 7,000 APMC markets in India. The National Farmers Commission (2004) recommended that 42,000 APMC markets are required in India. So, there is a need to create this infrastructure but some states like Bihar have abolished APMC.

MSP is definitely feasible. It is seen that when the government procures crops at MSP, the wholesale prices for most of those crops stay above MSP even one or two months after the harvest season. So, the government can possibly sell its procurement at even these wholesale prices to recover its expenditure.

The government does not need to procure all 23 crops from all states in the beginning. It can procure just one crop in Kharif as well as the Rabi season in each state. A lot of crops are not perishable and would not require any special storage. Gradually, they scale up MSP to more crops. In Punjab, Haryana, and Western UP, let the government procure the entire produce at MSP. MSP is effective for 11 crops but there is a practice of targeted procurement—the government agencies can procure just up to their set quota levels. However, this still helps in the price discovery or fixing up a floor price at which private trade occurs. This benefits even those farmers who couldn't avail MSP directly. That is because, if wheat sells in Punjab for Rs 2,000, it would sell in Bihar at Rs 1,500. But if wheat sells in Punjab itself at Rs 1,500, then it would sell for just Rs 1,000 in Bihar.

This cannot be done as the government is conforming to WTO's policies that prohibit direct market support within its Agreement on Agriculture (AoA). This is the reason these laws were brought in. But the government can make use of the peace clause[2] within WTO's policies. We need to support the peasantry on its demand for guaranteed MSP.

GX: *Besides MSP for all crops, what else should be done to minimise agrarian distress?*

SUKHPAL SINGH: In Punjab, it isn't as if farming does not yield any income. But this income is insufficient to meet expenses. With privatisation, services such as health, education, electricity etc. have become quite expensive. Also, unemployment is quite high in Punjab as there isn't any industry or service sector to provide jobs. Therefore, people choose to migrate to other countries. Because of all the chemicals used in farming, there has been an adverse impact on health along with the environment. So, MSP is also insufficient for the livelihood. All these issues are more aggravated where the market economy is more developed, i.e. both inputs and outputs are linked to the market. These linkages with the market, i.e. capitalist development of agriculture deepen the crisis.

Besides MSP, we need to promote the agro-processing industry. We must shift the workforce away from agriculture to industry and the services sector. Our educated youth should find jobs in these sectors. With mechanisation, employment opportunities within agriculture have shrunk. On one acre of farm growing wheat, there are just eight days of work. With paddy, there would be just 20 days of work. So, there are just 28 days of work per year in one acre of land. So, there are no avenues to get earnings for labour for the rest of the year. These avenues can be created if we invest in agriculture and promote agro-processing, dairy etc.

MSP does not mean we don't want farmers to go through transition. But the transition should not come about as a result of push factors within agriculture. Instead, it should be growth driven i.e. as a result of pull factors outside agriculture. If I hail from a peasant family and I become a professor, it is a pull factor. But if my brother becomes a labourer from a farmer, it's a push factor as he may have been pushed out of agriculture on account of mechanisation. Mechanisation should improve the status of a labourer to a technical labourer or service provider rather than turn him into a wage labourer. However, we are seeing that even farmers are turning into wage labourers.

We need reforms in agriculture, but only those reforms which focus on improving the livelihood of small and medium farmers, landless labourers and women. These three laws were not for the people, these laws didn't address the negative effects of the Green Revolution, rather they would have further deepened the agrarian crisis.

Endnotes

1. According to the findings of the 77th round of National Sample Survey (NSS) for January-December 2019 which were released on 10 September 2021, the average monthly income per agricultural household in Punjab for the same period has been calculated at Rs 26,701 which includes Rs 5,981 from wages/salary, Rs 2,652 from leasing out of land, Rs 12,597 from crop production, Rs 4,457 from farming of animals and Rs 1,014 from non-farm business.

2. The 'peace clause' in the Agreement on Agriculture (AoA) protects a developing country's food procurement programs against action from other WTO member countries in case subsidy limits are breached.

Farmers' and Workers' Education Happens in the Furnace of Struggle
RANDEEP MADDOKE, DOCUMENTARY FILMMAKER

> RANDEEP MADDOKE is an activist as well as a photographer and filmmaker from Punjab. His documentary film *Landless*, which is about the struggles of Dalit landless labourers in Punjab, has received widespread acclaim. He has also documented the struggles of Dalits in many other parts of India, like Tamil Nadu and Haryana, and also in Nepal. He was at the protest site throughout documenting the different moments and different dimensions of the farmers' movement.
>
> During the first phase of the struggle, WORKERS UNITY interviewed Randeep Maddoke at the protest site of BKU (Ekta-Ugrahan) at Tikri border.

WORKERS UNITY: *A question often raised about this movement is regarding the role and the participation of the landless farmers and agricultural labourers, majority of whom are Dalits. What are your thoughts on it?*

RANDEEP MADDOKE: A cursory view of the movement from outside may create an impression that this struggle completely ignores the issues faced by the landless farmers and Dalit agricultural labourers. However, let us consider one of the demands raised by the protesting farmers, namely, repeal of the Essential Commodities Act (ECA), 2020. If this act goes through, it will be devastating for all the toiling masses of this country, not only the landless farmers but also the urban and rural working class.

It is indeed true that this movement is being led by landed peasantry. However, by demanding the repeal of ECA, these farmers have clearly shown an awareness about a law which will adversely impact everyone from landless Dalits in villages to workers in towns and cities. In fact, even if the other two laws go through, the farmers will somehow try to survive, thanks to the land they own. However, if ECA goes through, it will bring unimaginable hardship on the landless labourers.

Our friends and comrades, who work among Dalits, criticise this movement as being led by upper-caste farmers. But how many of them have educated Dalits about the dangers of the ECA? How many of them have started campaigns demanding repeal of the ECA? It is these landed farmers who are raising and fighting for its repeal. So, I ask them, "Why don't you also fight for the repeal of the Essential Commodities Act?"

About the actual participation of the agricultural labourers and landless farmers in this movement, if you only visit the protest sites at Singhu border and Tikri border, you may feel that Dalit and landless are not part of the movement. But please go to Punjab. There are people protesting at hundreds of toll plazas. People have surrounded Adani's *silos* (hi-tech warehouses). There are protests going on outside the homes of BJP ministers. Such a massive statewide protest involves every section of the peasantry. Agricultural labourers face many issues. They are daily wage earners and cannot come and stay at the *morchas* (fronts) at the borders. They just don't have the means and the resources to do this. However, they are participating in local protests in Punjab. I can give you an example of a village in Punjab which has no farmer union but has a union of agricultural labourers. It is this union which is campaigning among the farmers of that village that they should all march to Delhi and join the ongoing protest at the borders.

On 7 January 2021, there is going to be a massive mobilisation of the landless farmers and labourers here at the protest sites. Why do you think they are coming? They are not being hired to come here! They are coming because they know that this movement is also against those laws which will bring havoc in their lives. We cannot deny that there are severe ruptures and tensions between labourers and landed farmers, however, from a tactical perspective, all the toiling masses must recognise who the biggest enemy is at this stage.

Apart from ECA, there is also the Electricity Amendment Bill which will ease the entry of private players in distribution of electricity. This is extremely dangerous as many of the rural families get free or subsidised electricity now and that will disappear if the amendment to t his bill is passed. We should remember that despite several issues and tensions, farmers and agricultural labourers are not enemies, the enemy is someone else, and it is time to form new camaraderie, new bonds and fight this common enemy together.

WU: *As we know, one day after the bills concerning the farm laws were presented, the four labour codes were also passed. What do you think the trade unions and various industrial workers organisations can learn from this farmers' movement?*

RANDEEP MADDOKE: Working class in India is facing an all-out frontal attack on their most basic rights by this government. But I want to ask their unions, if you do not want to stand in solidarity with these farmers, no problem, at least fight for your own rights. Why is the Maruti workers union so silent? Why is the Honda union so silent? Why is the working class in the entire Gurgaon industrial belt so silent? These supposedly landed farmers have opened up road for the working class movement by surrounding Delhi. Why are the worker unions not taking advantage of this situation that this fascist government is on a back foot and has been caught off guard by the farmers' movement?

There are many borders surrounding Delhi which are not yet occupied by the farmers. Why don't the worker unions occupy those borders and create a multi-faceted struggle against this government and its anti-people policies? Farmers have planted their flags at Singhu and Tikri and if workers also plant their flags at other borders, then this government which is already scared will retreat further and various other struggles will gain momentum.

WU: *There are many communist and Ambedkarite groups that are criticising this movement as a movement of upper-caste kulaks. That it does not represent the interest of landless peasantry, and hence they should not participate in this movement. What is your opinion and response to this critique?*

RANDEEP MADDOKE: I think that to actually come on the ground and participate in a people's struggle, facing a repressive state and hostile weather, is one thing. And sitting comfortably inside your homes with blankets wrapped around and doing activism via smartphones or laptops is another thing. It is all well and good that your activism is on Facebook and Twitter but then the importance and relevance of your criticism will also be limited as is your participation on the ground. This is my opinion: if some of these groups and individuals had raised these same criticisms working in the slums amongst Dalits, I would have taken their criticism with seriousness.

I do not want to say that these criticisms have no truth in them, they do have some truth. However, these intellectuals and scholars should also recognise the importance of tactics in a struggle and ask themselves: is this the right time to raise such criticisms? After all, issues that the Dalits are facing were not born during this movement. They have always existed for centuries. So why didn't these groups rise to support the demands and struggles of landless farmers in the past? If we look back at the writings of many of these so-called intellectuals, it can be easily seen that they never supported the struggles the landless farmers had been fighting in Punjab for years. Now it can very well be that for these intellectuals and the kind of politics they stand for, Dalits' demand for ownership of land is not revolutionary!

When Dalit farmers of Punjab were fighting for the ownership of land that they were tilling, I made the film *Landless* to document their struggle. Now when landed farmers are fighting against this fascist government, I am documenting their struggle. It is because the real enemy of the people is this fascist government and the capitalist class. Any movement which fights these fascists and their policies deserves our support, our participation, and investment of our intellectual and creative capacities.

And to those activists who are critiquing this movement sitting far away, I say: these *kulaks* have brought the biggest enemy of Dalits to its knees. A fascist government which is orchestrating pogroms against Muslims is now forced to reckon with the farmers. Till a few months back, when Muslims protesting the CAA (Citizenship Amendment Act) and the NRC (National Register of Citizens) faced a pogrom in Delhi, many people were feeling helpless as to how to fight these fascists. The farmers are showing how to fight them. If you stand for Dalits and workers and are not with landed peasantry, don't join this struggle but fight your own battle on the ground now that the fascists are on the defensive. And if you can, come to these protest sites, talk to farmers and listen to how they view this struggle not only as a struggle to repeal the three farm laws but as part of an overall anti-fascist struggle.

We should remember that this struggle and movement will not end with the repeal of these laws. Once these fascists are defeated in their pursuit of implementing these laws, their anger and hatred will be channelised towards the participants of this movement, and unless we are all united, it will be impossible to defeat them. So, I request all the intellectuals and activists to contribute to the movement constructively.

WU: *I would now like to ask you a little bit about your movie* Landless, *which received widespread acclaim. One of the reasons the film got a lot of attention is due to the unique struggles waged by the landless farmers of Punjab that you documented. Please tell us briefly about these struggles and the role communist revolutionary organisations played in these struggles.*

RANDEEP MADDOKE: Like every other state, the peasantry in Punjab is also fragmented into big, medium, small, marginal, and landless peasants. Most of the landless farmers are Dalit, which means that the issue of land-ownership is strongly correlated with caste. When Dalit agricultural workers of Punjab led by a couple of radical left organisations started fighting for their right to land, which was guaranteed to them on a lease basis by law, I naturally got very interested and documented it. There have been many historic struggles by landless peasants in India such as the Telangana movement and then the Tebhaga movement in Bengal. The current movement to claim ownership of land by the Dalits in Punjab is in my opinion among those historic struggles which will reverberate for decades to come.

I also want to add that the struggle by the landless and their practice of collective farming on the lands they acquire holds important lessons even for the landed farmers. As you know, in Punjab, farmers are in deep distress. It is high time that a more scientific approach that uses less resources is adopted by the Punjabi peasantry. In my opinion, the cooperative farming model adopted by those Dalit farmers can show the way.

If a landed farmer, say, has three acres of land, then generally he or she will go and buy a tractor or some high-tech equipment to increase the yield and his income. But to do this, they have to take loan, in most cases by mortgaging the land which in many ways defeats the purpose. As farmers with different land holdings meet during the present movement and exchange ideas, my hope is that farmers with adjacent land holdings will start sharing their resources like tractors and adopt a sort of cooperative farming model that the Dalit collectives who have acquired panchayat land in auctions are adopting. It is inevitable that small and marginal farmers will have to adopt that model. Otherwise, even after repealing the farm laws, holding on to their small individual land will become impossible due to the increasing cost of cultivation and declining returns.

For farmers and workers, their entire education—political, socio-economic and cultural—takes place in the furnace of a struggle. It is here that they earn their PhDs. I hope that this movement will not only lead to spread of anti-fascist and anti-imperialist struggle but will also generate creative ideas and scientific models of cooperative farming.

WU: *Can you elaborate on the cultural aspect of the movement emerging on these borders? Famous Punjabi singers like Cheema and Garhewal are writing songs on this movement and on the farmers—songs, which are becoming hugely popular even among the youths. How do you view this phenomenon?*

RANDEEP MADDOKE: There is an overall impression that peasant movements or in general movements which emerge primarily in the villages are very restrictive in many ways. For example, in the past it was mostly the elderly who participated in such struggles and the youths were not really interested. However, if you see today, the participation of youth in this struggle in various capacities, be it artistic or as a doctor or as a singer, is quite impressive. Sale of alcohol in Punjab has declined in the last few months and when you walk around these protest sites, you will not find a single youth taking drugs or drinking alcohol. This is one positive cultural development which has emerged. As far as singers and other artists are concerned, if today they do not stand with farmers, in future, how will they reach out to people? What will they write and sing and perform about if they do not respond to a historic people's movement like this?

And finally, we should always remember that a flood sweeps away everything in its wake. It evokes imagery of devastation, but a people's movement is that flood which sweeps off the repressive state and carries the people forward.

WU: *Do you finally have a message for filmmakers, artists, painters, singers of this country as to how they can contribute to this movement?*

RANDEEP MADDOKE: Certainly. A movement like this can only grow and widen as workers/teachers/cultural activists and artists come and participate. Teachers can come and educate, painters can come and hold exhibitions. A multi-faceted space has been created by the revolutionary potential of the farmers and it is fertile in more ways than we can anticipate.

The Most Essential Work Today is Not Only to Raise Our Fists but also Our Pens and Brushes

AMOLAK SINGH, CULTURAL ACTIVIST, PUNJAB LOK SABHYACHARAK MANCH

> AMOLAK SINGH is the President of the Punjab Lok Sabhyacharak Manch that was set up in 1982. He brings attention to people's issues through both poetry and theatre. He was closely associated with Gurucharan Singh, one of the most famous playwrights of Punjab. As an activist of cultural movement in the state, Amolak Singh has worked to build the relation between music, theatre and the common people of Punjab. He has been associated with the peasant movement for a long time.
>
> WORKERS UNITY interviewed Amolak Singh at the *dana mandi* (grain market) in Barnala, Punjab on February 21, 2021, on the eve of the Kisan-Mazdoor Ekta rally (farmer-worker unity rally) organised jointly by Punjab Khet Mazdoor Union (PKMU) and BKU (Ekta-Ugrahan).

WORKERS UNITY: *The artists and intellectuals in Punjab participated heavily in the farmers' movement. How do you see the impact of this on the culture and the youth in Punjab?*

AMOLAK SINGH: The mass culture in Punjab has changed a lot during this movement. We can see the kisan unions' flags being put up everywhere. Now when a *baaraat* (bridegroom's procession) is taken out the groom's sister puts a farmer union's flag on the *pagdi (*turban), instead of a traditional *kalgi (*feather embellishment) on the groom's head. The *boli* (lyrics) of the *gidda* (popular Punjabi songs) has changed. The themes of the songs now revolve around the farm laws, Modi, corporate loot, Hindu-Muslim-Sikh harmony, Punjab-Haryana botherhood and so on. There are lyrics like: *Ae Bhagat Singh aapka vatan abhi azaad nahi hua / Abhi Adani Ambani ka raaj hai* (Bhagat Singh, your country is not yet free / It is now under the rule of Adani-Ambani). The songs spoke about *Maai* (mother) Gulab Kaur[1] as well. Songs that used to glorify alcohol and drugs or objectify women are now being replaced, youths in Punjab are realising that songs that do not respect women cannot be called 'art or creation.' Those songs belong to the category of *lacchar sangeet* (derogratory music). Youth used to find pleasure in such *lachhar* songs and were ready to dance even with the noise of the generator! The culture of mindless drunken dancing to any sort of songs is changing in Punjab. But, these new songs of protest will have to pass the test of time. These songs have a long journey in front of them. And so do the youth who are with the movement today. We constantly request artists to create music and songs that focus on the unity of the workers and farmers rather than glorifying a particular religion, caste or regional identity.

BJP members are trying to spread a false narrative in the villages. They are telling Dalit agricultural workers that land will be taken away from the Jat land-owners and industries will come up on those land. This will create jobs for them. We are trying to counter such false narratives. We say, if you listen to those rumour-mongers:

Fasal ko bhi nuksaan hoga,
nasal ko bhi nuksaan hoga,
panchhi bhi bhukhe marenge
bhukh par vyapar hoga.

(The crop will be damaged,
so will your family,
and the birds themselves will starve.
They are but merchants of hunger.)

We tell people that the corporates want to monopolise paani (water) and roti (bread) as they have realised that these are the most essential things. But Punjab will not let this happen. It is the land of Baba Nanak, Baba Bulleh Shah, Baba Kabir, Baba Farid, Bhagat Singh, Kartar Singh Sarabha[2] and Guru Govind Singh.

During this movement, all over the world, wherever the Punjabi live, massive tractor rallies with thousands of peoples were organised in support of the movement—be it in Canada, Australia, New Zealand, or England. Earlier parents would send their children abroad, spending lakhs out of their pocket, with the hope that they will settle there and enjoy a good life. Today, those children are realising that even Kartar Singh Sarabha had gone abroad to study, but he returned back to Punjab and joined the Ghadar Party.

We have been doing a play in the villages. The play is called *Begaane Bohad Ki Chhaon* (shade of another's banyan tree). *Bohad* means tree in Punjabi. The play says: "How long can you put up your chair or *manji* (cot) in the shade of another's banyan tree? If it's someone else's tree, that person can at any time ask you to get up and leave." When you go and settle in a foreign land, they can throw you out at any time. So, this is our message for Punjab's youth who have settled abroad; they too should, like Kartar Singh Sarabha, return to their homeland and work to free it from the clutches of corporates.

WU: *What role are cultural groups playing in countering government's propaganda among agricultural labourers and mobilising people in support of the ongoing movement?*

AMOLAK SINGH: In Punjab, attempts are being made by the RSS/BJP government to confuse the agricultural workers by saying: "We will bring new jobs and industries. We will distribute land to everyone." These are nothing but *maha-jhooth* (big lies). We are trying to counter these lies through our plays and songs. We have written many songs as a counter to such attempts. We sing a song by poet Sant Ram Udasi[3] on farmers and labourers sharing their grief—*Gal lag ke siri de jatt roya, bohla vicho neer vagya. Lya tangli naseeba nu faroliye, toodi vicho putt Jagya.* (The Jat peasant cried while hugging his serf, Tears flew out of the heaps of grains. Bring the rake, let's explore our destiny out of the chaff, Oh my son Jagya!) These lines propagate unity between the Jat farmers and Dalit workers.

The contradiction between a land-owning farmer and a landless peasant/agricultural worker is very real and the BJP-RSS is trying to take advantage of it to weaken the movement. So today, we were very conscious of the nature of unity that must be practised. Instead of giving it a name like '*mahapanchayat*,' we are calling it *Mazdoor-Kisan Maha Rally*. You can see that we have consciously put the workers before the farmers.

We are talking not just about the farmers but also the agricultural labourers, industrial workers, and small shop owners; the laws are against their interests also. They have obviously been passed for the benefit of the corporates. It is not just about a particular Prime Minister or Chief Minister, but about the entire system. Over two lakh people are present here in this rally, you can see—farmers, workers, landless peasants, youth, artists, poets, intellectuals—all have come. In Punjab, we have performed at over 160 locations, even at protests outside the homes of the BJP leaders. We perform songs and street plays. Even today, a *kafila* (convoy) will arrive here after performing *nukkad-natak* (street-theatre) at many places. Many activists will also come here after singing in protest gatherings going on outside Adani and Reliance petrol pumps and malls.

Punjab Lok Sabhyacharak Manch has composed many songs to convey to the workers that they need to open their 'third eye' to the reality of the situation and what the BJP government at Delhi is trying to do to divide the movement. For example, attempts are being made to divide the people from urban and rural areas, to create divisions between Dalits and Jats, and these need to be tackled head on. In order to get Dalit vote, these parties are announcing Dalit candidate as the CM or Deputy CM, but this will not fool us. We saw what they did with Nodeep Kaur—how they forcefully arrested her and Shiva Kumar, and tortured both of them in police custody.

Minutes before Bhagat Singh was taken away for execution he had just turned a page of a book by Lenin [*State and Revolution*] that he was reading and he folded a corner of the page before leaving his cell. Today it is our duty to open that very same book and unfold that page. Through our theatre, we read out one of Pash's poem to tell farmers and workers what was written on that page in the book,

> *Jis din fansi dee gayi*
> *Unki kothri mein Lenin ki kitaab mili*
> *Jiska ek panna muda hua tha.*
> *Punjab ki jawani ko*
> *Uske aakhri din se*
> *Is mude panne se badhna hain aage, chalna hai aage.*
>
> (The day he was hanged,
> A book by Lenin was found in his bag,
> A page folded, a place marked.

> His last day,
> His marked page,
> From there Punjab's youth needs to begin.)

Bhagat Singh had said that we might get freedom for this country in some form, but that would not give freedom to the workers and farmers. Rather than the gun-wielding Bhagat Singh, we feel that it is this Bhagat Singh, the one who was reading Lenin's *State and Revolution*, that needs to be taken to the masses.

We have been giving slogans: *"Akele akele maar na khao, ikaththa ho kar aage ao"* (Don't stay divided and face the assault alone, unite and come forward) and *"Votan da bharam todo, lok takat jodo"* (Break the illusion of votes, build people's power).

We know that these slogans will resonate here today. This is a call for every worker to come forward. The government policies are taking away our schools, hospitals, roads, drinking water, railways and airports; even historical national monuments like the Red Fort are now being rented out to corporate houses! Even the Cellular Jail in Andaman-Nicobar will be given away. Thus, irrespective of your class, caste, and gender, you need to join this fight. Whether you are an intellectual or an agricultural worker, a man or a woman, you need to unite—that's the only way forward—this is what we are telling people.

We can see the impact of this unity. The government has put nails on roads, placed barricades on the highways and have mocked us as *aandolanjeevis* (those who make livelihood out of protesting). But people are not seeing these labels as slurs. Rather, they have appropriated these labels and take pride in them. We want to see *aandolanjeevis* emerging from every household in Punjab. That's our primary job now. The most essential work today is not only to raise our fists but also our pens and brushes to write songs and paint the walls with slogans.

WU: *This is our last question for you. How do you see this movement going forward in the path dreamed by Bhagat Singh?*

AMOLAK SINGH: Baba Guru Ravidas[4], who is seen as a great emancipatory figure by *Dalit* communities, expressed through beautiful couplets his yearning for equality among all:

> *Aisa chahun raaj mein*
> *Jahan mile saban ko ann*
> *Chhote bade jahan sam base*
> *Ravidas rahe prasan*

> (Such a society I want
> Where food is available for everyone.
> Where big and small live equally,
> There Ravidas is on cloud nine.)

His dream of '*ann* (food) for all' is being shattered by the corporates, who now dream to own all the *ann* through these farm laws. So, are they against Ravidas-*ji*'s thoughts? We are trying to expose precisely these contradictions to the masses. We are invoking the ideas of *saanjhi* (common/shared) as propagated by Ghadri Babas[5] and Guru Nanak, who came from the same *mitti* (soil) as us, the same heritage, history, and culture. By talking about their ideas, we are motivating people to fulfil the dreams of our revered Gurus and revolutionaries. We are telling the youths: "When you are painting the images of your life, why not—rather than committing suicide in despair or losing oneself in drugs and alcohol—create a new Punjab?"

Through this protest it has become clear that the real powers do not rest with our elected representatives– they are the *khalnayaks* (villains). It is the duty of us theatre artists to expose them, to drag them out from behind the curtains, where they hide their real faces. We tell the masses who the true villains are and who the real heroes are.

If weapons alone could win the world, Hitler and Mussolini would be ruling even today. This is what world history teaches us. Which is why we take this song from village to village:

> *Kya hua agar aayi patjhad?*
> *Tum agli ritu pe yakin rakhna.*
> *Main le kar aunga kuch kalamein,*
> *Tum phoolon jaisi zameen rakhna.*

> (So what if autumn has come?
> You keep believing in the next season.
> I will come with some grafts,
> You just keep the soil ready for flowers.)

Endnotes

1. Mai Gulab Kaur (1890-1941) was a freedom fighter from Punjab. She joined the Ghadar Party and, posing as a journalist, distributed arms to the freedom fighters. She was sentenced to jail in Lahore for two years by the British Government.

2. Kartar Singh Sarabha (1896-1916) joined the Ghadar Party at the age of 15, came back to India from San Francisco, where he was sent to study. In 1915, Kartar Singh was arrested along with other freedom fighters and hanged to death at Central Jail, Lahore, for his role in the movement. He was only 19 years old then.

3. Sant Ram Das Udasi (1939-1986) was a Dalit-revolutionary poet. His songs were sung at the Singhu and Tikri borders of Delhi.

4. Sant Ravidas was a poet and saint of the Bhakti movement in the late 15th and early 16th century. He was born in a Dalit family of *chamar* caste (leather-tanners), and preached caste and gender equality. His legacy lives on in a Dalit sect called Ravidasia.

5. All Ghadrite were popularly called Babas—revolutionaries, who had sacrificed comfortable material life for the establishment of an egalitarian society.

We Do Not Really Believe that Electoral Participation and Even Victory Can Solve Any Real Problems of the People

NODEEP KAUR, LABOUR ACTIVIST, MAZDOOR ADHIKAR SANGATHAN

> NODEEP KAUR, 26, hails from a Dalit agricultural worker's family based in Kandar village in the Muktsar Sahib district in Punjab. In 2020 she joined a glass factory in the Kundli industrial belt (Sonipat, Haryana) as a worker, and soon became an active member of the Mazdoor Adhikar Sangathan (MAS)—an organisation engaged in militant struggles for the rights of contractual workers. Singhu border, one of the primary sites of the farmers' movement, happens to be a part of the greater Kundli area, and MAS stood in solidarity with the farmers' movement. Nodeep Kaur along with Shiv Kumar, a fellow Dalit activist of MAS, were arrested and confined to prison for more than a month.
>
> GROUNDXERO interviewed Nodeep Kaur in February, 2022.

GROUNDXERO: *Assembly elections are to be held in Punjab soon. What are the issues that are being raised by the contesting political parties? Are they raising the issues concerning the Dalits, agricultural workers, and the farmers at all? What kind of impact is the farmers' movement having on the elections in Punjab?*

NODEEP KAUR: The primary sentiment in the elections is that Punjab needs to be saved. Almost all of the political parties, whether it is Akali Dal, Congress, BJP, or Aam Aadmi Party (AAP), are trying to impress upon the people that Punjab needs to be saved. This is basically the agenda on which all of them are conducting the election campaign everywhere in the rural areas.

The farmers' movement has had a deep impact on the masses, they are not with the BJP anymore. Many are even actively speaking out against RSS/BJP. But, there is no alternative in sight. The revolutionary left parties have failed to come up with any alternative in front of the people, so the only choice that they are left with is to elect a smaller thief to protect oneself from a bigger thief. So, the way people are thinking is like, it doesn't matter if we vote or do not vote, as one of these parties will assume power anyway. So let us elect someone who is relatively better. As a result, a lot of people in Punjab are talking about electing AAP, because the AAP government in Delhi under Kejriwal has a record of delivering free water and electricity, it has also made public transportation free. So, people see Kejriwal a bit differently.

But, many of those farmer unions which were part of the SKM, and the farmers' movement, are now fighting elections under the banner of Sanyukt Samaj Morcha (SSM). They, too, do not have any agenda. People are not getting any concrete political directions from them either. If you form a political party and want people to vote for you, you must have a clear agenda, and a clear stand on issues such as unemployment, re-distribution of land to Dalit agricultural workers, etc. As such, they are just like any other political party.

People understand this lacuna and they also know that these elections won't have any real positive effect on their lives. But, whatever little expectations they still have, based on that, they will cast their votes.

GX: *Do you think the revolutionary left farmer unions which were also part of SKM should have put up candidates for this election? Especially since these elections are being fought right after the historic movement and a clear victory for the farmers?*

NODEEP KAUR: We do not really believe that electoral participation and even victory can solve any real problems of the people. Even if you are in the Vidhan Sabha (State Assembly), under whose authority and power would you work? Whatever the dictates of the ruling class are, you would have to implement them. So, participation in elections is not really important and relevant, but I do feel that the revolutionary unions needed to come together with a unified call that they are not going to participate in elections, instead they will begin a long-standing fight based on the people's issues. A call for the election boycott should have been issued, and the revolutionary organisations should have come together to build up an even more militant people's movement. However, nothing like that has happened. So, the fact that the people of Punjab do not have any alternative is not their fault. In spite of such a huge victory for the farmers, I think that the revolutionary left in Punjab has not been able to do their work in the way it should have been done.

GX: *What is your understanding of the fact that the farmers' movement was withdrawn after the repeal of the three contentious laws? Because, as we know, some of the demands, including that of the legal guarantee of MSP for all crops, were not accepted by the Union government.*

NODEEP KAUR: The withdrawal of the movement was opportunistic in our opinion. As we have seen, quite a few of the prominent farmer leaders wanted to contest the elections and so they began to convince and put pressure on the other unions in SKM that as the three farm laws have been withdrawn, the farmers need to vacate the borders and go home. However, in my understanding, a significant number of farmers and several unions within SKM were not in agreement.

In fact, we should remember that even before these three laws came into being, the struggle for MSP (Minimum Support Price) had been going on. This struggle is much more important, especially if we have to understand why the farmers were killing themselves. For a long time, farmers all over India have not been receiving fair prices for their produce and hence they are burdened with debt. So, the demand for the MSP has always been one of the core demands of the Indian peasantry. We also need to remember and keep reminding the masses that till now, none of the recommendations of the Swaminathan Commission have been implemented. In fact, this movement was simply never only about the three farm laws. In fact, in the initial charter of demands, there were eight distinct demands. Later the charter was reduced to four, and then three, and then the movement was withdrawn based on fulfilment of just one demand, namely, repealing of the three laws. [Two demands relating to the withdrawal of the Electricity (Amendment) Bill 2020 and scrapping of the provision under which farmers responsible for stubble burning can be imprisoned for five years, besides imposition of a fine of up to Rs 1 crore, were already accepted by the Union government during the negotiation process]

I can only say that when viewed in totality, the leadership of the farmers' movement has harmed the interests of the farmers in the long run. The farmers were confident of their strength, they had the desire to carry forward the struggle, but the leadership made a big mistake in withdrawing the movement. Think of all the things the people did—closing off the toll plazas, preventing BJP and other political party leaders from coming to the protest sites, organising a *rail roko* (rail blockade), boycotting of corporate goods—and all of this created a situation of massive face loss for the Narendra Modi government. It is only then that they were forced to repeal the laws. In this context, withdrawing the movement, indeed, was a big mistake, if you ask our opinion.

GX: *How did you personally feel when the Prime Minister announced the decision to repeal the three laws?*

NODEEP KAUR: It came as an absolute surprise as I had not anticipated this. When it sunk in, I felt elated, it was a clear victory for the farmers' movement, even though a partial one. This victory came at a time when many falsehoods were being spread about the movement. There was propaganda from the right-wing that there was an ideological clash between the Sikh organisations and the Left unions. We were also hearing frequent news as to how Dalits and women were being attacked at Singhu and Tikri borders. Many rumours were being spread, and it was not clear for how long could people sustain the movement in such a hostile environment.

Keeping in mind the times we are living in, I do consider the repealing of the three laws to be a big victory for the people. Certainly, it is only a partial victory, as the demand for the MSP remains. But, the fact is that so many people were martyred, and it's their martyrdom that brought us this partial victory.

The movement has also given toiling masses, at least in states like Punjab, Haryana, and UP, a new kind of energy. The farm laws are not the only thing plaguing us right now. There are the educational reforms, the new labour codes and such, and now the people have begun to feel, if the farm laws can be repealed through struggle, why not the other anti-people laws. None of these repressive laws are permanent. If a law can be made by the ruling parties it can also be unmade by the people.

GX: *What, in your view, compelled Modi to repeal the three laws, as the ruling party and the media have carefully cultivated an image of Modi as that of a strong politician who never goes back on any of his decisions under pressure?*

NODEEP KAUR: There are two aspects here. We can talk about Modi's personal traits, but it is not merely an individual who determines the things we are talking about. What we should really see is, for whose interests and under what forces he works. In this context, the primary force is imperialism and the frontal organisations which formulate and put pressure to execute such imperialist policies are institutions like WTO (World Trade Organisation), IMF (International Monetary Forum), World Bank, etc. And what is the primary thrust behind the policies pushed by these organisations? Absolute privatisation, by turning every aspect of our lives into a commodity, which, in turn, would bring in new multinational companies into the country. This includes privatising the education and health sector, institutionalising the labour codes, and exposing Indian peasantry to global capital.

But against some of these imperialist policies like the three farm laws adopted by the BJP government, rural masses from the three states—Punjab, Haryana, and western UP—started mobilising in large numbers. In Punjab, the farmers directly targeted the corporates—the toll plazas on highways were blocked, mobile phone towers were uprooted, corporate owned shopping malls and departmental stores were shut down. The BJP and RSS activists were kicked out from the villages, the BJP leaders were being publicly heckled, the police were attacked, and it slowly became clear that if the laws were not repealed, more and more people would join this movement. The trade unions had already come forward with their support, as did the Muslim community.

This could have easily become a nationwide people's movement. Consequently, the BJP began to see that they were completely losing their credibility amongst the people, and they could have suffered more electoral losses. That is why they took the decision to repeal the laws.

BJP has got the popular support in places like UP, Uttarakhand, and Bihar. But, the farmers there also began to confront their own realities—that they have no MSP, the *mandi* (agricultural produce market) system has been completely destroyed, the farmers are being forced to leave farming and become informal workers. If the government had not repealed the farm laws, chances are, BJP would have also lost people's support in UP and Uttarakhand, places that have long been considered as BJP strongholds. In other words, they had begun to notice their own withering.

As such, BJP remains one of the largest agents of big private companies. The farmers' movement put them in a fix. They will make every attempt to re-implement these laws through different methods and in different forms. Maybe under different names. But, for now, the popular resistance has made them take back the laws.

GX: *The Singhu border was one the main sites of the year-long sit-in by the farmers. And you were already working in that area organising contract labourers. So, you saw the farmers marching towards Delhi, you actually witnessed the movement up close. As a political activist, what are your impressions of the movement?*

NODEEP KAUR: We used to live quite close to the Singhu border. So, when we heard that the farmers had begun to march towards Delhi, we decided to become a part of the movement. Because after years, the farmers, in such large numbers, were marching towards Delhi to seal it off. Even in the initial phase, we felt that it's so remarkable that people in such large numbers got together to claim their rights. We felt that the march of the farmers, in itself, was historic irrespective of the outcome of the movement.

Initially, we thought that they would enter Delhi and protest inside the city. If that had happened it would have been a historic moment. The government had proposed to the farmers to go and sit at a designated place. Some felt that it was okay. They had no problems moving into Burari ground. But others opposed such a plan. They said, we haven't come here to be surrounded, we have come to surround the government. Finally, the farmers decided to seal Delhi off, by occupying the highways at the Singhu and Tikri border.

Our organisation works close to the Singhu border. This is an industrial area with thousands of factories. It is an extremely crucial point for the production, as well as transport of goods from Punjab, Haryana, UP, and Bihar to Delhi. Cities like Delhi function due to industrial corridors like Singhu and the comfortable lives of the ruling class inside Delhi, cannot be sustained without goods coming through the Singhu border. This was the strategic reason as to why the farmers, who were coming in thousands on their tractors and trolleys, began to surround the city of Delhi via Singhu.

Tents were pitched on the highway, support began to pour in from all corners. The students began to participate, and women began to join in large numbers. We witnessed unity amongst the activists and cadres who were never able to work together inside Punjab. The farmer unions, which haven't been able to put up a united front in Punjab, came together on a common platform and succeeded in bringing together the students, the youth, and even a section of the landless peasants. In the beginning, the industrial workers weren't involved in the movement.

I was working with a team that was helping people through Khalsa Aid by providing them with food, clothes, shoes, etc. Arrangements were made for langar (community kitchen). If anyone got their clothes torn, sewing machines were provided to them. If you were sitting somewhere, people would come up to you, ask whether you have eaten, whether you had blankets. If you didn't have a warm jersey, someone would provide you with that. No one felt the scarcity of necessary material goods.

And it is not as if only the Punjabi Sikhs were protesting like one big family. Farmers from Punjab, Haryana, and UP, who had never known each other, formed the support base of this movement. Strangers before the movement, they sat together, shared ideas, and helped each other throughout the difficult year, to the best of every one's abilities.

Punjab's economy has been decimated thanks to the Green Revolution. The land has been completely exhausted, and consequently, a lot of people have left for jobs in other countries. And these people who had left, also began to send in their support in the form of financial aid and donations. As a result, an infrastructure could be set up in the camps, and a lot of essential things could be supplied to the protestors camping on the borders.

Most of the farmers used to come with the basic rations, and all other things were available at the protest sites. Afterwards, there were also efforts to set up libraries. Near the Singhu border, a library of radical and political books was built, reading rooms were constructed, courtyards and separate tents representing many different political groups and interests were set up, some even began to plant vegetables on the sideways. All the protestors collectively created a community and began to feel that it was their home, their common village.

I was struck by certain developments that I saw with my own eyes. The consciousness that takes years and generations to evolve, had emerged amongst the people in a matter of a few months. A movement can do that, and it was great to be a witness to such a process. People who had come from remote corners of the villages in this country, were talking about issues that were of global and historical importance. Those who were enemies in the villages, were eating together, sitting down to talk to each other, and finding common issues amongst themselves. Because of the community kitchen, food was being provided, and that gave everyone the time to engage in other activities. So, this was a huge achievement, which I haven't quite seen happen in this way inside any other movement space.

In the past, there used to be a rivalry between Haryana and Punjab. Punjab had always wanted to see itself as the Big Brother supplying water to Haryana. There were also mutual stereotypes about each other, and such notions are often created and kept alive by the state to prevent unity amongst the people. But as the movement started, a language and feeling of brotherhood emerged. Men were exchanging turbans and taking oath that they would never fight amongst themselves. There were conversations around the issue of water, and how such issues can be resolved amongst each other without taking recourse to courts and the state. The movement, thus, has altered the relationship between Punjab and Haryana, which might have deep effects in the region in the years to come.

Now, when people go to each others' homes, in social gatherings and family functions, conversations about the laws and corporatisation of agriculture start spontaneously. People discuss WTO, Ambani and Adani, how they are connected to each other, and how the government and the ministers are their mere tools.

So, people have learnt a lot. They have learnt who their enemies are, and how these enemies can be targeted. We recognise and accept that a particular movement cannot address each and every need of the people. But, this movement has given birth to a new political consciousness amongst the peasantry and struggling masses who participated in it.

There were way too many other things that I am skipping now. And to be frank with you, I think it is impossible to say in totality what this movement has produced. I cannot put in words and in language what I saw and experienced. It is more about how I felt. We often speak of Marx, Lenin, and Mao, who have imagined a different society, a different world. I began to feel as if socialism and communism had already arrived! At least at the Singhu border.

GX: *How did the movement impact the popular culture in Punjab as well as Haryana? What have you observed?*

NODEEP KAUR: There are remarkable changes that this movement has brought in the cultural space. Just look at how it has changed the popular music in Punjab. Earlier, the dominant trend in Punjabi popular music was to follow a fixed narrative. There was a stereotypical representation of Punjabi men picking up guns, engaging in drug addiction and these things were sprinkled with some doses of nationalism. Now, people have begun to become thoughtful in their music. There are deeper reflections of their own history, history of Sikhism, and its relationship to the state of Delhi. There are new plays being written and performed, new films are being made, which are trying to reflect on the current times. And, all of these cultural changes have happened because of the movement. As such, there have been changes in the music of Haryana too. New songs were composed in both Punjab and Haryana, and the songs soon became the weapons of protest by the peasants and the workers. These are important cultural changes in the region, and a lot more of such things are in the process. Only the coming days will reveal what this movement has achieved in different fields and spaces. In the future, we will see the real impacts of this movement on mass consciousness.

GX: *The land-owning farmers are not alone in facing the agrarian dis-*

tress. *The agricultural workers are in a far worse condition. Most of them are Dalits. Historically, they don't own any land. Will you talk from your personal experience about caste discrimination in Punjab and how it impacts the agricultural workers, particularly the women?*

NODEEP KAUR: Caste system was done away within Sikhism. The teachings of the ten gurus were precisely about the fact that the *chamars*, shoe-makers, weavers, etc. (all the lower castes) would be brought under one fold. Those proponents of Sikhism, who spoke about taking up arms, also talked about how no human being would worship another human being, how no person would be a "Guru" to another person. So, the caste system that exists in Punjab, especially within Sikhism, is different from the casteism that exists in the rest of the country, especially UP and Bihar. But, castes and casteism still exist within Sikhism. Just as there are Ravidasias (followers of Sant Ravi Das), who happened to be Dalits, there are also Jat Sikhs. The Dalit Sikhs are called *Majhabi*s, they are neither given access to land nor to other resources. But, there is no untouchability as such. For example, I have lived in Telangana for eight years, and even today, the upper-castes there practice untouchability. As the society gets modernised, the nature and face of oppression might change, but it does not fully disappear.

In Punjab, there are a large number of [Dalit] landless peasants and agricultural workers. In our village, the landless peasantry and agricultural workers are spatially segregated from the upper-castes and Jat zamindars. They don't share the same residential area. The upper-caste people are popularly called *baadewale log* (rich people). Even the gurudwaras have been segregated, based on caste. The environment of social discrimination runs deep, and open calls of social boycott of Dalits are issued by the upper-castes.

It happened in our village. Agricultural workers had come together and demanded a minimum *dihari* (daily-wage); a social boycott had been called against those who lead the movement. As it is, in Punjab, there are hardly any industries. So, people mostly work in agriculture. And, when social boycotts are announced, you won't be allowed to step into the fields, your source of livelihood is attacked. You are left without any options. Not everyone can leave for foreign lands. As such, it's only the children of the big peasants who can go abroad. That's not an option for the children of the landless and agricultural labourers. So, social boycott is an important weapon in the hands of the upper-caste zamindars to force agricultural workers into submission.

We should of course remember that casteism is always far more destructive for women. If a male worker is paid Rs 500, a woman worker is paid only Rs 300. But they continue working simply because there are no other alternatives. They do not have lands of their own. The monopoly on owning lands lies with only a few. In our village, almost all of the land is owned by two or three Jats. There are zamindars who own even 100 acres of land. They are the ones who also have a hold over the panchayat and the sarpanch. Even if someone comes from outside during elections, to seek our votes, that person will go to the zamindars who will decide what will happen, and the rest of the village would simply follow their decision. So, as you can see, there is still a lot of feudal control.

For example, once my mother had gone to the fields to get some grass, and because she was associated with an agriculture worker union, the zamindar began to abuse her. There were other women with her too, but no one dared to speak back. But, my mother did. The Jats said, "How dare you even speak to us?" But when the matter intensified further, my mother picked up the machete which she was carrying along for grass-cutting, and attacked them. This is not something that Dalit female agricultural workers ever do. The Jats organised themselves, and so did the Dalit agricultural workers. The latter demanded that the Jats apologise to my mother. A movement began to take shape, and for the first time ever, the Jats were forced to apologise. But as a whole, the situation continues to be precarious for Dalit women. The assault and rape of Dalit women have been normalised in many villages, including ours, and to raise voice against such incidences, is to risk being socially boycotted.

GX: *We have heard that the upper-caste farmers had also issued a call to boycott your family and your family had to leave the village and migrate to Telangana. What had actually happened?*

NODEEP KAUR: There was another incident in our village, a minor Dalit girl was raped by three sons of a zamindar. My family, along with two or three other families, got involved. They protested. Seven days after the incident, an FIR was lodged, and the three accused men were arrested. A social boycott was called against us, and it was announced by the Jat community that anyone who would assist and help us, would be boycotted too. We were not allowed to go into the fields to work. We were a big family, with four daughters and two sons, and it became difficult to keep on fighting by ourselves. Others were too afraid to come forward.

Around that time my father rented a small shop in Telangana, and that's where we went and lived for eight years. It was a shop for repairing machines. Then, we came back here [Punjab] again. You can understand that if this is the state of a family willing to fight, then what is being done to the ones who do not dare to protest. The truth is, the rich farmers have a lot of power and control, they suppress the landless, marginal and small peasants. In fact, the condition of a small peasant is often worse than the agricultural workers, because they are ashamed to work in others' fields. This is why the rate of suicide is so high amongst them. Their lands are small and debt larger. They neither belong to the landed peasantry nor to the landless.

In Punjab, because of the long history of organised struggles people gained a certain level of consciousness. They join organisations. This is the reason why they have been able to raise demands. But, caste divides people, it prevents them from building up an unified struggle. The Dalit workers have this deeply rooted in their psychology that they do not deserve to own land. And, it will take time to change this psychology. So, there is a fighting spirit in Punjab, but that fighting spirit is also fractured because of caste.

GX: *Does your family own any land of its own?*

NODEEP KAUR: No, and this is the reality for most Dalit families in rural Punjab. Dalits do not possess any land. Even if a few manage to do so, the land is almost always taken away from them in one way or the other. It is seen as an affront, as kind of a challenge, that the Dalits possess lands of their own. Even though, as per the law, certain parts of village common land must be allotted to Dalit peasant families by the panchayat, the reality is too complicated.

GX: *What's the state of the debt in Punjab among landless agricultural workers? Can you also speak about the presence of microfinance companies in this regard?*

NODEEP KAUR: It is not uncommon in Punjab, for landless, marginal or small farmers like my father, to owe a debt of one and half or two lakh rupees. Obviously, they cannot repay, and so they are compelled to work as bonded labourers, and then their sons are forced to shoulder the burden. At times, they are also forced to mortgage their homes. Often, the original loan amount gets doubled and tripled. The Jat zamindars never ever forgive the loans, therefore, the landless, small and marginal peasants are extremely scared to take loans from them. The nationalised banks do not offer any loans to them. Banks demand mortgaging documents of land ownership etc. to issue loans.

This is the background in which the microfinance companies have made their inroads into the rural areas in Punjab. They claim that they allow the farmers and labourers to repay the loans slowly. And, in the process, also loot them gradually. I have seen this not only in our village, but also in the neighbouring villages. Often, for example, a landless farmer would, say, receive a loan of Rs 20,000, and end up repaying Rs 40,000. The burden of loans weighed heavily on our family too. We had to take a loan of Rs 50,000 from HDFC bank, and now my mother is repaying it in instalments of two or three thousand rupees every month with lots of difficulty. On a loan of Rs 50,000, we will finally end up paying more than Rs 70,000.

But this is part of the state's strategy towards India's peasantry. If the Indian state's goal was to make the small and landless peasants independent, and help in their struggle to stand on their own feet, it would have given loans at zero interest rate and the reality of Indian agriculture would have been very different.

GX: *Can you speak a bit about the state of women agricultural workers in Punjab? Also, about the role of the Left parties in addressing this issue?*

NODEEP KAUR: It is easier to repress those who don't have anything. The Dalits are repressed, because they do not have land. But a Dalit woman is oppressed by three things working together—the patriarchal family, zamindar and the state. She is, in fact, chained to these three oppressive structures from three sides.

Take my mother, for example. She used to wake up at 4 am in the morning. We had around 10 to 12 buffaloes, so she would go to the fields to fetch grass for them. Our father, too, would leave home at 4 am and return after midnight. When we were young, we were not even sure if we had a father or not, as we barely saw him.

Our mother used to take care of us, tend the animals, and do all the household chores. Like most women, she, too, had become a free machine which provided service at no cost. An industrial worker gets something in exchange for the work that he or she does, even if it's not adequate. But, women like my mother, get nothing. If she ever earns anything, that money is spent on her children or husband. In villages (and I would assume it is similar everywhere in the Indian countryside), women are promised Rs 400 or 500 for the work they would be doing, but they would be paid only Rs 200 or 300. If anyone protests, she would not be hired again. Even when they go to work under MGNREGA, the women are made to work more than the men. I often picture life of a Dalit peasant woman like this: she is the one who would rear children, tend to the domestic animals, do all her household work, go to work for MGNREGA, can be sexually abused or even raped at work or in bed at home.

Who knows why she is alive? Perhaps, she is kept alive to give birth to heirs, to carry forward the family line.

On the one hand, there is the caste system. On the other hand, a woman takes for granted the fact that she will be abused. So, even if a woman gets battered by her husband every day, she isn't surprised. If on a particular day, her husband refrains from abusing her, she feels grateful! She also comes to take it for granted that outside the home, when she goes out to work in the fields, she will be abused, molested, or even raped by the landlord or his relatives. Such is the atmosphere in which a Dalit woman lives here, and such is the culture which she also has internalised.

As it is, we never had any honour, to begin with.

I have a lot of angst about the women's question: my anger primarily comes from the fact that even the revolutionary parties haven't been able to make much headway in dealing with gender issues. There hasn't been any change in their mindset, none of them has been successful in building up a political 'women's front.' And, if this is something in which they fail, I fear that nothing substantial and long lasting can be created by them. Because, in the revolutionary struggle, abolition of gender inequality and patriarchy is of prime importance. Even within the revolutionary parties, women are never given space. Once a year, a women's day is given to them to celebrate. I think, these are the issues on which we should begin to have open discussions.

GX: *What do you think of the struggle that's being led by Zameen Prapti Sangarsh Samiti (ZPSC) for acquiring land for the Dalit landless labourers in Punjab and the struggle for loan waiver of agricultural workers?*

NODEEP KAUR: ZPSC is doing commendable work in Punjab. There had been struggles in Punjab before on this issue, but there has never been any sustained struggle on this issue. So, it is great that they are taking forward this struggle for years and have also attained significant victories.

They started their struggle based on acquiring panchayati and *nazool* lands meant for Dalits. Their struggle is important, because through formation of Dalit collectives in villages, they have succeeded in building up some form of unity amongst those who are the most deprived. It is a departure from the usual norm in India where those who oppress and live off the poor, are united. But those who are oppressed are not. For example, even though the land-owning farmers have succeeded in building up the Samuykta Kisan Morcha, the agricultural workers do not have a Samyukta Mazdoor Morcha. In fact, a few months back, a united platform of the rural and agricultural workers was formed in Punjab, and it was a good start. I think such struggles should be built up not only inside Punjab, but also throughout the rest of the country. Without the unity of the workers, and a struggle that involves rural as well as urban working class, ultimately no radical movement will succeed.

Coming back to the work of ZPSC, they have started a serious and an important struggle over panchayati land. In Punjab, the government has made a law that one-third of the panchayati land should go to the landless, but in reality, that is not happening. The price of the land has also been hiked up. ZPSC started a movement to make it possible for the landless peasants to acquire such land at lower prices. And, this has raised the confidence of the Dalit agricultural workers considerably.

In a village called Jhaloor during one such struggle led by ZPSC, the Jat landlords had molested, groped, and beaten up the women engaged in the struggle, severed the arms and legs of the Dalit men and in fact chopped off the legs of a 72 year old Dalit woman. In Punjab, this incident is known as Jhaloor *kaand* (Jhaloor incident)[1]. So, you can imagine what kind of terror has been unleashed in the villages.

It has to be ensured that the lives of those comrades who were martyred in the land struggle do not go in vain. ZPSC is doing precisely this. Land redistribution amongst the landless is a must. And, the work that ZPSC has done in this regard is extremely inspiring. It gives us hope and strength.

GX. *The farmers' movement raised the slogan of farmer-worker unity. But, if we look closely into the realities on the ground in Punjab, what we see is that the urgent question of land ownership for the landless agricultural workers hasn't been addressed. Doesn't this slogan then begin to sound empty, more of a lip service to the idea of unity?*

NODEEP KAUR: The issue of caste is deeply ingrained in peoples' minds, and the issue is ultimately tied to the land question. The farmers' movement is really the first of its kind, and we have to remember that one of the three laws to be repealed also would have adversely affected the agricultural workers. But the primary thrust of this movement should be viewed as a resistance to anti-imperialist policies in the agricultural sector, which the working class too, needed to support and rally behind. But in villages, the primary enemy of a landless farmer is still the *zamindars* and rich peasants, and hence the fight against them will also continue simultaneously.

When the leadership of a movement is primarily constituted of feudal forces, they will naturally focus on their own interests. Why would they talk about the need to change the form of land ownership and demand land redistribution? Why would they speak about the labour codes? They will not speak for complete implementation of the Swaminathan Commission report, because this report does speak about the issue of landlessness and land redistribution. In fact, the reality is, the agricultural workers were never given a space in the farmers' protest, although their presence in the movement was sought after. When labour rights organisations mobilised about two thousand workers, and went to the protest site, they were given just five minutes to speak after waiting for two hours. And when we were attacked by goons hired by factory owners at a few kilometers distance from Singhu border, picked up by the police and then tortured and abused in police custody, the Samyukta Kisan Morcha (SKM) didn't quite come to our aid, didn't lend us the support it should have.

We feel that this movement has been led by the land-owning rich farmers and the feudal elements, and the revolutionary parties could not lead it. In fact, the agricultural workers and landless peasants participated in large numbers, but their issues were never raised. This is a failure on the part of the revolutionary left within the movement. In the late phase of the movement, many farmer leaders started calling for farmer-worker unity. Earlier, the workers were seen as a separate entity and were not paid heed to, by the big and small land-owners alike. Today, things have slightly changed, the small farmers are now saying publicly that agricultural workers have been wronged and their issues should be addressed.

However, I would once again like to emphasise that a single movement cannot resolve all contradictions. It cannot address everyone's needs and demands. And, we should not trust and expect big farmers and *zamindar* leadership to fight our battles.

GX: *To end our discussion, how did the farmers' movement impact the workers in the Kundli industrial belt where you worked in a factory and took on the task of organising the workers, most of whom are migrants from other states with roots in the agricultural economy?*

NODEEP KAUR: If we are talking about the workers from UP and Bihar, 40 percent of them are from peasant families. I have met many who have land, but can't afford a decent livelihood based on the income from that land. Some have come after selling off their land. Around 60 percent are Dalit, who have neither land nor permanent home. They go wherever they get work and that place becomes their address.

The company where I used to work, they wouldn't even let the workers talk amongst themselves. There was high surveillance within the factory. Workers have been punished because of talking to each other. Here, lunch breaks are only for 15 minutes, and if the worker ends up taking a few minutes more, they are punished, their wages are cut.

Here, forming a union is a far-fetched dream. On the other hand, the owners hire goons to keep the workers in line. If a worker leaves a job, he/she never gets the last month's salary. If the worker demands that salary, they are roughed up by the goons. In Kundli, there is no history of labour activism. At least in the Manesar area, some trade unions have been working for a considerably long time. Also, it becomes extremely difficult to build up a unified working class struggle only with migrant workers. You need local workers to do that. So far, we have failed, by and large, to build up such a network amongst the local workers.

Until the farmers' movement started, it wasn't in the imagination of the workers and working class activists, including our own organisation, that such a massive and long dharna could be organised. Many workers became part of the farmers' struggle—staying with the farmers, eating in the langars, working alongside them, walking in the rallies and listening to speeches, slogans and songs.

The workers would say, if we can organise something of our own as workers, because of the impact created by the farmers' movement, then, no doubt that something remarkable can happen. When the farmers were leaving, a lot of the workers were crying. It was a sight to behold, where the workers and farmers were crying together while holding each other in arms. During the days of the lockdown, when the workers did not have anything to eat, the ration that they were getting from the government were neither adequate nor of edible quality—the langars at the protest sites had provided them food. The medical camps at the protest sites provided the workers with the requisite medical help. So, there has developed this feeling amongst the workers that when the government didn't stand by us, the farmers did. The workers have begun to think that if people are given the opportunity and power to manage things on their own, they can do so better than the government. But one has to take all these lessons and use it to build up a working class struggle. But, it won't take any roots until and unless we succeed to evolve a distinct political program for the workers.

See, no union or a class struggle is ever built by sitting inside one's homes. Neither can symbolic protests accomplish much. One has to reach out to the workers, explain to them the implications of the labour codes, and encourage them to understand their own strength. But, we have become habituated in a culture of symbolic protests. Even the revolutionary organisations have failed to build up anything worthwhile amongst the workers. On top of that, there is the issue of caste, and oftentimes it seems, the trade union leadership simply doesn't want to understand this issue. Blaming only the SKM leadership can't hide our own shortcomings.

Endnote

1. Jhaloor *kaand* refers to the violent incident of attack and brutality on Dalit agricultural workers, including women, by the Jat farmers in Jhaloor village in Sangrur district on 5 October 2016. The workers were demanding their right over village common land, fraudulently usurped by the rich Jat farmers of the village. For details see interview of Gurmukh Singh, p-267-294 in this volume.

On October 12, 2021, Shaheed Kisan Divas was observed—*antim ardaas* (last rites) of the martyrs of Lakhimpur Kheri massacre were held in Tikunia village.
Photo Credit: Workers Unity.

A Simple Repeal of the Farm Laws Does Not Address the Existing Agrarian Crisis

PROF. RANJIT SINGH GHUMAN, ECONOMIST, GURU NANAK DEV UNIVERSITY

RANJIT SINGH GHUMAN is Professor of Eminence, Punjab School of Economics, Guru Nanak Dev University, Amritsar. He has worked extensively on the ecological crisis in agriculture, and the problems of landless farmers and rural unemployment in Punjab.

He has served at Punjabi University in various capacities including Head of Economics Department. He has been Chairman, Punjab Government Committee on MSP for agricultural produce. He has co-authored *Emerging Water Insecurity in India: Lessons from an Agriculturally Advanced State*.

This conversation with Prof. Ghuman is in two parts. Part I was conducted by WORKERS UNITY in August 2021 in Patiala (Punjab). Part II was done by HARSHITA BHASIN and SAHIL MEHRA of South Asian University in January 2022 for GROUNDXERO.

PART I

WORKERS UNITY: *You have worked extensively on a range of agrarian and ecological issues in Punjab over the years. I would like you to elaborate on the crisis we are facing in agriculture in Punjab and how farming is becoming ecologically nonviable.*

RS GHUMAN: We can understand the issue of agrarian crisis only if we go far back, to the years before the Green Revolution. While the Green Revolution emerged only in the 1960s, the idea had been laid down much earlier in the 1940s by the Rockefeller Foundation, Ford Foundation, etc. Budding agricultural scientists from the Third World were trained free of cost by these institutions in those years. PL-480,[1] which was a diplomatic instrument used by the US government as a 'Food for Peace' program, was also started. The Green Revolution is linked to all these developments.

There were some underlying reasons behind the idea of the Green

Revolution: global agri-business interests wanted to channel the efforts of the Third World countries towards agriculture over industry and also counter the possibility of social revolution in these countries. China had a communist revolution in 1949 and there was a threat of similar revolutions in other East Asian countries.

If we talk about ecology, then we must note that High Yielding Varieties (HYV) of seeds aren't exactly high yielding but actually only highly responsive seeds; they are mainly responsive to water. The first experimental lab for the Green Revolution was Punjab because of the abundance of river, canal and groundwater available for irrigation. Almost one hundred percent of cultivated land in Punjab is irrigated, as against just 45 percent at all India level. About 83 percent of the total geographical land (in Punjab) is under agriculture. But the situation of groundwater is now quite poor – "groundwater development" in Punjab was 149 percent in 2013 and 166 percent in 2017. This means that we did not recharge 66 percent of the groundwater which we extracted in 2017. Water is the key reason that the Punjab model of agriculture is unsustainable.

Besides water, the cropping pattern of Punjab is now concentrated towards just two crops—rice and wheat. This is another big reason underlying the agrarian crisis.

Also, the rise of mechanisation has displaced labour from farming. Even if we leave aside the work for agricultural labourers, even cultivators do not have more than two months of work in Punjab agriculture. It is livestock, especially dairy, which is safeguarding Punjab agriculture as about 40 percent of farm income is coming from dairy.

As per studies done by Punjab Agricultural University (PAU), Guru Nanak Dev University, and Punjabi University, there have been about 16,606 suicides by farmers and agricultural labourers between 2000 and 2016 in a small state like Punjab. A conservative estimate for the following four years would be around 4000 more suicides. So, we have had about 20,000 suicides by farmers and agricultural labourers which are symptomatic of the crisis within agriculture—lack of employment, insufficiency of income from agriculture, and heavy indebtedness.

In research from the year 2000, I found that per hectare income from agriculture in Punjab was increasing *at a diminishing rate*. Even as income is shrinking, the cost of cultivation has been rising. Because of the water crisis, farmers have had to deepen their bore wells at rising capital costs. If, five years ago, you had to spend two to three lakh to install a tube well, today it costs you about three to four lakh. Such high expenditures are not affordable for medium, small, and marginal farmers of Punjab. In India, about 86 percent of farmers are small and marginal. In fact, within the category of small and marginal farmers, about 69 percent are marginal, i.e. they cultivate less than 2.5 acres of land. Their average holdings come out to be just about one acre. We have to ponder how a farming household can sustain itself with farming income from such a meagre land holding—can they manage the health and education of their children even as the government's expenditure on health and education is falling? This puts a pressure on out-of-pocket health expenses of these families.

It is an amalgamation of all these factors that has created the current agricultural and farmers' distress, which has been deepening over time. In fact, the ongoing farmers' agitation is nothing but a symptom and manifestation of this crisis and the three agricultural laws enacted by the Indian Government are being perceived as augmenting the crisis.

WU: *You mentioned the displacement of labour on account of mechanisation in agriculture. You were part of a 2007 study on the status of local agricultural labourers in Punjab where you looked at the changing job profile of local as well as migrant agricultural labourers in Punjab. Can you elaborate on the findings of this study, while also discussing the impact of these changes on rural society?*

RS GHUMAN: We had conducted this study in 2007 when the Punjab State Farmers' Commission was headed by the notable agricultural scientist and ex-VC of PAU, Dr. Kalkat. He was very curious to learn what was happening to the local labour of Punjab given the influx of migrant labour in the state. Professor Inderjeet Singh and Professor Lakhwinder Singh also worked with me on this one-and-a-half-year-long investigation into the issue. We collected data from 36 villages spread across 12 districts of the state which was representative of the entire state. We found that the skill and education level of agricultural labour was abysmally poor, despite the perception of Punjab to be a developed state. In fact, 90 percent of the farm labour households did not have a single member who had passed Class 10. Amongst households across all categories, this figure was around 69 percent. Given the lack of education and skill, this labour can only take up unskilled jobs. One of our key findings was that these labourers could not find even 120 days of work in a year.

And if you ask about the non-farm sector, unlike the West, Punjab and really the entire country has not created suitable job opportunities outside agriculture. This is a critical issue which remains unaddressed. With less than 120 days of work a year, these labourers did not make much income at all, as we are talking about 2007 when even MGNREGA did not exist. We did another study after the introduction of MGNREGA in 2008 and found that MGNREGA also did not create much employment in Punjab. So, these workers don't have much choice—they take up seasonal work available in food-grain markets close to the villages or other small-time jobs.

Besides these agricultural worker households, two to three lakh cultivator households in Punjab have also left farming and seek work as labourers. All these households are trapped in low-paid and unskilled jobs in the informal sector. You can find such a scenario in industrial centres like Ludhiana—these households do not find work in such centres too on account of a skill mismatch. Migrant labourers, almost anywhere, are known to go to more prosperous regions and take up jobs that are unattractive to the local labour. This is seen to be true for Punjab as well: local labourers do not want to take up these jobs.

A farmer can sell half or one acre of land to send their children abroad but agricultural labourers do not have even this option. Mechanisation has reduced work in agriculture and there are hardly any employment opportunities outside agriculture. This has been a general trend everywhere with growing neoliberalisation. This explains why, in the last five years or so, about 50,000 youth (and maybe more, there is no reliable data) from Punjab have migrated to other countries each year after spending lakhs of rupees on legal as well as illegal routes. This just reflects how an individual may attempt to find his or her way out given the rising unemployment.

According to government statistics, Punjab has an unemployment rate of around 7.3 percent. Given that the size of the workforce is about 98 lakh, this suggests that about 7.2 lakh persons are unemployed in the state. However, according to our estimates the number of unemployed is about 22 lakh. If we add around three lakh marginal workers (having employment from one day to 90 days) this figure would go up to 25 lakh. The brunt of this huge unemployment problem is borne by vulnerable sections of the population, those who lack skill and education. All the labour agitations unfolding in Punjab, such as the one recently in Patiala [referring to the three day demonstration by farm and rural labourers at Patiala from 9 to 11 August 2021] are a manifestation of this labour crisis—they realise that there are no opportunities for them.

And forget about other solutions, we are not even realising the full potential of MGNREGA. If MGNREGA could provide them with 100 days of employment in off-season over and above the 100 days of seasonal work in farming, then they would have 200 days of employment. Similarly, there is a provision within MGNREGA where a marginal farmer can claim some wages for the work done on his own farm. But we are not making use of these avenues on account of a crisis of governance as well.

WU: *You have described the deepening crisis of the agricultural labourers. The large three-day rally in Patiala conducted by various agricultural worker unions is a manifestation of this crisis. The Zameen Prapti Sangharsh Committee has also led a large demonstration. Conversations with their leaders as well as their charter of demands reveal a range of issues that affect Dalit agricultural labourers: MGNREGA is not providing more than 12 to 15 days of work in a year; wages have seen a sharp decline, so much that it is difficult to find work even at wages of 200-250 rupees per day. This brings up the issue of unequal distribution of agricultural land in Punjab. A major demand raised by Dalit agricultural labour organisations is that the laws that earmark one-third of Panchayati land to be cultivated by Dalits is not implemented properly. Do you see land reforms as one of the possible solutions to the problems of agricultural labourers?*

RS Ghuman: As per NSSO data, about 65 percent of rural households are landless. Our own study on labour also revealed that 67 percent of rural households in Punjab are landless. There is also a large income disparity within these households. There isn't sufficient land available in Punjab which may be redistributed. Panchayati land (land under village council) is available; in fact, there is a law[2] mandating that one-third of this land should be leased out to SCs (Scheduled Castes) and 10 percent to BCs (Backward Castes). But this law isn't implemented properly. There is the issue of dummy candidates put up by rich Jat farmers from the village, this land is leased in the name of a Dalit, but the land ultimately goes to the rich farmers. In Punjab, there was a recent struggle by the Zameen Prapti Sangharsh Committee wherein they managed to gain access to such land in some villages and initiated cooperative farming on it. Such models need to be replicated.

But, a sizable amount of panchayati land in Punjab is under illegal occupation of influential people. There is indeed a need in Punjab that this panchayati land rightfully goes in the hands of the Dalit labourers as per the law. But how many lives can this change? Ultimately, we need to provide education, enhance skill sets, and create employment opportunities, such as self-employment or via promotion of agro-processing.

This crisis is systemic. Now, people are taking steps to collectively as well as individually, find solutions to the crisis. But the government is not doing what it should from sheer indifference to people. Just look at the farmers struggling for over a year, sitting in Delhi for the last eight months even as the Central government remains indifferent. We, a group of 12 economists, also wrote a letter to *Tomar ji*, the Union Minister of Agriculture, citing reasons that call for a repeal of the laws.

This insensitivity of the government can be resolved only via large social movements that can threaten the seat of the political leadership. Look at all the political parties in Punjab singing praises of the farmers. The Akali Dal had initially voted in favour of the laws and made a case for their merit but changed course when they feared a backlash from the electorate. This kind of political opportunism has been correctly recognised by the farmers.

WU: *The slogan of Kisan-Mazdoor Ekta is raised with vigour at Singhu and Tikri border protest sites. But, the day-to-day interactions in the* *villages reveal a different reality. There is an intense struggle over land and wages between the kisan and mazdoor. There is also the related issue of migrant labourers working at very low wages. So, we have a lot of fault lines vis-a-vis potential areas of cooperation. Do you see any resolution for these fault lines? Is there a possibility that any new or alternate politics may come about to take us past this systemic crisis?*

RS GHUMAN: The vested interests within the system would not want the differences between *kisan* (farmer) and *khet mazdoor* (agricultural worker) to get resolved. The marginal farmers may be like a large farmer in terms of the caste, but his economic position is in conflict with the large farmers and aligned with the labourer. But they do stay in conflict with labour on account of the caste system. Caste conflict isn't as severe in Punjab as in other parts of the country but it remains embedded in the psyche. Besides caste, there is a critical economic contradiction between farmer and labour as the farmer wants to extract labour at the lowest possible wages even as the labourer seeks higher wages for his work. This economic contradiction is tied to the mode of production (ownership of means of production and production relations). While it is not so easy to resolve this contradiction, it is possible to weaken it. This would require a social movement which advocates that the fundamental contradiction is with the neoliberal forces and not against each other. Such an understanding has been exhibited by the ongoing farmers' movement in their opposition to the neoliberal paradigm or growth model.

In the village, the farmers have camaraderie amongst each other, but only a functional relationship with the labourers. But when it comes to wages, they run into problems. It is the large farmers, not the small, who oppose *zameen prapti sangharsh* (land ownership struggle) of the agricultural workers. There are over 10 lakh operational holdings in Punjab of which approximately 60 percent are small and marginal farmers (up to five acres) operating only 9.69 percent of the total operated area. The relations between these small and marginal farmers and labourers should be better. If Punjab farmers would receive MSP as recommended by Swaminathan Commission i.e. 50 percent returns over C2 cost and not on A2 + FL cost which covers just cost of purchased inputs and imputed family labour, then they would have received an additional sum of over 14,200 crore rupees. If 10 lakh farmers of Punjab would get this additional sum, then it may be easier for agricultural worker unions to bargain for higher wages with the farmers. It is not right that farmers or labourers collude over wages, they should negotiate wages based on ground realities. The slogans of *kisaan-mazdor ekta* (farmer-worker unity) at Singhu and Tikri borders of Delhi do not reflect reality as the participation of farm-labourer unions and trade unions in the farmers' movement is not much. The government is also cognizant of this fact. If agricultural worker unions could have been brought on board, the movement would have become more stronger. However, these contradictions are difficult to diminish unless we understand the larger context.

PART II

GX: *There has been a lot of debate around the demand for MSP. A lot of experts feel that a legal guarantee of MSP is not very feasible. What are your thoughts on the feasibility as well as desirability of MSP?*

RS Ghuman: There were two major demands put forth by the farmers right from the beginning of this movement: legalised MSP and repeal of the three farm laws. The laws have been repealed which means that the farmers have prevailed over the government even though it was quite late.

When it comes to the feasibility of MSP, as an economist, I am of the opinion that MSP is feasible beyond any doubt. The opinion of the government, as well as of some experts supporting the laws, is that the government will have to spend Rs 17 lakh crore every year on MSP, if it is provided for all crops and across the country. I think this figure is highly exaggerated. At present, the government spends 2.5 to 3.5 lakh crore annualy to procure a few crops for the central pool even though only a very small percentage of farmers get MSP. If the government is ready to spend an additional one or 1.5 lakh crore, then it could make the whole issue feasible.

Farmers are not demanding that the entire produce of all the 23 crops for which MSP is currently declared by the CACP (Commission for Agricultural Costs and Prices) be procured by the government. They are demanding a Swaminathan-MSP, which is C2 (or comprehensive cost) plus 50 percent returns. Currently, the government is giving MSP equal to 50 percent of A2 cost+family labour. There is a huge difference between the Swaminathan-MSP and the MSP given by the government. The farmers are demanding that MSP should be legalised because it gives a reference point or a floor price. In the absence of such a floor price, the farmers are at the mercy of private traders or procurers (as has been happening over the decades) and get a much lower price than the MSP. Moreover, the farmers are not arguing that the government should procure each and every grain produced by the farmer but are demanding legal steps to ensure that the private traders do not carry out procurement below the MSP. If MSP is legal, then procurement below MSP will be recognised as an offence that is subject to trial in a court of law. Past experience also shows that whenever the government agencies enter into procurement (by purchasing some of the produce) the private players do start giving higher prices.

The government has taken care of bank NPAs or bad loans, running beyond Rs 10 lakh crore. They have undertaken a one-time settlement wherein the entire bad loan has been pardoned in lieu of just 20 percent of the amount. So, a burden of six to seven lakh crore has been passed on to the taxpayers. If this can be done, then why can't MSP be legalised for farmers? Agricultural produce being purchased (or to be procured in future) by the private traders from farmers is a tangible commodity which can be resold and/or processed. By adding value to the raw produce, the traders do charge remunerative prices from the end consumers. True, the government cannot and will not procure the entire produce of the farmers, but private traders/companies would certainly need the agricultural produce for reselling and processing to run their business enterprises.

So, legalisation of MSP is not only feasible but desirable as well. Farmers are justified in their demand for legal status to MSP. Many people ask me why the government is not giving legal status to MSP even if it's feasible. It is because the government wants to further the interests of private traders and big companies. The government does not want to put the private traders in trouble by legalising MSP.

GX: *It is well known that public procurement of food grains and MSP works well in Punjab. Yet, there are extensive reports of widespread eco-*

nomic distress and farmers' suicide in the state. How do you explain this? Does this suggest that MSP may not be a complete solution to the problem of agrarian distress in Punjab?

RS GHUMAN: Punjab's rice-wheat monoculture has led to agrarian distress and indebtedness in the state. There is no doubt that MSP is given to farmers in Punjab, however, in view of the increasing costs of cultivation and the shrinking unemployment in agriculture we have to go beyond the MSP to address the agrarian crisis and farmers' distress. There is an urgent need to have a comprehensive study of this and come out with viable solutions. Unfortunately, no government has taken any serious steps towards this. Had it been so, the National Farmers Commission's (popularly known as Swaminathan Commission) report (2004-06) would have been debated in the parliament instead of gathering dust for the last 16 years.

Over time, the costs of cultivation have increased at a higher pace relative to MSP. Also, the Green Revolution has led to higher aspirations and expenditure levels amongst the farmers on account of the prosperity created in the 1970s and 80s. However, the colour of the Green Revolution started fading by the mid-1990s, which means that the net returns per hectare started shrinking. There was a decline in the long-term growth rate as per a study I conducted in 2002. The aggregate return was increasing but at a diminishing trend of growth rate. The expenditure on crop cultivation and animal husbandry along with upkeep of farmers through expenses on health, education, etc. has increased. Even some of the consumption expenditure of the farmers is being met by taking loans. In economics, there is this famous theory put forth by Duesenberry[3] that once you achieve a certain economic standard of living, it is very difficult to slide downwards.

Since we are talking of Punjab in particular, non-farm employment did not expand in the state to absorb the surplus labour force among cultivators and farm-labourers in agriculture. In the absence of a dynamic rural non-farm sector, the shrinking opportunities in agriculture have led to a squeeze on the per capita incomes of farmers and labourers. Another supplementary cause is that the social fabric also weakened so farmers are finding themselves psychologically beleaguered. When we talk of costs of cultivation, the costs of ground water extraction especially have increased to enormous amounts with the decline in the water table.

GX: *If we talk about rice-wheat monoculture, what steps are really required so that Punjab moves away from this practice? Do you think MSP will have any role to play in ensuring crop diversification?*

RS GHUMAN: In Punjab, paddy wasn't a natural crop even prior to Independence. In the 1940s, only nine percent of the undivided Punjab's irrigated area was under paddy cultivation even though Punjab was much bigger at that time as it also included the Pakistani state of Punjab, Haryana as well as parts of Himachal Pradesh. Even until 1971, only nine percent of the net sown area was under paddy cultivation. At present, 85 percent of net sown area in the Kharif season is under paddy cultivation.

Paddy was not promoted in Punjab by the farmers but by the policy mix of the government on account of the food security of the nation. There used to be a phrase, 'ship to mouth,' during the PL-480 days. The policy mix I want to draw attention towards is HYV (High Yielding Variety) seeds for paddy and wheat, assured irrigation which was available in Punjab and assured procurement at the MSP by the Food Corporation of India (FCI) under PDS (Public Distribution System). There was an Agricultural Prices Commission which became the Commission for Agricultural Costs and Prices (CACP) in 1985. All this was aimed to work as an incentive to farmers of Punjab, Haryana and western Uttar Pradesh to grow more paddy and wheat, the final aim being to meet the food requirement of the country.

If we talk about ecological impact, then this wheat-paddy combination has destroyed the erstwhile diversified agriculture of Punjab which was there before the Green Revolution. If you look at the cropping pattern of the state in the 1970s, there was a substantial area under pulses, oilseeds and other crops. However, all these crops just vanished by the 1980s. Some experiments are being done to promote maize as a substitute for paddy but there is no MSP being given out for maize. The recommended MSP of maize is around Rs 1,880 but it is being procured at only Rs 1,100 or 1,200.

This leads us to your question—if MSP can play a role for diversification of agriculture in Punjab. I would say yes because paddy was promoted in Punjab by implementing MSP for the crop. Effective implementation of MSP (recommended by the CACP) for all the 23 crops would certainly work to promote much needed crop diversification. And if that is done for oil seeds and pulses, the country can save a lot on foreign exchange currently being spent on their imports. Punjab badly needs crop-diversification and if that happens, we will be able to save a lot of ground water as well. We did a detailed study, commissioned by the Indian Council for Social Sciences Research, from 2013 to 2015 wherein we found that the water table in 12 districts which mostly produced paddy had gone down from 6 to 22 metres between 1996 and 2016. Our dependence on ground water for irrigation is 73 percent at present. Of course, free electric supply for agriculture has also contributed to this high dependence on ground water for irrigation.

Actually, this free electricity meant for Punjab farmers often goes to consumers, mainly outside Punjab. There is a virtual water-export from Punjab—we do not export rice to the nation so much as our ground water. If we look at the total procurement of paddy in Punjab as well as total contribution towards the central pool, you will find that 80 to 85 percent of water consumed in production of paddy goes to the central pool.

Punjab's rice consumes more water than the national average. For example, Punjab consumes 5,337 litres of water to produce one kg of rice compared to a national average of 3,875 litre per kg. This figure is just 2,605 litres per kg of rice in West Bengal. We are certainly over irrigating our lands, which also contributes to overuse of groundwater. All this leads to an increase in costs of extracting ground water (such as installing deep tube wells etc.) which directly fall on the farmer as well as the bill of the electricity subsidy given by the government of Punjab to the farmers. If a farmer with five acres of land or less takes up a loan to install a tube well, he/she will never be able to repay it out of the income from agriculture.

In another 10 to 15 years, the water crisis may make Punjab's paddy cultivation economically unviable. Crop diversification is the need of the hour, not by arm twisting but through a policy mix. The same set of policies which promoted paddy in Punjab is needed to achieve crop diversification away from paddy. Way back in 1986, a Punjab government's committee (popularly known as Johl Committee) recommended crop diversification. The second Johl Committee in 2002 recommended substituting at least 20 percent of area under paddy for other crops. The committee recommended that the central government should bear the cost (around Rs 1250 crore per annum) for 5 to 10 years. Unfortunately, nothing has happened; instead, the Central government has also been advising the Punjab government to implement diversification on its own. Farmers or the Punjab government alone cannot achieve this. It is the responsibility of the nation to come up with a compatible policy mix as the present cropping pattern was developed by the Central government's policies. Along with crop diversification, we also need diversification of the rural economy without which Punjab is really in for a crisis.

GX: *In the farmers' movement, we saw solidarities across the existing divides of caste, class, and gender. Now that the movement has ended successfully, do you expect the solidarities lasting, or do you think that the traditional fault lines [between farmers and labourers as well as farmers and* arhtiyas] *are likely to reappear?*

RS GHUMAN: There are some perennial or fundamental clashes of interests which are going to stay on the scene even though the farmers' movement united all these sections—labourers, small and big farmers, etc. For instance, farmers' interest is to pay low wages whereas labourers expect high wages. Similarly, landless Dalit labourers are entitled to one-third of panchayati land but there have been clashes over it in the last few years.

There are more than 20,000 *arhtiyas* (registered commission agents in notified *mandis* in Punjab). Some people claim that there is a close relationship between *arhtiyas* and farmers as they are the ATMs of the farmers. But there is exploitation of farmers by the *arhtiyas* – economic exploitation at the time of procurement, charging high interest rates on the loans which range from 12 to 18 percent per annum but sometimes even exceed 20 percent as well. There is also the issue of direct payment to farmers which has been implemented in the last year or so. Some farmer unions demanded a direct payment to get rid of the *arhtiyas*. The three laws have for the time being subdued these differences. The *arhtiyas* have supported the farmers' movement in a big way.

Despite the fundamental differences, the external aggression has united these groups. Of course, this agitation has minimised these differences and there is a possibility that in the future, they may resolve these issues at their own level.

GX: *Now, the movement is being hailed for its success as the laws have been repealed and the government has also promised to set up a committee over MSP. But do you think that there exist structural issues in agriculture and rural economy that remain unaddressed?*

RS GHUMAN: Agrarian crisis and farmers' distress had been issues even prior to these farm laws, these laws would have just augmented those issues. A simple repeal of the farm laws does not address the existing agrarian crisis. As I have said, crop diversification is the need of the hour. The rural non-farm sector is also in need of development—the surplus workforce in agriculture which comprises both cultivators as well as labourers must be redeployed in the non-farm sector. There is also the issue of employability of those being pushed out of agriculture in the non-farm sector. We have to provide them with the skills which are demanded in the non-farm sector.

One of the pressing issues in Punjab is the migration of youths to other countries. In the years to come, you will realise that the cream of Punjab has left the state, creating a scarcity of youth to sustain even the traditional occupations.

Even a legal MSP won't be a lasting solution to the problems of Punjab's rural economy. So, what Punjab needs is cooperative farming—value addition in agriculture by way of processing through farmers cooperatives. Cooperative use of machinery is also very important – we have 14 lakh tube wells compared to two lakh tube wells in 1997. We don't need five lakh tractors—they remain highly under-utilised. Cooperatives can reduce the costs of cultivation of farmers so that their profit margins can increase. Processing can also generate employment as well as additional income.

So, there is a range of issues; for instance, the state's financial crisis and unemployment. Unemployment in Punjab is much higher than the national average. Youth unemployment is around 22 percent. The state's lack of orientation towards development, decelerating growth rate, financial mismanagement and governance-deficit along with huge unemployment and ever increasing public debt are some serious challenges which need to be addressed in a systematic manner.

GX: *You must be aware that some farm unions are considering contesting elections in Punjab. What are your thoughts over this—can they offer a new leadership that is much needed in Punjab or will it just dilute their goodwill?*

RS GHUMAN: So there are several sub-questions here. One is, if farmers should have jumped into electoral politics or not. In fact, people are fed up with the traditional political parties. There is a serious trust deficit in the traditional political leadership. There is hardly any expectation among people that they will improve Punjab's economy, agriculture, industrial development or tackle unemployment issues. It is common knowledge that they are using politics only for their business interests. On account of this, many people had been demanding farmer leaders jump into electoral politics even prior to the repeal of the laws.

I have been in constant touch with the farmers' agitation; I have addressed them at their Kisan Sansad[4] on their invitation, as well as at the Singhu and Tikri border. I have also written substantially in the media about their struggle. But I am not convinced that they should jump into electoral politics.

There is indeed a need for a new leadership which has a commitment towards Punjab's people as well as issues around its economy, culture and society. You see 22 (later some of them withdrew) farmer unions have recently come together and launched a political platform, Sanyukt Samaj Morcha (SSM), and they plan to contest in all the 117 assembly seats. If SSM is able to take along other farmer unions, they do have the ability to make a perceptible impact on the elections, as there are more than 60 to 70 constituencies wherein rural or agrarian populations can have a significant impact. However, this is subject to two conditions: their ability to take along other unions of the Samyukta Kisan Morcha

(SKM) and their ability to rope in the *samyukta samaj*. i.e., all sections of society. But this seems to be an uphill task as the traditional political parties have some committed vote banks and are also well equipped with election skills, besides muscle and money power. So, the issue is also if they will be able to outsmart these parties that are so well grounded in Punjab.

I really wish to see new and honest faces in the Punjab assembly so that Punjab can be resurrected. I am using a big word here as it is my considered opinion that Punjab needs resurrection on all fronts and that would be possible if persons with impeccable integrity and commitment to Punjab's all-round development are in command across all the fields, including politics.

GX: *What are your final thoughts on the way forward for Punjab's agriculture?*

RS GHUMAN: I have been pondering over this question with my colleagues and other experts over the years. I think we need crop diversification—we need to reduce the substantial area under paddy. Also, effective implementation of MSP for other crops as well as non-farm employment in the rural sector.

Of course, Punjab is a land-locked state and is facing a hostile border with Pakistan. It leads to a perception of constant threat to security and disturbance to peace. I feel that some border areas of Punjab should be given a special status. I have done a reasonable amount of research work on Indo-Pak trade relations, which is beneficial to both the neighbouring countries. We need to develop the trade route with Pakistan through the Wagah-Attari border so that we can access the market in as well as beyond Pakistan. Such an approach may also help in developing normal relations between India and Pakistan. Certainly, Punjab and some neighbouring states would benefit from such a move.

So, issues of farmers cannot be addressed entirely within agriculture. We need to integrate them with industry and services so that we can ameliorate the farmers' economic distress and also put Punjab on the development path with a new dynamism.

Finally, the issue is how to address the serious concerns of Punjab's economy. The Punjab government is itself under a heavy debt of over three lakh crores—nearly 40 percent of our annual revenue is being consumed in servicing debt. So, the Punjab government has very little left for capital expenditure or development. This adversely affects our agriculture, industry, governance and public investment. It also affects our private investment; it's a rule of thumb that high public investment also attracts private investment.

Endnotes

1. Public Law 480 (PL-480) also known as "Food for Peace" program was an American foreign policy tool to maintain and further its imperialist interests in many underdeveloped countries.

2. The Punjab Village Common Lands Regulation Act, 1961 has a provision that out of the total cultivable land, available with the village panchayat and which is proposed to be leased, "thirty percent, ten percent and ten percent, respectively shall be reserved for giving on lease by auction, to members of the Scheduled Caste; Backward Classes; and dependants of defence personnel killed in any war after the independence of India" (Government of Punjab, 1961).

3. James Duesenberry, American economist, made a significant contribution to the Keynesian analysis of income and employment with his 1949 doctoral thesis—*Income, Saving and the Theory of Consumer Behaviour*.

4. 'Kisan Sansad'—literally meaning farmers' parliament—was held at Jantar Mantar in New Delhi. It was called by SKM as part of the farmers' movement to highlight the absolute lack of attention and concern of the Union government towards the plight of more than 14.5 crore farmers in the country. The farmers had decided to argue their case against the three farm laws that directly attacked their livelihoods—just like they should have been debated in parliament. It started on July 23, 2021.

Kisan Shaheed Smarak: an art memorial at Ghazipur border in memory of those who died during the nationwide farmers' protest. **Photo Credit:** Workers Unity.

380 Days that Shook the Delhi Empire: A Chronology of the Struggle

On 15 May 2020, as India was emerging from the first wave of the COVID-19 pandemic and seeing an end of the lockdown, the Union Finance Minister announced the government's intention to enact three farm laws to accelerate 'reforms' in the agricultural sector. The three ordinances came into effect as they were approved by the Union Cabinet on 3 June and promulgated by the President of India on 5 June.

We attempt to present a chronology of the events that followed as farmers went on one of the longest and sustained protests ever in this country. We also attempt to cover the significant points in their negotiations and talks with the government, the police repression on protesters and more significantly, the responses and strategies of the farmers' movement. This is merely an overview of the trials and tribulations of their long journey of rebellion within which lie countless other stories and happenings.

PHASE I

FROM ROOFTOP PROTESTS TO TRACTOR RALLIES TO DELHI CHALO

JUNE 6, 2020

Farmers started protesting from their rooftops and common areas in their villages. Effigies of the NDA ministers were burnt in hundreds of villages in Punjab.

JUNE 14, 2020

The rooftop protests spread over 500 villages of Punjab and were held daily from 9 am to 10 am.

A press statement released by the BKU (Ekta-Ugrahan) objected to the ordinances stating that these would "kill farming." The statement expressed their fear of corporate takeover of Indian agriculture.

JULY 20-21, 2020

Effigies of members of the then SAD-BJP alliance were burnt in several villages by the 11 major farmer unions of the state, including BKU (Ekta-Ugrahan), BKU (Dakaunda) and Kirti Kisan Union. The next day, these 11 farmer unions joined hands to protest against the ordinances in a coordinated manner.

Prime Minister Modi made a statement in favour of the ordinances. As a result, the two day effigy burning program was extended till 26 July.

JULY 27, 2020

The 11 farmer unions organised a joint tractor march. Farmers travelled on tractors from their villages to submit memorandums to their MPs. In Bathinda, the march was led by 17-year-old Baldeep Kaur, who drove the tractor herself to submit a memorandum to the then Union Minister Harsimrat Kaur Badal, inspiring the youth into joining the farmers' protests.

JULY 29, 2020

The 11 farmer unions met again and decided to send another memorandum to PM Narendra Modi and Punjab CM Captain Amarinder Singh.

AUGUST 19, 2020

All the 31 farmer unions of Punjab, along with the agricultural worker unions, decided to work in coordination against the three farm laws. The 31 unions also decided to work in coordination with the AIKSCC.

AUGUST 25, 2020

BKU (Ekta-Ugrahan) organised *nakabandi* (blockade) in villages till August 29. Their posters gave the call to deny the SAD and BJP leaders entry into the villages.

SEPTEMBER 7-10, 2020

A *Jail Bharo* movement was organised by all 31 farmer unions and another memorandum was sent to the PM.

SEPTEMBER 9, 2020

Protests were held against FIRs lodged against farmers for violation of section 144 CrPC, Covid-guidelines.

SEPTEMBER 11, 2020

The police lathi-charged on farmers in Haryana when they were trying to reach a rally at Pipli (Kurukshetra, Haryana). This became a significant turning point. The next day, farmer unions in Punjab protested against the lathi-charge.

SEPTEMBER 12, 2020

The bridge of Harike Pattan and Beas were blocked by the Kisan Mazdoor Sangharsh Committee (KMSC) in Tarn Taran and Amritsar areas from September 12 onwards.

SEPTEMBER 14, 2020

The ordinances were tabled in the parliament. The 31 farmer unions organised *Lalkar* rallies on the same day at Phagwara, Patiala, Barnala, Amritsar and Moga. They asked Akali Dal to make its stand clear as the party was in alliance with BJP at the centre.

SEPTEMBER 15, 2020

BKU (Ekta-Ugrahan) started *pakka morcha* or permanent sit-ins outside the houses of former CM Parkash Singh Badal and in Patiala at CM Amarinder Singh's hometown. On the next day, the government announced that all FIRs against protesting farmers would be withdrawn.

SEPTEMBER 17, 2020

The ordinances were passed in Lok Sabha. MP and SAD leader Harsimrat Kaur Badal resigned as Union Food Processing Minister on the same day, citing the farm bills as the main reason.

SEPTEMBER 20, 2020

The ordinances were passed in Rajya Sabha by a voice vote.

SEPTEMBER 23, 2020

All 31 farmer unions in Punjab announced that they would start *rail roko* from October 1, along with dharnas outside malls, corporate-owned petrol pumps and residences of BJP leaders.

SEPTEMBER 24, 2020

The *rail roko* protest started on 24 September by Kisan Mazdoor Sangharsh Committee (KMSC) and BKU (Ekta-Ugrahan) at 12 locations in Punjab.

SEPTEMBER 25, 2020

The Punjab Bandh called by Punjab-based farmer unions met an unprecedented success: People from all sections of the society participated spontaneously in the Bandh.

SEPTEMBER 27, 2020

The President gave assent to the farm bills, and they were notified in the Gazette of India as Farm Laws.

The pressure built up by the farmers and youth compelled Shiromani Akali Dal to announce a break in its 27-year-old alliance with BJP.

OCTOBER 1, 2020

Protests intensified. In response to an indefinite *rail roko* call, all the railway tracks in Punjab were blocked from October 1; all toll plazas were occupied; products and services of Adani and Ambani were boycotted; dharnas were organised outside petrol pumps and shopping malls owned by them; demonstrations were held everyday outside the residences of BJP leaders.

OCTOBER 8, 2020

Leaders of farmer unions were invited to Delhi to learn about the benefits of the farm laws. They rejected the invitation.

OCTOBER 14, 2020

Leaders of farmer unions went to Delhi for talks but boycotted the meeting as no Union Minister was present.

OCTOBER 19, 2020

The Punjab government called a special session of the state assembly and passed a resolution opposing the farm laws. Barring the two BJP MLAs, the MLAs of all political parties joined a procession to submit a resolution opposing the farm laws to the state Governor.

NOVEMBER 5, 2020

A nationwide *chakka jam* (road blockade) took place.

NOVEMBER 7, 2020

A meeting of farmer unions was held in Gurudwara Rakab Ganj in Delhi. An umbrella body named Samyukta Kisan Morcha (SKM) composed of different farmer organisations opposing the farm laws from across the country, was formed. Rakesh Tikait from BKU (UP) and BKU (Ekta-Ugrahan) remained outside the SKM.

NOVEMBER 14, 2020

A meeting took place between farmer unions and the Union Agriculture Minister and Union Minister for Railways. In Punjab all goods and passenger trains had remained suspended though the farmer unions were willing to lift blockades on the goods trains. The Union Minister for Railways threatened to stop all supplies to and from Punjab. The meeting failed.

NOVEMBER 14-24, 2020

Preparations for *Delhi Chalo* began in full swing. Farmers started to decorate their tractors; equip their trolleys with all necessities and converted them into mobile homes.

NOVEMBER 25-26, 2020

Thousands of farmers marched towards Delhi, facing water cannons and tear gas as the police tried to disperse them at Haryana's Ambala border. The farmers, overcoming police repression and barricades, reached Singhu border. The police asked farmers to move to Burari ground in North-West Delhi. But farmers rejected the offer, demanding to hold the protest at Jantar Mantar; they sat on the roads, occupying the two major national highways at Singhu and Tikri.

PHASE II

THE 380 DAYS OF PROTEST ON DELHI BORDERS BEGAN

Tractors and trolleys were parked for several kilometers on both the Singhu and Tikri borders. Thousands of farmers from western Uttar Pradesh, Uttarakhand and Madhya Pradesh closed down two more national highways as they camped at the Ghazipur and Palwal borders. The response of the Union government made it clear that the struggle would be a protracted one.

NOVEMBER 28, 2020

Union Home Minister Amit Shah offered to hold talks with farmer unions as soon as the farmers vacate the borders and move to the designated protest site at Burari ground. However, farmers rejected his offer.

PM Narendra Modi in his *Mann Ki Baat* programme defended the farm laws as being beneficial to the farmers.

DECEMBER 3, 2020

Countrywide demonstrations by farmers. Landless farmers and agricultural workers from various villages of Punjab joined the farmers' protest at the borders.

The government held first round of talks with representatives of the farmer unions, but the meeting remained inconclusive.

DECEMBER 4, 2020

SKM announced Bharat Bandh to be held on December 8.

DECEMBER 5, 2020

Left parties issued a statement supporting the Bharat Bandh. Farmers burned effigies of Modi, Shah, Adani and Ambani in several parts of the country. The second round of talks with the Union government also remained inconclusive.

Uchana Khap boycotted BJP and JJP leaders in Haryana.

DECEMBER 8, 2020

Bharat Bandh called in support of the farmers' struggle got massive response in Punjab; SKM issued a call to boycott Adani and Ambani products and services.

DECEMBER 9, 2020
>SKM leaders rejected the government's proposal to amend the three laws and vowed to intensify the agitation for the repeal of the three laws.

DECEMBER 10, 2020
>World Human Rights Day was observed at Tikri border by the BKU (Ekta-Ugrahan). Farmers and activists demanded the release of public intellectuals and democratic rights activists held under UAPA in the Bhima Koregaon case.

DECEMBER 13, 2020
>Farmers from Rajasthan and Haryana blocked the fifth remaining national highway at Shahjahanpur.
>
>Army veterans from Punjab and Haryana collected over 5,000 gallantry medals to return them to the government in protest against the farm laws.

DECEMBER 14, 2020
>Farmer union leaders observed a one-day fast and two minutes of silence at all the borders to mourn the death of more than 20 farmers in the protest.

DECEMBER 16, 2020
>A large number of women from Punjab participated in the protest at Singhu border, holding photographs of male members of their families who had committed suicide due to indebtedness and agrarian distress.

DECEMBER 20, 2020
>The movement reached its 25th day. *Shradhanjali Divas* (Homage Day) was announced for the 33 farmers who had died so far during the movement due to accidents, illnesses, hostile weather and protest suicides.

DECEMBER 26, 2020
>One month of the farmers' protest was celebrated by demonstrations in front of malls, petrol pumps and retail outlets owned by the Adani and Ambani groups.

December 30, 2020

In the sixth round of talks between government and farmer leaders, the government agreed to exempt farmers from stubble burning penalty and drop changes in the Electricity Amendment Bill, 2020.

The death toll of farmers at protest sites crossed 50.

December 31, 2020

Kerala State assembly unanimously adopted a resolution against the three farm laws.

January 2, 2021

SKM issued an ultimatum to the government that it would march into the city of Delhi on 26 January if farmers' demands were not met. The event would be named the Farmers' Republic Day parade and would be held as soon as the official Republic Day celebration was over.

January 12, 2021

The Supreme Court stayed the implementation of the three farm laws for one and a half years. It set up a four-member committee of experts to make recommendations on the legislations after talking to all stakeholders. All the four experts had publicly supported the farm laws and advocated neoliberal reforms in agriculture. SKM reiterated its position of not participating in any such process.

Labour activist Nodeep Kaur was arrested at Kundli near Singhu border by Sonipat police on various criminal charges Her arrest and the arrest of her fellow comrade Shiv Kumar on 16 January was clearly because of their efforts to organise workers in support of the farmers' struggle.

January 18, 2021

Mahila Kisan Divas was celebrated at the borders. Hundreds of women drove in tractors and marched to the borders of Delhi.

January 22, 2021

The Union government arbitrarily broke off all talks with SKM after 11 rounds of talks failed. For the next ten months no more talks were held. Farmer unions stood firm on their demand to repeal the laws.

JANUARY 23, 2021

Subhash Chandra Bose's birth anniversary observed as *Kisan Chetna Divas*. Protests were held across many states in support of the farmers' movement. SKM gave a call for *mahapadavs* (sit-ins) and rallies before Governor houses from January 23 to January 26.

JANUARY 26, 2021

Lakhs of farmers marched on tractors decorated with the national flag and the flags of the kisan unions on the outskirts of Delhi. The Kisan Tractor Parade was organised in all the states. Several protesters from the Singhu and Ghazipur borders changed the designated route, and drove towards Delhi's ITO and Red Fort, where police resorted to tear gas shelling and lathi-charge. At Red Fort, a section of the protesters climbed poles and hoisted the Nishan Sahib flag. Navreet Singh, a young farmer from UP, died in clashes with the police. SKM issued a statement on the same day condemning the turn of events and asked farmers to return to their camps.

Following the incidents on 26 January, state repression was unleashed on farmers. The Delhi police filed hundreds of FIRs against farmers and farmer union leaders. Almost 121 farmers were arrested. Tractors were confiscated. The next day, the police attacked the protest camps. It evicted farmers from the Palwal borders and attempted to clear the Ghazipur border. At Singhu and Tikri, RSS-BJP cadres disguised as 'local villagers' stoned farmers, abusing them as anti-nationals and Khalistanis.

Protest sites were cordoned off by multiple layers of barbed steel wires, iron spikes, razor wire, wide trenches, concrete boulders and huge goods containers. Water, electricity and internet connections were cut off. Mobile toilets were broken. Armed commandos along with Rapid Action Force were stationed at all protest sites.

January 28, 2021

BKU leader Rakesh Tikait's emotional appeal resulted in thousands of sugarcane farmers from western UP marching to Ghazipur border to join the protest.

Sitabai Tadvi, an adivasi woman farmer of Lok Sangharsh Morcha from Maharashtra, passed away at the protest site. The death toll reached 171.

The West Bengal assembly passed a resolution against the three farm laws.

January 29, 2021

A massive *Mahapanchayat*, attended by thousands of Muslim peasants, was held at Muzaffarnagar. Ghulam Mohammad Jaula, the Muslim peasant leader, reminded the gathering of the assaults on Muslims in 2013. BKU President Naresh Tikait apologised for letting the Muslims down in 2013.

January 30, 2021

Mahatma Gandhi's martyrdom was observed by SKM to reiterate its commitment to truth and non-violence and highlight the role of RSS in his assassination.

February 4, 2021

The government slammed "celebrities and others" for comments in support of farmer protests, calling them "neither accurate nor responsible." This came after pop icon Rihanna, climate activist Greta Thunberg and Meena Harris, niece of US Vice President Kamala Harris, spoke out in support of the farmer protests.

February 6, 2021

SKM called a three-hour nationwide *chakka jam* in response to the government's various repressive measures, including internet ban at protest sites, following the events on 26 January.

February 8, 2021

PM Narendra Modi, while replying to the debate on the President's Address in parliament, called farmers *andolanjeevis* (professional protesters) and *parjeevis* (parasites). SKM condemned the Prime

Minister's speech in parliament.

FEBRUARY 14, 2021
SKM gave a call for nationwide torch rallies.

The Delhi Police arrested 21-year-old climate activist Disha Ravi for allegedly "editing" the toolkit shared by Greta Thunberg in support of the farmers' struggle. SKM condemned the arrest.

FEBRUARY 18, 2021
On SKM's call for a nationwide *rail roko* protest, trains were stopped, cancelled and rerouted at many places.

FEBRUARY 21, 2021
Kisan Mazdoor Ekta Maha Rally, attended by over one lakh participants, was organised by BKU (Ekta-Ugrahan) and Punjab Khet Mazdoor Union in the grain market of Barnala to expose government's propaganda to label the movement with Khalistani tag and build solidarity between farmers and agricultural workers.

FEBRUARY 26, 2021
The farmers' struggle completed three months. The day was observed as *Yuva Kisan Divas* to felicitate the role of peasant youths in the struggle.

FEBRUARY 27, 2021
The martyrdom anniversary of Chandrashekar Azad and birth anniversary of Sant Ravidas were observed as Worker-Peasant Unity Day.

MARCH 5, 2021
The Punjab Vidhan Sabha passed a resolution asking for the unconditional withdrawal of the farm laws in the interest of farmers, and to continue with the existing system of government procurement of food grains at MSP.

MARCH 6, 2021
Kundli-Manesar-Palwal Expressway blocked by farmers. The farmers' movement completed 100 days.

Rajbir Kaur, a 48-year-old farmer committed suicide at Tikri border. His was the eighth protest suicide at the Delhi borders. The overall death toll of farmers reached 248.

MARCH 8, 2021

Thousands of women from Punjab and Haryana observed International Women's Day at all protest sites.

A petition signed by over one lakh citizens in Britain compelled the British parliament to debate the situation in India regarding the enactment of the three farm laws.

MARCH 10, 2021

Farmer leaders participated in the *No Vote to BJP* campaign in West Bengal and gave an open call to defeat BJP in the assembly elections.

MARCH 15, 2021

SKM supported the call of the Central Trade Unions to observe Anti-Privatisation Day.

On the call of the Punjab Khet Mazdoor Union, thousands of agricultural workers held a meeting in a local grain market in Bathinda in support of the farmers' movement.

MARCH 23, 2021

The Martyrdom Anniversary of Bhagat Singh, Rajguru and Sukhdev was observed at protest sites. Youths from Punjab and other states reached the Tikri and Singhu border in large numbers.

MARCH 26, 2021

SKM called for a second Bharat Bandh in support of the farmers' struggle and received massive nationwide response. The day also marked the completion of four months of struggle.

MARCH 28, 2021

To mark the Holi festival, thousands of farmers at the borders as well as across the country made bonfires to symbolically burn the three farm laws.

April 1, 2021

Thousands of farmers, including a large number of women, blocked the Hisar airport and the corresponding highway for more than two hours, to prevent the Deputy CM of Haryana from coming out of the airport. This was done as part of a call by SKM to boycott the leaders of the BJP-JJP alliance.

April 5, 2021

Farmers gheraoed FCI godowns and offices in various states, as part of the *FCI Bachao Divas* to oppose attempts to dismantle both procurement at MSP and the PDS.

April 10-11, 2021

Thousands of farmers blocked the Kundli-Manesar-Palwal Expressway for 24 hours, to protest police lathi-charge on protesting farmers in Rohtak, Haryana.

On April 11, the birth anniversary of Mahatma Jyotirao Phule was observed at protest sites.

April 13, 2021

On the day of *Baisakhi*, the Jallianwala Bagh massacre was mourned at the Delhi borders.

April 14, 2021

Ambedkar Jayanti was celebrated as Save Constitution Day and *Kisan Bahujan Ekta Divas* at protest sites.

April 30, 2021

Farmers celebrated the 400th birth anniversary of Sri Tegh Bahadur, the ninth Guru of Sikhs.

A young woman activist from West Bengal succumbed to Covid in a hospital at Tikri border. Investigations revealed that she was sexually assaulted by members of a group called Kisan Social Army, with whom she travelled to the border. SKM denounced the organisation, removed its tent from the protest site and helped her family to file an FIR.

In the month of April and May, the deadly second wave of the Covid pandemic struck. The Union government used it as a ruse to evict farmers from Delhi borders. Media reports blamed farmers for spreading the virus, and highlighted Operation Clean—to drive away the farmers—after the assembly elections in five states were over.

SKM made arrangements to protect the protest sites from the virus, set up medical and vaccination camps. The farmers also arranged free food and shelter for migrant workers, distributed thousands of food packets to starving people at railway stations, bus terminals and patients at hospitals.

SKM gave the Phir Delhi Chalo *call as unions and organisations urged farmers, who had gone to their villages for the wheat harvesting season, to return to the borders from April 24, the 150day of the farmers' struggle.*

May 1, 2021

Kisan Mazdoor Ekta Divas was celebrated at all protest sites.

May 10, 2021

BJP's defeat in the assembly election in three states out of five, including West Bengal, was celebrated at the protest sites.

May 16, 2021

Police used lathis and tear gas on farmers in Hisar (Haryana) who were on their way to protest against the CM who was inaugurating a hospital. Over 50 farmers and 20 police personnel were injured.

May 26, 2021

Farmers observed Black Day to mark six months of the agitation and seven years of Modi's rule by burning effigies of the members of the Modi government.

Buddha Purnima was celebrated at protest sites.

June 5, 2021

Protesting farmers observed *Sampoorna Kranti Divas* (Total Revolution Day) to mark the first year of the promulgation of the farm ordinances. Farmers across the country burned copies of the three farm laws.

June 7, 2021

Farmers in Haryana gheraoed police stations in protest against lathi-charge and arrest of three farmers. The arrested farmers were released and the Haryana CM was forced to apologise.

June 14, 2021

Guru Arjan Dev's martyrdom day was observed. It also marked the 200th day of the farmer's struggle.

June 26, 2021

The day marked 46 years of imposition of Emergency. SKM observed it as Save Agriculture Save Democracy Day; the day also marked seven months of the struggle. Farmers in Punjab and Haryana marched to the Governor House. They broke police barricades in Chandigarh and faced lathi-charge and water cannons.

Farmers also celebrated Sant Kabir's birth anniversary.

July 8, 2021

Protests were held against hikes in fuel prices, with petrol and diesel prices touching Rs 100 per litre in many states.

Death toll of farmers during the struggle reached 537.

July 22 - August 9, 2021

Kisan Sansad or Farmers' Parliament was held at Jantar Mantar in New Delhi, parallel to the monsoon session of the parliament. It was called by SKM as part of the farmers' movement to highlight the lack of attention and concern the Union government had shown towards the plight of more than 14.5 crore farmers in the country. It started on July 22 and continued till August 9.

On July 26 and August 9, exclusive women farmers' sessions were held. The *Kisan Sansad* concluded by adopting a No Confidence Motion against the Modi government.

July 31, 2021
Shaheed Udham Singh's martyrdom day was observed and marked as Anti-Imperialist Day by farmer unions.

August 2-5, 2021
A delegation of farmers from Krishak Mukti Sangharsh Samiti of Assam and a delegation from Odisha participated in the *Kisan Sansad*. Farmers from the Andhra Pradesh Farmers Associations Coordination Committee and All India Kisan Sabha from Tamil Nadu joined as well.

August 3, 2021
Adani Logistics Services shut its inland container depot or dry port at Qila Raipur in Ludhiana, as its operations were suspended since January due to the farmers' dharna at the entrance of the facility.

August 7, 2021
Leaders of 14 opposition parties met at Parliament House and visited the *Kisan Sansad* at Jantar Mantar.

August 9-11, 2021
In Patiala, seven agricultural and rural worker unions, which had formed a *Sanjha Mazdoor Morcha* (United Workers Front) held a three-day demonstration to raise their eight-point demands, including waiving off Electricity Bill, granting residential plots and loans, and repealing labour codes and farm laws.

August 14, 2021
Massive dharna of landless agricultural workers, both women and men, was organised in Patiala by Zameen Prapti Sangharsh Committee (ZPSC), demanding waiver of all types of loans of agricultural labourers, including loans from microfinance companies.

August 15, 2021
Farmers celebrated the 75th Independence Day on India as the *Kisan Mazdoor Mukti Sangharsh Divas*.

August 17, 2021
Social boycotts and protests against BJP leaders extended to Uttara-

khand, after Punjab, Haryana and western UP.

Sugarcane farmers in Punjab protested on NH-1 demanding hike in prices and payment of pending arrears of Rs 200 crore. Farmers occupied railway tracks near the protest site (Amritsar-Kolkata line) until demands were met.

AUGUST 26-27, 2021

Nine months passed since the protest began on the borders. SKM's two-day All India Convention started at the Singhu border on this day. Over 1,500 representatives from 22 states representing more than 300 farmer and agricultural worker unions along with 18 all India trade unions, 9 women's organisations and 17 students and youth organisations joined. The convention concluded on August 27 after unanimously giving a clarion call to expand and intensify the agitation to every village and corner of the country. A call was given for a one-day Bharat Bandh on September 27.

AUGUST 28, 2021

Haryana Police brutally cracked down on farmers in Karnal, leaving several injured in a lathi-charge at the Bastara toll plaza. The farmers were protesting against a BJP meeting being attended by CM Manohar Lal Khattar and other state leaders of the BJP. One of the injured farmers, Sushil Kajal, later died in hospital.

AUGUST 29, 2021

The Tamil Nadu assembly passed a resolution supporting repeal of the three farm laws.

SEPTEMBER 5, 2021

A massive *Kisan Mazdoor Mahapanchayat* of over 10 lakh people cutting across caste, religion, state and language was held at Muzaffarnagar in UP. Mission Uttar Pradesh—SKM's campaign to defeat BJP in UP—was launched.

SEPTEMBER 7 - 9, 2021

Over two lakh farmers gathered in Karnal grain market despite implementation of Section 144 and suspension of the internet and laid siege to the mini-Secretariat. The farmers demanded Rs 25 lakh compensation to the family of the deceased farmer (Kajal) and a government job for his relative, compensation of Rs 2 lakh each for those injured in the lathi-charge and registration of a criminal case and stern action against the SDM and police personnel responsible for the lathi-charge.

SEPTEMBER 11, 2021

The Haryana government agreed to conduct a probe by a retired judge of the Punjab and Haryana High Court into the August 28 police lathi-charge on farmers and sent the former Karnal SDM Ayush Sinha on leave until the inquiry was completed.

SEPTEMBER 13 - 28, 2021

In MP, 26 farmer unions organised a motorcycle rally and torch procession. A Kisan convention was held in Bihar. A *Kisan Mahapanchayat* was organised in UP's Sitapur. *Mahapanchayats* were held in UP's Gorakhpur and Uttarakhand's Haridwar. A *Kisan Mahapanchayat* was organised by Chhattisgarh Kisan Mazdoor Mahasangh in Rajim. Farmer unions campaigned to garner support for the Bharat Bandh on 27 September.

SEPTEMBER 25, 2021

Two farmers were killed in police firing in Assam. Hemanta Biswa Sharma, the BJP CM of the state, hailed the police firing.

SEPTEMBER 27, 2021

The third Bharat Bandh in the farmers' struggle received huge support. There was complete shutdown in Punjab and Haryana, and good response in many other states. Thousands of farmers, workers, students, youth and civil society groups came forward in support of the Bandh.

SEPTEMBER 28, 2021

Shaheed Bhagat Singh's birth anniversary was observed at protest sites as well as across the country.

OCTOBER 2, 2021

Birth Anniversary of Mahatma Gandhi was observed by SKM, as it paid homage to the role of *satyagraha* and Gandhi's principles of *satya* and *ahimsa* (truth and non-violence) in the farmers' struggle.

SKM organised a *padayatra* (Lokniti Satyagraha Padayatra) from Champaran in Bihar to Varanasi in UP.

OCTOBER 3, 2021

A convoy of Ajay Mishra, the Union Minister of State for Home Affairs, that included his son Ashish Mishra, uncle and other goons, ran over protesting farmers in Lakhimpur Kheri of Uttar Pradesh. Four farmers—Gurvinder Singh (19), Lovepreet Singh (20), Daljit Singh (35), and Nachattar Singh (60)—were killed. A local journalist, Raman Kashyap, also died. SKM condemned the murderous attack on farmers. It demanded MoS Ajay Mishra to be dismissed immediately and murder cases to be imposed on both the father and son. Ashish was finally arrested on October 9.

Haryana CM while addressing a meeting of the BJP's *Kisan Morcha* in Chandigarh, encouraged BJP cadres to pick up sticks and attack farmers. SKM demanded that he apologise immediately and resign from his post.

OCTOBER 5, 2021

A video of the Lakhimpur Kheri massacre emerged showing the vehicles of the minister mowing down farmers. SKM demanded a judicial inquiry by a sitting judge of the Supreme Court.

OCTOBER 11, 2021

Maharashtra Bandh was called by the ruling Maha Vikas Aghadi and supported by all anti-BJP forces.

SKM paid its deep respects to Lok Nayak Jayaprakash Narayan on his 119th birth anniversary.

OCTOBER 12, 2021

Shaheed Kisan Divas was observed—*antim ardaas* (last rites) of the martyrs of Lakhimpur Kheri were held in Tikunia village. Farmer organisations and other progressive groups across the country marked the *Shaheed Kisan Divas* by organising prayer and homage meetings; in the evening, candlelight vigils were held as per SKM's call.

October 15, 2021

On Dussehra, effigy-burning of top BJP leaders like Modi, Amit Shah, Yogi, and others took place at hundreds of locations across the country.

A Dalit Sikh man was found brutally murdered, allegedly for desecration of Sarbaloh Granth (a Sikh holy book) at the Singhu border protest site by members of a Nihang sect.

October 18, 2021

A countrywide *rail roko* program was held to demand the dismissal of Ajay Mishra from the Union Cabinet and his arrest for his role in the Lakhimpur Kheri massacre.

The leader of the accused Nihang sect, Baba Aman Singh, was identified to be suspiciously close to BJP. His photos with Agriculture Minister and a dismissed cop and murder convict Gurmeet Singh Pinky went viral.

October 26, 2021

The farmers' movement completed 11 months. Death toll rose above 600.

In several states, *Shaheed Kalash Yatras* were taken out to pay homage to the martyrs of the Lakhimpur Kheri massacre.

October 28, 2021

SKM condemned the cancellation of OCI cards and long-term visas of NRIs supporting the farmers' movement.

Three women protesters were crushed to death by a speeding truck near Pakora Chowk at Tikri border while they were waiting for an auto-rickshaw. They were returning to their village Kheeva Dyaluwala in Mansa.

November 4, 2021

The farmers' movement observed Diwali and *Bandi Chhor Divas*. Homage was paid to over 650 martyrs by lighting lamps in their memory at protest sites.

November 7, 2021

A study conducted by Punjabi University at Patiala revealed that the majority of those who died during the protest due to harsh weather, accident, suicide and other reasons were marginal and small farmers.

SKM called *Mahapanchayats* in all state capitals, starting on 22 November in Lucknow, to mark one year of the farmers' movement against the three farm laws.

November 15, 2021

SKM opposed the WTO's proposal to impose limitations on public stock holding of good grains to 15 percent of the production in a country in the upcoming WTO meeting (MC12) in Geneva from 30 November to 3 December 2021. SKM rejected another proposal that food grains procured for public stock holding cannot be exported.

Birth anniversary of Adivasi freedom fighter Birsa Munda was observed by SKM.

November 16, 2021

Martyrdom anniversaries of Ghadar Party revolutionary Kartar Singh Saraba and Vishnu Ganesh Pingle and Dalit woman fighter of 1857 war Veerangana Uda Devi Pasi were observed by SKM.

November 19, 2021

PM Modi announced repeal of the farm laws. Spontaneous celebrations at borders and all over the country.

November 21, 2021

SKM in its first meeting after the PM's announcement of the repeal of farm laws decided to send a letter to the PM, listing the six major pending demands, namely, legal guarantee of MSP for all crops, withdrawal of draft Electricity Amendment Bill 2020/2021, removal of the penal provisions on farmers for stubble burning, withdrawal of all cases against the farmers over the course of the movement, dismissal and arrest of Minister Ajay Mishra, compensation to the families of the martyrs of the farmers' movement and allocation of land to build a memorial in their memory at Singhu border. SKM asked the government to immediately resume talks on these six pending demands of the farmers.

NOVEMBER 22, 2021

A massive Kisan Mazdoor Mahapanchayat was held at Lucknow. Family members of the martyrs of Lakhimpur Kheri Massacre also attended the *Mahapanchayat* and were felicitated.

NOVEMBER 24, 2021

It was reported by the Centre for Information Resilience that at least 80 fake social media accounts were being operated in a networked manner in names of Sikhs for maligning the movement; these accounts were suspended across social media.

NOVEMBER 26, 2021

The farmers' movement completed one year of its historic struggle. Tens of thousands of farmers assembled at protest sites on Delhi borders—Singhu, Tikri, Ghazipur and Shahjahanpur. Protest programs were held nationwide in support of the farmers' movement.

NOVEMBER 28, 2021

A massive *Kisan Mazdoor Mahapanchayat* took place at Azad Maidan, Mumbai, organised by the Samyukta Shetkari Kamgar Morcha (SSKM)—a platform of over 100 organisations of peasants, workers, students, youth and women—in solidarity with the farmers. This Mahapanchayat marked the culmination of the SKM-led *Shaheed Kalash Yatra* that began on 27 October from Mahatma Jyotirao Phule and Savitri Bai Phule's house in Pune. The ashes of the martyrs of Lakhimpur Kheri massacre were immersed in the Arabian Sea.

NOVEMBER 29, 2021

Both the Houses of parliament cleared the Farm Laws Repeal Bill, 2021 via voice votes, within four minutes, without any discussion.

DECEMBER 2, 2021

The President gave assent to the Farm Laws Repeal Bill, 2021.

December 4, 2021

SKM held a meeting to discuss the absence of formal response from the government regarding its pending demands. It reiterated its resolve to continue the agitation until a formal and satisfactory response came from the government.

DECEMBER 6, 2021

SKM celebrated *Mahaparinirvana Divas* of Dr Babasaheb Ambedkar and took oath in ceremonies across the country to protect the Constitution of India.

DECEMBER 7, 2021

For the first time in the year-long struggle, the government sent a written proposal to the SKM. SKM after discussion, sent concrete amendments to the government's proposal.

DECEMBER 8, 2021

The government sent a revised draft proposal to the farmer unions. SKM after discussion approved the proposal and sent it back to the government for finalisation.

DECEMBER 9, 2021

Farmer leaders met after receiving the official letter signed by the Secretary, Ministry of Agriculture and Farmers' Welfare. SKM called off the farmers' movement and formally announced lifting of the *morchas* at the borders. It announced that on 11 December, *Vijay Divas* (Victory Day) would be celebrated at all borders, toll plazas and protest sites across the country.

DECEMBER 11, 2021

After 380 days and nights of an unrelenting struggle, the victorious farmers started returning home from all the borders; the victory of the farmers was celebrated all over the country.

Sources of data: SKM website of press releases, When Farmers Stood UP by Ashok Dhawale, India Today, The Hindu, Interviews of Peasant leaders in this volume.

Glossary

AoA (Agreement on Agriculture): The AoA is a WTO treaty that was negotiated during the Uruguay Round of GATT in 1991 and ratified in 1994 at Marrakesh, Morocco. It came into effect in 1995. It was signed as part of the WTO deals giving market access, reducing export and government subsidies on agricultural products. India has been a WTO member since 1 January 1995 and is bound by the AoA, which views granting of subsidies like MSP to farmers as distorting global trade.

AIKSCC (All India Kisan Sangharsh Coordination Committee): The AIKSCC is an umbrella body of farmer organisations from across the country. The AIKSCC was formed in July 2017 following the death of six protesting farmers in police firing in Madhya Pradesh on 6 June 2017, in order to coordinate farmers struggles in different states for debt relief and remunerative prices.

AIKSCC drafted two seminal Bills—'Farmers' Freedom from Indebtedness Bill' and 'Farmers' Right to Guaranteed Remunerative Minimum Support Prices for Agricultural Commodities Bill.' These two Bills were placed in parliament as private members' bills in August 2018.

APMC (Agricultural Produce Marketing Committee): The APMC or *mandi* is a marketing board established by the state governments in India to ensure farmers are safeguarded from exploitation by large retailers or intermediaries and are not forced to sell their produce at extremely low prices. Presently, India's agricultural markets are regulated by the states under the Agricultural Produce Marketing Committee (APMC) Act. The states can establish agricultural markets, popularly known as *mandis*; the sale of agricultural commodities can occur only in those notified *mandis* through auction. The APMCs are managed by the Market Committees constituted by the State government. The sales process in *mandis* is regulated through registered commission agents who mediate between the farmers and traders.

For farmers in Punjab and Haryana, the APMC or *mandi* system is inextricably tied up with MSP procurement for wheat and paddy. The majority of farmers sell their produce in *mandis* and farmers fear that the amendment to the APMC Act allowing private *mandis* will deprive them of the MSP.

ARHTIYAS: The *arhtiyas* are registered commission agents in APMCs (notified agri-markets or *mandis*). They are linked to both the agricultural credit market and the product market in Punjab. The *arhtiya* facilitates the transaction between a farmer and the actual buyer, who may be a private trader, a processor, an exporter, or a government agency like the Food Corporation of India (FCI). Arhtiyas extended critical support to the farmers' movement against the farm laws.

BHARATIYA KISAN UNION (BKU): It was founded in the seventies by Chaudhary Charan Singh. Earlier known as the Punjab Khetibari Union, the Bharatiya Kisan Union consolidated itself as a platform of farmers' unions.

Following the demise of Charan Singh, BKU under the leadership of Mahendra Singh Tikait, in the 1980s, organised several protest movements for cheaper electricity and higher MSP for crops. In January 1988, BKU organised thousands of farmers who picketed the District Commissioner's office in Meerut town for over three weeks. Among the core demands were waiving of electricity and water bills, waiver of loans, and higher prices for sugarcane. The Meerut protest was followed by the historic Boat Club rally in Delhi in October of the same year. Over time, the BKU branched into separate units in different states; the separation in Punjab was determined along ideological persuasions of the Left. The BKU has largely maintained distance from electoral politics in order to bargain effectively with different ruling class parties.

DUNKEL DRAFT: It refers to the draft proposals of Arthur Dunkel, director-general of GATT (the General Agreement on Trade and Tariffs), at the Uruguay round of negotiations in December 1991. The draft put together the results of negotiations and provided a solution to issues on which negotiators failed to agree. The Dunkel Draft was accepted by negotiating countries, including India, and it became the foundation of the World Trade Organisation (WTO).

FCI (Food Corporation of India): It was set up under the Food Corporations Act 1964, under the Ministry of Consumer Affairs, Food and Public Distribution, to fulfil India's goal of achieving self-sufficiency in paddy and wheat following the Green Revolution. FCI was given the task of managing procurement and stocking of food grains to maintain a buffer-stock that supported a vast Public Distribution System (PDS). FCI conducts "open-ended procurement," which means it procures at Minimum Support Price (MSP) any quantity of wheat and rice from any farmer who comes forward to sell in government notified *mandis* (APMCs).

Freedom From Indebtedness Bill: This bill was introduced in 2018 in parliament as a private member bill by MP Raju Shetti. The draft was prepared by the All India Kisan Sangharsh Coordination Committee (AIKSCC). The bill conferred a right on indebted farmers to obtain an immediate one-time complete waiver of outstanding loan; right to obtain institutional credit; protection of debt trapped farmers suffering from natural disasters or distress and constitution of a National Farmers' Distress and Disaster Relief Commission and State Farmers' Distress and Disaster Relief Commissions with power to pass awards and recommend appropriate measures for relief to farmers in distress.

Green Revolution: The introduction of High Yielding Varieties (HYV) seeds and the increased use of agro-chemicals (fertilisers, and pesticides), tractors and irrigation facilities into the agricultural sector characterised the Green Revolution. Punjab was the laboratory of the experiment to increase crop yield needed to make India self-sufficient in food grains. A network of institutional funding through banks and non-institutional credit support was a significant marker to facilitate the commodification of agriculture that led to the debt traps within a few years. The myth of the Green Revolution began to fade as the excessive use of fertilisers and pesticides polluted water sources and killed beneficial insects. Rampant irrigation practices caused over-use of soil, rapidly depleted its nutrients and led to eventual soil degradation and depletion of water levels in the state.

Gurudwara Reform Movement: The Gurudwara Reform Movement or the Akali movement was a campaign to bring reform in the gurudwaras in India during the early 1920s. The movement started with the formation of the Central Sikh League in March 1919. The League in its periodical, the *Akali*, declared liberating gurudwaras from *mahant* control, as one of its main objectives. It demanded the administration of the Golden Temple to be transferred from the government to an elected representative body of Sikhs answerable to the *panth*, and in October 1919 took control of the Golden Temple and Akal Takht.

On 20 February 1921, about 130 people were killed, after the guards of the *mahant* of gurudwara Nankana Sahib, the birthplace of the first Sikh Guru Nanak, opened fire on a Akali *jatha* (band or group) without warning. The Nankana massacre turned the reform movement into a national liberation movement with the Shiromani Gurudwara Parbandhak Committee (SGPC), passing a resolution on May 1921 appealing to Sikhs to begin civil disobedience. The British government regarded this development as being dangerous and agreed to transfer the control of the Gurudwara Nankana Sahib to the *Akalis* on 3 March 1921.

The movement led to the introduction of the Sikh Gurudwara Bill in 1925, which placed all the historical Sikh shrines in India under the control of the Shiromani Gurudwara Parbandhak Committee (SGPC).

JAT: Jats are a large agricultural caste of North India. After post-Independence land reforms, Jats became the dominant landholding castes in many regions of North India. In Punjab and Haryana, land ownership is dominated largely by Jats. Punjab has the maximum proportion (5.28 percent) of big farmers (mostly Jats) owning more than 10 hectares of land among the states of India.

KHAP PANCHAYATS: Khap panchayats are quasi-judicial bodies, especially among Jats in villages of Haryana and Uttar Pradesh, and to some extent in Rajasthan and Punjab. In these regions the term *kisan* (farmer) is almost synonymous with Jats, and for more than a hundred years the Jat community form a bulk of the land-owning farmers and socially dominant castes. *Khap panchayats* have gained notoriety owing mainly for issuing certain controversial and regressive diktats such as honour killings against inter-caste love marriages. *Khap panchayats*, particularly in Haryana and western UP, declared support to the farmers' movement and played an important role in mobilising Jat farmers against the farm laws.

KISAN LONG MARCH (2018): It was the historic week-long farmers' march on foot led by All India Kisan Sabha (AIKS), the peasants' wing of the CPI(M). Beginning on 5 March 2018 in Nasik (Maharashtra) with over 25000 farmers—including agricultural labourers and indigenous (Adivasi) cultivators—it concluded in Mumbai on 12 March with over 50000 people. The march was successful in drawing people's attention to the plight of the peasantry in the country. The march elicited massive support and sympathy of the masses, including the middle-classes.

An estimated 2414 farmers had succumbed to suicide in the state of Maharashtra between January 1 and October 31, 2017. The state government had announced a conditional loan waiver amounting to Rs 34,000 crores but it was not implemented as promised. Nor were the other demands of the farmers fulfilled despite government assurances.

KISAN SANSAD: 'Kisan Sansad'—literally meaning farmers' parliament—was held at Jantar Mantar in New Delhi, parallel to the monsoon session of the parliament. It started on 22 July 2021 and continued till 9 August. It was called to highlight the absolute lack of attention and concern the Union government had shown towards the plight of more than 14.5 crore farmers in the country. The farmers had decided to argue their case against the three farm laws just like they should have been debated inside the parliament. On 26 July and 9 August, exclusive women farmers' sessions were held. The Kisan Sansad concluded by adopting a No Confidence Motion against the Modi government.

LABOUR CODES: Within a fortnight of passing of the three anti-farmer farm laws, the Modi government passed the remaining three of the four anti-worker Labour Codes—Industrial Relations Code, Social Security Code and the Occupational Safety, Health and Working Conditions Code—in the parliament. The Code on Wages was already passed, The four codes were set to replace the 29 existing labour laws—which had been won by the working class after decades of bitter struggles. Though passed in the Modi regime, constituents of the two major political alliances, both NDA and UPA, have been party to this exercise when in power. The Second Labour Commission in 1999 had first made the move to 'rationalise' labour laws and curtail the rights of worker unions and legalise hire and fire policy to facilitate investment.

LAND ACQUISITION AMENDMENT ORDINANCE, 2015: As soon as the Modi government came to power in December 2014, it brought in an anti-farmer ordinance to amend the Land Acquisition, Rehabilitation and Resettlement Act, 2013 (LARR Act, 2013). The pro-corporate ordinance was meant to make it easier for the corporate houses and state governments to acquire agricultural land from the farmers. A nationwide peasants' struggle began in February 2015 against the ordinance led by Bhumi Adhikar Andolan (BAA). The ordinance was withdrawn on 31 August 2015.

LAND REFORMS: Imposition of a ceiling on agricultural landholdings and redistribution of excess land by the government to landless people for cultivation is known as Land Reform. Since independence, there has been some state-initiated or mediated land reforms in several states of India. But land reforms have been successful only in certain pockets, as people holding excess agricultural lands have used loopholes in the laws to retain land in excess to the prescribed limit. Many militant and armed struggles of the peasants led by the revolutionary Left in India took place from time to time to occupy excess land of the landlords and redistribute it among the landless peasantry.

LANGAR: In Sikhism, *langar* is the community kitchen of a gurudwara, which serves vegetarian meals to all free of charge, regardless of religion, caste, gender, class, or ethnicity. People sit on the floor and eat together, and the kitchen is maintained and serviced by volunteers of the Sikh community. The concept of *langar* as a symbol of both *sewa* (service) and equality was introduced into Sikhism by its founder, Guru Nanak. *Langars* are set up by Sikh community volunteers during natural disasters, religious, social and political gatherings.

MAZHABI SIKHS: Mazhabis are supposed to be descendants of the Chuhra caste that was at the bottom of the caste hierarchy. It is believed that Guru Gobind Singh brought them into the Sikh faith in appreciation of their having carried the mutilated body of Guru Teg Bahadur from Delhi. There are other Scheduled Caste groups like the Rai Sikhs, Ramdasias, Ravidasias and Bairagis among others. Each community has its own self-identified claim as stories and folklore to trace its origin in the history of the state.

The term Dalit and "landless' is almost synonymous in Punjab. While five lakh hectares of land is under agricultural cultivation according to India's Agricultural Census 2015-16, Dalits, comprising 32 percent of the population of Punjab (highest in India, the national average being 16 percent), own only about 3.5 percent of private farmland.

MGNREGA: NREGA, later renamed as the "Mahatma Gandhi National Rural Employment Guarantee Act" or MGNREGA, is an Indian labour law and social security measure. This law was passed on 23 August 2005 by the Congress Party led UPA government of prime minister Dr Manmohan Singh.

The MGNREGA guarantees 100 days of work in a year to each above-18 person in rural India who volunteers to do manual work. Under MGNREGA, workers are entitled to get the statutory minimum wage applicable to agricultural labourers in the concerned state.

MSP (Minimum Support Price): The MSP is the price fixed by the government of India for the crops produced by farmers. It was first introduced in the 1965-66 season (July-June) for wheat, and now it covers 23 crops. MSP of all the 23 crops are fixed based on the recommendations of the Commission for Agricultural Costs and Prices (CACP). It is announced weeks ahead of the Kharif and Rabi sowing seasons. The MSP is a guaranteed price that safeguards farmers with a minimum profit for their harvest. It acts as a floor price for food grains to avoid distress sales by farmers.

MSP was announced in the 1960s to incentivise farmers in areas where the Green Revolution was introduced to boost their production when India faced a shortage of food grains. It is the price which the government agencies such as the Food Corporation of India (FCI) pays to the farmers to procure wheat and paddy for the central pool. In the case of maize, cotton, pulses and oilseeds, the government only steps in to procure them when their prices fall far below the MSP and farmers resort to distress sale. However, only a little over 14 percent of land-owning farmers in the country benefit from MSP. According to government data the number of MSP beneficiaries was about 2.1 crore during 2020-21.

NAZOOL LAND: The Nazool Lands (Transfer) Rules, 1956, Punjab, define "Nazool" lands as "land situated beyond two miles of the Municipal limits, which has escheated to the State Government and has not already been appropriated by the State Government for any purpose"; or it is "such other land as the State Government may make available for being transferred under these rules" (Govt. of Punjab, 1956).

Much of the Nazool land in Punjab comprises the remainder of land belonging to Muslims who migrated to Pakistan at the time of partition, after a part of this land was given to the Hindu and Sikh families that migrated from the Pakistani Punjab to the state. This land is meant to be leased to the scheduled castes and other backward castes for cultivation, provided this land has not been appropriated by the state government for any other public purpose. Some part of the Nazool land also comprises land that came to the government's account in cases where there was no heir to the land.

NEW ECONOMIC POLICY (NEP) 1990s: This refers to a series of policy measures and changes introduced by the Indian government to facilitate the liberalisation of the Indian economy. The key thrust of the reforms dictated by the World Bank and International Monetary Fund (IMF) were: liberalising industrial licensing and registration without restrictions, permitting large private entrepreneurs to set up industries in sectors which were previously reserved for only public sector and small scale enterprises, disinvestment and privatisation of PSUs, removal of controls on foreign trade, allowing foreign direct investment (FDI) to the extent of 100 percent without any restriction in most sectors, gradual reduction in custom duties and tariffs imposed on imports and exports and so on.

NIHANG: It is an order of Sikh warriors, characterised by blue robes, traditional arms such as swords and spears, and decorated turbans. According to Sikh historians, the origin of the order can be traced back to the creation of the *Khalsa Panth* by the 10th Sikh Guru, Gobind Singh, in 1699. The *Nihangs* strictly adhere to the form and content of the *Khalsa* as it was established by Guru Gobind Singh.

NISHAN SAHIB: The *Nishan Sahib* is a triangular saffron coloured flag outside a gurudwara. It has been associated with Sikhism and the *Khalsa* in history. It commands the respect and reverence of the Sikhs, symbolises Sikh sovereignty and identity.

OPERATION BLUE STAR: It was a military operation that took place in June 1984, ordered by prime minister Indira Gandhi at the height of the Sikh militant struggle for a separate state (Khalistan) to flush out armed militants led by Jarnail Singh Bhindranwale from Harmandir Sahib inside the Golden Temple complex in Amritsar. The operation ended with the killing of 492 civilians and 136 army men. Bhindranwale and Shabeg Singh were killed. The military operation inside the holiest Sikh shrine was viewed as an act of desecration by Sikhs all over the world. Four months later, Indira Gandhi was assassinated by Satwant Singh and Beant Singh, two of her Sikh bodyguards, in what is viewed as an act of vengeance. This was followed by an anti-Sikh pogrom in Delhi in which more than three thousand Sikhs were killed.

PACS (PRIMARY AGRICULTURAL COOPERATIVE SOCIETIES): A PACS is a co-operative credit institution at the gram panchayat and village level in India. The main function of the PACS is to provide short and medium-term purpose loans to its members. Farmers are provided seeds, fertilisers, agricultural equipment along with short term loans.

PAGDI SAMBHAL JATTA LEHAR (MOVEMENT): This is one of the most celebrated historical struggles of the farmers in Punjab. This movement was triggered by the passing of the Punjab Land Colonisation Act 1906 in the Punjab Legislative Council in February 1907. The Act had stringent clauses that 'forbade the transfer of property by will' and debarred the courts from 'interfering with executive orders.' One of the clauses that enraged the farmers and led to their revolt was that if a new settler (farmer) died without gaining occupancy rights, the land would revert to the colonial British government. The hostility of the farmers increased further with the passing of the Doab Bari Act of 1907 leading to an increase in the *abiana* (water tax). The farmers under the leadership of Sardar Ajit Singh, uncle of Saheed Bhagat Singh, fought tooth and nail against the threat of losing their land. Finally, The Punjab Land Colonisation Act was withdrawn after the Secretary of State vetoed it on May 26, 1907.

PDS (Public Distribution System): The PDS facilitates the supply of food grains through a network of more than four lakh Fair Price Shops (FPSs) in India, which distribute food grains to the public at subsidised prices, playing a critical role in ensuring food security to millions of Indians from various vulnerable sections. PDS is operated under the joint responsibility of the Union and the State/UT governments. The Union government, through the Food Corporation of India (FCI), has assumed the responsibility for procurement, storage, transportation and bulk allocation of food grains to the state governments. The operational responsibility including allocation within the state, identification of eligible families, issue of Ration Cards and supervising the functioning of the FPSs etc., rest with the state governments.

In 2013, the National Food security Act was passed, which was opposed by many member countries in the WTO. The BJP-led government at the Centre dissolved the planning commission and replaced it with Niti Aayog. Modi government is also in favour of dismantling the PDS and wishes to replace it with food stamps or direct cash transfer to beneficiary accounts, letting people buy food grains from the open market as is done in "free market" economies of advanced capitalist countries. These measures, already being experimented in many districts, are also as per the dictates of the WTO, which is pressurising the Indian government to reduce subsidy in agriculture and gradually do away with PDS and subsidised food prices.

Peace Clause: This clause in the Agreement on Agriculture (AoA) protects a developing country's food procurement programs against action from other WTO member countries in case subsidy limits are breached. The subsidy limit is fixed at 10 percent of the value of food production (*de minimis*) in the case of developing countries such as India. India was the first country to invoke the clause for breaching the subsidy limit for rice for the year 2018-19. In April 2020, India informed the WTO that the value of India's rice production was $43.67 billion in 2018-19 and India had given subsidies worth $5 billion.

PL-480 (Public Law 480): After Independence, India relied on supply of food grains from the United States under PL-480 against rupee payments, as India didn't have much foreign exchange at that time to buy large quantities of food from the international market. PL-480, also known as "Food for Peace" program, was actually an American foreign policy tool to maintain and further its imperialist interests in underdeveloped countries. India's dependence on America for supply of food grains became apparent in the mid-1960s, when the US suspended wheat supplies due to political differences at a time India was facing back-to-back droughts. On December 29, 1971, A.P. Shinde, the Union Minister of State for Agriculture, announced the government of India's decision to cancel all grain imports from the US under the existing PL-480 agreement.

PUNJAB LAND REFORMS ACT, 1972: This Act or law stipulates maximum permissible irrigated land-owning of 17.5 acres (about seven hectares) and 52 acres of barren land per family in the state of Punjab.

PUNJAB VILLAGE COMMON LANDS REGULATION ACT, 1961: The village panchayat or village council has a certain amount of land under its jurisdiction that is earmarked for use for purposes directed at the welfare of the people in the village. The Punjab Village Common Lands Regulation Act, 1961 has a provision that out of the total cultivable land, available with the village panchayat and which is proposed to be leased, "thirty percent, ten percent and ten percent, respectively shall be reserved for giving on lease by auction, to members of the Scheduled Caste; Backward Classes; and dependents of defence personnel killed in any war after the independence of India" (Government of Punjab, 1961).

SHAHEEN BAGH: The Shaheen Bagh protest was a peaceful sit-in at Delhi that began on 15 December 2019 and lasted until 24 March 2020. The protest was led by Muslim women who blocked a major road at Shaheen Bagh, located in Jamia Nagar, South-East Delhi, using non-violent resistance. The protest began in response to the passing of the Citizenship (Amendment) Act on 11 December 2019 in parliament and the Delhi police's atrocities on students at Jamia Millia Islamia University who were opposing the Amendment.

Shaheen Bagh soon became the site of the longest sit-in protests against the CAA, inspiring similar protests across the country. Leaders from farmer unions like BKU (Ekta-Ugrahan) from Punjab went to Shabeen Bagh to express solidarity. Following the communal riots in

East Delhi engineered by Hindutva forces in February and imposition of lockdown in Delhi on 23 March 2020, protesters at Shaheen Bagh were arrested and forcefully removed from the site by the Delhi Police.

SHANTA KUMAR COMMITTEE REPORT: Soon after coming to power in 2014, Narendra Modi set up a six member committee under BJP leader and ex-CM of Himachal, Shanta Kumar. The mandate given to the committee was to suggest restructuring or unbundling of FCI to improve its financial management and operational efficiency in procurement, storage and distribution of food grains. The Committee on 21 January 2015 submitted its report on restructuring of the Food Corporation of India (FCI) to the government. Its main recommendations were to:

* Reduce the number of beneficiaries under the Food Security Act—from 67 percent to 40 percent.

* Allow private players to procure and store food grains.

* Stop bonuses on Minimum Support Price (MSP) paid by states to farmers and adopt a cash transfer system so that MSP and food subsidy amounts can be directly transferred to the accounts of farmers and food security beneficiaries.

* Involve FCI in full-fledged grain procurement only in states with poor procurement and for others such as Haryana, Punjab, Andhra Pradesh, Chhattisgarh, Madhya Pradesh and Odisha, make the states do the procurement.

* Outsource the stocking of grains to private agencies.

It is against this background that the farmers in Punjab, Haryana and western UP, who depend on MSP procurement by FCI, perceived the three farm laws as a move to deregulate and 'bypass' *mandis* as an attempt to gradually dismantle the MSP system and withdraw state support from agriculture.

SWAMINATHAN COMMISSION REPORT: Chaired by Prof M.S. Swaminathan, a renowned agro-scientist, the National Commission on Farmers (NCF) was formed in 2004 and it submitted five reports between the years 2004 and 2006, suggesting ways to enhance productivity, profitability and sustainability of the major farming systems in India. In common terms, these reports are known as the Swaminathan report.

The fifth report of the NCF set up under his chairmanship first recommended that Minimum Support Price—which act as a floor price for food grains to avoid distress sales by farmers—should be "at least 50% more than the weighted average cost of production." This cost, called C2 (comprehensive cost), includes all assumed costs. The MSP which the government now gives is 50 percent returns over just the A2 cost plus family labour costs (FL), while the farmers are demanding C2 plus 50 percent.

APPENDIX I

A LIST OF THE FARMERS' UNIONS THAT LED THE MOVEMENT

The farmers' movement was led by the SKM—a platform of farmer unions opposed to the three farm laws. While the majority among them were from Punjab, the rest were from Haryana and Madhya Pradesh.

FARMER UNIONS FROM PUNJAB

1. Kirti Kisan Union
2. Bharatiya Kisan Union (Ekta-Ugrahan)
3. Bharatiya Kisan Union (Krantikari)
4. Bharatiya Kisan Union (Dakaunda)
5. Kisan Mazdoor Sangharsh Committee
6. Kisan Sangharsh Committee
7. Azad Kisan Sangharsh Committee
8. All India Kisan Sabha
9. Bharatiya Kisan Union Sidhupur
10. Bharatiya Kisan Union Kadian
11. Bharatiya Kisan Union Rajewal
12. Bharatiya Kisan Union Doaba
13. Bharatiya Kisan Union Mansa
14. Majha Kisan Committee
15. Punjab Kisan Union
16. Lok Bhalai Insaaf Welfare Society
17. Doaba Kisan Samiti
18. Doaba Kisan Sangharsh Committee
19. Ganna Sangharsh Committee
20. Azad Kisan Committee
21. Kisan Bachao Morcha
22. Bharat Kisan Union
23. Kul Hind Kisan Federation

24. Jamhuri Kisan Sabha
25. Jai Kisan Andolan
26. Krantikari Kisan Union
27. Indian Farmers' Association
28. Kul Hind Kisan Sabha
29. Bharatiya Kisan Manch
30. Bharatiya Kisan Union Lakhowal

Farmer unions from Haryana and Madhya Pradesh

1. Bharatiya Kisan Union Tikait
2. Bharatiya Kisan Union Chaduni
3. Bharatiya Kisan Union Mann
4. Rashtriya Kisan Mazdoor Mahasangh

The Four Common Demands of the Farmers' Movement

1. Complete repeal of the three new farm laws passed by the Union government. The three laws include the Farmers Produce Trade and Commerce (Promotion and Simplification) Act 2020, the Farmers (Empowerment and Protection) Price Assurance and Agreement on Agricultural Services Act 2020, and Essential Commodities (Amendment) Act 2020.

2. A legal guarantee by the Union government of Minimum Support Price (MSP) to ensure procurement of crops from farmers at MSP will continue.

3. Withdrawal of the Electricity (Amendment) Bill 2020.

4. Scrapping of the provision under which the farmers responsible for stubble burning can be imprisoned for five years, besides imposition of a fine of up to Rs 1 crore.

APPENDIX II

THIRTEEN-POINT CHARTER OF DEMANDS OF THE LEFT-WING FARMER UNIONS

Apart from the four common demands, BKU (Ekta-Ugrahan) and other Left-affiliated farmer unions had presented a thirteen-point charter of demands to the Union government in October 2020. The demands were:

1. Repeal the three recent agriculture laws besides the Electricity (Amendment) Bill 2020.

2. Implement universal Public Distribution System (PDS) throughout the country and include in it all essential food and non-food items of basic necessities.

3. Implement the formula recommended by Swaminathan Commission to fix profitable MSPs for all crops.

4. Legally ensure government procurement on MSP for all crops.

5. Also implement other pro-farmer recommendations of Swaminathan Commission.

6. Roll back steps directed towards deregulating and decontrolling trade and commerce of farm produce in favour of big Indian and foreign traders and multinational companies.

7. Put an end to farmers' exploitation by big traders and MNCs in agriculture produce markets (APMCs).

8. Put an end to monopoly of Indian and foreign corporate and multinational companies over trade of agriculture inputs. Make these inputs available to farmers at subsidised rates.

9. Immediately release detained and imprisoned intellectuals, democratic rights activists and student activists all over the country.

Withdraw false cases registered against them.

10. Withdraw all restrictions imposed against the right to struggle.

11. Repeal the ordinance imposing a fine of Rs 1 crore and imprisonment for five years on farmers burning paddy stubble.

12. Make full arrangements for harmless disposal of stubble according to directions of the Supreme Court and National Green Tribunal. Else, pay Rs 200 per quintal bonus on paddy in lieu of extra expenses for this purpose.

13. Marginal relief of not imposing interest over interest given to other loanees should primarily be given to farmers.

Source: https://www.indiatoday.in/india/story/know-about-the-kisan-unions-leading-the-biggest-farmers-agitation-in-delhi-in-30-years-1746468-2020-12-03

APPENDIX III

SANJHA MORCHA (UNITED FRONT) OF RURAL AND AGRICULTURAL WORKER UNIONS IN PUNJAB

To fight for their own demands seven rural and agricultural worker organisations in Punjab formed a united front named Pendu aur Khet Mazdoor Jathebandiyon ka Sanjha Morcha (United Front of Rural and Farm Workers' Unions). The *sanjha morcha* prepared an eight-point charter of demands and launched a campaign and protest movement in support of their demands. They held a three-day sit-in in Patiala from 9 to 12 August 2021 to raise these demands.

List of Rural and Agricultural Worker Unions in the Sanjha Morcha

1. Dehati Mazdoor Sabha
2. Punjab Khet Mazdoor Union
3. Krantikari Pendu Mazdoor Union
4. Pendu Mazdoor Union
5. Mazdoor Mukti Morcha
6. Punjab Khet Mazdoor Sabha
7. Khet Mazdoor Sabha

Eight-point Charter of Demands of the Sanjha Morcha

1. A plot of land of 10 *marla* be allocated to each needy labourer and a grant Rs 50,000 to them to build their homes on it.

2. Ensure availability of work for the whole year to all the eligible

workers through MGNREGA, pay Rs 700 daily wage and control corruption in MGNREGA.

3. Old age and widow pension of Rs 5,000 per month.

4. Write off all government and non-government loans, including those with micro-finance companies, on the heads of farm labourers and small farmers. Bring in new law to eliminate debt and provide government loans at low interest to the needy.

5. The government should make available one-third of panchayat reserved land on cheap contracts to the landless.

6. Strengthening of the Public Distribution System, kitchen utensils at affordable price to the landless labourers

7. Supply of cooking gas at half the market price, free electricity, water, education and health services.

8. Permanent government employment to all educated sons and daughters of farm labourers.

About the Original Publishers

GroundXero is an attempt to defend facts, reason and truth, and uphold them as acts of resistance. It is a platform for news, dialogue and debate aimed at holding the rulers and the state accountable, while staying fiercely independent of any kind of government/corporate funding and/or control of political parties.

WEBSITE: https://www.groundxero.in/
EMAIL: groundxero2018@gmail.com

Notes on the Academy is a magazine that aims to critically evaluate academic institutions and culture. Our efforts are directed at making the larger community admit that these problems are not one-off cases but are systemic. We hope that our efforts spark a conversation among your circles about how higher educational institutions may be re-imagined, and how we, as a community, might work to cure academia of its illnesses.

WEBSITE: https://notacademy.in
EMAIL: notacademy@pm.me

Workers Unity is a digital media initiative for the working class voice. Dedicated to spreading awareness amongst toiling masses and marginalised sections of the society about working class issues and challenges, it has created a huge buzz in the Hindi heartland. It is completely supported by workers and general masses who appreciate their work, and is free of any corporate or political party funding.

WEBSITE: https://www.workersunity.com/
EMAIL: workersunity18@gmail.com

www.ingramcontent.com/pod-product-compliance
Lightning Source LLC
LaVergne TN
LVHW092103060526
838201LV00047B/1561